ASSESSMENT

We dedicate this book to our families and especially—
To *Jo Ann Harrison* and
to the memory of *Miriam Shirom*

ORGANIZATIONAL DIAGNOSIS AND ASSESSMENT

BRIDGING THEORY AND PRACTICE

MICHAEL I. HARRISON
ARIE SHIROM

SAGE Publications
International Educational and Professional Publisher
Thousand Oaks   London   New Delhi

For information:

SAGE Publications, Inc.
2455 Teller Road
Thousand Oaks, California 91320
E-mail: order@sagepub.com

SAGE Publications Ltd.
6 Bonhill Street
London EC2A 4PU
United Kingdom

SAGE Publications India Pvt. Ltd.
M-32 Market
Greater Kailash I
New Delhi 110 048 India

Printed in the United States of America

Library of Congress Cataloging-in-Publication Data

Harrison, Michael I.
    Organizational diagnosis and assessment: Bridging theory
and practice / by Michael I. Harrison, Arie Shirom.
        p.   cm.
    Includes bibliographical references and index.
    ISBN 978-0-8039-5510-3 (cloth: acid-free paper)
    ISBN 978-0-8039-5511-0 (pbk.: acid-free paper)
    1. Organizational change. 2. Organization—Evaluation. I. Shirom,
Arie. II. Title.
    HD58.8.H3673   1998
    658.4'063—ddc21   98-9070

This book is printed on acid-free paper.

    07 08   13 12 11

Acquiring Editor: Marquita Flemming
Production Editor: Sanford Robinson
Editorial Assistant: Lynn Miyata
Designer/Typesetter: Janelle LeMaster
Indexer: Virgil Diodato
Cover Designer: Candice Harman

Contents

PART II: FOCAL AREAS

PART III: APPLICATIONS

PART IV: BRIDGING THEORY AND PRACTICE

Preface

The subtitle of our book, *Bridging Theory and Practice*, helps convey our objectives for the book and reflects the book's origins in our own work on both sides of the theory-practice divide. Most broadly, we want to show how applied researchers, consultants, managers, and policymakers can enhance their ability to diagnose organizational problems and challenges by drawing on a broad spectrum of current organizational research and theory and by examining organizations through divergent theoretical frames. We believe that our multiframe approach to diagnosis can contribute to decision making by practicing managers, in addition to improving diagnoses conducted by behavioral science consultants. Hence, our book should be useful to management educators, as well as to consultants and scholars of planned change.

More specifically, we seek to contribute to the theory and practice of planned change by developing a new approach to diagnosis that we call sharp-image diagnosis. Unlike the very broad forms of diagnosis that characterize much work in organization development, sharp-image diagnosis focuses directly on the forces that produce symptoms of organizational ineffectiveness and shape an organization's capacity to cope with critical challenges. This form of diagnosis can produce very powerful and useful findings without exhausting the resources of clients and consultants.

We have also sought to develop approaches and models for diagnosis and assessment that reflect the changing nature of the workplace, including important developments that have received limited attention in traditional treatments on diagnosis and assessment for planned change. These include organizational decline and other life cycle transitions; gendering; workforce diversity; the spread of interdisciplinary teams, flatter hierarchies, networks, and other new forms of work organization; growing reliance on information technology; and the growth of mergers and other types of strategic alliance among organizations.

In these ways, we hope to help managers, policymakers, and consultants break out of unproductive ways of thinking about organizational challenges. In addition, we seek to foster critical evaluation of managerial fads and fashions. At the same time, we propose to organizational theorists that they periodically apply a simple reality test to their work: Can their ideas help consultants, decision makers, and other organizational stakeholders find workable solutions to critical problems and challenges? Can their theories help decision makers learn how to handle future challenges?

The book's origins lie in the confluence of streams of work that each of us has done as academic researchers, consultants, applied researchers, university teachers, and trainers of managers and consultants. In the past few years, we have each been involved in analyses of health systems and health system reforms. These experiences made clear to us the potential contribution of diagnostic studies of macro systems to debates about major public policy issues. Moreover, our encounters with policy formation in health systems brought home the importance of strengthening diagnostic thinking and inquiry among makers of public policy.

We owe thanks to the following people who read drafts of book chapters or related papers: Peter Bamberger, Jean Bartunek, Jo Ann Harrison, and Dafna Izraeli. Thanks also to Sam Bacharach, Dov Eden, and Bruce Phillips for discussing with us some of the ideas presented in the book. In addition, we would like to thank Ms. Ettie Rosenberg for her help in preparing the figures that appear in the text.

PART 1 FOUNDATIONS

1 Frames and Models in Organizational Diagnosis

Managers in both the public and private sectors are investing growing amounts of time and energy in planning and managing organizational change. For help in introducing change, managers are employing rapidly rising numbers of internal and external consultants ("Survey," 1997).[1] These planned change efforts respond to challenges arising in very turbulent and competitive environments, to the claims and demands of vocal stakeholders, and to policy-makers who mandate change in the organizations under their jurisdiction.

Unfortunately, many efforts to plan and manage change—including many projects that employ teams of expert consultants—fail to deliver viable solutions to pressing organizational challenges and problems. Instead, change projects often waste precious time and money. Sometimes, applying the wrong techniques produces unanticipated and undesired results, which only add to an organization's problems.[2] In consequence, there is growing disappointment and disillusion with planned change and organizational consultation.[3]

One explanation for the high rate of failure of change efforts is that managers and consultants alike frequently fail to *diagnose* the needs of the organization and to examine feasible routes to change. Instead, they implement fashionable administrative techniques and new organization designs without carefully considering whether these tools will help them solve pressing problems and meet the challenges at hand. Nor do they consider whether proposed interventions fit the focal organization. Too often, standard change techniques are good for solving problems *other than the ones confronting the organization.* Or the tools may be useful for other organizations but *not for the one needing help now.*

The risks of attempting to improve or change an organization without an adequate diagnosis are well captured by Scott Adams's (1996) satirical blast at business consultants:

> Consultants will ultimately recommend that you do whatever you're *not* doing now. Centralize whatever is decentralized. Flatten whatever is vertical. Diversify whatever is concentrated and divest everything that is not "core" to the business. You'll hardly ever find a consultant that recommends that you keep everything the same and stop wasting money on consultants. And consultants rarely deal with the root cause of your company's problems, since that's probably the person who hired them. (p. 153)[4]

To help consultants, managers, and other organizational members diagnose root causes of organizational problems and challenges and to help guide change management, we introduce a distinctive approach that we call *sharp-image diagnosis.* Diagnostic practitioners who follow the sharp-image approach move quickly and decisively from initially stated problems and concerns to the identification of underlying forces that produce ineffective outcomes. In like manner, they can examine the forces affecting an organization's ability to meet critical organizational challenges—such as sudden changes in governmental regulations, major shifts in customer expectations, new competitive threats, or changes in the composition of the workforce. Then, they provide action-oriented feedback that takes into account the organization's capacities and prospects for planned change.

Managers who incorporate concepts and techniques of sharp-image diagnosis into their own decision making use a similar logic: They search for the sources of specific problems and challenges before acting on them. After deciding upon and implementing actions, they obtain periodic feedback on implementation processes and outcomes. They use this feedback to sharpen their understanding of their organization, its environment, and managed change. What is more, they rely on feedback to help them decide on further moves toward change and adaptation.

Sharp-image diagnosis bridges theory and practice by drawing a broad spectrum of organizational theory and research, yet also responding directly to the distinctive conditions shaping organizational operations and change options. The outcome of sharp-image diagnosis is a model that provides clients with a highly focused, multidimensional image of conditions underlying basic problems and critical challenges. This model contains clear implications for workable ways to resolve problems and to enhance future performance.

Our perspective on diagnosis draws on a growing body of academic work that encourages decision makers and their consultants to engage in empirically grounded and theoretically reflexive inquiry about organizational problems and challenges (Argyris & Schon, 1996; Gordon, 1996; Morgan, 1986; Schein, 1988; Schon & Rein, 1994; Senge, 1990; Smircich & Stubbart, 1985; Weick, 1979). Moreover, we draw on research that shows that unless a radical organizational transformation is envisioned, managerial initiatives are more likely to succeed when they fit the organization's current configuration of internal features and external conditions (Meyer, Tsui, & Hinnings, 1993; Ketchen et al., 1997; Ketchen, Thomas, & Snow, 1993; Tushman & Romanelli, 1985).

Diagnostic practitioners must attend simultaneously to three distinctive facets of diagnosis in order to provide decision makers with valid and useful data on organizational problems and challenges and to help clients find ways to improve their organizations: analysis, methods, and interactions between clients and consultants and among members of the focal organization (Harrison, 1994). This book concentrates on the core of diagnostic analysis— the framing and modeling of diagnostic issues and findings. These analytical processes critically affect the entire course of diagnosis. Yet these processes are often treated less thoroughly and comprehensively in the literature on planned change and behavioral science consultation than are data-gathering methods and client-consultant interactions (e.g., Block, 1981; Harrison, 1994). Because diagnostic analysis and thinking form the main concerns of this book, data-gathering techniques are mainly discussed when they are very problematic and closely related to analytical issues, as occurs in the diagnoses dealing with organizational culture, politics, and organization decline (Chapter 11).[5] In like manner, our discussions of client-consultant interactions stress links between these consulting processes, diagnostic techniques, and ways of framing diagnostic issues (Chapter 15).

To remedy the lack of attention to using theory and developing models in diagnosis, we survey, synthesize, and critique a wide range of theoretical frames and models from the literature on organizations and management that can help consultants, managers, and other organizational members diagnose organizational problems and challenges and plan for organizational change. We show how to combine more than one theoretical perspective so as to enhance the power and utility of diagnosis. Moreover, we draw on useful theoretical perspectives that are not often applied to organizational diagnosis and consultation. Also included are critical discussions of well-known approaches, such as open-systems theory, that provide the conceptual foundations for much current diagnostic work.

The chapters that follow present frames and models for diagnosing operations at the level of workgroups, major units within an organization, entire organizations, and networks of interacting organizations. Some of the analytical guides apply across levels, whereas others are tailored to specific diagnostic levels. Many of the frames and models presented, like those derived from open-systems theory, can be applied to most types of organizations and to many diagnostic issues. We also develop models designed to aid in the diagnosis of specific organizational functions, such as human resource management, strategy formation, and labor relations. For each frame and model, we strive to specify the organizational and environmental conditions affecting the applicability of the model.

Besides contributing to practice, we seek to contribute to the academic study of planned change in several areas. Most important, we apply divergent theoretical frames to understanding planned change (e.g., Chapter 7) and examine procedures for combining multiple frames in applied research and consultation (see especially Chapter 15). We also present new analytical models, including an integrative model for defining and assessing organizational effectiveness, a model for diagnosing entire societal sectors or networks of organizations (Chapter 14), and several models for diagnosing specific organizational functions and focal areas. Furthermore, we refine and specify new uses for research-based models and theories in areas such as team effectiveness (Chapter 6), workforce diversity (Chapter 9), gendering (Chapter 9), strategic human resource management, life-cycle transitions, and organizational culture.

More generally, we seek to contribute to the study of planned change by critically examining a broad range of procedures and models for diagnosing and assessing organizational operations, and by specifying organizational contexts in which specific diagnostic models and procedures are most appropriate. In these ways, our treatments of diagnostic models move beyond ideal-typical models of diagnosis and action, like those contained within some organization development texts. In doing so, this book joins a growing number of studies of the processes and conditions affecting the successful formulation and implementation of planned organizational change (e.g., Dunphy & Stace, 1988, 1993; Mintzberg, 1994; Pettigrew, Ferlie, & McKee, 1992). These studies of the contexts of managed change ultimately will provide more valid and useful ways of understanding planned change than do ideal-typical descriptions of change processes.

The rest of this chapter contains five main sections. The first introduces diagnosis and argues that diagnostic inquiry can contribute to management decision making even under very turbulent conditions. The second section examines the contributions of models and frames to diagnosis and cites some of the benefits of incorporating more than one theoretical frame into diagnosis. The third section outlines our procedure for conducting sharp-image diagnoses. The fourth part of the chapter examines variations in diagnostic approaches. These variations reflect differences in the contexts in which diagnosis is used, in diagnostic goals, and in the roles played by consultants and members of the focal organization. The chapter's conclusion discusses the contribution of framing and modeling to diagnostic effectiveness.

Diagnosis and the Management of Change

Although systematic diagnosis can contribute to the work of all consultants, this book is directed mainly at internal and external consultants trained in the behavioral and organizational sciences, as well as managers and other organizational members who want to diagnose their own organizations. Behavioral science consultants typically work with top-level or division-level managers and less often with other client groups, such as labor-management teams or members of community groups (e.g., Chisholm & Elden, 1993; Shirom, 1983).

We use the term *diagnosis* to refer to investigations that draw on concepts, models, and methods from the behavioral sciences in order to examine an organization's current state and help clients find ways to solve problems or enhance organizational effectiveness. Although the term *assessment* is sometimes used interchangeably with diagnosis (Lawler, Nadler, & Cammann,

1980; Seashore, Lawler, Mirvis, & Cammann, 1983), we use it to refer to more focused studies. For example, assessments can involve summative or formative evaluations of specific organizational projects or functions (Herman, Morris, & Fitz-Gibbon, 1987; Rossi & Freeman, 1993).[6] In addition, some assessments aim at gathering data that are useful to decision makers without diagnosing specific challenges and problems. The emphasis throughout this book is on the diagnosis of entire organizations or subsystems. However, several chapters discuss more narrowly focused assessments of predefined change projects and programs and even of very specific managerial practices (e.g., Chapters 5, 7, 8, and 13). Furthermore, many of the ideas developed in the book could contribute to more narrowly focused assessments and evaluations, as well as to organizational diagnoses.

Diagnosis usually forms a phase in strategic decision making even when the decision process is not highly structured (Mintzberg, Raisinghani, & Theoret, 1976). By diagnosing issues more systematically, and by examining options for action carefully, managers, policymakers, and other types of decision makers can break away from tried-and-tested practices that are becoming unworkable. At the same time, they can decide upon appropriate steps toward improvement and can avoid unselectively adopting managerial fads and fashions that offer "quick fixes" to fundamental organizational challenges (Abrahamson, 1996; Abrahamson & Fairchild, 1997). Moreover, through careful diagnosis, planning, action, and follow-up, decision makers can learn from experience and avoid the pitfalls that often accompany the unsystematic implementation of new forms of management.

Unfortunately, many managers and consultants show a bias for quick intervention and shortchange diagnosis. This tendency is mirrored by the neglect of diagnosis in research reviews of the impact of organization development interventions (Macy & Izumi, 1993; Newman, Edwards, & Raju, 1989). For example, in a meta-analysis of the effects of consulting interventions, Tett, Meyer, and Roese (1994) make no mention of diagnosis or of any other consulting stage prior to intervention. Future research may show that the effects of interventions depend greatly on the degree to which they are based on valid and robust diagnostic findings.

Research on the downsizing in the automobile industry provides one indication of the potential payoffs of carefully diagnosing the needs and prospects for change and of developing interventions that are tailored to prevailing conditions within the focal organization. A 4-year study of downsizing among 30 firms in that industry (Cameron, 1994; Cameron, Freeman,

& Mishra, 1991) showed that firms that planned and designed downsizing moves through systematic analyses of jobs, resource usage, workflows, and implications for human resource management were more likely to attain subsequent improvements in performance. Furthermore, these firms were more able to avoid common negative consequences of downsizing, such as loss of valued employees and declining morale among remaining employees.

Is it reasonable to expect managers to engage in systematic diagnosis and decision making when they face unfamiliar and rapidly changing situations? Can decisions still proceed through the classic sequence of diagnosis, planning, action, and evaluation when external turbulence reaches a state of "permanent white water" (Vaill, 1989)? The answer to these questions is that the very conditions that create barriers to diagnosis and systematic decision making also render them essential.

Managers and other decision makers run serious risks if they eschew diagnostic inquiry and systematic decision making altogether when uncertainty and pressure for quick action intensify. Unselective imitation of other organizations often wastes resources and delays effective actions. Inaction and reversion to familiar routines also can be dangerous. Managers facing major environmental threats often resist moving in new directions just when the need to do so is greatest (Staw, Sandelands, & Dutton, 1981). Another possibility, which also carries heavy risks, is that as external conditions worsen and organizational decline results, managers will act blindly without careful analysis of the likely effects of their decisions (Weitzel & Jonsson, 1989; see also Chapter 11). These unsystematic actions can undermine chances for recovery.

There is one viable alternative to inaction and to reorganizing without sufficient forethought: Managers facing rapidly changing and uncertain conditions can quickly and flexibly diagnose their situation, define the strategic direction in which they seek to move, choose appropriate actions, and begin to move in the chosen direction. Then, they can track the results of their actions and of their shifting context in order to assess the appropriateness of current steps and to decide when to modify them or to shift course altogether. Rather than relying on elaborate decision processes and time-consuming planning techniques, decision makers must move through this type of diagnostic inquiry quickly and experimentally—continually formulating, checking, and reformulating their interpretations and explanations (Schon, 1983). Frequent feedback on previous actions provides the basis for this learning process. When feedback or additional data fail to support their expectations about the environment and about their own organization, or when new opportunities arise, the managers can reassess their guiding strategy and rediagnose their operations (Pascale, 1984; Quinn, 1980).

Models and Frames in Diagnosis

Models and Frames

The theories and analytical perspectives adopted by investigators lead them to concentrate on some phenomena to the exclusion of others. Moreover, some theoretical perspectives lead analysts to favor particular research methods and different logics of proof and argumentation. Throughout this book, we use the term *framing* to refer to the ways in which theories shape diagnostic analysis (Bolman & Deal, 1991; Schon & Rein, 1994). The term *frame* is used broadly to include what others have described as paradigms, perspectives, and theory groups, and to capture differing perspectives embodied within specific diagnostic models and frameworks.

The discussion that follows presents the frames on which we rely most heavily and describes several levels of theory on which we draw in developing these frames. Theories consist of concepts, sets of statements about relations among these concepts, and basic assumptions—for example, assumptions about developing, testing, and applying theories. Formal theories (Bacharach, 1989), which state precisely the expected relations between their subcomponents, deal with a very limited subset of the issues generally considered in diagnosis.

Models, or theoretical frameworks, are less well specified and less deterministic than are theories. Models typically focus on a limited number of key concepts and on relations among them, and they may specify specific variables for operationalizing and measuring concepts. For example, one useful model explains intraorganizational power in terms of control over strategic organizational contingencies (Hickson, Hinings, Schneck, & Pennings, 1971). Another, partially overlapping model, specifies organizational power bases, such as legitimacy, expertise, and ability to reward others (French & Raven, 1959). Some models and theoretical frameworks refer to clusters of variables, such as leadership processes or external resource constraints, rather than isolating discrete variables.

Like theories, models help practitioners of diagnosis focus on a limited number of features of organizational life and account for organizational effectiveness and ineffectiveness. Models can thereby help decision makers examine the alternative points at which they might intervene to change their organization. Models can contribute more directly to diagnosis than can whole bodies of theory or formal theoretical statements, because models are generally simpler, less determined, and less fully specified. These features provide diagnostic investigators with more opportunities for attending to distinctive features of the focal organization that shape possibilities for action and for organizational improvement. Moreover, models serve as heuristic devices for organizing data for feedback and communicating it to participants in the focal organization (Lundberg, 1989; Schein, 1993). For these reasons, we present a wide range of potentially useful models in the chapters that follow and urge investigators to construct their own diagnostic models.

More abstract, but no less important than theories and models, are theoretical perspectives, which encompass entire sets of related concepts, models, and theories. During the past three decades, two divergent perspectives have informed most applied and basic sociological research on organizations in North America, northern Europe, and Scandinavia (Lammers, 1990). The first views organizations as *open systems,* whereas the second treats them as *political arenas* in which bargaining and exchange take place among internal and external stakeholders. A third, *structural* perspective remains influential in applied research and consultation, even though it enjoys less popularity within academic research. Derived from the theory of bureaucracy, the structural frame treats organizations as tools that can be designed to enhance goal attainment (Bolman & Deal, 1991).

The most abstract distinctions among theories concern entire paradigms—such as the Functionalist, Interpretive (social constructionist), Radical Humanist, and Radical Structural paradigms described by Burrell and Morgan (1979), and the groupings of theory and research described by Morgan's (1986) metaphors of organization.[7] Paradigms include sets of concepts, research, and theory that contain distinctive metatheoretical assumptions about the nature of social science, society, and organizations.

Until now, diagnosis has drawn almost entirely on the functionalist paradigm. In particular, behavioral science consultants have used the *open-systems frame* more widely than any other perspective as a guide to diagnosis. We follow this tradition but also criticize diagnostic approaches that rely exclusively on the integrative and systems-oriented streams within functionalism.

Hence, in the first part of the book, we recommend combining the political and systems perspectives to orient diagnosis. The *political frame* (Bacharach & Lawler, 1980; Lawler & Bacharach, 1983; Pfeffer, 1981b) helps investigators view organizations as fields made up of competing internal and external stakeholders. This perspective provides important guidelines for the definition and assessment of organizational effectiveness and for assessments of the feasibility of proposed organizational changes. The political perspective also contributes to understanding organizational conflict and bargaining in areas such as labor relations (Chapter 11).

In the second and third parts of the book, we supplement these frames with several variants on the *interpretive frame* and with a *negotiation frame*, which all contribute to analysis of organizational culture and of emergent organizational patterns. In addition, we draw on the *structural frame*, which is particularly useful in examinations of organizational design and of strategy. In the final chapter of the book, we discuss ways to combine these divergent frames. In addition, we examine the applicability to diagnosis of new and alternative paradigms, including postmodernism and feminism.

Using Multiple Frames and Models in Diagnosis

Consultants and managers may react with skepticism and surprise to the suggestion that a wide variety of organizational and managerial theories are potentially useful for diagnosis. Perhaps consideration of competing models, perspectives, and paradigms will just add confusion and make it harder to deal with real-world problems. Might not managers and their advisors be better off with a single diagnostic model that is easy to apply and universally applicable? Even the old saw about there being nothing so practical as a good theory seems to suggest looking for one good theory, not dozens!

These concerns are legitimate. Nevertheless, there are sound empirical, theoretical, and practical reasons for making the effort to use *multiple* and even competing frames and models in diagnosis (Chapter 15). Many organizational theorists now agree that no single model or frame fully captures the complexity and multifaceted nature of organizational reality (Morgan, 1986; Bolman & Deal, 1991). Each theoretical approach brings particular insights and emphases that might not be obtained through the use of other approaches. By applying divergent models and frames to a focal organization, managers and consultants can mirror more fully the complexity of organizational life and discover ways to meet critical problems and challenges (Morgan, 1997).

Case 1.1 illustrates some of the drawbacks of viewing organizational problems from a single interpretive frame and suggests potential benefits of using more than one frame:[8]

CASE 1.1

In a large, democratically run transport cooperative, a newly elected management team sought to bring about a major organizational transformation. In their view, the cooperative was handicapped by a tradition of paternalistic management, political infighting, and deal making. The team wanted to run the firm according to principles of business management, rather than political bargaining. The team asked a private behavioral science consulting firm for help in planning and implementing this transformation. One particular area of concern was that management felt overburdened with minor problems originating in the local branches and wanted to find ways to improve decision making and to enhance coordination of field operations. Members of the consulting firm interviewed managers in the field and at headquarters, culled company records for evidence on communication and decision-making processes, and observed local- and national-level meetings. The consultants recommended structural and administrative reforms that would reduce pressure on top management and would fit the firm's overall reorganization program.

Although these recommendations were appropriate from a design standpoint, many of the proposed changes threatened veteran rank-and-file members of the organization. The structural changes, along with the introduction of standardized personnel testing, threatened the ability of many local and national leaders to gain power through patronage. In the next round of elections, the leaders who felt these threats channeled resistance to reform into opposition to the incumbent managers. A new slate of managers was elected that identified closely with the traditions and practices that had prevailed before the reforms.

The reform-oriented managers had sought to turn the transit cooperative into a business with a strong orientation toward profitability and efficiency. The consultants had encouraged the new managers to think of the firm as an instrument—a structure that could be designed to enhance these business goals. The consultants understandably shied away from diagnosing the firm as a web of political alliances and exchanges, and they left political considerations up to the managers. But the consultants also underestimated the degree to which the proposed changes violated fundamental norms and values within the organization's culture. In retrospect, it is evident that successful implementation of the transformation required more than the redesign of structures and processes. Implementation turned on the ability of management to change the organizational culture. Furthermore, to gain the time and support required for such a long-term undertaking, management needed to reduce or overcome resistance before it produced electoral revolt. A more systematic diagnosis of the nature of the culture and of the politics of resistance among important organizational stakeholders might have helped management anticipate opposition to their initiatives and develop ways to cope with it.

As this analysis suggests, the use of more than one frame in diagnosis and decision making can help consultants and managers become more aware of the implicit assumptions that are embedded within their own mental maps of organizations (Huff & Schwenk, 1990). In like manner, using multiple models and frames can help investigators break free of the assumptions that are built into "off-the-shelf" techniques for diagnosis and change management. Too often, these techniques provide only a partial portrait of the focal organization and its problems and lead analysts to overlook important possibilities and problems that fall outside of the focal concerns of the chosen change technique.

Total Quality Management (TQM) packages, for example, build in the assumption that organizational success depends on satisfying the expectations of current clients and on continually improving the organization's products and services. In contrast, the strategic-intent perspective (Hamel & Prahalad, 1994), which focuses on an organization's ability to forge new environmental relations and discover new sources of competitive advantage, reveals a fundamental limitation of process-oriented techniques like TQM: Techniques that mainly enhance current production and service processes may have little impact on a firm's competitive standing or on its external market performance (Short & Venkatraman, 1992).[9]

Use of multiple analytical frames can also help consultants and managers avoid the common judgmental error of starting with a particular point of view and then selectively reading data and feedback on their own actions in order to confirm their initial viewpoint. For instance, managers often employ an implicit theory that attributes organizational successes to their own initiatives and treats failures as caused by unstable and uncontrollable external developments, such as market downturns (e.g., Bettman & Weitz, 1983). Use of a model that pinpoints the role of management in scanning and anticipating external developments calls into question this tendency to attribute difficulties to uncontrollable external causes.

By selecting their models from among a range of theoretical approaches, and by using more than one frame in a model, consultants and managers also increase their ability to find routes to organizational improvement that fit the goals of the consultation and that match the client organization's distinctive features and operating context. Research shows that managerial practices and organizational patterns that solve problems or promote effectiveness in one type of organization, such as a family business, will not necessarily produce the same results in another type of organization, such as a multidivisional corporation (Friedlander & Pickle, 1967). In like manner, organizational resource states, such as growth, stability, crisis, and decline, influence the outcomes of particular managerial practices (Whetten, 1987). Other crucial contingencies that affect the consequences of managerial actions include the organization's strategy, technology, culture, ownership, environment, workforce composition, size, degree of bureaucratization, and its life-cycle stage (Hall, 1987; Mintzberg, 1979; Mintzberg & Westley, 1992; Pennings, 1992). Furthermore, microlevel interactions among individual managers, and even rank-and-file employees, can affect performance and shape the course of organizational change. People shape the organizations in which they work by *interpreting* organizational conditions, challenges, and opportunities and by *acting* in response to these understandings (Hrebiniak & Joyce, 1985; Pennings, 1992; Weick, 1979).

The many macro- and microlevel contingencies affecting planned change introduce high levels of indeterminacy into the change process: We cannot say for sure what effects a particular organizational intervention will have. In consequence, there is much disagreement about the effectiveness and applicability of many popular managerial and consultant interventions. What is certain is that many once-popular structural interventions have failed to produce consistent results of the sort that their advocates anticipated. Among the prominent techniques that have undergone this type of reassessment are long-range planning, downsizing, just-in-time manufacturing, reengineering, total quality management, and the creation of highly diversified firms (Cascio, 1993; Cusamano, 1994; Hackman & Wageman, 1995; Halachmi, 1995; Lubatkin & Lane, 1996; Mintzberg, 1994).

In light of the complexity and indeterminacy of planned change, diagnostic models should be flexible and capable of reflecting both macrocontingencies and microprocesses, such as participant interaction and interpretation. Consultants would be well advised to present decision makers with options for action rather than push a pet change technique simply because it is fashionable or worked well elsewhere. Then, as they formulate change targets and techniques, clients and consultants can carefully consider pragmatic considerations, including the interactions among consultants and clients (Block, 1981), the organization's political system, and the resources available for change efforts.

Despite the many advantages of using multiple theoretical frames in diagnosis, the difficulties remain clear. The very range of possibilities burdens decision makers with ambiguity and uncertainty. Furthermore, many of the theoretical approaches now in fashion lack clear implications for consultation or for managerial practice.

These limitations must be weighed against those of traditional approaches to diagnosis, which only use one perspective. Many of the models that are specifically designed for diagnosis (Burke, 1994; Walton & Nadler, 1994; see also Chapter 4) apply only to a narrow range of issues or provide a superficial view of critical organizational processes and conditions. Moreover, some consultants remain committed to models that lead to favored interventions, even though these interventions have not proved themselves to be universally applicable or effective. Sometimes, the understanding gained when diagnostic practitioners adopt an additional analytical frame complements insights obtained from previous approaches. On other occasions, the added view clashes with former understandings and invites empirical testing of hypotheses derived from the conflicting perspectives. These possibilities are illustrated in the substantive chapters that follow. The concluding chapter considers alternatives for combining multiple frames in practice.

Organization of the Book

To help consultants and managers choose among the many possible approaches to diagnosis, we have selected a limited number of theoretical and research approaches that can be particularly useful in diagnosis and organizational problem solving, along with a few models that can contribute to understanding specific organizational functions and issues, such as human resource management. Some of the frames and models have already proved their value for consultation and managerial problem solving. Others, such as research-based models of organizational transitions and life cycles, contain unrealized potential for diagnostic work.

The organization of the book reflects these distinctions. The first part of the book, consisting of Chapters 1 through 5, presents our basic approach to diagnosis, compares it to other approaches, and discusses frames, models, and analytical approaches that set foundations for most diagnostic work. Chapter 2 examines the open-systems approach, whereas Chapter 3 contrasts several theoretical approaches to assessing organizational effectiveness. Chapter 4 critically examines prominent diagnostic models that were derived from the open-systems frame. Chapter 5 examines the diagnosis of organizational politics. Chapters 6 through 10, which constitute the second part of the book, present models and frames for diagnosing specific features that are present in all organizations and often become targets for diagnosis. These focal features include workgroup processes, organization design, human resource management, emergent behavior and relations, and organizational culture. Client concerns and the nature of the most pressing problems and challenges facing the organization usually will dictate whether or not diagnosis explores one or more of these areas in depth.

The third part of the book, which includes Chapters 11 through 14, considers applications of diagnosis to specific topics and diagnostic issues that are not applicable to all organizations. These include life-cycle changes; strategy formation and implementation; organizational innovation and learning; management-union relations; and the diagnosis of entire organizational networks or sectors, such as health and education. The book's fourth part consists of a concluding chapter that examines prospects for using multiple theoretical frames in diagnosis. In elaborating on this central theme, we suggest that attention to new developments within organizational and management studies can make diagnosis more responsive to rapidly changing organizational conditions and more able to contribute to client and consultant learning.

Sharp-Image Diagnosis

A review of the literature on diagnosis, our own experiences, and the experiences of our students suggest that consultants who conduct diagnostic studies can benefit by starting with one or more broad analytical frames, such as the open-systems and political frames, and then developing more sharply focused models to guide analysis, additional data-gathering, and feedback. This approach combines the advantages of starting with a rich and broad view of the organization with those of providing clients with a tightly focused diagnosis of critical problems and challenges.

We use the term *sharp-image diagnosis* as a metaphor for this diagnostic approach. The metaphor is inspired by two very different technologies for producing visual images. The zoom lens allows photographers to start with a broad view of a scene and then to zoom in on a main character or critical detail. In like manner, practitioners of sharp-image diagnosis start with a broad scan of an organization but then select core problems and organizational challenges for close-up examination. After choosing these core issues, investigators shift to a mode of analysis resembling another imaging technology—magnetic resonance imaging (MRI). MRI goes below the surface of the body to produce three-dimensional cross-sections showing the condition of body tissues, blood flow, and even of the contraction and relaxation of internal organs (Banta, 1995). In the same way, sharp-image diagnosis typically uses two or more theoretical perspectives or frames to go below the surface of presented problems or organizational challenges to examine underlying system features and their dynamic interactions. By doing so, practitioners can discern sources of ineffectiveness and discover forces that clients can mobilize to generate productive change.

Our description of diagnosis in terms of metaphors drawn from the field of photography and imaging is meant to convey that diagnostic analysts play a very crucial role in deciding what to study, how to look at chosen phenomena, how to account for them, and how to create images of them for use in diagnostic feedback. Readers familiar with photography will have little difficulty in thinking of additional ways in which photographers recreate and define their subjects (e.g., by choosing filters and lighting effects). While accepting this implication of our metaphor, we nevertheless retain the premise of realism by assuming that in diagnosis—as in most types of photography—images reflect external realities.

Steps in Sharp-Image Diagnosis

Sharp-image diagnosis is typically preceded by two entry stages that are similar to those in most types of organizational consultation (French & Bell,

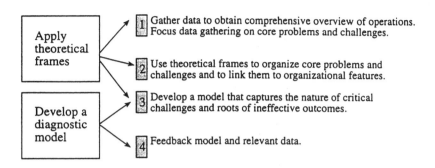

Figure 1.1 Steps in Sharp-Image Diagnosis

1995; Nadler, 1977). During the first stage, which is often called *scouting,* potential clients and consultants explore expectations for the project. The clients present problems or challenges that are to be examined in the diagnosis. The consultant seeks to clarify the nature of these issues and develops a preliminary view of organizational strengths and weaknesses. During these contacts, the consultant also tries to judge the likelihood that members of the organization will cooperate with data-gathering activities, the prospects for involving participants in the diagnosis, and the clients' receptiveness to feedback.

If the results of these preliminary discussions are favorable, clients and consultants move toward *contracting,* during which they negotiate and reach agreement on the goals and design of the diagnosis. Contracts typically specify at least the time frame for the diagnosis, the organizational resources required, the nature of the remuneration, and the form of the feedback. Misunderstandings can often be avoided if, at this stage, the parties involved also spell out the goals of the study, the criteria for evaluating it, and its design—including the degree and nature of participation by members of the organization, procedures for feedback, and the uses to be made of the diagnostic feedback and data. Contracting can also include preliminary discussions about possible ways to frame the problems or issues presented by clients.

Once contracting is completed, investigators are ready to undertake a sharp-image diagnosis. This process is shown in a series of steps in Figure 1.1 and is discussed below in the sequence provided in the figure.

In the first step, the people responsible for conducting the diagnosis *design procedures for obtaining data* on organizational problems or challenges and their probable sources, and they *gather the needed data.* Particular attention is given to core problems and challenges. Methods are chosen that fit the diagnostic issues, relations between consultants and clients, and the culture of the focal organization. Analytical frames help investigators decide which topics, features, and units to study, other than those that appear to be closely related to the problems presented by clients. Particularly useful orienting frames include the open-systems frame; SWOT analysis (strengths, weaknesses, opportunities, and threats), which derives from an instrumental and strategy-directed approach; and stakeholder analysis, which derives from a political perspective. The open-systems frame, the use of which is illustrated below in Case 1.2, directs attention to dominant features of the focal organization, its environment, and interactions between them. The systems frame facilitates orderly data gathering while sustaining a broad view of organizational features and performance. Moreover, the system frame can help consultants take note of conditions that may be producing problems presented by clients.

During the second diagnostic step, investigators *use frames to organize core problems or challenges and to link them to other organizational features.* At this point, we encourage practitioners of diagnosis to make a strategic choice: Rather than aiming at a comprehensive approach toward organizational improvement, consultants can focus directly on ineffective features and outcomes—analyzing what is hurting members of the organization and the organization's clients most—on problems and points needing improvement, and on their likely causes and facilitating conditions. If practitioners adopt this approach, they directly examine links between organizational problems or challenges and other system features.

Solving problems stemming from ineffectiveness can contribute more directly and dramatically to organizational survival and short-term success than can the enhancement of effectiveness. Hence, analysis of sources of ineffectiveness is more critical to key decision makers than the assessment of sources of effectiveness (Cameron, 1980, 1984; see also Chapter 3).[10] Ineffective elements (i.e., problems and points in need of improvement) are also easier to identify and describe than are the many dimensions and sources of effectiveness, and they are less controversial. Therefore, decision makers can reach agreement on them more readily. Focusing on ineffectiveness is also very appropriate in "permanently failing" organizations (Meyer & Zucker, 1989) that are characterized by chronically low levels of performance. These organizations can survive for many years without ever attaining high levels of effectiveness.

Several diagnostic models in the literature use this strategy of focusing on ineffectiveness (e.g., Porras, 1987; Shirom, 1993; Weisbord, 1976). In addition, the approach fits well with the emphasis in TQM on identifying and reducing sources of high costs or high variability (Deming, 1986). In a similar fashion, the theory of constraints (Goldratt, 1990) concentrates on removing forces that block improvement efforts.

Critical organizational challenges, including both strategic threats and opportunities, can also galvanize the attention and energy of decision makers and their subordinates. Strategic-oriented consultations often start from clients' desires to find ways to meet critical external challenges, such as changes in competition or in markets. Internal events, such as executive succession, can also pose critical challenges.

By examining the links between organizational problems or challenges and major system features, consultants and managers can distinguish between symptoms of underlying conditions and the conditions themselves (Senge, 1990). Underlying conditions affect major system features or are affected by them. The systems approach also facilitates the identification of core or major organizational problems, as distinct from superficial ones. Problems that lead to expressions of dissatisfaction with organizational outcomes among both internal members (Ostroff, 1993) and powerful external clients, customers, or stakeholders (Savage, Nix, Whitehead, & Blair, 1991) can eventually affect resource flows to the organization and even its long-term survival (Beckhard, 1969; Weisbord, 1976).

In the third step shown in Figure 1.1, consultants *develop one or more focused models of the conditions sustaining ineffective outcomes or shaping the organization's ability to meet critical challenges.* These models summarize the factors that produce central organizational problems, such as the inability to provide services or products that satisfy customers, or the failure of the organization to obtain competitive advantage within its environment. The models concentrate on patterns and forces that have the greatest impacts on ineffective outcomes or that most directly affect the capacity to meet challenges, as well as on those forces that are most likely to be amenable to intervention.

Consultants sometimes find that research-based models from the organizational literature (e.g., Howard, 1994) help them identify sources of ineffective outcomes. For example, if consultants have identified rapid employee turnover as a core problem of the client organization, they may draw on a research-based model that identifies the causes of turnover (Bluedorn & Keon, 1985). Although the use of existing models is appealing, this approach also has significant drawbacks. Because they aim to generalize across organizations, research-based models cannot adequately reflect the unique causal patterns prevailing within any given organization. If diagnostic investigators rely heavily on existing research-based models or on existing diagnostic models, they may fail to attend closely to important cultural, environmental, and organizational features that are not contained within the original model. Similarly, investigators may be tempted to discard or discount diagnostic data that do not fit the expectations contained within the original model. Therefore, we suggest that consultants use existing models with caution and be prepared to extend and modify these models to make them directly relevant to the focal organization and the diagnostic problems.

In most cases, it is easier and more satisfactory to create a diagnostic model to match the observed organizational conditions by using inductive processes of inference and data gathering used in process consultation (Schein, 1985, 1988) or in grounded theory construction and qualitative field studies (Glaser & Strauss, 1967; Van Maanen, 1979).[11] One helpful approach to isolating the crucial sources of ineffective outcomes is to trace the links of each identified problem, representing an ineffective outcome, to the organization's system components and subcomponents. It is often useful to chart these linkages graphically. Comparisons of the charts can point to common underlying conditions, in a manner analogous to that advocated by Porras (1987) in his stream analysis (see Chapter 4 and Figure 4.2). For example, in Case 1.2 below, the consultants traced dissatisfaction among the internal and external clients of a hospital admissions department (AD) to delays and breakdowns in communication between units, to AD's structural fragmentation, and to a lack of adequate administrative procedures for interunit coordination. If necessary, additional data can be gathered to confirm or disconfirm a hypothesized linkage. The discovery of a common source of ineffectiveness then provides the basis for the construction of the final diagnostic model.

To construct diagnostic models, consultants usually have to supplement their diagnostic data with available evidence and insights from the organizational and management literature and with their own experience and intuition. Assumptions about organizational functioning, like the open-systems principles discussed in Chapter 2, can help guide the development of such models.

Nevertheless, there is no codified body of knowledge and practice concerning the etiology of organizational problems that can help investigators quickly identify the sources of ineffectiveness underlying observed problems. Hence, practitioners of diagnosis cannot readily match symptoms to underlying causes and conditions, as physicians sometimes can. The complexity and indeterminacy of organizational life, along with the noncumulative nature of most organizational research, all block the path to such a development.

In addition to providing a convincing and valid explanation of the sources of organizational problems, diagnostic models need to identify feasible points of intervention to alleviate problems. As they prepare their findings for feedback, consultants become increasingly concerned with the action implications of their findings. Sometimes, one or more major causes of ineffectiveness cannot be altered, whereas other causes of problems are amenable to intervention. For example, work rules and job assignments covered by labor-relations contracts may not be subject to negotiation. On the other hand, there may be room for discussions of the ways that employees apply these rules, and there may be opportunities for creating new mechanisms for coordinating the work of individual employees or of entire units.

In the fourth diagnostic step, consultants provide clients with *feedback,* which is cast in terms of the emergent diagnostic model. The model points to ways to reduce ineffectiveness, cope with challenges, and enhance effectiveness, even if the consultant does not make explicit action recommendations. In many instances, consultants can present feedback by graphically mapping the connections between sources of ineffectiveness and organizational problems or types of ineffectiveness (Burke, 1994; Howard, 1994). The research literature provides ample illustrations of techniques for developing such graphic presentations (e.g., Checkland & Scholes, 1990; Miles & Huberman, 1994; Nelson & Mathews, 1991).

The goal of feedback is the channeling of client energy toward decisions and actions that are likely to provide the broadest organizational benefits (Block, 1981; Neilsen, 1984). Feedback facilitates change, if it "unfreezes" opposition to change, by leading recipients to recognize the need to change current practices and helping them discover appropriate ways to achieve change. To facilitate these processes, consultants sometimes select portions of their diagnostic model and findings for feedback, rather than presenting all of their findings. Moreover, consultants encourage their clients to accept ultimate responsibility for decisions and plans flowing from the feedback discussions.

In some instances, consultants can develop a highly focused diagnosis within a matter of hours. More often, diagnosis takes several weeks. Consulting teams can undertake longer studies of very complex issues, but they run the risk that organizational conditions may change during the course of the study and that clients may lose interest in the study.

Case 1.2 describes an application of the sharp-image approach.

CASE 1.2

Mr. Nir, the newly appointed manager of the Admissions Department in Municipal Medical Center (MMC), decided to invite a team of consultants to help him find ways to make the department more "user friendly." MMC is an 800-bed acute care hospital located in one of Israel's major cities. After a period of steady growth, many of its departments, and particularly its outpatient clinics, were suffering from a variety of "growing pains." The Admissions Department (AD) is an administrative department employing 35 people in the Department Manager's Office and in physically separate units: Emergency Room Admissions, Children's Hospital Admissions, Elective Hospitalization Admissions, and the Collections Unit. AD handles both inpatient and outpatient admissions, settlement of hospital bills with sick funds and insurance companies, and collection of direct payments by tourists and other private patients.

Before undertaking the project, the consultants discussed the nature of diagnosis and organization development with Nir. They agreed to form a collaborative relationship so as to better understand the problems facing AD. With Nir's support, the consultants conducted semistructured interviews with the managers and with half of the employees. Then, a questionnaire was distributed to all administrative employees. Statements about work in AD assessed the prevalence of ineffective outcomes that had shown up in the original interviews. The consultants also examined written documents, including AD's annual reports to MMC's director and the regulations covering its operations; participated in the management staff meetings; and observed service delivery to patients, insurers, and to other hospital units. Data collection focused on effective and ineffective outcomes; on problematic features of AD's structure, processes, inputs, and external relations; and on suggestions for possible improvements.

The consultants then organized the diagnostic data within an open-systems framework. Next, they identified ineffective outcomes and sought the outcomes' roots in the many areas that respondents said needed improvement. To identify the most influential causes of problems, they ranked possible causes in terms of their probable proximity to the ineffective outcomes. For example, group processes such as communication and decision making were ranked as more immediate causes of customer complaints than were the competencies of entry-level employees, because group processes are closer in time to complaints than are personnel characteristics. In addition, group processes affect complaints more directly. The consultants considered organizing and presenting the data in terms of several available diagnostic models but eventually decided to retain the open-systems frame and to focus directly on organizational problems, their causes, and possible solutions. Many of the root causal conditions could be described in terms of system gaps, misfits, or inadequate management of interdependencies (see Chapter 2). This type of modeling of the problems and causes directed attention to organizational processes rather than to the faults or mistakes of individuals. The model thereby provided a basis for feedback that would suggest workable action alternatives without directly threatening the client or other members of the organization.

The consultants presented their diagnostic findings in oral feedback sessions with Nir and his assistants and thereafter with the entire management team, which included the heads of AD's four subunits. Administrative employees received written feedback directly from the consultants and oral feedback from their immediate managers. The consultants defined the purpose of the initial feedback to Nir and his assistants as enabling AD's managers to make data-based decisions about steps toward improving AD's effectiveness. During feedback, the consultants described a broad range of effective outcomes—including low rates of uncollected debts compared to other hospitals, streamlined work processes that took advantage of new computer software, and successfully renovated work spaces. In addition, the consultants pointed out that the employees were very committed to providing quality service and to ensuring client satisfaction.

Then, the feedback presented ineffective outcomes and their roots. One set of problems concerned the quality of services to external and internal customers. For example, insurers and sick funds complained that they had received confused written statements from several AD units. In addition, customers complained that AD employees often sent them shuttling back and forth between physically distant AD units instead of providing the required service on the spot. The consultants showed clients how customer dissatisfaction stemmed in part from misfits between two sets of interactions: those between AD management and internal clients —such as MMC top management and heads of clinical departments—and those between the heads of the AD field units and external clients. There was also a lack of fit between AD's structure and its external clients' need for continuous processing of bills and of hospital documents. AD's four field units were physically distant and were run as independent, self-contained units, each of which had its own management structure and work culture. Formal communications between the four units were slow, and there were few additional mechanisms for coordinating their operations. Nir accepted the diagnosis that customer dissatisfaction stemmed from fragmentation in AD's structure and managerial processes. Therefore, he decided to seek help from the hospital's Human Resource Management Department in introducing several integrating mechanisms, including regular all-department meetings, systematic job rotation, and streamlining of communication flows among the four units.

Case 1.2 illustrates many of the features of sharp-image diagnosis discussed above. After initial data gathering (Step 1), open-systems analysis helped consultants focus on customers' complaints and other ineffective outcomes of AD operations, and it helped them find links between these signs of ineffectiveness (Step 2). Then, the consultants narrowed their focus to just a few of AD's system characteristics, including the department's structural fragmentation and its lack of interunit coordination, and they showed how these features led to the ineffective outcomes (Step 3). Once the consultants developed a clear model of the sources of ineffectiveness in the AD, they could afford to ignore other system features that lacked clear implications for reducing ineffectiveness. This model provided the basis for feedback (Step 4) and for the client's development of a plan for action to improve AD operations.

In practice, consultants do not always follow the order shown in Figure 1.1 and described in Case 1.2. Instead, they move between phases of diagnosis in response to diagnostic findings and analysis, evolving relations with clients, and developments within the focal organization and its environment. Case 1.3 illustrates ways in which diagnostic studies can loop back to analytically and chronologically prior stages of diagnosis as the inquiry unfolds. In this instance, as consultants began to understand the forces underlying the problems presented to them, they had to renegotiate project goals and problem definitions with their client and needed to gather additional diagnostic data.

CASE 1.3

The owner and president of 21C, a small high-technology firm, asked a private consultant to examine ways to improve efficiency and morale. The client and consultant agreed that staff from the consulting firm would conduct a set of in-depth interviews with divisional managers and a sample of other employees. The first interviews with the three division heads and from the assistant director suggested that their frustrations and poor morale stemmed from the firm's lack of growth and the president's failure to include divisional managers in decision making and in strategy formulation. In light of these findings, the consultant returned to the president, discussed the results of the interviews, and suggested refocusing the diagnosis on relations between the managers and the president and on planning and strategy formulation within the firm.

In the 21C project, analysis (Steps 2 and 3 in Figure 1.1) and feedback (Step 4) began before data gathering (Step 1) was completed. The preliminary findings led the consultant to renew the contracting process, through which he sought the client's approval to redefine the project's main focus and to change the research design.

Advantages of Explicit Models

Sharp-image diagnosis aims to develop explicit diagnostic models, rather than relying solely on broad classification schemes, analytical frames, or implicit and intuitive models. There are several advantages to making diagnostic models explicit (Burke, 1994; Howard, 1994). First, practitioners of diagnosis enhance their ability to obtain a comprehensive understanding of organizational problems and their underlying conditions when they conceptualize them in terms of explicit models. Reliance on intuitive models encour-

ages selective attention to problems and relations that fit one's prior experience and knowledge. Second, the use of an explicit diagnostic model that is
based on systematic data gathering and analyses provides the consultant, other
consultants, and members of the client organization with a basis for evaluating
and improving the quality of the diagnosis. Other investigators can check more
readily whether an explicit model adequately covered key issues and organizational features and whether adequate attention was given to linkages between problems, relationships among organizational features, and possible
roots of problems. Moreover, the use of explicit models makes it easier to
judge whether a diagnostician's hypotheses about important causal relations
are correct. In addition, explicit models can be modified more readily than
implicit ones, so as to enhance the model's validity (Tichy, Hornstein, &
Nisberg, 1976).

Third, the use of explicit models motivates consultants to engage in orderly
diagnostic work and to avoid rushing ahead with recommendations for
change. Otherwise, consultants and clients may be tempted to hop on the
bandwagon of planned change before a systematic and logically sequenced
diagnosis has been completed. A sound diagnosis will bring out organizational
strengths that may be undermined by change efforts and will illuminate the
complexities of accomplishing change. Explicit diagnosis can thus discourage
consultants and clients from unjustifiably recommending high-risk projects.

Fourth, explicit models can serve as powerful tools for management development. The use of a holistic and logically organized model of the organization's core problems can help decision makers learn a new way of looking at
their organization (Howe, 1989; Lowstedt, 1993). Moreover, feedback based
on clear models can help clients develop their abilities to diagnose problems
on their own. The development of a broad, integrative view of organizational
affairs and the ability to engage in self-diagnosis can, in turn, contribute to
organizational learning and the capacity for organizational self-renewal.

Diagnosis in Context

Consultants and decision makers shape the focal concerns of diagnosis and
its processes and methods in response to the decision issues facing them, to
diagnostic objectives, and to the interpersonal and organizational contexts in
which diagnosis occurs. Comparisons among alternative diagnostic goals and
roles for consultants capture many of these important variations.

Diagnostic Goals

Behavioral science consultants and researchers use diagnostic techniques in the pursuit of several goals besides the reduction of organizational ineffectiveness. Traditionally, organization development consultants defined their project goals as the enhancement of organizational effectiveness or the improvement of overall organizational health (e.g., Beckhard, 1969; Cummings & Worley, 1993). Diagnosis then becomes a means of helping consultants identify ways of enhancing effectiveness and of deciding which types of consultant and managerial interventions are most likely to yield desired improvements (Kolb & Frohman, 1970). This approach to diagnosis and to consultation in general seems to be most appropriate when organizations are stable or growing and when clients can reach agreement on definitions of effectiveness (see Chapter 3).

Diagnoses can also aim at providing periodic feedback on organizational functioning (e.g., Nadler, 1977). Feedback from these periodic assessments then can be used to reduce ineffectiveness or to enhance effectiveness. Periodic assessments of this type can contribute substantially to organizational learning if the recipients of feedback develop the capacity to critically assess data on their organization's operations in light of managerial, social, technological, and economic changes (Cummings & Worley, 1993; Nadler, Mirvis, & Cammann, 1976; Torbert, 1981; Wildavsky, 1972). On the other hand, learning will be blocked if feedback and analysis cover a very narrow set of measures that does not adequately reflect critical dimensions of organizational performance and adaptation to change (Kaplan & Norton, 1992, 1993).

In most instances, consultants and clients view diagnosis as contributing to problem solving and incremental organizational change. But diagnosis can also provide input into efforts to bring about fundamental, strategic change, in the sense of shifts in resource allocation, structural design, and other practices that have major consequences for internal operations and environmental relations. In some cases, these strategic changes aim at systemwide organizational transformations (Bartunek & Louis, 1988; Kilmann et al., 1988), which involve basic changes in the organization's goals, structures, strategies, and culture and in relations among these features. Transformations usually require members of the organization to bend or break out of accepted ways of thinking and acting and to develop new frames for understanding their work and evaluating it (Bartunek & Moch, 1987; Nadler, 1988). Changes like these evolve over a period of several years under the leadership of top management (Tichy & DeVanna, 1986). Efforts to achieve transformations often follow major shifts in organizational power alignments or crises that threaten the organization's survival. To accomplish such fundamental changes, management may draw on the advice of consultants with expertise in many different areas.

Diagnostic studies can help decision makers deal with many of the most important phases of programs for strategic change or organizational transformation. The diagnostic investigator can provide feedback and guidance on the need for radical change, the organization's capacity for change, ways to enhance this capacity, and on feasible routes to change (see Chapter 13). Furthermore, diagnostic investigators can assess progress toward program implementation (e.g., Chapter 7) and can help managers revise their plans and goals in light of internal and external developments during the transformation period (Nadler et al., 1995).

The Contemporary Health Facilities project described in Case 1.4 shows how consultants can help clients assess the need and prospects for organizational transformation. The case illustrates well the interplay between diagnostic framing and client-consultant interactions. The project's two clients initially envisioned a different diagnostic goal from the one they ultimately adopted. They redefined their goals through dialogue with each other and with the consultant.

CASE 1.4

The head of training of a national health care system received a request from the director of one of its member organizations—here called Contemporary Health Facility (CHF)—for an ambitious program that would train CHF employees to undertake a major organizational transformation. The transformation proposed by the director would radically redefine the goals and mission of CHF. Moreover, it would alter CHF's patient characteristics, personnel, size, structure, and its relations with other health care organizations. The director was worried that CHF's nursing staff and administrative employees would oppose the far-reaching changes that he envisioned for CHF. Unconvinced that the training program was justified, the head of training reached an agreement with the CHF director to ask an independent consultant to assess the situation. After discussions between the consultant, the head of training, and the top managers at CHF, all parties agreed to broaden the study goals to include assessment of the feasibility of the planned transformation and the staff's readiness for the change. Training was to be considered as only one of the possible steps that might facilitate the change.

Over a period of 3 weeks, the consultant conducted in-depth interviews with CHF's three top managers and with seven staff members who held positions of authority. In addition, he conducted group interviews with 12 lower-level staff members; made site visits; and examined data on CHF's personnel, patient characteristics, and administration. The consultant analyzed and presented these data within the context of a guiding model (derived in part from Tichy, 1983) of the preconditions for strategic organizational change. The major finding was that the transformation was both desirable and feasible, although accomplishing it would be risky and difficult. In his report and oral feedback to the CHF management and to the director of training, the consultant conveyed these conclusions and some of the findings on which they were based. Moreover, the consultant recommended steps that the director of CHF should take to overcome opposition and build support for the proposed transformation of CHF and ways of implementing the transformation. The report also recommended ways to improve organizational climate, enhance staffing procedures, and improve other aspects of organizational effectiveness *with or without* implementing the program to transform CHF.

The director of training originally phrased the diagnostic problem in terms of assessing the need for the training program requested by CHF's director. The consultant helped reframe this issue into two more basic issues: assessing the feasibility of accomplishing the organizational transformation envisioned by the director, and discovering steps that the management could take to facilitate the transformation. This redefinition of the diagnostic problem thus contained an image of the organization's desired state that fit both client expectations and social science knowledge about organizational transformations. Moreover, this reformulation helped specify the issues that should be studied in depth and suggested ways that the clients could deal with the problem that concerned them initially.

There is growing evidence that many systemwide changes in areas such as quality assurance, teamwork, and reengineering do not attain many of the ambitious objectives set for them. It seems likely that diagnostic studies of the need and prospects for change, like the one conducted at CHF, can help managers decide whether or not to launch far-reaching programs of change and can enhance their capacity to implement appropriate programs (Mitroff, Mason, & Pearson, 1994; Nadler et al., 1995).

Roles of Consultants and Members
of the Focal Organization

The roles that clients, consultants, and other actors take in a diagnosis also shape its focus and processes. Diagnoses of the sort described in this book are conducted most frequently by in-house or external behavioral science consultants who specialize in organization development, applied research, human resource management, or related fields (Church & Burke, 1995). Whether or not these diagnoses follow the sharp-image approach, they typically incorporate preparatory, data-gathering, analysis, and feedback stages.

As already noted, managers and other decision makers can engage in diagnostic inquiry as part of their ongoing decision-making process, without the aid of external or in-house consultants. For instance, managers adopt a diagnostic approach if they carefully examine the current and projected future state of their organization and its environment as a prelude to reformulating strategic or operational objectives.

In some cases, members of an organization formalize diagnostic activities in self-study projects (e.g., Beer & Eisenstat, 1996). Members of an organization can conduct a self-diagnosis without the aid of a professional consultant if they are open to self-analysis and criticism, and if some members have the skills needed for the gathering and interpretation of information. Case 1.5 illustrates a modest self-diagnosis (Austin, 1982, p. 20):

CASE 1.5

The executive director of a multi-service youth agency appointed a program-review committee to make a general evaluation of the services provided by the agency and make recommendations for improving its effectiveness. The committee included clinical case workers, supervisors, administrators, and several members of the agency's governing board. The director of the agency, who had technical knowledge of how to conduct such a study, served as an advisor to the committee. She asked the committee members to look first at the agency's intake service, because it was central to the operations of the entire agency and suffered from high turnover among its paid staff. Besides examining intake operations, the committee members decided to investigate whether clients were getting appropriate services. They interviewed both the paid and the volunteer intake staff and surveyed clients over a three-month period. Their main finding was that there were substantial delays in client referral to counseling. They traced these delays to the difficulties that the half-time coordinator of intake faced in handling the large staff, many of whom were volunteers, and to the heavy burden of record keeping that fell on the intake workers. This paperwork was required by funding agencies but did not contribute directly to providing services to clients. To increase the satisfaction of the intake staff and thereby reduce turnover, the committee recommended that the coordinator's position be made full time and that paperwork at intake be reduced. The executive director accepted the first recommendation and asked for further study of how to streamline the record-keeping process and reduce paperwork.

As this case suggests, during self-diagnosis, members of the organization temporarily take on some of the tasks that would otherwise have been the responsibility of a professional consultant. Many of the diagnostic frames and models described in this book, and in other treatments of diagnosis (e.g., Howard, 1994; Manzini, 1988), could contribute to such self-studies. People who want to conduct a self-diagnosis or act as consultants should be skilled at handling the interpersonal relations that develop during a study and at giving feedback to groups and individuals, as well as at gathering and analyzing diagnostic data.

One of the most important dimensions of variation in consultants' roles in diagnosis concerns the degree to which consultants intervene actively in the focal unit or organization. Intervention during diagnosis is partly an unintended or uncontrolled by-product of the substantive focus of the diagnosis and of its data-gathering techniques. Even if consultants restrict their role to gathering and providing diagnostic feedback, their activities entail at least a minimal intervention into the everyday life of the members of the organization (Argyris, 1970). Diagnostic activity interrupts organizational routines, may affect members' expectations concerning change, and may influence how they think about themselves and their organization. For instance, the questions asked by consultants and the types of data that interest them can create "experimenter effects" on those from whom information is being collected. In addition, the very fact that a diagnosis is being conducted creates expectations of change and may lead participants to act on their hopes, fears, and assumptions about likely changes. The process of diagnostic inquiry can also focus participants' attention on specific issues or problems. Sometimes, diagnosis can lead participants to adopt different frames for analyzing their activities and their organization. These effects can stem from interactions that occur outside of the formal feedback process, as well as during feedback.

In some instances, by raising members' expectations, consultants intentionally encourage the development of a positive, self-fulfilling prophecy, which leads to behavioral and cognitive changes that complement the goals of planned change (Eden, 1990). On other occasions, participants react to diagnosis in unforeseen ways that diverge from project goals. Moreover, when participants do not feel that tangible improvements followed the diagnosis, they can become more frustrated and less trusting of management.

Consultant intervention is not just a by-product of diagnostic work. Consultants sometimes choose to use the diagnostic process as a way of intervening to promote organizational change. In *process consultation* (Schein, 1988), for example, consultants provide diagnostic feedback on group processes to heighten awareness of these processes and thereby lead participants to seek ways to improve them. In a similar vein, Miller (1992) and other practitioners from the Tavistock Institute seek to provide feedback that helps clients view the organization as an open system. Other diagnostic interventions seek to promote teamwork and facilitate planning and decision making through *diagnostic workshops* for management teams or steering committees responsible for change projects. During the workshops, the consultants may lead participants to examine their organization's culture (Lundberg, 1990); clarify their goals and strategies (Jayaram, 1976); or choose and implement appropriate organization designs (Stebbins & Shani, 1989).

Once they have completed a diagnosis, consultants may end their relationship with the clients, or they can continue to fill a wide range of roles aimed at promoting change within the focal unit (Harrison, 1991; Nees & Greiner, 1985). In traditional organization development projects, diagnosis was regarded as a stage leading to the planning of additional interventions by behavioral science consultants and their clients (e.g., Kolb & Frohman, 1970).

Another variation in consulting roles involves the degree to which consultants actively involve members of the client organization in the diagnosis. Many practitioners of organization development and action research favor client-centered or collaborative approaches, such as the diagnostic workshops just described. Collaborative approaches encourage clients or members of the organization appointed by them to become actively involved in most phases of diagnosis (Chisholm & Elden, 1993; Lawler & Drexler, 1980; Turner, 1982). These approaches enable members of the focal organization to contribute their insider's understanding and expertise to the study as they share in problem definition, research design, data gathering, and analysis. To enhance member involvement in diagnosis and change, special steering committees can be set up that are parallel to, but outside of, the operating hierarchy of the organization. These steering groups may define project goals, conduct all or part of the diagnosis, plan interventions, and supervise project implementation (Rubenstein & Woodman, 1984; Stein & Kanter, 1980). In formal action-research projects, applied researchers and members of the organization plan the diagnostic study together. Then, the investigators conduct the formal research study with or without the aid of participants, and they provide feedback before, during, and after planned changes.

Collaborative and client-centered approaches contrast with the tendency of many consultants to minimize members' participation in diagnosis. Consultants who define themselves mainly as substantive experts, rather than as facilitators of interpersonal and organizational processes, usually adopt a very consultant-centered approach to diagnosis. In these instances, consultants contract with clients concerning the nature of the diagnosis and then assume primary responsibility for study design, data gathering, analysis, and feedback. In these projects, formal relations between clients and consultants typically end with the delivery of the diagnostic report. Subsequent negotiations determine whether the consultant will continue to work with the clients on other phases of the change project.

There are many practical and methodological drawbacks to involving members of the client organization in the design, gathering, and analysis of diagnostic data (see Chapter 4). Moreover, this type of involvement may be incompatible with the organizational culture and with the clients' change goals and their tactics for implementing change. However, if client-centered diagnosis is appropriate and feasible, it can substantially enhance the credibility and salience of diagnostic findings. Moreover, participation in diagnosis can help members develop the capacity to assess their own operations and thereby contribute to organizational learning (see Chapter 13).

Effective Diagnosis

Consultants and clients can assess the success and effectiveness of diagnosis and assessment in two ways. The first examines whether diagnosis helps clients meet agreed-upon objectives. Diagnoses can aim at attaining highly focused goals, such as solving specific organizational problems; midrange goals, such as eliminating critical ineffective outcomes or helping organizations meet specific challenges; and very broad goals, such as enhancing organizational learning and facilitating organizational transformations (Turner, 1982). The sharp-image approach to diagnosis aims mainly at midrange goals, which seem realistic and appropriate for most diagnostic projects.

The second way of evaluating a diagnosis examines its contributions to client and organizational effectiveness, regardless of the initial objectives that were set for the diagnosis. From this standpoint, diagnosis is effective when it motivates and empowers managers to reduce critical forms of ineffectiveness and face challenges; when it contributes to client learning and to the adoption of a diagnostic approach to problem solving and decision making; and when it contributes to organizational flexibility and adaptation to environmental change.

Effective diagnosis, whether defined in terms of goal attainment or organizational contributions, turns on the ability of diagnostic practitioners and members of the focal organization to frame and diagnose problems and challenges in ways that are both useful and valid; on the use of appropriate methods for data gathering and analysis; and on the development of constructive relations between clients and consultants and among members of the client relations. All of these facets of diagnosis must generate support and motivation for change among the heads of the units undergoing change and other influential clients.[12] This book focuses on the ways that framing and analysis of diagnostic issues contribute to effective diagnosis. Diagnostic framing deserves close attention because it has been examined less thoroughly than have diagnostic methods and client-consultant interactions. Moreover, many consultations and managerial initiatives appear to fail because of inadequate diagnoses of problems, challenges, and change prospects. Despite its importance, incisive framing and analysis of diagnostic issues is insufficient to promote organizational improvement. Instead, diagnostic framing must also promote—or at least not harm—client support and motivation for change and should contribute to good working relations among all those taking part in the diagnostic project.

Sharp-image diagnosis seeks to respond simultaneously to the analytical tasks of diagnosis and to the requirements for sustaining a constructive consultation. In Case 1.2, for example, the consultants took care to ensure that the client understood and accepted the diagnostic approach to be used. The consultants deepened the client's commitment to the project by focusing quickly on the specific problems and ineffective outcomes that were most troubling to members of the organization and to their clients. Then, the consultants developed an explanatory model that distinguished symptoms of ineffectiveness and presented problems from their underlying causes. This model helped the client discover feasible ways of removing these causes of ineffectiveness. Furthermore, the model used in feedback helped motivate the client to undertake change by pointing to solutions that did not directly threaten the client or his colleagues.

The chapters that follow present models and frames that can enhance the effectiveness of diagnosis, other forms of applied research, and managerial decision making. In many instances, diagnosis can benefit by developing empirically grounded models of core problems and organizational challenges. In other cases, diagnosis can form part of assessments of prospects for strategic change (e.g., Chapters 7 and 13) or can help decision makers evaluate the operations of one or more critical organizational functions (e.g., Chapter 8).

The examinations of organizational models and frames in the chapters that follow can also enhance academic understanding of planned change and of organizational effectiveness. Several of the chapters develop or refine models that are applicable to nonapplied research, as well as to consultation. Moreover, the book as a whole contributes to scholarly efforts to map the critical contingencies affecting the prospects for planned organizational change and shaping the organizational consequences of change techniques and managerial interventions. This contextualized view of planned change serves as a corrective to earlier attempts to characterize the causes of organizational effectiveness and the nature of planned change in highly generalized and ideal-typical terms.

Notes

1. In a study of the competencies that American managers in 1,500 firms expected from their colleagues in human resource management, the domain relating to managing change was the most important for assessment of success as a human resource professional (Ulrich, Brockbank, Yeung, & Lake, 1995). See McMahan and Woodman (1992) for surveys of the roles of organization development consultants in large firms.

2. References on drawbacks and failures of popular change techniques appear later in this chapter and in Chapters 6 and 7.

3. Consultant-bashing ("Survey," 1997) and attacks on management fads have now reached such proportions that they are becoming an influential fashion in their own right (Abrahamson & Fairchild, 1997).

4. With due respect to Adams's wit, telling clients that they are the root of the problem will probably lead them to become defensive and to resist taking constructive steps toward change. For an alternative approach, see Case 1.2.

5. Cross-references to chapters will be used primarily to show the location of treatments of topics that are not listed in chapter headings.

6. See Harrison (1994) for distinctions between diagnosis and evaluation.

7. In a similar vein, Astley and Van de Ven (1983) distinguish Natural Selection, Collective-Action, System-Structural, and Strategic-Choice views of organization and management. Reed (1992, 1996) discusses six metanarratives in organizational theory.

8. When no references are provided for a case, they are based on the experiences of one of us, who acted as the main consultant or as a member of the consulting team. All of the reported cases in which we participated involved organizations in Israel.

9. This same criticism applies to other internally focused techniques, such as reengineering.

10. Further support for the preference for examining ineffectiveness comes from prospect theory, which argues that people are more willing to take risks when they are dissatisfied with their current situation and view themselves as operating below a desired reference point (Fiegenbaum, Hart, & Schendel, 1996). In contrast, when they view themselves as above the reference point, managers are more apt to become risk averse. In like manner, research shows that organizations tend to make strategic changes when their performance is declining but avoid major changes when performance is good or improving. It should be noted, however, that decline can also produce rigidity and resistance to change (McKinley, 1993; Staw et al., 1981).

11. Harrison (1994) reviews other research designs and techniques used in diagnosis.

12. See Beer and Eisenstat (1997) for a listing of diagnostic requirements that stresses the comprehensiveness of diagnosis, rather than its focus, and stresses the importance of fostering collaboration within the focal organization and between clients and consultants. In our view, the feasibility of both types of collaboration depends on the nature of the diagnostic project and of the focal organization (see Dunphy & Stace, 1988, 1993; Harrison, 1991).

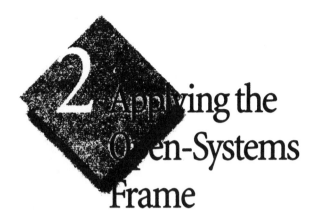

2 Applying the Open-Systems Frame

During the 1960s and 1970s, the open-systems (OS) approach (Katz & Kahn, 1978) swept through the social sciences, informing both applied and basic research and providing a conceptual foundation for behavioral science consultation. Adoption of a systems frame helped researchers in the social sciences to discover commonalities with fields such as biology and engineering, and it provided a basis for an interdisciplinary approach to organizations. According to the OS perspective, any group or organization can be viewed as a system obtaining inputs from its environment, processing these inputs, and producing outputs. OS theory posits that systems have certain common operating principles, including their tendency to run down (negative entropy) if not provided with additional resources from the environment and their tendency to retain a state of equilibrium if not disturbed (Ashmos & Huber, 1987).

After a brief overview of the background to OS analysis and of current variants on the systems approach, this chapter examines advantages and disadvantages of using OS analysis in diagnosis. Analytical frameworks derived from the OS approach can help guide the early phases of diagnosis by facilitating a comprehensive view of the focal organization, its major subcomponents, and its environment. After developing this overview, the diagnostic practitioner can zero in on specific features, problems, and challenges. The second part of the chapter presents a basic OS framework and discusses its use as an orienting frame for diagnosis. Special attention is paid to relations between system levels and to the assessment of organizational strengths, weaknesses, opportunities, and threats (SWOT). The third part of the chapter synthesizes and critically reviews three diagnostic procedures that add analytical power and specificity to the OS frame and thereby can contribute directly to sharp-image diagnosis. These procedures involve *assessing fits* among system components and subcomponents, *examining critical interdependencies,* and *identifying gaps* between current and desired system outcomes and states.

Background

The OS frame originally drew on General System Theory (Bertalanffy, 1968) and on several variations on the systems idea, including the work of Boulding (1956) and Miller (1978). Many of the early streams in systems theory continued to develop independently (Kline, 1995). Among the earliest contributors to the systems approach was cybernetics, with its concern for system control and feedback (Ashby, 1956; Beer, 1985). Hard-systems thinking of this sort often considered issues of scheduling and inventory control and later on cost-benefit analysis (Jackson, 1992). Work on system dynamics (e.g., Forrester, 1961) continued and elaborated the interest in feedback processes and interdependencies among system components (Senge, 1990). Sociotechnical systems (e.g., Cummings, 1993; Rice, 1963), yet another application of the systems approach, emphasized the interdependence of human and technical elements within the organization and gave rise to several important diagnostic models.

A fundamental theme in much of the OS work cited in this chapter concerns the need for organizations to adapt to environmental conditions. Many studies showed that organizational success depends on adapting to external change, producing outputs that are valued by external stakeholders, and selecting supportive environmental niches in which to operate.[1] Systems thinking and research also directed attention to the crucial impact of information about the environment on managerial decision making and to the complex interplay of forces for system stability and change.

Several recent streams within systems thinking stress the importance of organizational cognition and of the processes through which members learn about and interpret system operations (Senge, 1990).[2] Soft-system methodology (Checkland, 1981; Checkland & Scholes, 1990), for example, advocates constructing several system models that reflect the cognitive maps of participants in organizational problem solving. Comparisons among these maps can contribute to organizational learning and to consensus building among divergent stakeholders (Jackson, 1995). A further contribution of soft-system methodology is its proposal to move from unstructured to structured definitions of problems, and then to construct a causal analysis of the sources of structured problems. This approach contributed directly to our view of problem framing and model construction in sharp-image diagnosis.

In response to this outpouring of systems theory and research, practitioners of management education and development drew extensively on the OS approach. OS was seen as a useful way to help managers view their organizations in more productive ways and to learn to diagnose and solve pressing problems (e.g., Senge, 1990).

Similarly, practitioners of organizational diagnosis recommended using OS to guide problem definition, data gathering, analysis, and feedback of diagnostic data (Beer, 1980; Beer, 1985; Nadler & Tushman, 1980a; Neilsen, 1984; Walton & Nadler, 1994). The OS perspective can contribute to diagnosis in several important ways. First, the OS framework is widely applicable. It is possible to analyze *any* focal organization, subunit, or set of organizations in terms of the flows of inputs—such as cash, personnel, and information—the processing of these inputs, and the creation of goods, services, and other outputs. Similarly, it is possible to trace links among basic system components of environment technology, structure, culture, and behavior (see Figure 2.1) and among their subcomponents. The OS frame thus provides a useful starting point for diagnosis regardless of the focal organization's size, complexity, purpose, technology, life cycle stage, ownership, or cultural and institutional context.

A second contribution of the OS frame to diagnosis is that it leads consultants and managers to adopt a holistic approach (Jackson, 1992) by examining the overall environmental and organizational contexts within which problems arise and within which steps toward organizational improvement are enacted. The OS approach can thus help practitioners of diagnosis consider all components of the organizational system and their interactions, rather than just examining specific issues and problems that are easy to study or are widely discussed within the organization. Holism can also help consultants and managers avoid seizing on popular or readily available change techniques that are not likely to provide sufficient leverage to bring about systemwide change.

Third, the OS frame can help consultants and clients deal with the complexity of organizational performance and change and thereby resist the temptations of management fads. Many fads encourage simplistic thinking: Introduce Program X and you will achieve the outcomes you desire—excellence, quality, client satisfaction, profits, and organizational prestige. In contrast, the systems approach encourages more complicated thinking, which recognizes contingent relations and examines interactions between units, levels, and subsystems within an organization.

Fourth, systems-based diagnosis can help consultants and clients distinguish symptoms of ineffectiveness from underlying, systemic causes (Senge, 1990). By tracing presented problems to misfits and problematic flows among system components, as is done in sharp-image diagnosis (Chapter 1) and in stream analysis (Porras, 1987; see also Chapter 4), consultants can discover enduring system features that account for acute problems and may even lead to organizational crises.

Fifth, the OS perspective alerts consultants and their clients to look for possible side effects of actions—unanticipated and hard-to-diagnose consequences that can alter the status quo within the system (Senge, 1990). These unanticipated outcomes can occur when changes in one system component lead to developments somewhere in a distant, but interdependent part of the system. For example, the introduction of computer networking capacity can create opportunities for some people and groups to obtain and communicate information that was previously unavailable to them and thereby increase their influence over communication and decision-making processes. The change in computer technology can unintentionally lead to unanticipated shifts in the distribution of power within the organization and can gradually alter decision processes and outcomes.

There are also significant limitations on the use of the OS frame in diagnosis and in management development. Some of the system laws and principles that were articulated by early OS theorists, such as Katz and Kahn, proved too abstract to be useful in research and consultation. For instance, the concept of integration or fit among system components requires more definition and specification than it was given in early formulations of systems ideas.

Furthermore, some of the underlying assumptions of OS theory bias the investigator toward a particular view of organizational conditions before these conditions have been investigated empirically. Moreover, acceptance of the a priori assumptions of OS theory can lead investigators to overlook important organizational features and processes (Burrell & Morgan, 1979). In particular, early researchers and consultants who drew on the systems perspective tended to pay too little attention to the political forces operating in and around organizations, to the dynamics of organizational change and conflict, and to the processes through which participants assign meanings to organizational conditions and external developments (Abrahamsson, 1977; Silverman, 1970). To compensate for the omission of political forces, consultants and applied researchers added political concepts, such as that of the dominant coalition, to the original OS frame (e.g., Beer, 1980).

A further limitation of the OS frame is that its very universality and abstractness can lead researchers and consultants to adopt a superficial approach that overlooks important details of organizational operations and ignores significant differences among organizations and among organizational contexts. Yet sensitivity to a firm's distinctive history, people, setting, and practices can prove crucial to good consulting, just as this type of responsiveness to detail is vital to good management. Managers and consultants sometimes learn from the school of hard knocks that it is simply not true that if you have seen or run one organization, you have seen them all.

In summary, the OS frame provides a means of looking at organizations and describing them using common terminology, rather than an explanatory model of how organizations work. To specify the causes of ineffectiveness or of effectiveness and to identify possible solutions to problems, investigators must conduct empirically grounded investigations like the ones described in Case 1.2. Or they may draw on well-researched propositions and additional theories that specify links between conceptual elements within the frame and between these elements and manifestations of ineffectiveness.

The OS frame can provide a useful guide to the first two phases of sharp-image diagnosis described in Chapter 1 (see Figure 1.1). But we must analytically and empirically specify the frame further before constructing highly focused models for analysis and feedback. The second part of this chapter, as well as Chapter 4, take up the task of analytical specification, as do several later chapters in the book. In addition, to develop valid and useful diagnoses, consultants need to supplement the OS frame with other diagnostic frames. Chapters 3 and 5, along with several chapters in the second part of

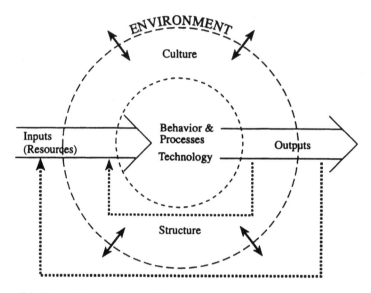

Figure 2.1 Open-Systems Framework
Key: Broken line shows system boundary; dotted line shows feedback loops.

this book, present these additional useful frames, whereas Chapter 15 addresses the challenge of combining frames.

Framework for Open-Systems Analysis

Figure 2.1 presents an OS framework that has proved itself useful in diagnosis.[3] The framework shown in the figure, and the definitions of system components that follow, will serve as reference points throughout the remainder of this book.

System Components

Here are the main system components, along with some of their most important subcomponents, and some major aspects of system dynamics:

Inputs (Resources)—raw materials, money, people (human resources), equipment, information, knowledge, and legal authorizations that an organization obtains from its environment and that contribute to the creation of its outputs.

Outputs—products, services, and ideas that are the outcomes of organizational action. An organization transfers its main outputs back to the environment and uses others internally. *Productivity* and *performance* measures examine the quantity and occasionally the quality of outputs. *Human outcomes* constitute important by-products of system functioning. These include behavioral outcomes such as absenteeism, work effort and cooperation, industrial disputes, turnover, and employee health and safety. In addition, there are subjective outcomes, such as employee satisfaction and perceived quality of working life.

System Processing (Transformations)—the ways in which the organization transforms inputs into outputs. Transformations in human service organizations involve treating, training, and classifying clients. Two main components contribute to system processing: *Technology* refers to the tools, equipment, and techniques used to process inputs. *Organizational behavior and processes* refers to the prevailing patterns of interaction between individuals and groups, which may contribute directly or indirectly to transforming inputs into outputs. Transformative processes include mental procedures, such as medical diagnosis; social procedures, such as group work in psychotherapy; as well as the applications of tangible technologies, such as medications. Subcomponents of behavior and processes that are particularly important for handling functional challenges include processes of cooperation, conflict, coordination, communication, controlling and rewarding behavior, influence processes and power relations, supervision, leadership, decision making, problem solving, information gathering, self-criticism, evaluation, group learning, and goal setting. Members' goals and objectives often refer to their expectations for current system performance or for desired future states of inputs, processes, outputs, and other components.

Environment—the *close (task) environment* includes all the external organizations and conditions that are directly related to the system's transformative processes and its technologies. These external organizations and forces encompass funding sources, suppliers, distributors, unions, customers, clients, regulators, competitors, strategic partners (e.g., in joint manufacturing ventures), markets for products and resources, and the state of knowledge concerning the organization's technologies. The *remote (general) environment* includes institutions and conditions having infrequent or long-term impacts on the organization and its close environment, including the economy, the legal and political systems, the state of scientific and technical knowledge, social institutions such as the family, population distribution and composition, and local or national cultures within which the organization operates.

Structure—enduring relations between individuals, groups, and larger units—including role assignments (job descriptions, authority, responsibility, privileges attached to positions); grouping of positions in divisions, departments, and other units; standard operating procedures; established administrative arrangements for handling key processes such as coordination (e.g., committees, weekly meetings); control, human resources management, rewards, planning; job designs; and physical arrangements. Emergent structural patterns (e.g. informal cliques, coalitions, power distribution) can differ substantially from officially mandated ones. Structure constrains and focuses behavior without determining it.

Culture—shared norms, values, beliefs, and assumptions, as well as the behavior and artifacts that express these orientations—including symbols, rituals, stories, and language. Culture includes norms and understandings about the nature and identity of the organization, the way work is done, the value and possibility of changing or innovating, relations between lower- and higher-ranking members, and the nature of the environment.

System Dynamics—the system framework shown in Figure 2.1 contains dynamic features, including *feedback* of information and demands from within the organization and outside it. Feedback loops appear as dotted lines in Figure 2.1. System dynamics not depicted in the figure, but discussed in later chapters, include processes of growth, contraction, development, adjustment, innovation, learning, and changes in basic configurations of system components and subcomponents.

Key Features of the OS Frame

The OS frame contains several important ideas for diagnosis:

1. *The OS frame can be applied at several analytical levels,* ranging from interacting networks of organizations that produce a particular product or service (e.g., Chapter 14), total organizations, interdepartmental groups (e.g., divisions), face-to-face teams (e.g., Chapter 6), and individuals. Viewing units located at the same analytical level as systems facilitates diagnostic comparisons between them. Examining interchanges between levels shows that conditions, processes, and outcomes at any given level are often influenced by those at higher and lower levels (Miller & Miller, 1991; Rashford & Coghlan, 1994; Rousseau, 1985). Nevertheless, phenomena at a higher system level cannot be adequately reduced to those at another, lower level, nor can lower-level phenomena be fully captured by analyses of higher levels.[4]

When the system model is applied to an organization or unit, such as a project team that is nested within a larger organization, other units within the organization will constitute much or all of the focal unit's task environment. Caution is necessary in applying the systems framework to supportive or regulatory subunits that do not contribute directly to the production of goods and services. These subsystems do not display all of the properties of potentially independent, viable systems (Beer, 1985). For example, they do not necessarily contain mechanisms for maintaining equilibrium.

2. *Any organizational system may be described as made up of interdependent components like those shown in Figure 2.1.* The organization also can be viewed as consisting of subsystems whose functions are delineated in abstract terms, such as system maintenance and adaptation, or more concretely in terms of functions, such as human resource management and research and development. Developments within one component within these systems and subsystems can have consequences for other components.

3. *An organization's effectiveness and success depend heavily on its ability to adapt to its environment, shape that environment, or find a favorable environment in which to operate.* External conditions influence resource flows and the reception of outputs. External forces can also directly affect work processes, structure, and other internal system features (e.g., when regulatory agencies define standards for safety, packaging, or advertising). Figure 2.1 depicts the possibility for direct impacts on internal operations by showing a broken, permeable boundary around the organization. The external feedback loop depicts environmental responses to products or services that affect inputs.

Organization-environment relations form a major focus for OS-guided diagnosis and consultation. In addition to assessing adaptation to external constraints, diagnosis can examine the ways that members of an organization can shape their environment. For example, they may form alliances with other organizations or influence the behavior of clients, customers, and regulators.[5]

4. *Organizations use many of their products, services, and ideas as inputs to organizational maintenance or growth.* This feature is shown in Figure 2.1 by the feedback loop within the organizational boundary. A computer firm uses its own machines and software, and a university employs some of its doctoral students as instructors. Individual and group outcomes also feed back into the organization.

5. *People are a vital system resource.* They bring skills, knowledge, experience, and energy to the organization and continue to develop and change after joining it. The background, orientations, and accumulating experience of members contribute to emergent forms of organizational behavior and culture (Chapters 9 and 10).

6. *An organization's effectiveness depends substantially on its ability to meet internal system needs—including tying people into their roles in the organiza-*

tion, conducting transformative processes, and managing operations—as well as on adaptation to the environment (Katz & Kahn, 1978). These "system needs" do not necessarily correspond to the interests or priorities of top management. The nature and intensity of these system requirements vary across the organizational life cycle (see Chapter 11).

7. *Developments in and outside of organizations create pressures for change, as well as forces for inertia and stability.* Employee behavior and interpretations can reinforce or alter current practices. Change can result from visible pressure (e.g., union demands) and from hidden bargains and alliances. Change can also occur almost imperceptibly as people reinterpret their jobs and their work environments. Change that occurs in response to internal or external problems and pressures is *reactive,* whereas *anticipatory* (proactive) change entails conscious efforts by members to improve environmental standing or internal operations before pressure for change becomes acute. *Incremental changes* do not alter the main features of the seven system components, whereas *strategic changes* entail basic changes in one or more critical components—such as structure, environment, or culture—and in relations among these components (Nadler & Tushman, 1989).[6]

Applying the OS Framework

The OS framework can help practitioners of diagnosis develop a broad overview of the focal organization and its challenges. The discussion that follows sketches three applications of the OS frame that are particularly useful in the early phases of diagnosis. First, the OS framework can serve as a guide to gathering basic organizational information.[7] To follow this approach, investigators use the framework to generate a detailed outline of relevant information to be obtained on system components, important subcomponents, and on system dynamics. Preliminary information on these components and on system dynamics can come from a few knowledgeable members of the organization and from organizational records and documents.

By way of illustration, consider the nature and sources of basic data on system inputs, environment, and dynamics. Data on system inputs would come from records of sales, services, or funding allocations. Further data on inputs could reflect financial and capital assets, along with human resource indicators, such as the numbers of employees by category, their levels of training, and their work experience. Basic data on the organizational environment includes information on the organization's ownership, affiliations, and strategic alliances. In addition, the investigator seeks information on the major organizations and conditions in the focal organization's task environment. During preliminary interviews, the investigator can also ask members to describe the ease with which the organization can obtain needed resources from its environment, the extent of competition with other organizations, and important pressures or threats coming from the environment. The investigator can also note critical physical, geographical, and institutional conditions affecting the organization's operations and its future prospects. Important system dynamics to consider include data on the growth or contraction of organizational operations and on the flows of inputs and outputs. Some knowledge of the history of the organization will also prove useful, particularly if it sheds light on life cycle dynamics like those discussed in Chapter 11.

A second application of the OS frame that is often used in strategy formulation examines four crucial features of the focal system or subsystem—strengths, weaknesses, opportunities, and threats (SWOT)—and the interactions among these four features. By focusing on threats and opportunities, SWOT analysis draws attention to major internal and external forces that can enhance or undermine system effectiveness or that are likely to do so in the future. Threats refer to conditions that produce or are expected to create ineffectiveness by producing declines in system inputs, throughputs, or outputs, or in some combination of the three. Opportunities refer to situations that members might exploit in order to overcome threats or enhance organizational effectiveness in the future.

Identifying system strengths and weaknesses helps pinpoint features affecting the organization's ability to respond to threats and opportunities. System strengths can be thought of as current success factors—features that contribute to the organization's ability to obtain resources, process them efficiently while attaining high levels of quality, and provide services or products that are highly valued by the environment. Strengths can also refer to features that contain an unrealized potential for helping the organization make internal changes or enhance its environmental position. For example, a highly trained and flexible workforce could be a potential strong point in a firm that is introducing new technologies or entering new markets. Weaknesses are internal forces or features of environmental relations that lead to ineffective performance or block plans to enhance current operations. A poorly trained workforce or one accustomed to inflexible work rules would constitute a weakness for a firm facing a major technological change.

The SWOT approach quickly directs attention to fundamental strategic questions concerning the ability of the organization to obtain and maintain a favorable competitive position in its environment (see Chapter 13). A limitation of SWOT analysis is that its categories are very broad. Users must rely on their own experience and insights when specifying relations between the components in the scheme. Hence, users of the scheme may be tempted to make diagnostic generalizations that lack empirical support and do not reflect sufficiently the complexity of the focal organization.

A third use of the OS framework directs attention to interactions among system levels (Rashford & Coghlan, 1994). This type of diagnosis examines interactions among the levels of the environment, total organization, interdepartmental groups (e.g., divisions), face-to-face teams, and individuals. By examining interlevel dynamics, practitioners of diagnosis can sometimes discover causes of ineffective behavior that are not recognized by members of the organization. For instance, in one organization familiar to us, poor communication and limited cooperation among members of project teams can be traced to divisionwide reward contingencies that stress individual achievement rather than group performance. This reward system encourages employees to "look out for number one" and to resist time-consuming, "unproductive" work with project colleagues. By tracing the forces affecting a problem across organizational levels, investigators can sometimes identify feasible points at which to intervene in a problematic situation. In the case just mentioned, for example, it may be cheaper and more effective to encourage teamwork by providing occasional cash bonuses for successful project outcomes than by sending all project participants to training courses in teamwork.

Examination of organizational phenomena at several levels of analysis can also shed light on discontinuities between levels. Units at each level of analysis cope with environmental forces that differ from one another and from the environment facing the total organization. Local firms within multinational corporations, for example, adapt to national environments that diverge from one another and from the global environment facing the corporation as a whole (Ghoshal & Bartlett, 1990). Similarly, members at lower system levels within an organization sometimes fill organizational and extraorganizational roles and maintain network ties that link them to different people in the environment than those with whom higher-level managers maintain contact (Rousseau, 1985). Emergent behavior within subunits also leads to very different patterns from those mandated by organizational authorities, who make decisions affecting the organization as a whole (see Chapter 9).

Exclusive reliance on broad OS frameworks like those just described can lead to the gathering of a lot of data that are hard to analyze and will be hard to use. These difficulties are evident in one bold effort to construct a diagnostic scheme and instrument that faithfully reflect the entire OS framework. The assessment scheme developed by Van de Ven and Ferry (1980) has four levels of analysis: the macro-organization, work units in the focal organization, individual jobs, and the relationships among jobs and units within the organization and with other organizations. For each level, practitioners of diagnosis are called upon to collect survey data for five modules that cover effectiveness, structure, workgroup processes and tasks, job design, and interunit interdependencies. Each module contains several variables, such as context, structure, design, and outcome variables. The masses of data that may result from each assessment project may obscure rather than help identify the organizational factors that should be the targets of planned interventions. To help practitioners of diagnosis avoid difficulties like these, the following section, Chapter 4, and many of the subsequent chapters in this book discuss ways to modify and sharpen the focus of the OS frame.

Diagnostic Principles and Procedures

To make the OS frame more useful, practitioners of organizational diagnosis often follow one or more of three analytical procedures, each of which can contribute to sharp-image diagnosis:

1. Assess system fits.
2. Examine interdependencies among system components and levels.
3. Locate system gaps.

Each procedure rests on a set of assumptions or theoretical principles that describe how organizations operate as open systems. Consultants can better evaluate and apply existing diagnostic models if they understand the potential contributions of these principles, as well as the difficulties and drawbacks of applying them. By critically applying these principles, consultants also can better develop their own diagnostic models.

Although useful, the application of system principles can be quite difficult. Some important system concepts are ambiguous and overlapping. Hence, it is often hard to discover a single, logically unambiguous link between system principles and diagnostic practices. In addition, consultants and applied researchers do not always state clearly the theoretical principles that guide their diagnostic practices. By noting these problems, we hope to point to ways to develop and apply system-based models more critically and more successfully.

Assess Fits Among System Components

System Fit

Researchers and consultants have used the terms *fit, congruence, consistency, alignment,* and *matching* to describe a wide range of relations among internal system components and between organizations and their environments (Bluedorn, Johnson, Cartwright, & Barringer, 1994; Fry & Smith, 1987; Venkatraman, 1989). According to many formulations of the systems approach, good fit between system components—such as environment, technology, structure, behavior, and culture—means that system parts reinforce one another rather than disrupt one another's operations (Thompson, 1967, pp. 147-148).

More generally, according to OS theory, organizations can more readily adapt to their environments when internal organizational characteristics are compatible with environmental conditions. For example, the contingency approach, which derives from OS theory, anticipates that organizational structure must be sufficiently complex to mirror environmental complexity (e.g., Lawrence & Lorsch, 1969). In practice, organizations often achieve this type of fit by creating separate units or functions to deal with different types of clients and markets. In like manner, contingency theory anticipates that organizations will use one or more techniques for coping with environmental uncertainty, including the creation of cross-functional linking mechanisms, enhancement of information-processing capacities, and the creation of semi-autonomous decentralized units (Galbraith, 1977).

Good internal and external fit is expected to yield higher quality and greater efficiency of operations than will poor fit. Because system parts are necessarily interrelated, incompatibility among system parts or levels leads to losses of system energy or resources (Porras & Robertson, 1992).

Two major approaches to defining fit emerge from this literature, both of which are potentially useful in diagnosis.[8] The first approach treats fit in terms of conformity of organizational features and conditions to a *configuration,* or overall pattern (Ketchen et al., 1997; Meyer et al., 1993). These configurations, most of which derive from contingency theory, characterize expected features of several internal system components—such as structure, behavior and processes, technology, and occasionally culture—along with environmental conditions or organizational strategy. The configurations can be specified on the basis of past research and theory or developed inductively from data on samples of organizations (e.g., Miller & Friesen, 1984b). This configurational approach guides assessments of the alignment of the administrative system of an organization (structure, behavior, and culture) into mechanistic or organic types, as well as examination of the fit between these types and the organization's environment, technology (i.e., work processes), human resources, and effectiveness criteria (see Chapter 7). Another configurational approach examines the extent to which organizations possess a cluster of internal features that are expected to promote high levels of employee involvement in work (Lawler, 1986).

Rather than examine entire configurations, the second approach looks at the match or fit between one or more pairs of system components or subcomponents. Sometimes, this approach focuses on fits between analytically defined variables, such as environmental uncertainty and the degree of planfulness (i.e., intended rationality) in strategic decision processes (Harrison & Phillips, 1991; Miller, 1992). Fits and misfits between pairs of subcomponents, functions, or variables can be predicted deductively from theories, data, and experience, or fits can be examined inductively.

The match between two or more system parts is then assessed in terms of some outcome criterion, such as the time or energy needed to coordinate activities, or the effect of fits or misfits on system performance. Different units, components, or functions fit poorly if their activities erode or cancel each other; if exchanges between the components lead to avoidable losses of time, money, or energy; or if exchanges and links between these units harm their performance. For example, there is poor fit between a firm's marketing and its human resource functions if efforts to market technically sophisticated equipment are undermined by a poorly trained sales force that fails to explain the equipment's features and advantages over competing products. Poor fit is also evident when changes or variations in one part of a system produce uncontrolled and intolerable oscillations in other parts (Beer, 1985). Consider, for example, interchanges between a college admissions office and other parts of the college administration. Big and unpredictable fluctuations in the number and type of students admitted each semester can make it impossible for administrators to anticipate revenue flows versus expenses, allocate classroom and dormitory space, and assign faculty in keeping with demand.

Fits between system components, as opposed to misfits, can also refer to two additional types of links (Porter, 1996). *Reinforcement* occurs when activities in one area contribute directly to the pursuit of activities in another area. For example, a company can bundle products or services so that the delivery of one type of service, such as hotel accommodations, reinforces marketing and sales in others, such as travel services and discount merchandise ("All in the Same Bunch," 1997). *Optimalization* of fits occurs when coordination and information flows between activities or system components eliminate redundancy and wasted effort. By creating reinforcing and optimalizing fits, companies can create a situation where the whole chain of system links is greater than the sum of its parts. This outcome produces a form of strategic advantage that has often been overlooked (Porter, 1996): When activities reinforce each other, competitors cannot simply copy one part of the chain, such as an advertising campaign. They would have to duplicate the entire chain—advertising, human resource development, service production, and marketing strategy—in order to achieve the same result.

Whether they define fit in terms of configuration or matching, investigators can usefully examine contextual conditions that mediate fits. For example, according to contingency theory, alignment of system features into a mechanistic configuration will promote efficient performance only if environmental conditions are predictable and if the operations that contribute to system processing are well established and well understood. In contrast, when the environment is unpredictable and processing operations are not well understood, a mechanistic configuration will prove inefficient and ineffective. Similarly, the match between reward patterns and employee norms can be mediated by the cultural environment in which the firm operates. For example, the practice of linking rewards directly to individual performance appears to fit well with norms in many North American firms, but it fits poorly with the norms of most Russian factories (Welsh, Luthans, & Sommer, 1993).

Applications

The principle of fits leads consultants to diagnose system fits and to help clients search for ways to improve fits that are critical to organizational performance and organization-environment relations. Assessment of fits provides a foundation for several models of organizational diagnosis (e.g., Beer, 1980; Blake & Mouton, 1964; Kotter, 1978; Nadler & Tushman, 1980a, 1980b). For instance, the author of one well-known model (Tichy, 1983, p. 152) describes the purpose of diagnostic work as gathering sufficient information to determine which organizational alignments need adjusting. More recently, practitioners of reengineering (Hall, Rosenthal, & Wade, 1993; Hammer & Champy, 1993) have counseled radical steps to align organizational structure and administrative practices with strategy.

To use fit assessment as the basis for a broadly focused diagnosis, investigators can assess fits among all of the system components shown in Figure 2.1. Organization-environment links are among the most important fits for assessment. Diagnosis of environmental relations can make a major contribution to organizational decision making and planning for change (Mealiea & Lee, 1979). A basic premise of OS theory is that organizational effectiveness depends on adaptation to environmental conditions. Following this lead, practitioners of diagnosis can examine whether the organization's structures and processes appear to match environmental conditions in ways predicted by contingency theory.

More generally, diagnosis of organization-environment fits can assess whether critical inputs, such as personnel, match the requirements of organizational technologies, behavior, and processes. It is also possible to examine the alignment between organizational services and products and the demands and expectations of customers or clients. To illustrate misalignment with the environment, consider a publicly funded medical school that continues to train new physicians despite declining demand for new physicians. Gradually, such a poor fit between outputs and environmental demand will probably affect one of two vital inputs—admissions candidates or funding. Diagnosis of poor fits between the organization and its environment can lead to recommendations or decisions concerning internal organizational adaptations and to efforts to change the environment. For instance, the medical school might alter its environment by campaigning to place graduates in new areas, such as health care administration and preventive medicine, and in firms developing new medical technologies.

Fits among internal system components also can be examined. One practical way to assess internal fits is to examine the compatibility of operational requirements, needs, or procedures of different units or system parts. Incompatibility between units and system parts also shows up in divergent or conflicting messages about the kinds of behavior required. For example, there is poor fit between the production subsystem and the reward system if a firm custom designs products and delivers them in response to customer needs but calculates pay bonuses on the basis of daily sales results.

Organizational research can provide useful guides to constructive and ineffective fits among internal system components (e.g., Miles & Snow, 1978; Mintzberg, 1979; Nightingale & Toulouse, 1977; see also Chapter 7). For instance, research and practice on the design of sociotechnical systems (Cummings, 1993; Passmore, 1988) developed an entire paradigm based substantially on the enhancement of internal system fits. In particular, this paradigm stresses the need for fit between the technical and human sub-systems. The technical system consists of technology, raw materials, and production methods. The human (or social) subsystem consists of the employees, their work roles, and their attitudes.

Fit assessment can also follow the sharp-image approach developed in Chapter 1. In this case, diagnosis concentrates on fits that directly affect aspects of the system that clients view as problematic, ineffective, or challenging. For example, a diagnosis of disruptions and delays in a hospital emergency room could examine the fits between the emergency unit and other units on which it depends directly for support, such as the laboratory and diagnostic imaging. The fits are weak if the emergency room staff do not receive rapid and accurate results on the tests requested. Once such misalignments are found, the specific reasons for inaccuracies and delays can be investigated in detail.

Limitations

Consultants need to be aware of difficulties in applying the concept of fit to diagnosis. First, no developed body of knowledge and practice specifies which types of fits form necessary preconditions for organizational effectiveness and which types of misfits cause serious forms of ineffectiveness. Although there are many cases in which lack of fit seems to undermine performance, systematic research on the links between fit and performance has produced mixed results. What is perhaps the most comprehensive study to date (Huselid, 1995) failed to find support for the intuitively appealing notion that firms perform better financially when their human resource management practices are well aligned with one another and with the firm's organizational strategy. A further difficulty with the concept of fit is that organizations may be unable to achieve fits among their internal system features at the same time that they develop good alignments with their environments (Miller, 1992). In like manner, organizations that simultaneously pursue mutually conflicting goals or strategies cannot simultaneously attain good fits between system components and all of their important strategies (Quinn & Cameron, 1988). One solution to these dilemmas is to pursue fits sequentially rather than simultaneously.

In light of these complexities and ambiguities, applied researchers and consultants should seek direct evidence of the costs and benefits of enhancing a particular form of fit before recommending interventions aimed at improving fits. Consultants also need to rely on their past experience and their professional judgment in deciding which fits are most critical for a particular organization and are most likely to influence organizational effectiveness. To make such assessments, it is necessary to select criteria for effectiveness that reflect the expectations of clients and other powerful stakeholders and are compatible with the goals of the diagnostic project (see Chapter 3).

Second, it is a mistake to assume, as many diagnostic models seem to, that limited fit always produces ineffectiveness. Most organizations change constantly as their subcomponents interact with one another and interact with divergent sectors of the environment. Moreover, no two parts of an organization change at exactly the same rate or in exactly the same way. Hence, there is always some lack of fit in any organization that is not in a state of stagnation. Evidence that low levels of fit do not necessarily spell ineffectiveness comes from studies of loosely coupled organizations (Orton & Weick, 1990; Weick, 1979, 1985). These studies show that loose coupling can buffer organizations from external pressures (Meyer & Rowan, 1977) and can facilitate professional work (Mintzberg, 1979). Furthermore, managers sometimes seek to foster creativity and innovation by allowing for "productive redundancies" among overlapping research and development units, rather than striving for the tight coupling of such units with one another and with other organizational functions. High-tech firms may tolerate and even encourage ambiguous definitions of roles and jobs and allow for high levels of infighting and politicking in order to sustain and encourage creativity and initiative (e.g., Kidder, 1981; Kunda, 1992).

Third, organizations can suffer from too much system alignment, as well as too little.[9] When assessed in terms of the organization's capability to adjust to environmental changes, many organizations may be considered to be too tightly, rather than too loosely, aligned (Katz & Kahn, 1978, p. 174). Successful adjustment to a particular set of technological and environmental conditions, with its attendant tight alignment of system features, can lead large, mature organizations into a "success trap" and render them unable to deal with major environmental changes (Tushman & O'Reilly, 1996). The managers of such well-aligned organizations often seek to ride out new environmental developments or make only incremental adjustments to them, rather than undertake the radical changes needed to deal with them. This pattern of resisting fundamental change appears to have been characteristic of America's automobile manufacturers during the 1970s.

Fourth, both research and practice support the premise of equifinality—that several combinations of system components can produce nearly identical outcomes (Ashmos & Huber, 1987). Therefore, improvements in fit may not produce improvements in effectiveness. Instead, these changes may simply generate unjustified costs, because they substitute one moderately effective combination for another.

To recapitulate, diagnosticians need to exercise caution in assessing fits. On occasion, this procedure will help consultants identify misalignments that disturb and hamper effective system functioning. However, it is important to apply clear criteria of effectiveness and ineffectiveness when assessing fits, and to assess directly the degree to which misalignments cause ineffectiveness. It is also useful to pay close attention to the types of fit and misfit that frequently characterize organizations that the client organization resembles.

Examine System Interdependencies

Interdependency

In systems thinking, the principle of interdependency postulates that change in any one system component, subcomponent, or level brings about or is associated with complementary changes in other components (Ashmos & Huber, 1987). System operations are typically recursive, because the parts and levels of a system are highly dependent on one another and not just loosely related. As is the case for fit, interdependency can refer to bivariate relations between system components and subcomponents or to links between multiple components or features. Much of contingency theory rests on assumptions about the interdependence of system components such as structure, technology, and environment (Van de Ven & Drazin, 1985). Evidence for interdependence comes from the results of such contingency research, as well as from studies that document the clustering of organizational features into distinctive configurations (Meyer et al., 1993). Further support comes from findings that many organizations retain stable structural and systemic configurations over long periods of time until they are disturbed by environmental shocks or internal upheavals (Gersick, 1991; Tushman & Romanelli, 1985; see also Chapter 11).

Applications

Several diagnostic models explicitly refer to the principle of interdependency (Burke, 1994; Nadler & Tushman, 1980a, 1980b; Tichy, Tushman, & Fombrun, 1980). Moreover, the concept is implicit in many extensions and applications of the system perspective. The most prominent implication for diagnosis of the principle of system interdependence is that consultants and decision makers need to anticipate the ways in which interventions or gradual changes in one part of a system are likely to affect other parts of the system. When managers and consultants assess how action in one part of a system can affect other parts, they need to recognize that there may be forces resisting or delaying these effects (Senge, 1990).

For example, managers need to be aware that their firm's capacity to benefit from new information technologies depends greatly on the recruitment and training of employees who can use these technologies to full advantage (Morton, 1991). Even if managers do not face resistance to introducing the new technology, they should anticipate delays in obtaining performance improvements. These delays will stem from the need to change many operations in order to take advantage of the new technology. In addition, even properly trained operators need time to get acquainted with the technology's quirks and its potential uses.

In many cases, delays in feedback from one part of a system to another create the mistaken impression that actions affecting one system component have no consequences for other components. Consider, for example, a public social service agency that radically cuts client services. Although these cuts do not produce any immediate response among clients or other stakeholders, the reductions may gradually feed public frustration and disillusion with the agency. Gradually, this disillusion can give rise to political pressures to divert public funds from the unpopular agency to other service providers.

A further diagnostic implication of the principle of interdependency is that some interdependencies are more critical than others. Changes in critical interdependencies produce major consequences throughout an organization. Some of the most critical interdependencies concern exchanges of inputs and outputs with the environment. When changes occur that affect the flows of critical resources or the reception of primary outputs, these changes will probably be felt throughout the organization. The reduced demand for medical graduates mentioned above illustrates such a critical interdependency.

Diagnosis can help managers and other clients enhance their organization's standing in its environment by providing data on critical external interdependencies and assessing the effectiveness of current methods for managing these interdependencies (Harrison, 1994). After mapping out the parts of the environment that impinge most directly on operations, the investigator examines the availability of crucial resources, responses to and demand for major outputs, and demands placed on the organization by external groups or agencies. The next step is to assess how the organization currently manages these external linkages, and to examine the implications of current conditions and practices for internal system operations. Feedback from this type of analysis can help clients consider ways to improve their management of external relations, and it can lead them to examine trends and developments that are likely to affect organization-environment interdependencies in the future.

Analysis of system interdependencies can also facilitate the implementation of technical and administrative innovations. By identifying critical interdependencies, consultants can help clients anticipate undesired effects of innovations and can provide the support needed for successful implementation. Planning for potential repercussions of innovation is especially necessary when radical innovations, which will produce consequences throughout a system, are envisioned. In contrast, less planning is needed for routine innovations, such as the introduction of fax machines, which do not greatly affect other parts of the organization (Nord & Tucker, 1987). Unless radical innovations are introduced into receptive contexts or are carefully managed, they can produce much disruption without contributing to productivity or other organizational goals. For example, many efforts to introduce TQM appear to have faltered because the TQM projects were not accompanied by supportive changes in the organizational culture and structure (Argyris & Schon, 1996, pp. 231-236; Hackman & Wageman, 1995).

Limitations

Because the principle of interdependency has not been discussed widely in the literature on diagnosis, consultants will have to rely heavily on their experience and insight in applying it. One useful rule of thumb is that interdependencies are critical to diagnosis when they directly block effectiveness. For instance, the interdependence of information technology deployment on human resource training is critical only if the human resources function cannot readily catch up with the new needs created by the introduction of the new technologies.

Another difficulty in applying the principle of interdependency is that the degree of interdependence varies between and within organizations. In loosely coupled organizations, structures and activities in one part of the organization vary independently, rather than directly affecting one another (Aldrich, 1979, pp. 82-86). When organizations are only loosely coupled to their environments, as occurs in many not-for-profit organizations, the internal structure need not respond promptly or directly to environmental forces. Moreover, external stakeholders may be satisfied by symbolic responses, as opposed to changes in operating procedures and norms (Meyer & Rowan, 1977).

Some organizations contain tightly coupled functions, such as production, alongside loosely coupled ones, such as research and development (Lawrence & Lorsch, 1969). There often is only limited interdependence between these functions, so that each is buffered from developments affecting the other. In examining system interdependencies, consultants need to be attentive to these possibilities so as not to impose inappropriate empirical and normative assumptions on the client organization.

Locate System Gaps

Gaps

When information enters and flows through a system, it provides feedback on the system's internal state and on its exchanges with its environment. This feedback either meets current standards and thereby confirms the acceptability of current operations, or it reveals gaps between expected and actual conditions. In response to such gaps, managers and other members of an organization can try to restore equilibrium through minor corrective actions or through more basic changes (Beer, 1985).

The analysis of gaps thus forms a major step in the maintenance of system equilibrium and in reactive organizational change. Gap analysis can also provide a platform for strategic, proactive change. This type of change occurs when organizational members redefine their standards and objectives in response to feedback about current practices. Strategic change also occurs when members of an organization make substantial changes to narrow the gap between anticipated future conditions and desired conditions. In system terms, these moves may be thought of as attempts to achieve a new equilibrium state.

Most students of planned organizational change assume that organizations can improve their current functioning by closing gaps between actual and expected system states. Furthermore, the process of organization development and planned change is sometimes viewed as one in which consultants help clients define desirable future system states and decide on steps that will narrow the gap between current and desired future states (see French & Bell, 1995). Force field analysis (Lewin, 1951; see also Chapter 5) also employs comparisons between present and preferred conditions.

Applications

Organizational effectiveness is often evaluated in terms of gaps between current and desired states of performance or between current performance and that obtained by other, comparable organizations (Chapter 3). In keeping with this approach, diagnosis frequently uses the procedure of locating system gaps and suggesting ways to close them (Chapter 4). During diagnosis, consultants directly solicit clients' views of desired organizational states, or they ascertain these views inductively. Then, the investigator gathers data that shows the current or likely future gap between desired and actual conditions. Feedback on gaps can help recipients define issues requiring action and consider steps toward closing gaps.

For example, diagnosis can point to a gap between the current rate of employee turnover and some preferred level. Similarly, in strategic analysis, gaps are analyzed between current activities and the projected strategic intent (e.g., Hamel & Prahalad, 1989). Firm resource theory also concentrates on the gap between the current and needed levels of internal firm resources, such as physical and human resources (Barney, 1991). Benchmarking, another popular change technique, involves setting external comparison points for an organization that will identify gaps between current results and desirable, yet presumably obtainable, ones (Chapter 8). To use gap analysis as a means of encouraging planning for the future, consultants can encourage clients to develop workable future scenarios and then move to close the gap between these scenarios and present system states (see the discussion of open-systems planning in Chapter 4).

Feedback on gaps can generate strong motivation for change. Indeed, most models of motivation or goal-seeking activities refer to the discrepancy between current conditions and those that ought to be or that people would prefer (Kluger & DeNisi, 1996). Recognition of gaps motivates members of the organization to aspire to improvement and to work toward it.

One popular form of gap analysis that can motivate desire for change provides feedback on gaps between officially espoused or mandated behavior and actual practice (Weisbord, 1976; see also Chapter 9). Actual practices often reflect managers' theories in use as opposed to their espoused theories (Argyris & Schon, 1974, 1996). Managers may, for example, espouse full and honest communication, while in practice, they punish subordinates who reveal mistakes. Open discussion of the discrepancy between espoused theories and theories in use can help clients develop the capacity to examine and criticize their own behavior in the future. This type of discussion can thus pave the way to self-corrective, double-loop learning (Chapter 13).

Because the concept of gaps can be applied to any aspect of organizational functioning, practitioners require guidelines as to which gaps are most important to diagnosis. We suggest concentrating on measurable gaps in the acquisition of crucial resources and capacities or in organizational performance. Following this lead, diagnosis of gaps within the human resources function would concentrate on performance indicators, such as the outcomes of recruitment or training programs. If resources are the focus of diagnosis, the consultant could examine current levels of skills or human capital compared to desired levels. This focus on performance gaps is well illustrated by the efforts of TQM programs to narrow gaps between current quality levels and the quality standards or expectations of customers and clients (Grant, Shani, & Krishnan, 1994).

Another promising approach to choosing gaps for diagnosis and action is to start by examining gaps that can be closed using existing resources in very short periods of time (Schaffer, 1988). This approach is practical and easy to apply but may discourage consultants and their clients from facing more important challenges and from striving to enhance organizational capacities

for learning and growth (Turner, 1982). Alternative approaches include focusing on gaps that appear to pose the greatest threats to organizational performance or survival. A further possibility is to examine gaps that are of greatest
concern to powerful clients.

Limitations

Gap analysis can provide a powerful tool for diagnosis and change provided that it contains an orientation to anticipated and desired future states.
Consultants have sometimes concentrated on the analysis of current gaps
while neglecting likely gaps in future performance. Because organizations and
environments are constantly changing, concentrating solely on closing current
gaps in performance or resources is like trying to hit a moving target. If
diagnosis does concentrate on current gaps, it may be best to emphasize
chronic gaps, which point to enduring sources of ineffectiveness. Furthermore, if current gaps become a major focus for diagnosis, consultants should
encourage clients to view the closing of a particular gap as one cycle in a
repeating process of diagnosis and problem solving.

Another possible limitation of diagnosing gaps is that gaps lie in the eyes
of the beholder. Different people and groups will define an organization's
desirable, yet realistic, future states in different ways, in keeping with their
own goals, memberships in subunits, interests, and interpretive perspectives
(Cyert & March, 1963; Frost, Moore, Louis, Lundberg, & Martin, 1991; see
also Chapter 10). For instance, managers in a firm's finance department may
strive to increase liquid assets, whereas those in research and development
would like to accumulate fixed assets in the form of new technologies. There
are several ways that consultants can respond to divergences in goals, interpretations, and priorities among members of the client organization. The
consultant can provide feedback on differences of this sort to encourage
members to deal constructively with them. If consensus is needed, the consultant can ask clients to achieve a working agreement on desired states prior
to the diagnosis. The developing of such a working consensus can, in turn,
facilitate strategic decision making.

A third difficulty in diagnosing gaps lies in the risk that focusing too
narrowly on gaps in measurable features of performance will encourage
decision makers to develop counterproductive systems of control and rewards.
When people are subjected to very narrow measurements of performance and
of resource states, they learn quickly how to produce results that look good in

terms of the standards being monitored. However, they neglect unmonitored behavior that can be equally important in the long run. Too much stress on monthly sales results, for example, can lead sales personnel to neglect aspects of customer service that will show up only in yearly figures or in measures of the proportion of repeat customers.

Conclusion

The OS framework can help consultants and other diagnostic investigators develop a comprehensive view of the focal organization within its environment. The framework provides widely applicable concepts that can guide the gathering and analysis of data on entire organizations or on organizational subunits. The OS approach justifiably directs attention to the need for organizations to adapt themselves to environmental requirements and to adjust to environmental change. Today, many organizations face even more intense pressures for adaptation to rapid environmental change than was the case a few decades ago, when organizational diagnosis first embraced the OS approach.

Despite the benefits of the OS perspective, its very abstractness and comprehensiveness can prove disadvantageous as well as helpful. If investigators rely very heavily on the general OS frame, they may gather too much data and may analyze organizational features in terms that are very distant from the problems and issues facing clients. This type of very broad and overly abstract analysis can fail to pinpoint critical sources of ineffectiveness or effectiveness and fail to motivate action for organizational improvement among the recipients of feedback.

To overcome these difficulties, we introduced several ways of specifying and adding analytical power to the OS frame. First, we considered SWOT analysis and the examination of interlevel dynamics. These analytical techniques can best contribute to the examination of organizational problems and challenges during the early phases of diagnosis. Then, we surveyed three diagnostic procedures that can further sharpen and narrow the focus of systems-based diagnosis and thereby contribute to sharp-image diagnosis— *assessing fits* among system components and subcomponents, *examining critical interdependencies,* and *identifying gaps* between current and desired system outcomes and states. These three procedures inform many popular diagnostic models and much applied research. Although they all have some analytical and empirical limitations, the procedures help investigators move beyond broad description toward a sharp image of critical forces shaping ineffectiveness and effectiveness. The highly focused feedback generated by these three types of analysis, and in particular by gap analysis, can enhance the motivations of organizational decision makers to take steps toward reducing ineffectiveness and improving organizational functioning.

Like any theoretical approach, OS thinking directs attention to certain organizational features and tendencies at the expense of others. In particular, classic OS work paid little attention to interactions among interest groups and stakeholders in and around the organization. To remedy this weakness, Chapters 3, 5, and 12 introduce the political frame into organizational diagnosis. This approach helps us examine how prevailing definitions of effectiveness and ineffectiveness, goals, strategies, processes, and even structures reflect influence struggles among stakeholders in and around the organization.

Much of the early OS work placed little emphasis on the role of interpretive processes in system functioning. Today, theorists and practitioners alike recognize that organizational members act in response to their own interpretations and definitions of organizational reality rather than to objective conditions. Another limitation of some early OS work was its almost exclusive stress on passive adaptation to environmental conditions. This approach did not leave room for the possibility that managers could actively choose and shape their environments (Astley & Van de Ven, 1983). To overcome these limitations, Chapter 10 deals with the implications of interpretive processes for diagnosis, and Chapter 13 examines the diagnosis of strategy formation and proactive moves to enhance competitive advantage.

Notes

1. Organizational survival, as opposed to effectiveness, appears to depend much less on the adaptation by individual organizations to their task environment than OS theorists assumed (see Baum, 1996; Meyer & Zucker, 1989).

2. Unlike early OS work, recent treatments of organizational cognition and strategy stress that managers partially define, choose, and shape the environments in which they operate rather than simply reacting to them (see Chapters 10 and 13).

3. The framework and the discussion that follows are adopted from Harrison (1994). Goals and strategies are no longer included in the framework, and a narrower and simpler definition of technology has been adopted.

4. Beer's (1985) treatment of recursion seems to invite an overly deterministic view of the influence of higher levels on lower ones.

5. Early OS formulations did not give sufficient attention to the ways that organizations can actively manage environmental dependencies (Pfeffer & Salancik, 1978), symbolically enact their environments (Starbuck, Greve, & Hedberg, 1978; Weick, 1979), and exercise strategic choices affecting environmental relations (Child, 1977). These possibilities are discussed in subsequent chapters.

6. For finer-grained distinctions among types of change, see the section on organizational learning in Chapter 13, as well as Bartunek and Moch (1987).

7. Harrison (1994) discusses basic data to gather on all system components, along with methods for data gathering and analysis.

8. The discussion that follows reworks distinctions that appear in Venkatraman (1989). Our discussion of matching between components or variables includes the types he calls matching and covariation types. Our configurational category encompasses the types he calls profile deviation and gestalt. Our discussion of the contexts affecting fits is parallel to his treatment of fit as mediation.

9. For a discussion of the issue of fit versus flexibility within the context of human resource management, see Chapter 8, Assessing HRM's Strategic Contribution.

3 Assessing Effectiveness and Ineffectiveness

This chapter provides consultants and other participants in diagnosis with a guide to choosing criteria of effectiveness or ineffectiveness and assessing these phenomena during diagnostic studies. Conceptions of effectiveness underlie most types of diagnosis and planned change, including the process of sharp-image diagnosis described in Chapter 1 and the diagnostic principles and procedures described in Chapter 2. Similarly, after clients receive feedback from a diagnosis, their decisions about the objectives and processes of planned change reflect their conceptions of effectiveness and ineffectiveness.

If participants in diagnosis and decision making about change fail to anchor their analyses in clear effectiveness criteria, they will evoke shifting, ambiguous, and conflicting analytical standards. In the end, their decisions may be hard to implement because they are riddled with inconsistencies or because they reflect standards that clash with the goals, priorities, or strategies of the main clients for diagnosis and of other powerful decision makers.[1]

It is helpful to use a political frame to understand effectiveness and ineffectiveness, as well as to use open-systems and structural frames. The political frame helps practitioners of diagnosis and their clients see how particular effectiveness criteria—including those derived from the open-systems perspective—may support or undermine the interests of specific actors or subgroups in and around an organization. Insights derived from the political perspective can also help consultants choose assessment criteria that are appropriate to the client organization. The political frame contains other diagnostic implications that go far beyond the topic of this chapter. For example, as shown in Chapter 5, the political frame illuminates possible impacts of diagnosis on internal politics and suggests ways to assess the prospects for the implementation of planned change.

After introducing the political frame, we examine major issues confronting investigators as they move from abstract considerations concerning types of effectiveness criteria toward operationalization and empirical assessment. These issues are presented in a decision tree, which can help diagnostic practitioners engage in both deductive and inductive decisions about assessing effectiveness.

Political Approaches to Diagnosis

Stakeholders and Organizational Politics

The political frame views organizations as arenas encompassing diverse, competing groups of stakeholders who have distinctive interests and objectives (Bolman & Deal, 1991; Hall, 1987; Morgan, 1986). *Stakeholders*—who are also termed constituencies, interest groups, and political actors—are those individuals or groups that experience or are likely to experience harm or benefit from an organization's actions (Donaldson & Preston, 1995). Primary stakeholders maintain formal, official, or contractual relations with the organization and have a direct economic impact on it. Secondary stakeholders include all other groups that can influence an organization or are affected by it (Savage et al., 1991).

Organizational stakeholders engage in politics—actions aimed at acquiring, enhancing, and using power to obtain preferred outcomes in organizational decisions (Pfeffer, 1981b, p. 7).[2] Political actions in and around organizations typically aim at influencing budgeting decisions and other forms of resource allocation, shaping goals and programs, promoting or resisting personnel changes and changes in organizational throughputs or outputs, determining the resolution of conflicts and crises, and gaining power and influence (Burns, 1961; Pfeffer, 1981b; Zald & Berger, 1978). The terms *power* and *influence* refer here interchangeably to the ability to get people to do things that they might otherwise not do and to the capacity to get things done (Finkelstein, 1992; Kanter, 1977; Mintzberg, 1983, p. 5).

The political frame provides diagnosis with additional vantage points and greater depth in analyzing organizational dynamics than does that provided by the open-systems frame. According to the political perspective, organizational dynamics derive substantially from moves by powerful political actors and from the rise and fall of coalitions among them—rather than from abstract interactions among system forces or from powerful environmental pressures.

The political frame thus alerts consultants and managers to forces that can shape the outcome of programs of planned change and to the inherently political character of diagnosis and consultation (Cobb, 1986; Greiner & Schein, 1988). In particular, the political perspective shows how consultants engage in offstage political activity—recruiting and maintaining support for their work among key stakeholders, assessing how their interventions may affect organizational politics, and using their power as consultants (Chapter 5) to contribute to an effective consultation project.

The political perspective leads consultants and other practitioners of planned change to anticipate disagreement among stakeholders about the desirability of managerial decisions and proposals for planned change and about the criteria for judging an organization's actions. This frame further suggests that members' conformity to managerial mandates can depend on the power of management to overcome resistance and enforce conformity, as well as on management's ability to generate support for its programs. Stakeholder analysis recognizes that differences among political actors reflect cultural divergences—in values, norms, beliefs, and interpretations—and not just raw self-interest (see Bartunek, 1993, and also Chapter 10). These cultural differences can lead to divergent views of organizational success and effectiveness, as well as to very divergent interpretations of events and organizational conditions.

Consider, for example, gaps that emerged among stakeholders involved in a quality of work life (QWL) project in a large baked goods plant (Bartunek, 1993; Bartunek & Moch, 1987; Moch & Bartunek, 1990). The consultants who introduced the project expected QWL to enhance trust, communication, and respect among personnel, and probably would have included these dimensions in their assessment of project effectiveness. In contrast, line employees had a very different idea of what would make the project effective: They showed little interest in cooperative decision making and instead interpreted QWL as promising greater responsiveness of management to their requests for better working conditions—such as better food and parking. Corporate management, on the other hand, judged the QWL project's effectiveness solely in terms of its prospects for enhancing productivity. Other stakeholding groups opposed the project altogether, fearing it would undermine their power. These and other differences among stakeholders led to conflicts during implementation. At the end of the first year, corporate management responded to these conflicts and to productivity declines by absorbing the QWL program into current management operations rather than canceling it altogether.

Diagnostic studies need to take such stakeholder differences into account in formulating measures of effectiveness and in seeking workable steps toward organizational improvement. When diagnosis and plans for change fail to deal with subgroup differences that block the formation of consensus and common objectives, these differences are likely to crop up during implementation and may completely disrupt the change program.

Main Features of the Political Frame

Because of the practical difficulties of distinguishing interpretive and political sources of subgroup differences, for the purposes of diagnosis, it is often useful to encompass subcultural differences within an extended version of the political frame. Here are the frame's main assumptions, each of which sets it apart from the open-systems approach:[3]

1. People and groups in and around organizations differ in their interests, priorities, objectives, values, preferences, beliefs, information, and perceptions of reality. When these orientations are anchored in subcultures and personal biography, they change slowly.

2. Organizations operate as coalitions made up of divergent individuals and stakeholder (or interest) groups. Interest groups can form among people belonging to the same hierarchical level (e.g., middle management), department or functional unit, occupational subgroup, gender and ethnic group, geographical and national background, and among members of an organization that is joined to another through a strategic alignment or merger.

3. Most important decisions in organizations affect the allocation of scarce resources. They are decisions affecting "who gets what, when, how" (Lasswell, 1936).

4. Because resources are scarce and differences among interest groups enduring, much of organizational life consists of exchanges and conflicts among individual and group stakeholders.

5. Power becomes a critical resource in these struggles, in addition to serving as a means to obtaining other resources and objectives.

6. Organizational goals, priorities, and strategic decisions emerge through bargaining and negotiation among stakeholders in and around the organization.

7. The stakeholders who actively seek to influence one decision may not necessarily take action to influence other decisions. Those individuals and groups that routinely exercise substantial influence over major decisions form the organization's *dominant coalition.*

These assumptions have substantially influenced our approach to defining and assessing effectiveness—processes that form the central topics in this chapter.

Choosing Effectiveness Criteria

Consultants and applied researchers draw on a very wide range of definitions and measures of organizational effectiveness. To contribute to successful diagnosis, the effectiveness criteria in use should be appropriate to the focal organization and to the diagnostic issues under study. The political and open-systems frames can help managers and consultants make these choices.

The many definitions and measures of organizational effectiveness reflect its multidimensional nature (Denison & Mishra, 1995). For example, among the criteria used to assess the effectiveness of health maintenance organizations (HMOs) and sickness funds are the medical quality of the services delivered, the HMO's ability to hold down health care costs, and patient satisfaction with HMO services.[4] Different stakeholders often use divergent effectiveness criteria to assess the same organization. This tendency toward pluralistic views and demands by stakeholders is particularly evident in not-for-profit organizations (Kanter & Summers, 1987) and in publicly contested areas, such as health care. Top managers in HMOs, for example, are likely to view effectiveness largely in terms of profitability or after-cost revenues and in terms of their organization's ability to attract members and increase market share. Patients, on the other hand, seek convenient and unlimited access to quality care. Physicians working for HMO organizations put more stress than do other stakeholders on financial and logistical support for high-quality clinical services, professional autonomy and freedom from managerial constraints, and the acquisition of state-of-the-art medical technology. Governmental regulators are often most concerned with ensuring that HMOs and sickness funds provide legally mandated services, hold down costs, and accept all applicants without regard to age and health status.

How are practitioners of diagnosis to deal with the many possibilities confronting them when they choose and apply effectiveness criteria? One way to make systematic decisions about assessing effectiveness is to proceed deductively from basic choices about types of criteria to more operational decisions about measurement and standards for assessment.

Figure 3.1 presents these choices in a decision tree, which orders effectiveness logically. The figure gives illustrations for an assessment of the effectiveness of a photocopy service unit.

As they conduct a diagnosis, investigators often attend to these effectiveness choices in sequences other than the one shown in the figure. They can, for example, move back and forth between the choice points shown in the figure as they reassess their earlier decisions in light of additional understandings of the focal organization and the diagnostic tasks at hand. Diagnostic practitioners can also proceed inductively from available or readily gathered data to decisions about the types of effectiveness criteria and effectiveness dimensions that can reasonably be measured with these data. The discussion that follows examines each of the choice points in the order shown in the figure.

Assessment Approach

The first decision facing diagnostic practitioners concerns the basic assessment approach or combination of approaches to be adopted. Figure 3.1 lists four major approaches, which are discussed below, and illustrates the steps involved in applying the output-goal and stakeholder approaches. Each major theoretical approach to assessment leads to different types of assessment criteria. Moreover, divergent theoretical approaches and sets of effectiveness criteria embody very different images of preferred organizational states and reflect divergent assumptions about the conditions that promote these desired states (Cameron, 1980, 1984; Daft, 1995; Hall, 1987; Kanter & Brinkerhoff, 1981; Lewin & Minton, 1986).

Table 3.1 surveys four main approaches to effectiveness found in the literature, the major effectiveness domains emphasized by each approach, and criteria for specifying these domains.[5] Domains are sets of conceptually related criteria, such as those measuring output quality or those dealing with

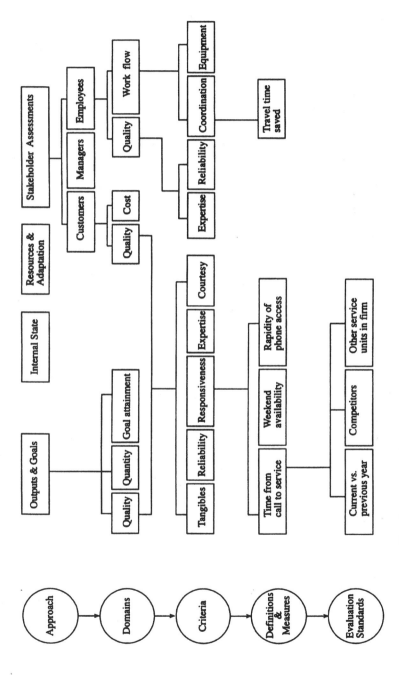

Figure 3.1 A Decision Tree for Assessing Effectiveness of a Photocopy Service Unit

Table 3.1 Effectiveness Approaches and Definitions

Approach and Domains	Criteria
1. Output Goals	
Goal attainment	Achievement of main objectives (e.g., airport construction)
Outputs—quantity	Productivity (number or value of sales, services—sometimes per unit or cost of labor); profits, revenues
Outputs—quality	Reliability (e.g., rejects, returns); reputation (customer satisfaction, expert ratings); institutional standards (e.g., approval by quality assurance body)
2. Internal System State	
Efficiency and costs	Efficiency measures (e.g., output value ÷ cost with constant quality); wastage; costs per unit of output
Human outcomes	Quality of work life (satisfaction with pay, working conditions); work effort and commitment (low absenteeism, turnover); employee health and safety; motivation; organizational image; citizenship behavior
Consensus/conflict	Goal and procedural consensus; cohesion (mutual attraction and identification with work group and organization); cooperation within and between units; conflict behavior (work stoppages, protests, flights)
Work and information flows	Work coordination (smooth flow of products, information between units; few delays and snags); adequacy and quality of information, multidirectional flows
Interpersonal relations	Trust; moderation of status differences (reduced prominence of status symbols and executive perks); openness, honesty of interpersonal communication, acceptance of diverse backgrounds and orientations
Employee involvement	Empowerment; participation in decision making
Fits	Alignment of internal system, components, subcomponents, and features
3. System Resources and Adaptation	
Resources—quantity	Size (employees, physical, financial, capital assets); resource flows (sales, budget allocations)
Resources—quality	Human capital (training, experience of work force); staff reputation; knowledge base; desirability of clients (e.g., college selectivity)
Adaptation	Ability to cope with external change and uncertainty; crisis management capabilities

Table 3.1 Continued

Approach and Domains	Criteria
Proactiveness	Impact on environment—clients (e.g., demand), competitors, suppliers, regulators; entrepreneurialism
Innovativeness	Technological and administrative innovation; implementation of new techniques and ideas
Legitimacy	Support by community and by public agencies or regulators; compliance with legal, professional, regulatory standards
Competitive position	Standing compared to competitors (e.g., market share); reputation for leadership in industry or sector
Fit	Alignment of internal system with environment
4. Multiple Stakeholder Assessments	
Standards	Effectiveness domains and criteria selected and defined by stakeholders
Satisfaction	Satisfaction with organization on standards specified by stakeholders; stakeholders' overall level of satisfaction with organization

the efficiency of important processes (throughputs). Table 3.1 also provides some illustrations in parentheses of ways to operationalize specific criteria.

The *output-goal* approach to assessing effectiveness derives from an instrumental frame that views organizations as goal-attainment devices and assesses effectiveness in terms of the attainment of clearly defined objectives and the production of specific outputs. Organizations contain multiple and even competing sets of goals and objectives that are often advocated by divergent internal and external actors. Hence, several output-goal domains, and multiple criteria specifying these domains, can all be relevant to a single organization. For example, the domains of quality, quantity, and goal attainment are all relevant to the photocopy service unit referred to in Figure 3.1. Nevertheless, only the quality domain has been elaborated in that figure. Effectiveness in output production can often be measured using continuous variables like those noted in Table 3.1 and illustrated in Figure 3.1. In other cases, goal criteria are expressed dichotomously in terms of the success or failure to achieve some end, such as the design of a cost-effective, electric-powered car or the development of a workable plan for rezoning a city district.

Despite the wide popularity of output-goal criteria, measures of effectiveness based solely on output goals suffer from many limitations, which are discussed later in this chapter.

The second approach, which focuses on *internal system states,* draws on the open-systems and human resources frames (Bolman & Deal, 1991). Sometimes, consultants and clients define internal system criteria, such as employee satisfaction and quality of work life, as ends in themselves. More often, consultants introduce these criteria into diagnosis because they assume that organizations can attain their output goals more readily when internal processes, such as coordination and communication, operate smoothly and efficiently, and when these processes enhance the motivations and capacities of members. Furthermore, many consultants argue that robust internal processes that are well aligned with one another help organizations to adapt to changing objectives, technologies, and environmental conditions (Beckhard, 1969; Campbell, 1977). From this standpoint, improving quality of work life, satisfaction, and motivation yields long-term benefits, as well as immediate performance improvements. The development of a loyal and flexible workforce helps organizations weather crises and enhances employee cooperation during periods of strategic change.

The third approach stresses *system resources and adaptation.* It derives mainly from open-systems theories that evaluate effectiveness in terms of the organization's ability to obtain scarce and valued resources from its environment, adapt to external change, and obtain a favorable competitive position within the environment.[6]

The fourth approach focuses on the assessments made by *multiple stakeholders* (or multiple constituencies). This approach defines effectiveness in terms of the organization's ability to satisfy a diverse set of internal and external constituencies (Connolly, Conlon, & Deutsch, 1980; Gaertner & Ramnarayan, 1983; see also Chapter 8). The multiple stakeholder approach, which derives from the political frame, has become widely accepted in organizational research (Bedeian, 1987; Kanter & Summers, 1987; Zammuto, 1984). Accumulating evidence indicates that organizations that are more responsive to the expectations of multiple stakeholders are generally more adaptable than are comparable organizations in which less attention is given to stakeholders (Tsui, 1994).

Stakeholder theories of effectiveness rest substantially on the normative assertion that internal and external stakeholders have legitimate interests in the substantive and procedural aspects of corporate activity (Donaldson &

Preston, 1995). From this standpoint, private firms, and not just publicly funded and regulated organizations, are ultimately responsible to a wide range of stakeholders, including customers, community members, and employees from disadvantaged groups, and not just to the organization's stockholders or owners. Support for this normative claim is growing throughout North America and Europe. This support shows up in court decisions, scholarly discussions, laws and legal regulations, and in the programs of social and political movements. An example of this trend is laws passed by many state legislatures in the United States to protect consumers from cuts in health insurance that were introduced by for-profit HMOs. These laws require the HMOs to expand insurance coverage in areas such as emergency care and childbirth—areas in which many HMOs had reduced coverage to levels that violated popular conceptions of reasonable care (Bodenheimer, 1996).

When the stakeholder approach is adopted, assessment of effectiveness begins with the identification of those groups or individuals who act as stakeholders for most of the actions of the organization or unit under study (see Chapter 5). For instance, in Figure 3.1, the three main stakeholders of the photocopy service unit are listed on the right side of the figure. The choice of stakeholding groups depends on the substantive focus of the diagnosis and on its level of analysis. For example, a broad assessment of an electric company's organizational effectiveness might reasonably treat political groups fighting air and water pollution as company stakeholders. These same groups could be excluded from a narrower assessment of the company's human resource function.

Effectiveness Domains and Criteria

The second decision shown in Figure 3.1 concerns the choice of effectiveness domains. The third decision concerns choices and nominal definitions of criteria for assessing each domain. In practice, there may be little correlation between effectiveness domains that fall under the same theoretical rubric or even between criteria belonging to the same domain (Hall, 1987; Rousseau, 1997). In fact, as a survey of Table 3.1 will show, there are many possible sources of tension between theoretically related domains and criteria. Consider, for example, the domains listed under the System Resources and Adaptation heading. Access to more revenues and budgetary flows may indeed be a sign that the organization handles critical external relations effectively. However, resource growth can lead to ideological stagnation and the extension of hierarchies that block innovation and effective adaptation to change. Similarly, there may be tensions between widespread employee involvement and administrative efficiency—two very different domains within the System State grouping. No matter what type of effectiveness domains and criteria they use, people can simultaneously favor conflicting effectiveness standards. They may remain unaware of the conflicts between standards because they do not evoke them simultaneously or do not fully spell out their operational implications.

The implications of any given assessment domain depend directly on the nominal definition of its criteria. An important case in point is the definition of objectives for service quality (Davenport, 1993, p. 266). As Figure 3.1 shows, quality of service processes can be defined in terms of tangibles, such as the appearance of personnel and service facilities; reliability of services rendered; responsiveness, including both timeliness and helpfulness; expertise of service personnel; and the courtesy with which they treat customers or clients. A service unit might be staffed with expert repair personnel and provide very reliable service, while at the same time, this service suffers from lack of courtesy and from slow responses to service calls.

If the multiple stakeholder approach is adopted, organizational effectiveness is defined nominally as the ability to operate in ways that all stakeholders view as effective. The definition of what is meant by effective is left up to members of each stakeholder group. Figure 3.1 illustrates a case in which stakeholders agree on some effectiveness domains and criteria but not on others. Employees in the service unit agree with customers that quality is a crucial aspect of unit effectiveness, but the employees do not share the customers' view that cost is an important criterion for evaluating the unit's performance. Moreover, the employees are sensitive to the flow of work within the unit, a domain including work scheduling, provision of adequate supplies and equipment, and other group features that are hidden from the customers' view. A further difference between these stakeholders reflects their definitions of the quality domain. Both customers and employees consider reliability and expertise as relevant to quality, but the employees do not include courtesy, responsiveness, and tangibles in their definition of service quality.

Operational Definitions and Measurement

The fourth decision point shown in Figure 3.1 concerns the operational definition and measurement of the selected effectiveness criteria. In principle, the procedure for deductively developing systematic measures of effectiveness is identical to that of developing any kind of measure (Judd, Smith, & Kidder, 1991). After clarifying the concept at the nominal level, the investigator specifies concretely which phenomena will be considered indicative of effectiveness and chooses measures that fit this operational definition.

Suppose, for example, that the practitioner who is assessing the photocopy service unit defines service responsiveness in terms of timeliness, measured by elapsed time between service calls and service delivery. Then, a sample of clients could be asked to report how long they usually have to wait after placing a service call. The investigator might also calculate the time elapsed between receipt of calls and completion of service, as reported in the unit's service log. Although reasonable, these operational definitions neglect other aspects of responsiveness that may be very important to clients, such as the unit's responsiveness to calls for after-hours or weekend service, or the amount of time that callers must remain on hold or punch their way through a maze of voice mail options before they can even record or explain a service request.

Diagnostic practitioners often have to define and measure effectiveness in ways that allow them to analyze data that are available or can be gathered quickly and inexpensively. Unless investigators keep clear conceptual and operational definitions of effectiveness in mind when working with these less-than-perfect data, they may interpret their findings incorrectly and may overlook important phenomena that are not covered by these measures. For example, data on pupils' performance on standardized achievement tests might be readily available to consultants conducting a diagnosis of an elementary school. Unfortunately, these tests do not measure many important educational outcomes, such as development of critical thinking and skills for self-study. Yet data on these outcomes and on internal system processes might actually be more relevant to the diagnosis than the outcomes measured by the standardized tests. A further problem with available data arises when data were originally designed to evaluate the performance of employees or units. In such cases, members may have learned to perform in ways that make them look good on the measured criteria (such as the number of sales completed) while neglecting other desirable forms of behavior (such as customer satisfaction or service) that are less closely monitored (Lawler & Rhode, 1976).

Another issue in measuring effectiveness concerns the value of using objective, behavioral measures of effectiveness (e.g., number of strike days), as opposed to subjective measures reflecting the judgments of participants or experts (e.g., descriptions of the quality of labor relations in the plant). In practice, this distinction often turns out to be far from clear-cut (Campbell, 1977, p. 45). Suppose that commercial accounts at a bank grew by 5% over the past year. Are these results substantial or lackluster, in light of the efforts and investments made and in comparison to what competitors have achieved? In the final analysis, the kinds of objective data that managers collect and pay attention to, and their evaluations of these figures, depend heavily on their subjective priorities and evaluative standards.

The multiple stakeholder approach to assessing effectiveness rests on subjective assessments obtained from members of stakeholding groups. One assessment technique involves using an abstract measure, such as perceived organizational effectiveness, which allows respondents to refer to their own implicit definitions of effectiveness. An alternative technique involves asking representatives of major stakeholders to define effectiveness or to select preferred definitions from a list of effectiveness criteria. This technique generates substantive data on the dimensions of effectiveness that are important to members of each stakeholder group, whereas the first technique provides data only on levels of stakeholder satisfaction.

Assessment of stakeholder views of *ineffectiveness* can follow a similar path. The diagnostic investigator directly asks members of important stakeholder groups to specify features of the organization's operations or its outcomes with which they are dissatisfied or that they view as ineffective. Then, for each ineffective feature, the investigator asks respondents a question like this: "What level of improvement [in the ineffective feature] would satisfy you?" To incorporate stakeholder views into diagnosis of feasible routes to change, the diagnostic practitioner can add a question like the following: "How could [the group with which the respondent is most closely identified] cooperate with [other powerful stakeholders] to achieve this degree of improvement?"

Evaluative Standards

The fifth and last choice point on the decision tree in Figure 3.1 relates to the standards to be used in analyzing and evaluating data on effectiveness and in providing feedback (Cameron, 1980). Each of the following comparisons can generate standards for evaluation:

- Current versus past levels of effectiveness (e.g., rates of growth and development)

- Effectiveness levels among units within the same organization (e.g., comparisons of efficiency ratings, accidents, quality)
- The client organization compared to others in the same industry or field (e.g., comparisons of profitability or sales to industry figures)
- The organization's current state versus some minimum standard (e.g., conformity to federal environmental standards)
- The current state compared to an ideal standard (e.g., innovativeness or community service)

Without standards of evaluation, findings on effectiveness can be meaningless. For example, we can create an apparently objective measure of the productivity of a primary health care clinic by calculating the number of patients treated per week, divided by the number of full-time staff. But we must have a standard—such as an average for strictly comparable units—to provide a basis for judging whether the figure is high, low, or about right.

The time frame used in assessments of effectiveness can vary from hours or days to years, depending in part on the organizational feature being assessed. Different time frames also can be applied to the same measure of effectiveness. For instance, a firm's financial performance may look good when judged in terms of its current quarterly profits or quarterly return on investment. However, if that firm achieves these results by aggressive cost cutting or by pricing its services or products below market, it may be unable to sustain these results for long. Moreover, neglect of the investment in the development of new products and services will gradually take its toll on sales and profits (Hayes & Abernathy, 1980).

Making Choices About Effectiveness

Many considerations guide practitioners and their clients as they confront choices like those shown in Figure 3.1 (see Cameron, 1984; Campbell, 1977; Connolly et al., 1980; Goodman & Pennings, 1980). These are summarized here under five guiding questions about effectiveness criteria.

First, *how applicable and appropriate are particular effectiveness criteria to the focal organization?* Output-goal measures are most applicable when goals can be defined in terms of clear, measurable objectives and when members of the client organization agree about the meaning and importance of these goals. Similarly, efficiency measures must be based on agreed-upon and accurate measures of inputs and quality of outputs, as well as on output quantity. In the absence of acceptable quality measures, it is risky to assume that improvements in productivity (outputs per input) signify the attainment of greater efficiency. Because they are so hard to define and measure, output-goal criteria and efficiency measures often are not readily applicable to human services and cultural organizations. For instance, even if decision makers and other stakeholders of a municipal health unit agree on the desirability of improving public health, they are likely to differ on the operational meaning and measurement of this goal and on assessments of the quality of public health services.

Stakeholder criteria can be applied to any organization. Moreover, the stakeholder approach is particularly appropriate to organizations where strategic decisions are highly contested. This approach can make a vital contribution to the diagnosis of organizations in which dissenting stakeholders are powerful as well as very vocal. In these instances, members of the dominant coalition place their organization's operations and legitimacy at risk if they ignore their stakeholders' concerns.

System adaptation and resource criteria are easier to apply in diagnoses where clients are high-level managers who have the authority to try to improve the environmental standing of an entire organization or semiautonomous division. In contrast, the criteria dealing with the internal system states can be applied to operations within departments or subunits that have little control over their environments. Criteria relating to smooth internal processes and cooperative relations are particularly relevant when work requires high levels of mutual consultation and adjustment, as in professional and management teams.

A risk in concentrating exclusively on internal system criteria is that they may lead consultants and clients to underestimate the impact of environmental relations on organizational performance and success. Furthermore, focusing mainly on internal harmony and smooth coordination can distract attention from the potential contributions to organizational adaptation of internal pluralism, tension, and conflict. Internal conflict may be too low, rather than too high, if work standards are lax, if members submit automatically to authority, or if they avoid confronting the challenges and problems facing their organization (Robbins, 1978).

Second, *how well do specific effectiveness criteria fit the goals and focal concerns of the diagnostic study?* Diagnostic practitioners need to choose their basic assessment approach and the specific effectiveness criteria for diagnosis so that they will best contribute to the strategic decisions facing clients (Campbell, 1977). The simplest way to choose among the wide range of possible criteria is to seek concepts and develop measures that are likely to generate feedback that directly addresses the goals of the diagnostic study and helps clients understand the nature of the problems and challenges that concern them most. For example, the internal system approach is likely to fit a diagnosis focused on ineffective coordination between departments. The system resource approach will probably contribute to a diagnosis of a voluntary social service organization facing declining support from local government.

In addition, investigators need to consider the appropriateness of possible concepts and measures to the basic design of the diagnosis. For example, measures of output-goal attainment, of efficiency, and of inefficiency in work and information flows suit the highly focused approach of sharp-image diagnosis (see Chapter 1). Output criteria are also well suited to assessments of the ways that important customers and clients evaluate organizational performance. Abstract criteria, such as internal system fit and adaptiveness, are less well suited to sharp-image diagnosis. However, as suggested in Chapter 2, analyses based on these criteria can help consultants discover the underlying sources of problems and challenges presented by clients.

Third, *how relevant are effectiveness criteria to clients?* Including criteria favored by clients enhances support for the study and client motivation to act on diagnostic feedback. Diagnoses should, therefore, incorporate criteria that directly reflect the concerns and views of clients and of other powerful actors within the client organizations, as well as criteria derived from the consultant's own analyses and approaches to effectiveness. The main clients for a diagnosis are the people who will have responsibility for deciding what actions to take in light of the diagnostic findings and for planning and implementing such actions. To identify criteria favored by clients, consultants can directly ask clients to specify their objectives and priorities. Clients can also be asked directly to explain what effectiveness or ineffectiveness means for their organization. In addition, consultants can sometimes observe the effectiveness criteria and priorities that clients actually use.

If disagreements among participants or contradictions in the effectiveness criteria used by clients are very great, they may undermine the investigator's efforts to develop effectiveness dimensions for use in diagnosis. In that case, the diagnostic practitioner may suggest defining effectiveness in terms of stakeholder satisfaction. Another option is to ask clients to develop a working consensus about organizational priorities in order to provide the consultant with guidelines for choosing effectiveness criteria (e.g., Beckhard & Harris,

1977). Clients can then meet to define their priorities for the diagnosis with or without the help of the consultant. If this approach is impractical, consultants may have to link efficiency and ineffectiveness criteria to the goals and priorities of the most powerful clients and then seek ways of enhancing effectiveness or reducing ineffectiveness that will bring benefits to the broadest possible spectrum of members and stakeholders.

In deciding how to deal with clients who favor or use conflicting standards of effectiveness, diagnostic practitioners should bear in mind that many organizations successfully pursue contradictory goals and evaluative standards (Cameron & Quinn, 1988; Quinn, 1988). For example, industrial firms can seek to promote both product quality and cost reduction (Eisenhardt & Westcott, 1988). In fact, some research indicates that organizations are most effective when they simultaneously balance competing values and satisfy multiple performance criteria (Denison & Spreitzer, 1991; Quinn & Rohrbaugh, 1983). Balancing competing values means simultaneously meeting the requirements of environmental adaptation, maximizing outputs, maintaining organizational stability and continuity, and developing human resources.[7]

Organizations sometimes develop tolerance for conflict between objectives and performance standards by accepting satisfactory levels of performance on some standards, as opposed to striving for uniformly optimal performance. Loose coupling among organizational units often accompanies this type of suboptimalization.[8] Under loose coupling, units can pursue divergent and even conflicting objectives or standards—such as enhancing customer satisfaction versus reducing the life expectancy of products so as to increase resales. Because the links between units are not tight, conflict among standards and objectives need not reach proportions that force members to choose between them.

There is yet a fourth, related issue to consider in making choices about effectiveness: *Are there strong normative or value reasons for preferring particular criteria, measures, or comparison standards?* As the discussion of stakeholder assessment indicated, norms and values in and around an organization can lead investigators to favor one assessment technique or procedure over another. To cite another example, in many European hospitals, the norms among hospital physicians rule out providing anyone other than the doctors in a medical unit with data that might document inadequate medical practices in that unit. In such a normative climate, it might prove very difficult to gather and give feedback on ineffective processes or outcomes within hospital units. On the other hand, the physicians might be more receptive to data on the ineffectiveness or effectiveness of the hospital as a whole—provided these data were not distributed outside of the hospital and were not used to evaluate individual physicians.

Fifth, and perhaps most important, *will feedback based on the selected criteria contribute to constructive problem solving?* Diagnostic feedback contributes to organizational improvement and client learning when it leads recipients to decide which organizational features, if any, require improvement; what steps to take toward improvement; and how to assess progress toward change targets. Rather than galvanizing members toward action, feedback based on assessment criteria that contradict one another or point to many unrelated possibilities for improvement can foster confusion and inaction. Hence, consultants who do not develop consensual criteria for assessing effectiveness may wish to select a limited number of important dimensions of effectiveness for emphasis during feedback.

Feedback on organizational ineffectiveness, as opposed to effectiveness, often focuses client attention and motivates action for change more successfully than does feedback on effectiveness. The motivating power of feedback on ineffectiveness appears to reflect the ability of actual or anticipated negative outcomes to produce more emotional, cognitive, and behavioral activity and to lead to more cognitive analysis than do neutral or positive events (Khaneman, Slovic, & Tversky, 1982; Taylor, 1991).[9] Members of a client organization can often agree more readily about the meaning of feedback on ineffectiveness and about the need to combat ineffectiveness than they can reach agreement about feedback on effectiveness (Cameron, 1984). In public-sector organizations, for example, members may disagree on organizational goals and effectiveness criteria but nevertheless concur about the need to cope with budget cuts, drops in client demand and satisfaction levels, or interference with organizational operations by regulators or external pressure groups. Furthermore, solving problems stemming from ineffectiveness can contribute more directly and dramatically to organizational survival and short-term success than can enhancing effectiveness (Cameron, 1980, 1984). Hence, reducing ineffectiveness can often prove more immediately relevant to key decision makers than can enhancing effectiveness.

Consultants can further contribute to consensus about the meaning and importance of feedback on ineffectiveness by providing clients and other stakeholders with data about the organizational costs of ineffectiveness and by pointing to the risks of continuing to perform poorly. Moreover, consultants can contribute to consensus about the need for change by helping clients find actionable routes to improvement that will benefit most powerful stakeholders or minimize harm to them. In addition, data on effectiveness are more likely to promote constructive problem solving if they focus clients' attention on group and systemwide outcomes and processes, which can only be improved through cooperation, rather than pointing to the inadequacies of individuals or small groups of people. The latter type of data feed into cycles of blame and defensiveness that can block problem solving and action.

Data from stakeholder assessments of effectiveness can help clients and other decision makers become aware of the divergent standards that stakeholders apply in evaluating the focal organization. In addition, these data help clients see how well they are meeting the expectations of stakeholders. However, data from multiple stakeholder assessments often fail to help decision makers find ways to cope constructively with the gaps among stakeholders' values and interests. A further limitation is that some stakeholder analyses report only the levels of perceived effectiveness or ineffectiveness among stakeholders, without providing feedback on the criteria that members of each group used in evaluating the organization. In these instances, recipients of feedback are left to argue about the meaning of the findings, as well as about their implications for action.

The standards for comparison used in interpreting data on effectiveness and ineffectiveness can directly affect the contribution of diagnostic feedback to constructive problem solving. When data about an organization or unit are compared to data from other, similar settings, the recipients of the data see that higher levels of effectiveness can be obtained, and they are motivated to try to improve their comparative standing. This type of comparison process underlies the techniques of survey feedback (Hausser, Pecorella, & Wissler, 1975) and also operates in many benchmarking activities (see Chapter 8). Comparisons of present levels of effectiveness or ineffectiveness to past ones can also generate motivation for change. Improvements over the past show that change is possible, whereas feedback on performance declines or rising ineffectiveness can sound an alarm that action is needed to halt further deterioration.

Conclusion

The choice of standards for evaluating and diagnosing organizations brings the practitioner face to face with stakeholder diversity and with organizational politics: Internal and external stakeholders advocate divergent effectiveness criteria and assign different meanings and degrees of importance to any given performance measure. The evaluative standards in use within an organization reflect the priorities and values of members of the organization's dominant coalition, as well as practices inherited from the past.

Further challenges to assessing effectiveness come from the academic literature, which proposes a myriad of divergent, and often conflicting, theoretical criteria and measurements. This chapter provided diagnostic investigators with a guide to confronting these academic and political complexities as they develop measures for assessing effectiveness. Five sets of issues facing investigators of effectiveness were presented. These were illustrated through a decision tree (Figure 3.1) that delineated the process of developing effectiveness measures. Investigators of effectiveness face decisions about underlying theoretical approaches to effectiveness, major domains for defining effectiveness, specific criteria, operational definitions, and standards for evaluation. Increasingly, top managers of organizations face conflicting demands and expectations of multiple stakeholders.

Whenever possible, practitioners of diagnosis should consider including a multiple stakeholder approach to effectiveness in their studies. This approach reflects most fully the constraints on managerial decision making that stem from the expectations of all powerful stakeholders. Diagnostic practitioners may also use the system resource and adaptation approach to focus attention on the focal organization's ability to meet the expectations of major external stakeholders.

In many instances, assessing ineffectiveness will prove more fruitful than will attempting to assess a broad range of dimensions of effectiveness. Clients can often agree more readily about criteria of ineffectiveness, and other stakeholders are more likely to agree with these criteria than with standards of effectiveness. Furthermore, findings on ineffectiveness frequently contain more immediate implications for action than do assessments of effectiveness.

In the final analysis, the choice of an assessment approach and of effectiveness criteria in diagnosis or the choice to concentrate on ineffectiveness depends on the specific needs and character of the client organization and on the goals of the diagnostic study. In many cases, several approaches and criteria can be used during data gathering, and their order of importance can be decided during the analysis of the findings and the formulation of plans for action. Whatever approach investigators take, they should try to reach an understanding with clients as early as possible about the focus on effectiveness or ineffectiveness, specific criteria to be applied, time frames, and comparison standards. Doing so increases the chances that clients will regard the diagnostic data and recommendations as worthwhile and useful.

Notes

1. Sometimes, ambiguity over goals and effectiveness criteria facilitates implementation of change. In these instances, actors reach agreement about operational steps toward improvement while continuing to differ over more abstract issues. These possibilities are discussed in Chapter 15.

2. This broad and nonpejorative definition of politics contrasts with definitions (e.g., Mayes & Allen, 1977) that stress the pursuit of nonlegitimated, personal, or subgroup goals at the expense of ends that are widely shared or legitimated.

3. This list modifies and expands that given by Bolman and Deal (1991, p. 186).

4. Most American HMOs operate on a for-profit basis, whereas sickness funds in Germany, the Netherlands, and Israel operate on a not-for-profit basis. Both sickness funds and HMOs are responsible for providing (or purchasing) care and for insuring patients. Sickness fund managers, like their American colleagues, experience strong incentives to maximize revenues and minimize costs of care.

5. The approaches shown in Table 3.1 correspond roughly to the goal, system-resource, internal process, and strategic constituency models described by Cameron. We have incorporated what he calls the legitimacy model into the System Resources and Adaptation category and have placed more emphasis on organizational adaptation than he does.

6. This approach also draws on work in business strategy (e.g., Porter, 1980), which incorporates a structural frame along with an open-systems frame, and on resource dependency theory (Pfeffer & Salancik, 1978), which includes open-systems and political concepts.

7. According to Quinn and McGrath (1982), each of these sets of activities reflects a different cluster of underlying values, which in turn corresponds to one of the four major perspectives on organizational effectiveness. Adaptation fits open-systems concerns; output maximization fits the rational goal approach; stability reflects internal process approaches; and concern for human resource development derives from the human relations approach. The competing values model focuses on managerial concerns rather than those of multiple stakeholders. Moreover, it neglects issues of resource acquisition, which should not be equated with those of system adaptation.

8. See the treatment of loose coupling in the discussions of Assessing Fits and Examining System Interdependencies in Chapter 2.

9. To discourage recipients from minimizing the psychological impact of feedback on actual and anticipated negative events (Taylor, 1991), consultants need to help recipients interpret negative feedback in constructive ways.

4. Diagnostic Models in Use

Diagnostic models powerfully influence feedback provided to clients, shape choices about interventions for change, and help determine the effectiveness of diagnosis and consultation. Hence, the choice and development of a diagnostic model is one of the most important decisions facing consultants and other practitioners of planned change (Howard, 1994; Tichy et al., 1976). The preceding chapters took several steps toward guiding decisions about diagnostic models. Chapter 1 explored advantages of using explicit diagnostic models as opposed to relying solely on implicit models or broad frames and metaphors. It also provided an introduction to sharp-image diagnosis, a method of developing a diagnostic model that begins with signs of ineffectiveness or challenges that directly concern clients and then examines the forces affecting these problems and challenges. Chapter 2 explored principles and procedures that can provide the foundations for diagnoses based on the open-systems frame, and Chapter 3 examined ways to choose and apply appropriate criteria of organizational effectiveness and ineffectiveness.

To further facilitate the choice and development of appropriate diagnostic models, this chapter discusses analytical requirements for developing models. Also considered are considerations relating to the contributions of models and techniques to the consulting process and to interactions among clients. Then, we review several diagnostic models based on the open-systems frame. These models have enjoyed prominence within the literature on applied research and consultation and helped influence our own views on sharp-image diagnosis.[1] These models depart from broad, open-systems frameworks (e.g., Figure 2.1), which many authors continue to recommend as diagnostic models (e.g., Cummings & Worley, 1993, pp. 85-93). Unlike those broad schemes, the models reviewed below apply gap analysis and some of the other diagnostic principles and procedures treated in Chapter 2. The models reviewed here also illustrate important alternatives for assessing effectiveness and variations in consultant roles. Several of the models surveyed can be used in diagnostic interventions in which participants in diagnosis move directly from feedback and analysis into the planning of steps toward organizational improvement or strategic change.

All of the models reviewed here derive from the action research tradition, which encourages participation by users of diagnosis in as many phases of the diagnosis as possible—including problem definition, study design, data gathering, and analysis. When conditions favor participation by clients and other organizational members in the diagnostic process, participation can enhance acceptance of diagnostic findings and commitment to action recommendations stemming from them. Moreover, participation by members can help ensure the relevance of the diagnostic model and findings to participants' concerns. Unfortunately, consultants often face serious constraints regarding involving clients and other members of the organization in diagnosis.

Open-systems planning, the search conference, and the six-box models for diagnosis are presented immediately after a discussion of requirements for diagnostic models. These approaches rest on simpler and older diagnostic models that have continued to be useful and appealing to consultants and other practitioners of diagnosis. The Stream Analysis model presented subsequently is newer and more analytically sophisticated. Nevertheless, this model and other complex models (e.g., Tichy, 1983) do not appear to be used as widely by trainers and diagnostic practitioners as are the simpler models.

What Makes a Good Diagnostic Model?

In selecting available models or developing ones that are tailored to the focal organization, consultants seek to meet two types of requirements. The first applies to virtually all models in the applied behavioral sciences. The second set of standards is distinctive to models used in consulting for organizational change. First, all behavioral science models (Gilfillan, 1980), including diagnostic ones, are more likely to prove valid and useful if they clearly specify the level of analysis, the conceptual boundaries of the model, relations among variables or analytical domains (e.g., system components), effectiveness criteria, and other evaluative standards. It is also desirable that models use consistent explanatory principles rather than conflicting ones. The principles of diagnostic fits and gaps, for example, are generally compatible with each other. In contrast, there can be incompatibilities between theories that explain effectiveness in terms of consensus and intergroup harmony and theories that view disagreements and even mild conflicts as contributing to effective adaptation to environmental complexity and change. If a model incorporates incompatible principles or interpretive frames, then consultants need to make explicit the procedures used for dealing with these incompatibilities (see Chapter 15).

Models that are derived inductively and are specified during data gathering and analysis can meet the above analytical requirements just as readily as models that are fully specified prior to diagnosis. Moreover, as was suggested in Chapter 1, empirically grounded and highly focused models contain substantial advantages for diagnosis over models that are standardized in advance.

Second, besides meeting these general analytical requirements, consultants need to ensure that their models generate useful feedback. Ideally, feedback should also contribute to organizational improvement and learning (see Chapter 13). In particular, diagnostic feedback should help clients and other members of the client organization to understand the nature and sources of organizational ineffectiveness and to focus on more promising levers for introducing change. To encourage acceptance and motivate change, feedback should be provided in as pragmatic and nonthreatening a fashion as possible (Block, 1981; Nadler, 1977). For instance, it is often possible to enhance acceptance and understanding of feedback on ineffective outcomes by sandwiching this feedback between findings on effective organizational features. This presentation helps recipients recognize that they and their organization possess the capacity to improve their performance in the problematic areas.

In addition to addressing the requirements for effective diagnosis discussed in Chapter 1, consultants face a choice between models that are generally applicable to a whole class of organizations and models that are unique to the focal organization (Nadler, 1980). Unlike research models, which sometimes apply to an entire class of organizations, diagnostic models need to reflect the nature of crucial conditions prevailing within the focal organization and its environment. By doing so, diagnostic models will enhance their users' insights into sources of ineffectiveness and into routes to possible improvement. To illustrate, a research-based model might define environmental uncertainty as an abstract variable to be measured using universally applicable and reliable measures. On the other hand, unless interorganizational comparisons were planned, a diagnostic model that includes environmental uncertainty could concentrate on issues of direct relevance to the focal organization. Consider, for example, a diagnosis of a high-tech firm that frequently loses highly skilled engineers to competitors. This study could examine how well human resource personnel cope with unpredictable variations in the supply and qualifications of candidates for engineering positions.

An important tactical and professional issue arises when consultants tailor their models directly to the concerns of clients: Can consultants appropriately start their study by accepting definitions of organizational problems and challenges provided by clients or by other powerful members of the organization? Furthermore, should consultants agree to confine their investigations to causal factors that clients define as important and thus implicitly allow clients to determine the diagnostic model? Focusing directly on client concerns helps consultants win clients' support. However, the concerns presented by clients during the entry stage in a project often reveal only the tip of the iceberg. These presented problems and explanations reflect clients' personal dissatisfactions as shaped by their emotions and their own personal and interpersonal goals. Moreover, the clients' dissatisfaction can be affected by whether they focus on themselves or on the organization, the extent that their statements reflect self-presentational concerns, and their possession of internal or external loci of control (Kowalski, 1996).

A further difficulty is that clients' explanations of ineffectiveness reflect their own attribution processes (Bettman & Weitz, 1983; Staw, 1975). Thus, we have found that top executives frequently blame failure on other members of their organization or uncontrollable external causes, rather than on organizational features or themselves. Consider statements like the following, which managerial clients made during our projects and training sessions: "You don't have to talk to anyone else here. My subordinate managers are a bunch of incompetent malingerers, and most of them need to be speedily replaced. . . . Indeed, that's what I want you to help me do." "All these losses are the fault of the local works committee [i.e., union], which blocks all our initiatives. Therefore, I want you to help me get rid of the union in this firm."

"The organization that owns our operation blocks our development in new directions."

Consultants cannot in good conscience allow client explanations like these to define the diagnostic agenda and set the scope of diagnostic investigations. However, consultants can make sure that their diagnostic models and feedback directly address their clients' concerns and attributions. In the case of the manager at odds with the union, the consultant might, for example, provide data on the performance of other firms facing equally militant unions. If these data reveal that comparable firms show greater initiative than the client firm and turn handsome profits, they could lead clients to reframe problems and could motivate desire for change. Or, the diagnosis might show that union representatives only block certain types of initiatives and that other action possibilities have not been explored sufficiently. Comparative feedback like this can encourage clients to understand and question their own attribution processes and to recognize that ineffectiveness stems from organizational and systemic sources, not just from the behavior of a small group of people.

When constraints of time and other resources are paramount, consultants may reasonably agree in advance to exclude some system components or types of variables from their diagnosis. To illustrate, to save time and money, consultants might agree to exclude time-consuming, hard-to-study facets of organization-environment relations from the study—provided that these interactions were judged to be unimportant to the main diagnostic questions. Links to competitors and suppliers, for example, could be excluded from a sharp-image diagnosis that focused mainly on discovering how internal organizational processes contributed to customer dissatisfaction. This kind of mutually negotiated and acknowledged narrowing of the scope of the diagnosis is, of course, a far cry from passively accepting the clients' initial statements as a valid diagnosis of organizational problems and possibilities for change.

Collaborative Applications of Open-Systems Models

Like the open-systems framework presented in Chapter 2, the models examined in this section use open-systems theory as a guiding scheme for the gathering, analysis, and feedback of diagnostic data. However, unlike the approaches discussed earlier, the models reviewed here assume that members of the client organization can and should take an active role in diagnosis and action planning. Moreover, these models place far less emphasis on the development of elaborate data-gathering schemes than do comprehensive open-systems approaches, such as those proposed by Van de Ven and Ferry (1980).

The models discussed here have their roots in efforts by organization development consultants to make diagnosis interactive and collaborative (Bartunek, 1984; Bartunek, Lacey, & Wood, 1992; Susman, 1981; Tichy & Hornstein, 1980). Advocates of collaborative diagnosis argue that members of any organization develop their own lay theories about major sources of inefficiencies in the organization, their likely causes, and the most appropriate remedial actions (Argyris & Schon, 1974). These schemata can be made explicit, that is, stated in formal terms and thereby opened to scrutiny by others (e.g., Nelson & Mathews, 1991). Doing so helps participants understand their own perspectives and those of others. Once made explicit, the participants' understandings can serve as inputs to collaborative diagnosis and action planning.

This collaborative approach seeks to democratize diagnosis and consultation. It defines clients as proactive agents in diagnosis and assigns consultants the role of facilitator. During collaborative analysis sessions, the consultant assembles the requisite "raw materials," much of which were generated by participants, and provides participants with enough analytical structure and continuity to engender constructive analysis by participants. Responsibility for both diagnosis and action planning thus fall squarely on the shoulders of those participants in the focal organization who will have to live with and be accountable for any consequences flowing from these interventions. The collaborative approach further directs consultants to focus participants' attention on the future of their organization rather than on solving short-term problems (Susman, 1981; Weisbord, 1988).

Open-Systems Planning

Open-systems planning (OSP; Beckhard & Harris, 1977, pp. 58-69; Burke, 1982, pp. 65-70; Fry, 1982; Jayaram, 1976) is a future-oriented, diagnostic process designed to achieve the above aims. During OSP, participants actively identify gaps between current conditions and desired future states, and they move gradually toward planning ways to attain these desired futures. OSP seeks to avoid the complexity of consultant-centered diagnoses of organization-environment relations by relying on participants' perceptions of the focal organization's environment and the organization's interchanges with the environment. Although this form of environmental assessment suffers from methodological limitations, it can contribute to the participants' awareness of the diverse environmental domains affecting the focal organization, as well as the different criteria for assessing relations with these domains.

In OSP, consultants conduct a series of workshops with members of an organization or subunit. Those participating in these workshops have the responsibility and authority to make decisions affecting the organization's strategic relations to its environment. The workshop participants diagnose their organization's current situation and decide which steps to take to deal with external challenges and opportunities. The consultant facilitates and guides the discussions, records and summarizes them, and gives feedback without dictating the content of the diagnosis and the planning for action. Groups whose members are familiar with the background and approach of OSP may also use it without the aid of an external consultant. The summary of the main steps in OSP shown in Box 4.1 contains instructions to participants in the planning process.[2]

OSP requires participants to use constructive problem-solving techniques to discover and deal with differences in their priorities and objectives. As Jayaram (1976) notes, this approach can work well only when members trust and cooperate with one another. Only then can they use OSP successfully to assess the organization's current strategic stance toward its environment and to plan changes in this stance (see Beckhard & Harris, 1977, for examples). In addition, to use OSP effectively, participants must have the power to put their plans into action. Otherwise, the whole process may frustrate and ultimately alienate and embitter participants. To conduct OSP, consultants need to be skilled in working with groups in training-type situations.

Search Conference

The Search Conference was developed by Emery and Trist (1973) as part of sociotechnical systems theory (Cummings & Worley, 1993, pp. 352-361; Jimenez, Escalante, & Aguirre-Vazquez, 1997). It is used most often in planning for sociotechnical interventions, but it can also be used as a diagnostic intervention. The Search Conference, like OSP, convenes participants in small groups to examine an organization's current state and its future. However, unlike OSP, search conferences start from the sociotechnical assumption that bureaucratic organizations are inimical to learning, and that new organizational forms must be developed to facilitate adaptation to environmental

Box 4.1
Steps in Open-Systems Planning

1. *Analyze current environmental conditions.* Create a map showing the external conditions, groups, and organizations in the task environment, as well as the demands, problems, and opportunities created by these forces.

2. *Analyze current responses to the environment.* Describe the ways that the organization currently handles these environmental demands and conditions. Consider all important transactions with the task environment.

3. *Analyze actual priorities and purposes.* Define current goals, values, and priorities by examining current responses to the environment and the organization's internal system components (structure, processes, culture, etc.). If possible, reach agreement on the organization's current guiding mission.

4. *Predict trends and conditions.* Predict likely changes in external conditions over the next 2 to 5 years. Assess the future awaiting the organization if it maintains its current responses to the environment.

5. *Define an ideal future.* Create scenarios for an ideal future state. These scenarios can envision changes in the organizational purposes and priorities, in external conditions, and in responses to the environment.

6. *Compare current and ideal states.* In light of projected trends (Step 4), define gaps between current and ideal future states in goals and strategies, external conditions, and organizational responses. These gaps may be thought of as differences between where the organization seems to be going and where you want it to go.

7. *Establish priorities.* Assign priorities to the gaps between ideal and current conditions. Define areas of working agreement and identify disagreements about values, priorities, and purposes.

8. *Plan appropriate actions.* Plan ways of moving toward agreed-upon future states by narrowing the most important gaps identified in Steps 6 and 7. Plan both immediate actions and those that will be undertaken after 6 months and 2 years. Consider actions for resolving disagreements. Create a schedule for following up on actions and updating plans.

change. In the Search Conference, many organizational members and stakeholders interact in small groups over an extended period of time, often from 2 to 3 consecutive days, in order to examine the focal organization's current state and to search for creative ways to envision and improve its future. The participants use open-systems concepts like those discussed in Chapter 2 but also scan their environment with techniques like "futuring" and "visioning," which resemble the procedures used in OSP. These techniques entail mapping systematically the demands and expectations of stakeholders (see Chapter 5), such as rank-and-file employees, stockholders, customers, and community groups. For this purpose, it is recommended that representatives of stakeholding groups take part in the conference.

Search Conference participants analyze the interface between the focal organization and its environment in a sequence of steps. They start with relations among environmental elements that exist independently of the organization but impinge on it, continue to develop learning cycles from these environmental elements, proceed to action planning with respect to environmental elements, and then deal with system relations within the organization. The outputs of Search Conferences are proposals for change that must then be negotiated with broad groups of stakeholders.

Besides OSP and the Search Conference, there are many other forms of collaborative diagnosis based on system frameworks. Weisbord (1988), for example, favors a "practice theory" that directs consultants to assess the potential for action, involve most of the focal organization's members in the diagnostic process ("get the whole system in the room"), and focus attention on the future of the focal organization—that is, avoid solving short-term problems. Weisbord's guidelines emphasize collaboration in diagnosis between consultants and the focal organization's key decision makers.

OSP, Search Conferences, and Weisbord's practice theory all stress the importance of envisioning possible futures for the organization and planning to meet them. Like the scenario-planning techniques sometimes used in strategic planning (Chapter 13), the open-systems techniques described here encourage decision makers to adopt a proactive stance toward their environments rather than just reacting to environmental changes and constraints.

OSP, Search Conferences, and practice theory encourage consultants and members of the focal organization to share their implicit diagnostic models and strategic assumptions and to make them explicit. This process reaffirms the core organization development value of reducing the focal organization's dependency on external consultants. Involvement in collaborative diagnosis also increases the exposure of participants to central values in organization development, including appreciation of others' points of view and commitment to collaborative forms of problem solving. When employees share actively in diagnosis, this democratization of diagnosis epitomizes the organization development ideal that employees should exercise control over decisions affecting their own worklife (Woodman, 1989).

Consultants and clients who would implement client-centered and collaborative forms of diagnosis and action planning, like OSP, need to be aware of the many contingencies affecting the success of these techniques (Tichy et al., 1976). Diagnostic workshops require participants to invest considerable time and energy. Moreover, these workshops function best when participants are already skilled in system thinking, problem solving, and teamwork. In the absence of these skills, consultants will have to devote time to training participants prior to starting the workshops. If participants do not acquire these skills during the workshops, they will not be able to engage in subseqent diagnoses once consultants leave the scene. In addition, collaborative techniques require participants to be committed to the idea of collaborative diagnosis and decision making. Moreover, teamwork within the diagnostic teams requires a climate that sustains honest sharing of views and cooperative problem solving.

Clearly, many organizations, and, in particular, those undergoing crises or suffering from serious forms of ineffectiveness, lack these preconditions for collaborative problem solving. Instead, these organizations may be divided into competing cliques and groups of stakeholders that do not trust one another and are unable to agree on organizational ends and means. Programs such as OSP are likely to fail if participants in the diagnostic process are divided in these ways. A further problem is that personal predilections and organizational culture often lead clients to resist investing personally in diagnosis and action planning. Instead, they prefer to cast the consultant in the role of expert and have him or her bear almost sole responsibility for executing the diagnosis.

Yet another limiting condition for using collaborative techniques such as OSP and the Search Conference is that they are best applied in face-to-face problem-solving groups. This requirement restricts their applicability to large organizations unless participation is restricted to top management. That solution undermines the possibility of broad employee involvement in diagnosis and planning for change. It is possible to convene many face-to-face groups, but then problems arise in coordinating group outputs.

Finally, OSP and some other workshop-based approaches may fail to meet two of the analytical criteria for diagnostic models reviewed above. First, there is a risk that relations among variables and system domains will not be specified very clearly and will be left up to the interpretation and judgment of participants. Yet without the ability to sort out causal connections between variables, participants cannot decide what steps to take to close gaps between current and ideal future states. Hence, they risk reaching invalid diagnostic conclusions. Second, effectiveness criteria may not be defined clearly. Without clear effectiveness criteria, participants may find it hard to assess the impacts of gaps and reach agreement on action priorities.

Making Systems Simple: The Six-Box Model

Weisbord's (1976) "six-box" model is one of the most straightforward and easy-to-use system models in the literature. In presenting it, Weisbord sought to distill years of consulting experience and to provide users with "Six Places to Look for Trouble with or without Theory." The model's ease of comprehension, its intuitive appeal to managers, and its potential uses in management development and in courses on organization development combine to make it perhaps the most popular diagnostic model.[3] The six-box model is widely cited in organization development texts (e.g., French & Bell, 1995, pp. 124-126) and has been recommended as the diagnostic model of choice when diagnosis is done under time constraints or when organizational participants do not have prior knowledge of open-systems concepts (Burke, 1982, p. 173).

The point of departure for use of the model is identification of those organizational outputs with which both the external customers and the internal "producers" are dissatisfied. Identification of these outputs then leads participants in the diagnosis to search for the sources of dissatisfaction inside the model. Internal producers are the relevant set of key decision makers in the focal organization. Cameron's (1984) model of organizational ineffectiveness also starts with the same general notion of focusing on dissatisfactions with key organizational outcomes. This feature of both Weisbord's and Cameron's models is specifically emphasized because it is one of the key ideas that inspired our approach to the construction of sharp-image models.

The six boxes shown in Figure 4.1 are postulated to contain the possible causes of dissatisfaction with organizational products or services. Each box represents a cluster of frequently occurring organizational problems.[4] The box labeled Helpful Mechanisms refers to internal procedures for coordination, control, communication, and information management that are intended to help employees in their work roles. The box labeled Relationships covers relations both within and among organizational units, including conflict resolution arrangements.

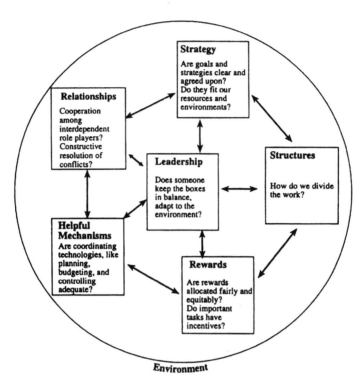

Figure 4.1 Six-Box Model
SOURCE: Weisbord (1976).

For each of these boxes, consultants are encouraged to diagnose the following types of gaps: (a) gaps between what exists now and what ought to be; (b) gaps between what is actually done and what employees and managers say that they do (i.e., gaps between the official and emergent aspects of organizational behavior); and (c) gaps among organizational units and layers—including gaps within and between boxes. These procedures rest on the assumption that the greater the gaps, the more problematic the functioning of the focal organization.

The leadership box in Figure 4.1 appears as a hub connecting the other five boxes because Weisbord assumes that leaders and their choices, including those concerning the organization's mission and strategy, exert pivotal influences over organizational effectiveness. Leaders are defined as key decision makers or top managers. They are assigned responsibility for reducing diagnosed gaps and for realigning relations between the areas defined by the surrounding boxes. The consultant's role in diagnosis is likened to that of an air traffic controller watching a radar screen (i.e., the model shown in Figure 4.1), which shows blips when gaps occur. Data on these blips are provided to organizational leaders, who then decide what action to take to reduce gaps.

The central position of the leadership makes the six-box model very appropriate whenever consultants diagnose top management's leadership style or behavior and whenever consultants view managerial behavior as a primary factor accounting for the organization's ills. On the other hand, consultants who doubt the model's assumptions about the role and influence of top management will probably decide not to use the model. Although there is some empirical support for the model's assumptions about the impacts of leadership (Gersick, 1991), many scholars question these premises. Organizational ecologists (e.g., Hannan & Freeman, 1984), for instance, argue that managerial choices have only slight impacts on organizational outcomes and that it is very difficult for managers to plan and bring about changes that contribute to organizational survival and enhance performance. Mintzberg (1984) has argued that the impact of leadership and the effectiveness of particular leadership styles depend on the life cycle stage in which the organization is located (see Chapter 11 for a similar position).

A major weakness of the model is that it lacks a firm theoretical foundation. Weisbord did not provide clear guidelines for determining whether a gap exists, which gaps exercise greater influence over organizational effectiveness and ineffectiveness, and how consultants should cull and integrate data on gaps. The model is thus deceptively simple (Burke, 1994). To apply it, consultants need to analyze and synthesize findings on a complex array of different types of gaps.

An even more serious threat to the model's robustness is the lack of a clear path for moving from statements of dissatisfactions regarding the focal organization's products or services toward systematic explanations of the intraorganizational causes of these dissatisfactions. Yet another limitation is the model's rather narrow view of effectiveness. By stressing the importance of agreed-upon goals and objectives and of smooth internal coordination among system components, the model downplays the significance of resource acquisition and adaptation criteria, along with criteria favored by powerful internal and external stakeholders. Moreover, the model takes a more optimistic view of the possibilities for attaining smooth internal coordination and consensus than do most current approaches to organizational politics.

A further limitation of the model is its failure to encourage users to examine several potentially crucial areas for diagnosis. These include the organization's economic foundations and resource flows, its technology, and its culture. The environment remains unspecified in the model, and the linkages among the boxes and environmental factors are underdeveloped. Lack of serious attention to the environment is a severe handicap, given the importance of diagnosing the ever more turbulent and competitive environments that most organizations face, as well as the predominance of multiple stakeholders in these environments.[5]

Diagnosis in Stream Analysis

Porras's (1987) diagnostic approach, which we refer to as the stream organizational model, is embedded in a comprehensive theory of diagnosis and planned change known as Stream Analysis. The main steps in Stream Analysis are diagnosis of organizational problems, construction of interventions to bring about planned changes, and evaluation of the interventions' outcomes. The evaluation phase is intended to enable organizational members to learn effective change approaches and techniques. The diagnostic model and Stream Analysis as a whole are grounded in systems theory and in the study of organizational cognition.

Users of the stream organizational model start by collecting and classifying symptoms of ineffectiveness and tracing linkages among these symptoms. Problems and symptoms are categorized into one or more of four system components, or *streams,* that characterize any focal organization: organizing arrangements, social factors, technology, and physical setting. Construction of the diagnostic model then progresses to identification of core problems that cause or affect symptoms and problems throughout the system. These core problems then become targets for planned change efforts. Action planning and management of planned change focus on the four system streams listed above.

Stream Analysis requires active participation in diagnosis by key organizational decision makers and internal stakeholders. Porras (1987) suggests forming a steering committee whose membership reflects a cross-section of the focal organization's functions, levels, and product lines. This committee guides the diagnosis, gathers the data, and is responsible for the analysis. This committee may or may not be assisted by an outside consultant. Porras recommended using consultants because of their expertise, their broader

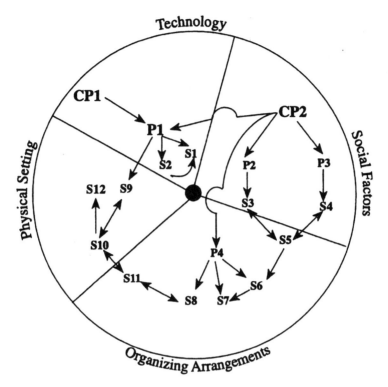

Figure 4.2 Stream Diagnostic Chart
Key: S = Symptom; P = Problem; CP = Core Problem

perspective, and their skill in facilitating the whole diagnostic process. However, he anticipated that participation in diagnosis would empower participants and train them to carry out future diagnoses independently of external consultants.

The major components of the diagnostic model are portrayed in Figure 4.2.[6] Two of the streams in the figure portray process components. These encompass social factors, which refer to human processes, and technology. The other two streams represent the structural components—organizational arrangements and physical setting. The relative size of the sectors in the figure can be adjusted to reflect the diagnostic importance assigned to them by the steering committee.

The four streams shown in Figure 4.2 are given special attention in diagnosis because they can be changed through planned change interventions

(Porras & Silver, 1991). These streams, in turn, affect individual organizational members, shape their behavior on the job, and thereby shape organizational outcomes. According to this logic, at any given point in time, the streams both reflect previous interventions and form targets for future interventions.

The steering committee begins its diagnosis by sorting current problems into the four streams or sectors. Subsequently, the participants in diagnosis try to reach consensus on the relations among the problems identified in each sector. To do so, the committee members discuss each problem and decide if it is a symptom or a more basic problem. Some of the identified problems (and symptoms) may be reciprocally related, whereas others may be arranged in a causal chain, with one problem leading to another. The diagnostic skills and expertise of the consultants and the other members of the steering committee find expression in the identification of core problems, which are responsible for other organizational problems.

Figure 4.2 denotes symptoms by the letter S, problems by P, and core problems by CP. A double-headed arrow symbolizes a reciprocal relation between symptoms and problems, whereas a single-headed arrow represents a unidirectional path of influence. In Figure 4.2, the second core problem (CP2), which is located in the Social Factors sector, directly and indirectly leads to other problems and symptoms among social factors, along with problems and symptoms in other sectors. Consequently, an intervention that resolves this core problem will produce effects throughout the organization.

Construction of the stream diagnostic chart, the main vehicle for understanding the underlying dysfunctions of the organization, follows a straightforward procedure. The steering committee identifies problems within the four streams and gathers data on them; organizes problems into categories (i.e., Ss, Ps, and CPs); identifies interconnections among symptoms and problems; and portrays these relations in a chart like that shown in Figure 4.2. The findings can then be shared with others in the organization and can serve as input into action planning and implementation. The process of planning specific change activities, implementing planned changes, and evaluating the results of these actions can all be undertaken within the analytical framework just presented. Thus, the stream diagnostic chart, which provides a visual representation of the diagnostic findings, helps leaders of planned change activities to identify those change levers that seem most important and relevant to the focal organization. The diagnostic model and chart can also provide a framework for analyzing the outcomes of planned change.

The stream organizational model contains insights and practical features that recommend it to consultants. In our approach to sharp-image diagnosis, we sought to incorporate the first two of these features while avoiding several drawbacks to Stream Analysis, which are discussed below. The first advantage of the stream organizational model is its focus on assessing ineffectiveness within organizational structures and processes (see Cameron, 1984, and Chapters 1 and 3). The second advantage of the model is its usefulness as a visual aid to diagnosis and feedback. Graphic presentation of the diagnostic analysis helps those responsible for diagnosis and recipients of feedback to understand complex system relations between symptoms, problems, and other organizational features. Construction of the diagnostic chart can readily become a collaborative activity in which consultants and other participants modify the chart during diagnostic sessions. Third, the diagnostic model is theoretically integrated with other phases of consultation and planned change. As noted, a derivative of the diagnostic model shown in Figure 4.2 can be used for both the intervention and evaluation phases of the consultation project. Fourth, the stream model is part of a theory of planned organizational change (Robertson, Roberts, & Porras, 1993) that has received some support from assessment studies designed to test a few of the theory's main tenets (Robertson et al., 1993).

Despite its strengths, the stream organizational model contains some limitations. Most important, there appears to be a basic flaw in the theoretical rationale underlying the selection of the four streams or system components. In Stream Analysis, diagnosis starts by examining variables that can be manipulated through planned change and may have been subject to past interventions. These variables, which are contained within the four streams, are assumed in advance to be the ones that can and should be changed to solve problems and to enhance critical organizational outcomes. This assumption prejudges the causes of effectiveness and ineffectiveness. Furthermore, this assumption can lead to the selection of change levers without reference to their feasibility and appropriateness to the organization and the problems at hand (see Chapter 5). In contrast, it seems more reasonable to begin diagnosis by examining critical ineffective outcomes, then tracing the underlying causes of these outcomes, and subsequently deciding how best to intervene in order to change these causal factors. This latter path is the one we recommend for sharp-image diagnosis.

Another serious weakness is that the stream organizational model can divert attention from critical system features that are not included or highlighted by the definition of the four streams. These include critical organizational inputs and outputs and stakeholder positions. More generally, the model fails to direct attention to environmental change, to external constraints, and to the ways that the organization manages its external relations. Porras cites environmental shifts as triggers for organizational change (Porras & Silver, 1991), but his model does not lead practitioners of diagnosis to study systematically how organizations cope with environmental threats and opportunities.

Yet another disadvantage of the model is its limited application of diagnostic principles and procedures like those discussed in Chapter 2. Surprisingly, the stream organizational model hardly applies the principles of gaps or fits. The model does call for the examination of interdependencies among system elements and components. Unfortunately, environmental interchanges are not discussed, and internal interdependencies are examined only in a rudimentary fashion. Finally, the model may turn out to be much harder to apply than might be supposed. Considerable experience and knowledge of the area of organizational behavior will be needed for users to distinguish symptoms from problems and to identify core problems. For this reason, organizational members who take part in diagnosis may find the model hard to use. In the end, the model may be better suited for consultant-led diagnosis than for client-centered diagnosis or for self-diagnosis by organizational members.

Conclusion

Choosing a diagnostic model is one of the most crucial judgment calls facing consultants and other practitioners of diagnosis. The model that is chosen not only influences data gathering and feedback, but it also shapes clients' and consultants' decisions about subsequent interventions into the client organization and about the entire course of planned change. As a guide to the choice of an existing diagnostic model or to its custom development, this chapter discussed requirements for diagnostic models that apply to all types of behavioral science models and requirements that are specific to models used in consulting and applied research. Then, the chapter critically reviewed several published models. The models selected for examination contributed directly to our thinking about sharp-image diagnosis, as outlined in Chapter 1. In reviewing the models, we pointed to positive features that we sought to incorporate into our own approach, and to drawbacks that we sought to overcome.

One drawback characterizes many standardized diagnostic models, including those reviewed here: In attempting to create explicit models that are universally applicable, the creators of diagnostic models necessarily develop analytical categories that are quite distant from daily realities in the focal organization and from the specific problems and expressions of ineffectiveness of greatest concern to clients. Consultants who use standardized, abstract models like the ones described in this chapter will have to make a special effort to ensure their relevance to client concerns. This problem is most pressing in diagnoses based on broad models, such as the open-systems framework underlying open-systems planning. In contrast, Weisbord's six-box model and Porras's stream model treat sources of dissatisfaction and problems as focal concerns for diagnosis. In like manner, our approach to sharp-image diagnosis · advocates beginning with an assessment of organizational problems and challenges and then moving to their underlying sources.

An additional difficulty with universally applied models, such as those surveyed in this chapter, is that they may fail to reflect the focal organization's goals and strategies and may overlook critical contingencies impinging on the organization. Key contingencies include ownership, organizational culture, growth patterns, environmental context, technology and material conditions, past history, and stage in the organizational life cycle. For example, Weisbord's six-box model would not be very helpful in diagnosing an organization in transition from a family-run, entrepreneurial firm into a shareholder-owned and professionally managed firm. There is nothing in the six-box model to inform its users that entirely different managerial styles are appropriate to the entrepreneurial and formalization stages of the organizational life cycle (see Chapter 11).

No predefined model can deal adequately with the distinctive sets of contingencies and member orientations that set organizations apart from one another and mark off one phase in an organization's history from another. Only custom-designed models can adequately reflect the individual character of a client organization. Hence, our approach to sharp-image diagnosis discourages consultants from choosing a diagnostic model at the start of the project. Instead, we advocate developing an empirically grounded model that focuses directly on the nature and causes of the focal organization's current problems and challenges.

The developmental approach of sharp-image diagnosis also helps the consultant build client commitment and motivation for action during the diagnosis. In contrast, the models presented in this chapter assume client commitment and motivation from the start of the project. In addition, these models assume that agreement is reached in advance about all of the major parameters of the project—such as who will be interviewed, by whom, and who will receive feedback. In practice, these issues are often negotiated while diagnosis takes place. The unfolding, developmental character of sharp-image diagnosis more readily incorporates these possibilities. Furthermore, the process of gradually developing a highly focused diagnostic model provides consultants with opportunities to assess and cope with political forces that can greatly affect the course of the diagnosis.

The impacts of organizational politics on diagnosis and planned change are crucial concerns for consultants. Yet they are neglected by all of the models presented in this chapter and by many other popular diagnostic models. Chapter 5 addresses these issues and discusses ways to assess power relations and political processes within focal organizations.

Notes

1. Another influential model, Lewin's force field analysis, is presented in Chapter 5.

2. This summary, which synthesizes and slightly adapts Jayaram's (1976) approach, also draws on Burke (1982, p. 66) and Plovnick, Fry, and Burke (1982, pp. 69-70). The main advantages of Jayaram's approach over that of Beckhard and Harris (1977, pp. 58-69) is that it allows the definitions of purposes and priorities to emerge from the discussions of the current and ideal states, and it requires only the achievement of working agreements about operating priorities. This approach to defining goals and priorities seems more realistic than expecting participants to agree in advance on the organization's core mission (see Fry, 1982).

3. Another very popular model is the somewhat similar 7-S model developed by the McKinsey group (Waterman, Peters, & Phillips, 1980; see Assessing and Guiding Strategic Processes in Chapter 13).

4. All of the boxes in the figure are labeled according to Weisbord's terminology, except for Strategy, which was originally called Goals. For clarity, we have changed some of the original entries that appeared within each box and have reconfigured the arrows that appeared in the original figure.

5. Since the publication of the six-box model, Weisbord has moved on to develop a more dynamic family of diagnostic models (Weisbord, 1988), labeled "third wave consulting."

6. Figure 4.2 modifies the original presentation of the stream organizational model. Each of the streams (system components) is now represented by a sector of the circle, rather than by rectangles. This presentation helps users view the streams as interrelated components. Furthermore, the circular arrangement places more emphasis on the importance of "core" problems.

Diagnosing Organizational Politics

Organizational politics can greatly influence the progress and outcomes of diagnosis and of other types of consultation. Sometimes, political forces undermine behavioral science consultations and block efforts by clients to implement planned change (e.g., Kakabadse & Parker, 1984; Mirvis & Berg, 1977; Tushman, 1977). More often, political conditions determine the effectiveness of interventions and change methods selected by clients and consultants. For example, innovations such as quality circles for production or clerical workers are likely to be effective only if supervisors and managers are willing to give real power to the members of quality circles. Similarly, there are political preconditions for the successful use of many organization development techniques, including process consultation and team building. Because these techniques require high levels of trust and interpersonal openness, they are not very effective in settings in which power differences and fundamental conflicts of interest prevail.

When consultants understand an organization's power structure and its politics, they may be able to work in ways that are in keeping with these political conditions without compromising the consulting relationship. If they ignore these political realities, they are likely to encounter resistance to their diagnoses and may recommend interventions that cannot be implemented or

111

will produce negative consequences. Thus, by assessing the politics of consultation and planned change, consultants can help their clients identify feasible steps toward change goals, find ways to enhance support for planned change, and overcome resistance to it.

This chapter employs the political frame, which was introduced in Chapter 3, as a basis for the diagnosis of the sources of support and resistance to consultation and planned change. The first section explains why diagnosis, like other organizational interventions, often becomes a political issue within an organization and sometimes arouses strong opposition. By anticipating such political responses to diagnosis, consultants become more able to avoid them or to cope with serious political barriers to a diagnostic project. The second section presents two models for diagnosing the political prospects for planned change and for helping decision makers plot an appropriate course toward their change targets. The third section addresses the diagnosis of political features in their own right, rather than just as facilitants or barriers to interventions by consultants and clients. This section concentrates on assessments of power distribution and the uses of power.

Politics of Diagnosis

Diagnosis, like any type of organizational consultation, and like manager-guided change, entails intervention into the organizational status quo. Diagnosis interrupts organizational routines, can affect members' expectations concerning organizational change, and can influence how they think about themselves and about their organization (Argyris, 1970). Members of a client organization often respond to diagnostic projects much as they would to anticipated managerial interventions into that organization, because they expect diagnosis to lead to those managerial actions. Suppose, for example, that employees in a firm fear that management plans to downsize. When a consultant is brought in to do a diagnostic study, the employees will quite naturally assume that the study will justify cutbacks and perhaps also identify their victims.

Political Implications of Diagnosis

As this example suggests, diagnostic studies rarely affect all stakeholders in the same way. Diagnosis, like other forms of consultation, holds prospects of benefiting some organizational members and external stakeholders while harming others. Outsiders often remain unaware of the possible benefits or threats of diagnosis and consultation unless management announces that its plans for action are based on consultants' recommendations.

The most obvious reason that diagnosis may threaten some members of an organization is that it can uncover weaknesses in their performance or that of their units. In addition, diagnostic recommendations or decisions stemming from them can lead to the enhancement of the resources or authority given to particular individuals or units. Diagnosis can also have a differential impact on particular members or units: The very process of providing people with additional information and understanding about their organization's operations may increase their power or their ability to take particular actions. Moreover, those who get feedback earlier sometimes gain advantages over others who receive the information later.

Even apparently neutral diagnostic recommendations can support particular interests or value positions at the expense of others. For example, there can be hidden power implications in the ways in which clients and practitioners define problems and selectively focus on some organizational levels or features (e.g., examining sources of high labor costs among lower-level employees while ignoring managerial practices and organization designs that generate hidden costs and reduce productivity). Or, consider the popular and often justified recommendation that decisions be made as close as possible to the operational level, and that all relevant members provide input into decisions. These recommendations can clash with the values and interests of managers who benefit personally from the current concentration of power.

Sometimes, the political impact of diagnostic feedback is quite different from that envisioned by the investigator. For example, performance comparisons between comparable units may direct client attention—and wrath—toward managers heading low-performing units, even if the consultant finds the explanation for unit performance in different variables. It should come as no surprise, then, that organizational members often react to a diagnosis according to their expectations of the study's effects on their own interests.

The Power of Stakeholders—and Consultants

The greater the power of stakeholders who oppose or support a diagnosis or intervention, the more they can determine the course and outcomes of the project. Assessment of the potential influence of stakeholders over diagnosis can draw on the same techniques used to assess the ability of stakeholders to support or oppose any type of organizational intervention. These techniques are discussed in detail in the next section of this chapter.

In considering the power of stakeholders over consultation, consultants should also bear in mind their own potential sources of organizational power. Consultant power typically derives from combinations of the following factors:[1]

- Expertise
- Personal and professional stature, as assessed by members of the client organization
- Control over operationally or politically valuable information
- Access to powerful members of the organization
- Ability to develop mutually beneficial exchanges with powerful members
- Support by powerful internal and external stakeholders

Most consultants draw on several power sources. The sources and degree of consultants' power depend on the practitioners' own background and characteristics, objective features of the organization, the nature of the consulting project, and the consultants' choices about how to define their roles in the organization. Some consultants seek greater involvement in the political system of the client organization, whereas many prefer the limited involvement required of outside experts and trainers.[2] Consultants who rely almost exclusively on their own expertise typically develop very limited contacts with members of the organization and make little effort to ensure that clients regard the consultants' recommendations as feasible.

Weighing the Political Consequences of Diagnosis

Without surrendering to either Machiavellianism or paranoia, consultants can benefit from an awareness of both the political implications of diagnosis and of the political constraints upon it—for example, political conditions affecting the feasibility of collaborative diagnostic studies (see Chapter 3). Awareness of conditions like these and of the political impact of diagnosis can help consultants choose more workable and potentially constructive forms of consultation.

As consultants become aware of the political implications of their work, they begin to face one of the fundamental professional dilemmas of diagnosis:

Who is to benefit from diagnosis—one or more individual clients who originally initiated or sponsored the study; a particular organizational stratum, such as top management; all members of some unit or group whose problem was originally presented to the consultant; or the entire organization, including external stakeholders?[3]

Consultants have proposed three possible solutions to the dilemma posed by the possibility that diagnosis will benefit some stakeholders at the expense of others. One classic solution, which is still popular among some organization development consultants, seeks to deny the existence of the problem by arguing that consultation furthers the overall health or effectiveness of the organization—a result that benefits all members. Although much admired, such win-win outcomes are remarkably rare in planned organizational change. A second and nearly opposite approach argues that behavioral science consultants, like any type of outside experts, owe their loyalties primarily to the client who hired them. This ostensibly simple solution raises serious ethical issues and often founders on the definition of the main client. In response to these difficulties, many consultants seek broad sponsorship and supervision of the diagnosis so that members of divergent stakeholding groups accept responsibility for resolving the political implications of the study.

A third, more appealing resolution of the dilemma argues that the main obligation of consultants is to provide clients with valid information and to allow them the freedom to decide whether and how to act upon this information (Bowen, 1977, based on Argyris, 1970). This approach discourages consultants from trying to impose their values and recommendations on the client organization. Instead, consultants accept that the power and responsibility for acting on diagnostic findings lie with members of the organization and not with the consultant. On the other hand, this approach does not specify sufficiently what constitutes valid information or who the real clients are. Therefore, this resolution of the issues facing consultants may encourage them to underestimate the political impacts of their work and lead them to blame clients for failure to enact recommendations.

A less elegant but more realistic resolution of the quandary begins with the assumption that consultants are responsible to a limited number of clients and that these clients need to define a clear set of expectations and priorities for diagnosis. A first step, therefore, is to require clients, with or without the aid of the consultant, to define goals for the study and criteria for assessing organizational effectiveness and ineffectiveness. Consultants or other diagnostic practitioners then can introduce additional criteria that are compatible with client goals and standards. In addition, consultants can propose problem definitions and solutions that benefit the widest possible range of groups and individuals but still fall within the boundaries set by client concerns and priorities. According to this approach, consultants may advocate particular effectiveness criteria and may favor particular solutions to organizational problems as long as their recommendations help reduce ineffectiveness or enhance effectiveness in ways that respond to client needs. The final responsibility for interpreting and acting on diagnostic findings lies with the client.

A major drawback of this approach is that it can encourage consultants to gear their work too closely to their clients' expectations, rather than making a comprehensive and independent assessment of the needs of the client organization. In consequence, diagnosticians may fail to discover sources of ineffectiveness and routes to organizational improvement besides those that their clients have already considered. An additional drawback is that consultants may have to choose among several individuals who assert that they are the "real clients" or among several people who share the role of client.

How, then, should consultants decide who is the appropriate client? One answer is that they should look for a person or group having both the authority and the expertise needed to use the diagnosis as a means to organizational improvement. The ideal client from this standpoint is often the highest manager who is concerned with the operations of the unit being studied—usually the chief executive officer (CEO) or the head of a semiautonomous division. This ideal client can also be the head of a function such as human resources, who has been assigned responsibility for handling the challenges and problems being examined in the diagnosis.

This way of defining the client helps consultants decide with whom they should try to work closely in planning a diagnosis and making recommendations. On the other hand, consultants may not know at the outset of a project whether or not particular functionaries have both the power and expertise to interpret diagnostic feedback and implement recommendations successfully. Moreover, this approach requires practitioners of diagnosis to make the strong assumption that their clients can define clear, overriding organizational interests or goals and will act on them. A further limitation of this solution to the politics dilemma is that it effectively excludes subordinate groups like labor from participating directly in the definition of project goals or the development of recommendations for action. To overcome this limitation, steering groups, which include representatives of labor and other stakeholding groups, can be assigned responsibility for coordinating a diagnosis and for planning actions based on diagnostic feedback.

In practice, some individuals and groups will usually gain from diagnosis and any subsequent changes, whereas others will lose. Hence, consultants and their clients need to confront the political implications of diagnosis in order to chart a course of action that is acceptable to them, their clients, and, if possible, other members of the organization. If practitioners anticipate the political impact of their work, they may be able to reduce the risk that opposition will undermine the study or prevent the implementation of its recommendations.

Diagnosing the Politics of Planned Change

Some consultants assess political processes primarily to facilitate their own diagnostic work. Others incorporate these assessments into diagnostic feedback and are even willing to help clients decide on tactics to enhance support and overcome resistance to change. Two models are presented here that can be used by consultants to help clients deal with organizational politics.

Successful planned change, as many consultants and scholars have observed, involves at least three distinct processes: unfreezing, changing, and refreezing of accepted understandings and practices (Kanter, Stein, & Jick, 1992; Lewin, 1951; Mintzberg & Westley, 1992; Tichy & DeVanna, 1986). First, members of an organization undergoing change must free themselves from the hold of previous conceptions and behavior patterns. Second, they develop new visions and programs. Third, they implement these programs and turn them into stable organizational routines. Participants in planned change typically engage in these processes in an iterative fashion, rather than sequentially. As they reject old ways of doing things, they often inductively discover new ones (e.g., Pascale, 1984). Gradually, they envision the state they want to obtain, plan ways to get there (Nadler & Tushman, 1989), and implement their plans. It is too early to speak of successful change until innovations and programs of change create new organizational routines, which are taken for granted by members of the organization and its environment (Yin, 1981).

Diagnosis can contribute to all three facets of planned change. Here, we focus on issues that consultants and managers can examine during the first two change phases, in which past practices and conceptions begin to unfreeze and members move gradually toward the envisioning and planning of change. Chapters 7 and 13 consider ways that diagnosis can contribute to the implementation of change.

Stakeholder Analysis

Stakeholder analysis, a technique originally developed to facilitate consideration of the politics of strategic decision making, provides a procedure that is useful for assessing the political forces impinging on any type of intervention or planned change.[4] Box 5.1 presents the main steps for identifying key stakeholders affected by an intervention and assessing their capacity to oppose or cooperate with proposed interventions. In analyses of the politics of strategy formation, the term *strategic moves* would be substituted wherever the term *intervention* appears in Box 5.1.

Clients and consultants can appropriately consider the issues raised in Box 5.1 in a collaborative fashion. Consultants can also make independent assessments of the issues listed there. These assessments would then serve as inputs into decisions by clients about what changes to pursue and what tactics to use to support their successful implementation.

Identifying Stakeholders

The first step shown in Box 5.1 can draw on several techniques. To follow the approach suggested by the questions in the box, investigators would analyze official lines of authority and contractual ties to the organization in order to identify primary stakeholders, such as owners, strategic partners, suppliers, and regulators. Then, through interviews with people holding divergent views and positions within the focal organization, investigators can identify influential secondary stakeholders. Internal secondary stakeholders often converge around important structural categories—including those based on rank and authority, function, department, geographical location, employment status (e.g., salaried versus hourly), and job categories. In addition, people can sometimes form an active stakeholder group on the basis of subgroup or background characteristics, such as gender and race. Once stakeholders are identified, the analysis focuses on those who are directly concerned with the proposed intervention or likely to be affected by it. In some cases, investigators can streamline the identification process by directly asking their informants which groups are likely to be affected by the intervention.

Box 5.1
Stakeholder Analysis

1. Identify key stakeholders.
   1a. Primary stakeholders: Which groups have formal (e.g., contractual) relations with the organization and exercise direct authority or economic influence over it?
   1b. Secondary stakeholders: Which other groups can exert influence over the organization and are affected by it?
   1c. Which stakeholders are likely to view the proposed intervention as important?

2. Examine the positions of each key stakeholder.
   2a. How did stakeholder act in the past on comparable issues?
   2b. What is stakeholder's position on the current intervention?

3. Examine stakeholder power.
   3a. Does stakeholder control resources that are crucial for the organization?
   3b. Can stakeholder exercise other sources of power over the organization?
   3c. All told, is stakeholder or the organization's top management more powerful?

4. Examine each stakeholder's capacity for action.
   4a. Can the stakeholder act in support of the organization?
   4b. Can the stakeholder act in opposition to the organization?
   4c. Can the stakeholder form a coalition with other stakeholders?
   4d. Can the stakeholder form a coalition with the organization?
   4e. How inclined are the leaders of stakeholding groups to take each of the above actions?

5. Assess stakeholder impacts.
   In light of the above, what is stakeholder's potential for resistance to or cooperation with the proposed interventions?

Another approach to identifying stakeholders involves specifying the interests and concerns of groups or individuals who play five crucial roles in the process of planned change (see Kanter et al., 1992, pp. 375-381 on strategists, implementors, and recipients).

1. *Change strategists,* who often include CEOs, top managers, and their consultants, create the overall vision for planned changes. Change strategists are usually the most powerful actors within an organization and act together as a dominant coalition. Sometimes, owners, the courts, or governmental administrators also act as change strategists and seek to impose changes on an organization. Change strategists are usually concerned with the ways that proposed changes will improve the organization's competitive position in its environment or will ensure the flow and efficient use of public funds.

2. *Change agents* include consultants, members of the organization who are recognized as having special expertise in planning and implementing change (e.g., human resource personnel, strategic planners), and other members of the organization or outsiders who encourage participants to undertake change and facilitate the development of change strategies and tactics. Change agents typically focus on change processes, as well as on outcomes.

3. *Implementors,* who are drawn from the top and middle ranks of the organization, have responsibility for managing day-to-day programs for change. Implementors often raise concerns about operational implications of interventions that were overlooked or poorly understood by strategists and external change agents.

4. The *recipients* of planned change, most of whom are located in the middle and lower ranks of an organization, usually have little say in the development of interventions of strategic programs and must react and adapt to plans and steps that come from higher up in the hierarchy. The recipients' reactions can make or break a program, because this large group of people must implement change on a daily basis.

5. Besides these three sets of participants in change, there are *nonparticipating stakeholders,* who are affected by interventions but do not participate in their development, implementation, or operation. Customers, clients, regulators, and community groups often fall into this category, as do employees in parts of the organization that do not undergo change.

Examining Stakeholder Positions

As shown in Box 5.1, the second step in stakeholder analysis entails assessment of the stand of each group toward proposed interventions. At this point, most investigators focus on the expressed attitudes of stakeholders. Caution is needed in interpreting these findings, because these attitudes may not predict very accurately how stakeholders will act once an intervention is implemented. Unless attitude measures are constructed very carefully, they do not consistently and powerfully predict peoples' behavior (Fishbein &

Ajzen, 1975; Krauss, 1995). What is more, peoples' attitudes toward a proposed change may shift during its implementation as they discover that the costs and benefits of the change differ greatly from what they anticipated. Hence, periodic reassessments of stakeholder positions may be needed once implementation begins. Despite their drawbacks, attitudinal data can reveal previously unnoticed hostility toward programs of change. To add validity to attitudinal assessments, it is helpful to check how stakeholders acted in the past when faced with comparable interventions.

Sometimes, investigators gather systematic attitudinal data on proposed interventions or strategic changes. For example, to assess the orientations of internal stakeholders, Floyd and Woolridge (1992) propose gathering questionnaire data from the people responsible for implementing strategic plans at the top, middle, and operational levels of the organization. These data are used to map areas of consensus and disagreement concerning managerial assessments of external conditions, goals, and strategies. Both cognitive and emotional differences are considered. It is possible, for example, that middle managers understand the intentions of top management but disagree with them or feel threatened by them. Once gaps among the orientations of actors responsible for implementation have been identified, the analyst can decide whether these gaps are likely to affect implementation. This decision will necessarily reflect the content of the organization's strategies, its recent experiences in implementing strategy, and the type of organization. For instance, bureaucratic organizations, which usually rely on top-down initiatives and controls, will face difficulties implementing strategies if there are big gaps in strategic understanding or commitment within or between management groups. On the other hand, attitudinal gaps among units and between levels are endemic to professional organizations such as hospitals and universities, and they may not be the most critical determinant of implementation prospects.

By taking an experimental and incremental approach to planned change, consultants and managers can sometimes make more accurate assessments of stakeholder reactions than can be obtained from attitude studies. This experimental approach can also help change strategists and change agents cope with difficulties that show up during implementation. For instance, consultants can implement behavioral science interventions in stages, beginning with some preliminary activity (such as an off-site meeting with top managers to plan changes) in order to learn from members' reactions to each stage how they may react to subsequent stages. Alternatively, management can introduce administrative or technological changes as experiments in just a few units within an organization. After a period of running in and an assessment of the consequences, the innovation can be modified in light of this experience and then diffused to other parts of the organization. Managers often take this approach when introducing costly technological innovations, such as robotics, or when trying out risky structural innovations, such as the substitution of self-checks for traditional forms of quality inspection (Eisenhardt & Westcott, 1988).

Unfortunately, stakeholders sometimes react very differently to interventions that are widely diffused than they did to pilots and experiments. Sometimes, middle managers implement pilot programs to show that they and their units are forward-looking or to benefit from the prestige or added resources that accompany such programs, even though they have little enthusiasm for the program itself. Furthermore, when diffusion is attempted, managers and employees who did not participate in the pilot may resist the predetermined solutions provided by the pilot program and fail to display the "deep learning" that went on during the experimental stages of the program (McKersie & Walton, 1991, p. 274). Finally, the enthusiasm created by the newness and uniqueness of a program can wear off once formerly innovative activities become widespread and routine.

Examining Stakeholder Power

The third step in stakeholder analysis requires an assessment of the power of each stakeholder and a comparison of the stakeholder's power to that of top management or some other agent responsible for implementing the change program.[5] Unfortunately, assessments of power in stakeholder analyses often rest on impressionistic judgments by a limited number of clients and other informants. These unsystematic judgments sometimes lead decision makers to underestimate the capacity of lower-ranking members and external stakeholders to wield power over management. Therefore, careful assessments of the power of stakeholders are very worthwhile. In addition to its contribution to stakeholder assessment, power assessment can help consultants identify the most powerful actors in a system, whose views must be considered during diagnosis and consultation. Moreover, power assessment can contribute to diagnoses of organizational politics like those discussed in the third part of this chapter.

For these reasons, the discussion that follows examines in detail alternative methods for assessing the power of stakeholders and other political actors. To assess the power of political actors directly, investigators need to follow the treatment of specific issues in different parts of the organization and examine political struggles directly. Because this kind of information is rarely available, it is usually necessary to look for overt manifestations of power (Kanter, 1977).

Table 5.1 directs attention to such overt indicators of power and lists techniques for gathering relevant information on them. The questions in the table refer to stakeholders and other political actors, but they could readily be modified to guide an assessment of the power and mobilization capacity of *potential* actors. For instance, many of the questions could be used as guidelines for assessing the potential power of women within an organization.

If some stakeholders appear to be powerful according to one type of criterion, such as centrality in emergent networks (Brass & Burkhardt, 1993; Ibarra, 1993), but not according to another, such as formal position or access to top decision makers, investigators will need additional information.[6] It will then be possible to determine whether a particular indicator is invalid or whether there are several distinct power bases within the organization but no single group of most powerful actors.

The sensitivity and informal character of political power and influence processes make them hard to measure. Members of an organization may not know much about its politics or may be reluctant to tell what they know. Moreover, powerful people often prefer to work behind the scenes, thereby avoiding challenges by critics in and around the organization. An additional difficulty is that power can be multifaceted. Actors who have power over one issue or area, such as influencing budget allocations, can lack power in another, such as determining long-term strategy. For these reasons, it is best to assess power using multiple measures and data-gathering techniques. Moreover, it is best to use issue-specific measures (Enz, 1989), along with general, global indicators.

Despite the difficulties in using questionnaires to assess subtle and sensitive topics, some authors have developed standard questionnaires for identifying powerful groups or individuals, delineating coalitions, describing prevalent influence tactics, and measuring power distribution. Many of these instruments use reputational techniques in which respondents are asked to rank the power of other groups or individuals (Enz, 1989; Moch, Cammann, & Cooke, 1983; Nelson, 1988; Price & Mueller, 1986). Respondents usually

Table 5.1 Assessing Stakeholder Power

Indicators and Guiding Questions	Research Methods
Resources: What kinds of resources are most important to members: funds, equipment, personnel, information, knowledge? Who gets disproportionate shares? In what units or job categories are pay and benefits particularly generous?	Observe (and/or interview) key resources and their distribution; examine budget allocations, salary scales.
Who controls resource acquisition and distribution?	Examine organizational charts, job descriptions
Centrality: Which technical and administrative processes are vital to everyday operations? Which are critical to success? Who influences and participates in them? Which individuals and groups do people consult for vital information, advice, and help in influencing key decisions?	Interview unit heads: study organization charts, job descriptions; analyze reports from interviews and workshops on troubleshooting, crises, failures, success; examine network ties through interviews and questionnaires; interview on emergent practices and routines.
Who handles contacts with powerful external organizations, units, and groups? Who holds central positions in important networks?	Interview, examine organization charts; interview or survey unit heads on external contacts and network ties.
Irreplaceability: Who is regarded as irreplaceable?	Interview knowledgeable members; survey members of relevant units.
Structure: Who holds top positions (titles) in the hierarchy? How many titles does each person have? How much is the person paid compared to others in the organization? What share of ownership does he or she have?	Examine organization charts, reports and records
Participation and Influence in Decision Making: Who participates in key official and unofficial decision-making forums? Who gets access to top decision makers?	Examine organization charts, job descriptions, reports on membership in decision-making bodies; observe participation patterns; interview on access and participation.
Whose views dominate major decisions? Who has won in power struggles and conflicts?	Analyze decisions as reported in documents, press, interviews, workshops.
To whom do members turn for sponsorship projects, career development?	Interview, analyze successes, failures reported in interviews, workshops.
Symbols: What are the main symbols of status and power (e.g., titles, office decor)? Who displays these symbols?	Observe nature, use, distribution of status symbols; interview knowledgeable members.
Reputation: Which groups, units, individuals are regarded as especially powerful?	Survey members for rankings; interview; observe attention, deference granted to individuals, groups.
Which units do people join in order to get ahead fast? With whom do members try to develop contacts? Whom do they try to impress?	Interview; examine executive career lines to find units that provide avenues to the top.

124

have little difficulty in ranking the power or influence of their peers. Nevertheless, the data from studies like these are often not valid enough to stand alone (Pfeffer, 1992).

As Table 5.1 suggests, a wide range of qualitative and largely unobtrusive techniques can supplement or substitute for questionnaire data on the power of political actors. These techniques include examining access to status symbols, representation in powerful decision-making bodies, and the ability of certain units or functions to serve as training grounds for people moving on to high-level positions. Each of the measures of power referred to in the table contains limitations, which can often be overcome by using multiple measures.

Examining Capacity for Action

The fourth step in stakeholder assessment involves examining each stakeholder's capacity for action in support of programs or in opposition to them. Even a relatively powerful group may lack the capacity to act on a particular issue or may face limits on available tactics. For example, members of a powerful labor union may bitterly oppose a planned relocation of their workplace, which will require a long commute to work. However, if labor laws restrict the union's ability to strike or use sanctions to influence issues directly covered in labor contracts, neither the union's power nor its members' feelings raise serious barriers to the relocation. Capacity for mobilization of stakeholding groups and the tactics available to them depend on many conditions that are only indirectly related to power (Gamson, Fireman, & Rytina, 1982; Jenkins, 1983). These include interaction and com- munication links among members sharing common interests, leadership, access to information, and possession of other necessary resources. Mobilization also depends on the emergence of a shared set of interpretations that defines joint interests or grievances and justifies joint actions. Finally, mobilization turns on the degree to which organizational authorities and other political and legal actors support mobilization or resist it.

As indicated in Box 5.1, assessments of capacity for action need to consider the possibility that actors who cannot alone affect managerial decisions will form powerful coalitions with other actors. For example, a broad coalition of external stakeholders used legal and procedural means to delay the construction and opening of a nuclear power plant on Long Island, near New York City. The coalition succeeded in delaying the project for so many years and raising its costs to such an extent that management ultimately abandoned its plans for operating the plant.

Limited compliance is a critical form of stakeholder action that is often overlooked. Even when they lack the power or authority to block the introduction of interventions, the people responsible for their implementation can undermine a program through defensive behavior (Ashforth & Lee, 1990), such as playing it safe and protecting their own turf, as well as by active resistance. In one major industrial concern studied by one of our students (Spanier-Golan, 1993), a program to introduce quality circles empowered rank-and-file workers to make proposals about quality improvements and efficiency. This new decision process threatened the authority and status of lower- and middle-level managers, who had traditionally had the main responsibility for administrative decisions. Most managers did not outwardly resist the program, but they failed to provide full operational support for the quality circles and were slow to process proposals initiated within the circles. As a result, most of the circles gradually went into decline and stopped meeting within a few years of their establishment.

Assessing Stakeholder Impacts

The fifth and last step in stakeholder analysis involves assessing the likely impact of tactics used by stakeholders. For example, can management count on support from suppliers and customers when it moves to just-in-time manufacturing? What will be the effects of this support? If management contemplates moves opposed by workers, can it weather work stoppages, adverse publicity, appeals to higher organizational and legal authorities, and low levels of commitment and compliance among the people who must implement a project?

Action Planning by Clients

Approaches like stakeholder analysis provide clients with feedback that can affect their decisions about how to handle the politics of change and can ultimately affect power alignments in and around the organization. Consultants vary in their willingness to take an active role in such highly politicized decisions. The appropriateness and feasibility of consultant involvement in organizational politics also depends greatly on the nature of the consulting contract, the types of challenges facing the organization, and conditions within the client organization (Harrison, 1991).

After assessing the potential for threat and cooperation among key stakeholders, decision makers usually consider tactics for mobilizing support for their programs and for defending themselves against opponents. Sometimes, managers can realign reward and control systems so as to generate incentives for compliance with planned changes. Managers who must confront opponents can consider the possible impacts of alternative ways of handling resistance—such as bargaining, threats, and sanctions to force compliance (Kotter & Schlesinger, 1979). One bargaining option is to collaborate with groups having a high potential for cooperation, even if these groups also have a high potential for threat (Savage et al., 1991). By cooperating with stakeholders who have the capability to both threaten and support them, management may diffuse potential opposition. For instance, involving powerful unions in decisions concerning reorganizations may diffuse the threat of labor opposition to the reorganization.

Force Field Analysis

Like stakeholder analysis, force field analysis (FFA) provides a model for mapping the balance of forces for and against a planned intervention. However, unlike stakeholder analysis, FFA uses the outcome of this assessment as a direct input into a systematic analysis of tactics for enhancing support and reducing or overcoming resistance to change. Consultants who adopt the sharp-image approach to diagnosis described in Chapter 1 can introduce FFA after the feedback stage in order to help clients decide how to act on feedback and plan appropriate interventions.[7]

Like the models presented in the previous chapter, FFA draws on a conception of organizations as systems (Lewin, 1951) and views change as a disruption of a temporary state of equilibrium (Lewin, 1958). Moreover, like those diagnostic models, FFA focuses client attention on ways to bridge gaps between current and desired future states. According to the FFA approach, once the forces supporting and restraining have been identified, decision makers can engage in rational and systemic planning for interventions that will lead toward the desired state of the organization. Restraining forces are those that work to maintain the status quo. Supportive or driving forces are those that advance the system toward the desired state—the change goal.

In principle, the interventions in question may aim at reducing the forces that restrain change, augmenting the driving forces, or both (Chin & Benne, 1985). For example, to augment the driving forces for change, consultants can provide feedback showing that the organization and its members face serious risks if they do not make changes soon. In addition, consultants and top managers can sometimes help rival power groups discover common interests—such as avoiding a takeover or ensuring competitiveness in the global marketplace—and work together toward mutually beneficial solutions.

In most cases, it seems preferable to focus on the forces restraining change. This preference for concentrating on ways to unfreeze restraining forces corresponds to the original view of Lewin (1951), who argued that strengthening or adding to the driving forces for change usually leads to the formation of countervailing, restraining forces. The tilt toward concern for restraining forces also fits with recent work on planned change that emphasizes the importance of understanding the sources of employees' resistance to change. In particular, Strebel (1996) proposes focusing on the reasons that employees perceive proposed planned changes as disruptive and intrusive. This type of analysis would examine the psychological and social contracts that exist between employees and the focal organization prior to change, as well as the formal contracts. It could well be that it is as valid to concentrate on driving forces, such as incentives and control systems, as it is to examine restraining ones. Organizational and situational contingencies, along with the specific change targets, may determine which emphasis is more appropriate.

The following explanation of steps for consultants to follow in applying FFA reflects our own uses of FFA and one of the more thorough discussions of the model in the literature (Morris & Sashkin, 1976, pp. 130-139).

1. *Define the desired state for the organization and state precisely and operationally which steps or interventions are to lead to the desired outcomes.* A precise and complete operational definition of the planned interventions is a prerequisite to the identification of driving and restraining forces.

2. *By gathering information from relevant participants in the focal organization, identify those groups or individuals who interact or are associated with the change goal and with planned interventions.* These actors (or stakeholders) are capable of wielding formal authority or informal influence over important aspects of the intervention process. Methods for identifying relevant actors were discussed in the preceding treatment of stakeholder analysis. Although FFA concentrates mainly on actors who exert restraining forces, the feedback diagram used in FFA customarily shows both supportive and restraining actors (see Figure 5.1, below).

3. *Map the driving and restraining forces associated with each influential actor, omitting neutral actors.* This step is analogous to the assessment of stakeholder positions during stakeholder analysis. It is very important to specify the restraining and driving forces in operational terms. Otherwise, it is very difficult to plan an intervention to reduce or eliminate restraints to change. For example, little useful information is provided by listing the "climate of opinion between labor and management" as a restraining force. In contrast, future attempts to deal with employee resistance will be facilitated if the listing specifies something like "union representatives distrust management's claim that the intervention will improve employees' quality of work life."

4. *For each restraining force, determine its strength and assess its amenability to change.* The strength of each force may be assessed by specifically asking members of the organization to rate the power of actors associated with it or by any of the other techniques just discussed for assessing stakeholder power. Amenability to change reflects the likelihood of changing an actor's position on a given issue. Forces that are amenable to change are those that could be reduced or removed by reshaping the organizational reality, people's perception of it, or both. Judgments about amenability are generally made by people familiar with the actor in question, but consultants may also gather information on actors' commitment to their positions.

5. *Create a diagram showing the interplay of forces restraining and driving change.* This diagram will show the present and desired state of the organization at the ends of a vertical arrow representing the change process. The actors creating restraining and driving forces are arrayed on opposite sides of the column, with the most powerful actors listed higher up. Groups of actors who are internally divided or who possess ambivalent views on proposed changes can be shown as both restraining and driving change. The forces deriving from actors who are unlikely to change their position are shown with solid arrows, whereas the forces created by actors who are more amenable to change are shown as broken arrows. An illustration of this type of diagram appears in Figure 5.1, which is based on Case 5.1 below. Note that the consultants have been shown in the figure as supporting the proposed changes but being amenable to altering their position should the proposals prove unworkable.

6. *Judge which interventions might change or remove sources of resistance to change.* By analyzing the attitudes, concerns, and interests of actors who oppose proposed changes, clients and consultants seek to determine concrete steps that might meet these actors' concerns and alter their change orientation. Sometimes, it is feasible to modify the change program in order to reduce resistance without harming progress toward the change target. Suppose, for example, that an industrial firm that plans to merge two divisions and lay off employees faces bitter opposition by a powerful union. Management might reduce the union's resistance without abandoning the merger plan by offering to retrain and reassign employees whose jobs will be eliminated, rather than simply firing them.

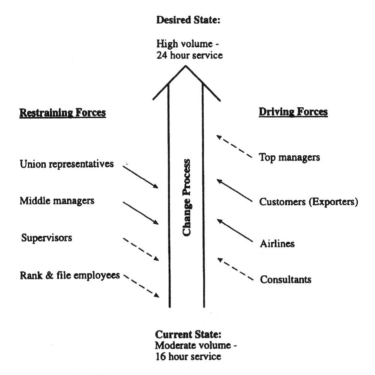

Figure 5.1 Force Field Diagram
Key: Solid lines show low amenability to change; broken lines show moderate to high amenability.

It is easier to reduce opposition through solutions like these when change is incremental than when organizations undergo radical transformations or must cope with declines and crises. Emotions often run high during decline, political relations become more polarized, and managerial credibility drops (Cameron, Kim, & Whetten, 1987; Gray & Ariss, 1985; Krantz, 1985). Hence, resistance to change may become very intense among both internal and external stakeholders. Under conditions like these, top management often must act directly to overcome resistance and impose change, rather than seek ways to reduce resistance (Dunphy & Stace, 1988).

The above listing of the steps in FFA may create a false impression that the analysis typically proceeds as a linear process. However, the balance of forces for and against change often changes. Hence, an FFA constructed at any given moment must be treated as subject to future modifications. Case 5.1 illustrates some of the dynamics that enter into FFA applications and some ways of gathering the data needed to conduct this type of analysis.

Case 5.1

The managers of a large air cargo transhipping company, located near a major airport, decided to move from a two-shift work schedule to one based on three shifts. There were many reasons for this planned change, including growth in the volume of exports and pressures by customers and airlines for an around-the-clock work schedule. Moreover, it was hoped that the change would increase the speed and quality of handling delicate agricultural exports, which formed the bulk of the items handled by the company. Several actors would be affected by the proposed change. The exporters welcomed the move to three shifts as a way of reducing transhipment time and enhancing quality. Implementation of the proposed schedule change was contingent on the agreement of the local union representatives, which was by no means guaranteed. Another group of actors who would be affected was middle managers. They were very resistant to the idea, fearing, among other things, loss of overtime pay that was easy to get under the two-shift system. The shop-floor supervisors also seemed resistant to the idea of working the night shift. The company's management decided to call in a group of consultants for help in making the transition. These consultants conducted a series of interviews with all managerial staff, with employees' representatives, and with a sample of rank-and-file employees. On the basis of the information gathered, they constructed a force field analysis that included the analytical steps listed above. This analysis showed that most of the restraining forces were internal and most of the driving forces were external to the company. Examples of restraining forces included the unwillingness of supervisors and rank-and-file employees to work on the third shift because of disruptions to their family life, fears of loss of status among middle managers, union demands for extra pay and benefits for employees on all shifts, and the reluctance of top management to risk a major confrontation with the local union over the planned change.

Following this diagnosis of forces resisting and supporting the planned change, an FFA diagram was prepared and fed back to top management. Upon discussion of the major implications of the findings, top management decided to focus on reducing resistance from middle managers and supervisors. Extensive group interviews were conducted with middle managers, with top managers attending. During these group meetings, the top managers asked about the forces of resistance that were more relevant to the middle managers and supervisors—and, in particular, about night work. These discussions revealed that most of the supervisors were adamantly opposed to working night shifts. However, the few supervisors who were willing to work at night were sufficient to staff the night shift's supervisory positions. When all of the supervisors heard about this solution to the problem, they became quite amenable to the proposed change. The supervisors' agreement to the plan made it hard for middle managers to continue to oppose it. Supervisors and employees were then asked to volunteer for the night shift. Top management then went to the local union with lists of employees and managers who had volunteered to work on the new shift. An agreement that allowed for the introduction of a third shift was arrived at after the leadership of the local union got some additional concessions from management.

FFA's major advantage lies in systematizing the assessment of forces advancing or hindering the introduction of specific interventions and in focusing client and consultant energy on the steps needed to facilitate change. When FFA is conducted after a diagnosis of organizational problems and challenges, it can help clients decide which steps toward change goals are most feasible and how they may best reduce resistance to change. For clients to apply the decisions flowing from FFA, they must be good negotiators and committed to avoiding unnecessary confrontations with groups opposing their plans.

Diagnosing Organizational Politics

Rather than treating political conditions mainly as contingencies affecting diagnosis and the implementation of change, consultants sometimes view power relations and political processes as focal topics for diagnosis. This diagnostic focus is particularly appropriate when preliminary findings link political features directly to critical forms of organizational effectiveness or ineffectiveness. For example, consultants conducting a sharp-image diagnosis might trace problems of lack of initiative and poor work quality among administrative employees to the employees' inability to influence their work processes, that is, to low levels of empowerment.

The political face of organizational life contains many features that can lead to ineffectiveness or contribute to effectiveness. Here, we consider the diagnosis of three important features of political action in organizations: organizational consequences of political activity, dominant influence tactics and their effects, and employee empowerment.

Organizational Consequences of Politics

Rather than assuming that any attempt to influence or manipulate the behavior of other people is by definition undesirable, consultants and their clients often need to accept the essentially political nature of organizational life and look directly at the organizational consequences of the politics within the client organization. Even though political activity is universal, its expressions and organizational outcomes vary greatly. Some organizations are reduced to a state of paralysis by conflicts among powerful internal and external stakeholders. In others, people spend so much time planning and parrying political maneuvers that they have little time and energy left for anything else. On the other hand, political action can be a force for development and organizational adaptation. Members of an organization can use power to champion changes that will benefit many groups within the organization, as well as external stakeholders. For example, in many organizations, proposals for new products and other innovations get accepted only when powerful managers strive hard to convince decision makers to provide the resources needed to develop a new idea and then fight to overcome opposition to its implementation (Frost & Egri, 1991; Kanter, 1983). Sometimes, champions of new concepts violate official directives and procedures—for example, by fudging budget entries and diverting resources to new product development (Peters & Waterman, 1982).

Practitioners of diagnosis can only evaluate the consequences of political activity from the viewpoints of particular actors within the organization and in terms of specific effectiveness criteria. Consider, for example, a situation in which workers join forces with local politicians to delay the closing of an unprofitable plant until a joint labor-management committee can draft a reorganization proposal. If a consultant to the management of the firm concentrated solely on finding ways to improve the firm's profitability, the consultant would view the workers' action as harming organizational effectiveness. In contrast, a consultant to the union would probably view the workers' actions favorably (e.g., Alinsky, 1971; Chesler, Crawfoot, & Bryant, 1978), as might a consultant to management who placed greater stress on job security, worker morale, and the standing of the firm in the community.

Influence Tactics

Besides evaluating the consequences of politics, diagnosis can assess the effects of the tactics that people use to influence others. People who have formal authority or control over valued resources may try to influence others and to accomplish things by explicitly directing those subject to their authority to act in a particular way and by shifting the flow of material and social rewards to encourage the desired behavior. Other influence tactics, which can be used by those possessing and those lacking formal authority, include the following (Benfari & Knox, 1991; Dalton, 1959; Porter, Allen, & Angle, 1981; Schilit & Locke, 1982):

- Adherence to rules
- Directing requests to higher authorities
- Appeals to logic and standards of rationality
- Appeals based on shared beliefs, standards, or values
- Stress on informal ties (e.g., reliance on interpersonal attraction, or similarities in subgroup memberships or social background)
- Manipulation through the provision of selective information or through hidden pressure
- Formation of coalitions
- Use or threat of sanctions
- Informal exchanges of goods and services (e.g., trading shifts, arranging for fringe benefits, offering bribes)

Appeals to standards of rationality and other types of standards are among the most important and widespread forms of influence, yet the subtlety of these processes makes them easy to overlook. Of particular importance are the ways that people convince others that a particular issue or problem deserves attention. By putting some topics on the agenda for discussion and action, as well as by keeping other issues off the agenda, top managers and other powerful actors can shape decisions and actions significantly. Yet they often exercise this form of influence without arousing much opposition. For example, by generating concern over the need for faculty members to bring revenue into the university, a university vice president can boost the standing of faculty members willing to conduct applied research for commercial purposes at the expense of colleagues dealing with less applied areas. By keeping off the agenda discussions of the academic contribution and validity of commercially sponsored research, the vice president helps to protect the applied researchers from collegial criticism and supervision.

As this example suggests, powerful actors exercise influence through the definitions and interpretive frames that they impose on issues (Bourdieu, 1989). In the above example, the university vice president framed the issue in such a way as to imply a particular set of values and priorities—that raising external funds was more important than obtaining peer recognition for nonapplied (and often esoteric) activities. This way of framing issues also implied a particular diagnosis of the sources of the problem—the failure of faculty members engaged in nonapplied work to obtain outside funding. The diagnosis, in turn, suggests particular solutions—redoubled efforts by nonapplied researchers to tailor their work to the interests of nonprofit granting agencies or diversion of their activities into commercially viable areas.

To assess the impacts of particular influence tactics and other uses of power, practitioners need to consider issues like these:

- How do those who are subject to a particular influence tactic react to it?
- Does the use of this tactic increase tensions or conflicts between groups?
- Do political deals or appeals to personal connections and loyalties undercut efforts to improve performance and maintain standards of excellence?
- Do the methods used to resolve conflicts produce lasting solutions that are regarded as fair?

Unfortunately, many powerful forms of influence, and, in particular, those that people regard as illegitimate, can be hard to observe. Coalition formation, agenda setting, and informal bargains, for example, can be hidden behind discourse that presents decisions as following rational procedures. Investigators who want to understand the actual, emergent practices of organizational politics will have to look closely at organizational documents, take note of interaction patterns among members of the focal organization, and listen carefully to what their informants tell them (see also Chapter 9).

To gather data on influence processes, consultants often have to rely on interviews or discussions during meetings or workshops. In workshops or interviews, consultants can ask members to provide detailed accounts of critical incidents, including organizational successes, the resolution of past organizational problems and crises, and the development of new ideas or proposals. In providing these accounts, members may, of course, justify and improve upon their own behavior and that of others to whom they are loyal, and they may exaggerate the failings of those they hold in low esteem. Still, when conducted and analyzed with sensitivity to these possibilities, interviews and group discussions can provide insight into members' perceptions of political processes, key political actors, and influence tactics in use. To develop an understanding of power relations and processes that is independent of the perceptions of particular members, practitioners will have to carefully cross-check members' reports with one another and with other kinds of information.

Case 5.2 illustrates the methods and findings of one such in-depth investigation of the politics underlying the adoption of an elaborate flexible manufacturing scheme (FMS) in a large aerospace firm (Thomas, 1992a, 1992b).

Case 5.2

The researcher was at first puzzled by discrepancies between internal memos from the Research and Development (R&D) unit expressing concern about the failure of more experienced companies with advanced FMS systems like these and proposals that R&D circulated to corporate executives. These proposals featured very explicit and appealing calculations of anticipated return on investment for FMS. On the face of it, the corporate documents showed that top management chose the innovation after carefully assessing its expected return on investment. In contrast, retrospective interviews with participants in the decision helped uncover the political sources of initial support for FMS and revealed how its backers pushed through the decision on the system's acquisition.

The R&D engineers who advocated buying the FMS stood to benefit from its acquisition by fulfilling their department's formal mandate in a more dramatic way than they ordinarily could and thereby attracting the attention of top management to themselves and their unit. The operations manager who approved the proposal wanted to be "the guy who did it first." To convince top management of the potential benefits of the system, the engineers framed their proposal as a solution to acknowledged problems of antiquated technology and inadequate process control and as a way to bring about top management's objectives of cutting staff and costs and boosting productivity. In fact, nobody knew if the FMS would really produce those results. To ensure support for the FMS, the engineers doctored the figures needed to justify the acquisition in terms of anticipated returns on investment. They also formed a coalition with allied functions that supported FMS and coopted potential opponents from the shop floor by including them in a "user group." The union was kept out of the picture until after the FMS was installed, but the user group gave participants a feeling of being involved in an important decision.

In the end, the system produced few of the expected benefits. In fact, it required additional staff members, rather than allowing for the promised staff reductions. Eighteen months after installation, the system had not yet been thoroughly evaluated. Despite the poor results, the operations manager who backed FMS had received a promotion.

The FMS case vividly illustrates how political processes can lie beneath many apparently rational decisions and shows how ostensibly rational documentation and discussion can camouflage political processes.

Empowerment

People and groups use power to accomplish tasks and meet organizational objectives, as well as to oppose them. Hence, a critical issue for diagnosis concerns the degree to which particular groups are empowered—in the sense of having sufficient resources, knowledge, skills, and influence to accomplish their tasks (Bowen & Lawler, 1992; Kanter, 1977). Lack of power can make it hard for individuals, teams, or entire categories of employees, such as women and minorities, to exercise influence over organizational operations and get difficult things done (Mainero, 1986). Lack of power among entire subgroups of employees can stem from location in the formal hierarchy, as well as from lack of access to emergent channels of information and influence.

It is possible to distinguish degrees of empowerment for any particular task or set of similar positions. Bowen and Lawler (1992), for example, distinguish three degrees of empowerment among employees of service organizations that use mass production principles (e.g., fast-food restaurants). Each degree of empowerment is associated with a different innovation in organizational design. The first design leaves job definitions intact but encourages employees to make suggestions about improving their work and takes employee input seriously. The second design further empowers employees by redesigning jobs and introducing teamwork. The third design, which gives the highest degree of empowerment, involves front-line service employees in the operations of the firm as a whole and not just in the management of their own tasks. In these rare instances, employees get information about the firm's operations and become involved in business operations through profit sharing or employee ownership.

More fine-grained investigations can uncover variations in empowerment among work teams or among individual tasks within a single organization. Investigators can, for example, question employees about their feelings of competence, self-determination, and ability to have an impact on strategic, administrative, or operational outcomes at work (Spreitzer, 1996; Thomas & Velthouse, 1990).[8] A more direct approach is to examine the actual behavior of employees during critical incidents. For example, Mainero (1986) asked respondents to describe what they did when they faced frustrating situations in which they found themselves dependent on others at work. He then analyzed the factors affecting whether respondents remained passive or acted assertively.

Diagnostic investigators can also assess the degree to which people or teams work under *empowering conditions*. These conditions provide opportunities for autonomy and for exercising influence over the task, group, or entire organization. This approach to assessing empowerment can be applied to individual tasks, sets of similar tasks, work teams, and larger units or categories of employees. Here is a list of the contextual conditions that are likely to promote employee empowerment (Brass & Burkhardt, 1993; Ibarra, 1993; Spreitzer, 1996):

- Performance of tasks that provide room for individual discretion and autonomy
- Working under a manager who has a broad span of control
- Working under a manager who values individual initiative, delegates considerable authority and responsibility, and does not exercise tight personal control over subordinates

- Access to important information about the task, workgroup, and organization
- Access to needed resources—including funds, material, space, and time
- Exposure to normative support for employee involvement in decision making
- Evaluation by reward and control systems that encourage discretion and initiative
- Location within emergent networks that provide information and political support

Diagnosis will necessarily examine the costs and benefits of empowerment, as well as its depth (Bowen & Lawler, 1992). Most commentators concentrate on the damage caused to organizations that constrain employee power and on the benefits that can flow from empowering employees. From this standpoint, lack of power stifles employee contributions at all organizational levels. First-line supervisors, for example, often cannot do their jobs adequately because they cannot control or influence the lines of supply to their units, they lack vital organizational information, and they cannot advance within the organization (Kanter, 1979). Because of their lack of power, supervisors become resistant to managerial initiatives, administer programs mechanistically, and achieve low productivity. Middle managers also need to acquire power to do their jobs well (e.g., Izraeli, 1975). American managers increasingly report suffering from the imposition of tight constraints over their decision making in operational areas, such as purchasing and staffing (O'Reilly, 1992; Pfeffer, 1992). Staff specialists, such as behavioral scientists and planners, often lack both the formal authority and the informal standing needed to get their ideas implemented (e.g., Phillips, 1991)—nor can engineers and other technical specialists contribute fully to their organization if they lack power. To promote innovation, management must empower people who are capable of developing new ideas and technologies (Delbecq & Mills, 1985; Kanter, 1983).

The anticipated benefits of empowerment include higher employee motivation and satisfaction, quicker and more personal responses to clients and customers, more creativity, and more personal initiative. Empowering employees can enhance organizational performance by increasing individual productivity and allowing the people who are close to organizational problems to solve them. These people sometimes have more or better information and knowledge than do higher-level managers or specialists who are distant from the problems.

Possible benefits of empowering a particular group of employees must be weighed against possible costs. Empowering first-line service employees, for example, can add to the costs for selèction, training, and pay. Empowerment can also make service delivery less consistent and can create opportunities for employees to give away company resources or otherwise deviate from official rules in order to please customers (Bowen & Lawler, 1992). Other possible costs involve the expenses associated with redesigning operations to enhance empowerment.

Equally worrisome are the costs and risks of empowerment in the eyes of the very people who are supposed to reap its benefits. Rather than welcoming the prospect of greater employee input, many managers appear to be threatened by the prospect. As the creator of the Dilbert cartoons puts it (Adams, 1996, p. 61), for many managers, "Employee Input = More Work = Bad." On a more serious note, managers and functional experts who view proposals for empowerment against the background of the recent wave of downsizings may understandably fear that increased initiative and independence among rank-and-file employees will reduce supervisors' functions and render them vulnerable to dismissal. Furthermore, both skilled and unskilled employees may well be concerned that programs to empower them will lead to extra responsibilities and work for no extra pay. Even worse, the resulting improvements in productivity could render some of them redundant.

Managers or consultants who seek to assess prospects for empowerment can weigh possible costs of the process against its expected benefits. This assessment depends very much on the choice of effectiveness criteria, which in turn reflect client priorities and the contingencies to which the organization is subject. Organization designs that create tight control over powerless service workers fit with low-cost, high-volume competitive strategies involving short-term service transactions, routine technologies, and predictable environments. On the other hand, empowerment and Theory Y approaches to motivation fit better with differentiation strategies, which often require customized and personalized service (Bowen & Lawler, 1992). Similarly, where environmental conditions are unpredictable and technology is nonroutine or complex, empowering workers can enhance effectiveness (see Chapter 7).

If diagnosis points to contingencies appropriate to empowerment and potential benefits from it, consultants can use techniques such as stakeholder analysis or FFA to examine the sources of support and resistance to proposed empowerment programs. This knowledge can help managers consider ways to overcome resistance to empowerment programs or create positive incentives for the implementation of programs of empowerment.

Conclusion

By examining consultant and client interventions into organizations from a political standpoint, consultants can develop an awareness of political conditions shaping the process of diagnosis and impinging on the implementation of change. The models presented in the second part of this chapter can help consultants assess support and opposition to planned change and guide clients in their choice of feasible routes toward their change targets. Political conditions can also become objects of diagnostic study in their own right when they directly or indirectly lead to ineffective outcomes. The third part of this chapter focused on assessing the organizational consequences of politics and discussed ways to diagnose the organizational outcomes of prevailing influence processes and patterns of employee empowerment. Power relations and uses are sensitive topics in most organizations and can be hard to assess. Still, political assessment is worth the effort: Attention to issues like those raised in this chapter can substantially enhance the relevance of diagnostic findings and recommendations to client concerns, and can increase the prospects for successfully implementing needed organizational changes.

This chapter brings to a conclusion the first part of the book, which examined frames, models, and techniques that provide foundations for most behavioral science diagnoses. In addition, this part of the book introduced our method of sharp-image diagnosis and noted advantages of this approach over other well-known diagnostic procedures. The second part of this volume examines applications of sharp-image diagnosis and other procedures to the diagnosis and assessment of critical focal areas. These areas can be chosen by clients and consultants at the start of a diagnosis or may emerge as focal concerns during scouting and initial data gathering.

Notes

1. All of the factors, except for stakeholder support, are discussed by Pettigrew (1975). He defines support in terms of backing for internal consultants from their own department.

2. On consultants' political involvement in planned change, see Cobb and Margulies (1981) and Greiner and Schein (1988). Harrison (1991) synthesizes this literature and provides a typology of forms of consultant involvement in change.

3. See Harrison (1994, pp. 127-132) for a more extended discussion of this dilemma and for relevant references to possible resolutions.

4. Box 5.1 and the following discussion derive with modifications from Savage et al. (1991). The discussion of techniques for assessing stakeholder power derives from Harrison (1994, pp. 102-105).

5. The following treatment of assessing stakeholder power draws on Pfeffer's (1981b, pp. 35-65, 199; 1992, pp. 49-68) two treatments of the topic. See also Finkelstein (1992) and Brass and Burkhardt (1993) on formal, structural sources of power, and Ibarra (1993) and Brass and Burkhardt (1993) on centrality in emergent networks.

6. Some research studies have found substantial agreement among independent measures of power, and reputational measures have been shown to be related to objective measures, such as promotions (Brass & Burkhardt, 1993; Pfeffer, 1992). Nevertheless, it seems unwise to assume without evidence that most actors in a complex organization can be ranked along a single underlying power dimension.

7. This recommended use of FFA differs from some texts in the area of organizational development that advocate using FFA as an all-purpose diagnostic model (e.g., Cummings & Worley, 1993, pp. 124-125).

8. These authors also propose measuring the felt meaningfulness of work because they conceptualize empowerment in terms of intrinsic motivation. We prefer to view subjective empowerment more narrowly in terms of the individual's perceptions of opportunities for exercising power and influence.

PART II FOCAL AREAS

Group Performance

"Why do some cabin crews earn praise from travelers, whereas others get nothing but complaints?"

"The mayor thought it was a great idea to bring social workers, teachers, parents, and pupils together in the committees for promoting drug-free schools. But after 6 months of meetings, only one committee has come up with any concrete action plans."

"Several of our international marketing groups keep losing their top members, while the less promising ones stay on. What can be done to reverse this pattern?"

"Can't we stop arguing about the same issues during our weekly program-review meetings and start making real progress?"

"We want to bring clients and engineers together right at the start of the production planning, but we don't know how to set up these teams."

"How should we design the management team that will coordinate the work of the firms taking part in the new joint venture? Should team members recruit and select additional members, or should recruits be assigned by their home firms and functional departments?"

These statements illustrate typical concerns about workgroups among managers and team members.[1] The first four statements express concerns about group ineffectiveness, whereas the last two solicit help in designing teams to handle new challenges. Because formal workgroups form the building blocks of most large organizations, managers, consultants, and applied researchers have sought ways to improve workgroup effectiveness for many years (Guzzo & Salas, 1995; Guzzo & Shea, 1993).

In the past two decades, managers, consultants, and researchers have become increasingly interested in designing new types of workgroups, like those illustrated in the last two statements above. Particularly noteworthy is the rapid growth in self-directed, semiautonomous teams (Lawler, Mohrman, & Ledford, 1992) and the growth of cross-functional and multidisciplinary teams (Galbraith et al., 1993).

When consultants follow the sharp-image approach to diagnosis, client concerns about team performance or design can lead directly to the investigation of forces underlying core forms of workgroup effectiveness and ineffectiveness. In like manner, managers and consultants following other diagnostic approaches often look closely at workgroups. Work teams are a popular focal area for diagnosis, because performance variations in workgroups are noticeable and measurable and because the structure and operations of groups seem amenable to interventions by managers and behavioral science practitioners.

To facilitate these inquiries, the first part of this chapter applies the open-systems framework to the assessment of effectiveness in workgroups and to the diagnosis of forces underlying ineffective teamwork. We point to both contributions and limitations of that framework and suggest ways of specifying it so as to make it more useful in diagnosis and action planning. The second part of the chapter continues this specification process by critically examining Hackman's (1987, 1991) Action Model of Group-Task Performance. This model provides guidelines for diagnosing team functioning and for planning, forming, and maintaining effective work teams.

Systems Framework for
Diagnosing Group Behavior

Many forces in and around organizations can shape patterns of team behavior like those illustrated in the statements listed at the start of this chapter. Figure 6.1 summarizes a multilevel framework for diagnosing team effectiveness and its impacts.[2] At the bottom row in Figure 6.1, the arrow labeled Human Resources refers to characteristics and traits that employees have acquired in the past. These inputs include the knowledge and skills that people bring to

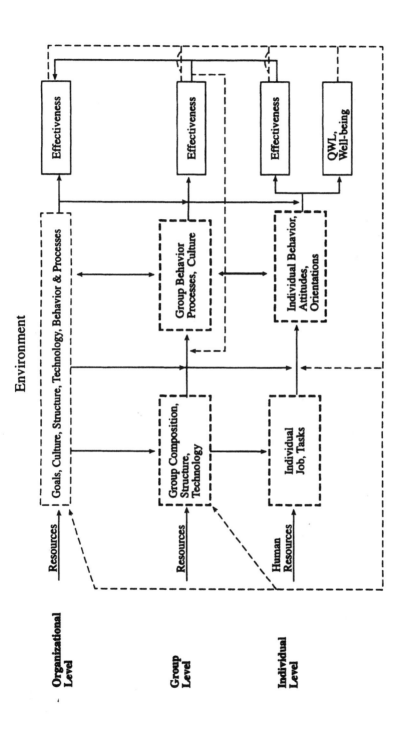

Figure 6.1 Framework for Diagnosing Group Behavior

Key: Solid lines show main lines of influence. Broken lines show feedback loops.

to their individual tasks and to the teams in which they work. The two boxes at the center of the bottom row of the figure depict main forms of organizational behavior that can shape group and individual outcomes. The second level in Figure 6.1 concentrates on group features, behavior, and culture. Many of these group-level characteristics are discussed in detail in the second part of this chapter. For simplicity, Figure 6.1 does not distinguish between division- and organization-level phenomena, but this distinction may be important if divisions differ substantially from one another.

Drawing on the discussion of system effectiveness in Chapter 3 and on the work of Hackman and his colleagues (Hackman, 1987, 1991), we define group effectiveness in terms of three components:[3]

1. *Outputs.* These are output-goal criteria for assessing team performance. They refer mainly to the quantity of outputs, their timeliness, and their quality (including features such as innovativeness).
2. *Satisfying the expectations of internal and external stakeholders.* The actors who have a stake in a workgroup's operations often include its members, internal clients (i.e., other units within the organization who receive the group's outputs), external clients, and top managers.
3. *Process criteria.* Like the Internal System State criteria listed in Table 3.1, these criteria relate to the ability of members to work together effectively at present and in the future.

Diagnosis can often benefit by concentrating on indications of team *ineffectiveness,* rather than effectiveness. Ineffectiveness can be defined in terms of each of the above three components. A detailed discussion of ways to define and assess effectiveness appears later in this chapter.

Assumptions

The framework presented in Figure 6.1 rests on several important assumptions, only some of which can be presented graphically. These assumptions further specify system characteristics discussed in Chapter 2.[4]

Direct and Mediated Effects

Inputs at the individual and group levels can directly affect outcomes, as well as affecting them via group processes. For example, members' skills and prior experience can directly shape team outputs, in addition to being mediated by group conditions, such as the degree of support and training provided to members.

Interaction Between Levels

As Figure 6.1 shows, there are interactions between all three system levels. Effectiveness at one system level, such as the individual level, can affect outputs at other levels, such as the group level. Moreover, lower-level forces, such as individual behavior, can affect higher-level phenomena, such as group processes and culture, as well as be influenced by them.

Under favorable conditions, individual and small-group initiatives and contributions can make a difference to an entire organization (House, Rousseau, & Thomas-Hunt, 1995, pp. 98-101). The impact of such initiatives is likely to be greater when actors have more power and status and when an organization is undergoing a crisis or threat. Bottom-up initiatives by individuals or teams are most likely to affect other people and units and to have organizationwide effects when group or organizational norms and practices are not well-defined, as well as when organizational changes create opportunities for renegotiation of previously taken-for-granted forms of acting and thinking. Groups that are more tightly coupled to one another are also more likely to influence one another than are loosely coupled groups.

Feedback

Effectiveness and other outcomes at all three system levels can, in turn, shape group interaction and individual behavior, as well as be shaped by them. For instance, individual or group productivity can enhance individual satisfaction and team cohesion, in addition to or instead of being affected by these subjective states. Poor results can undermine team cohesion and collaboration just as much as poor group relations.

Internal and External Constraints

Many critical determinants of individual, group, and organizational effectiveness lie beyond the control of consultants and practitioners. The broken lines around the components in the figure represent their openness to constraints from other units or levels within the focal organization and from the environment. Both types of constraints define the boundaries within which managers usually choose their interventions into current arrangements. Managers cannot, for example, violate labor agreements or employee welfare regulations without risking sanctions. But managers do have some room for choice in other important areas—such as the types of information they obtain and communicate to others.

Workgroups are subject to both intraorganizational and external constraints. The schemata held by members form one type of subtle constraint on group-level interventions. Schemata exist at the individual, group, and organizational levels (Dutton & Dukerich, 1991). These shared frames of reference lead group members to attend to particular aspects of their experiences and not to others. Most change efforts in organizations assume that the meaning of various organizational events remains unaltered during the change process (Bartunek, 1993). Hence, change agents implicitly or explicitly treat shared schemata as constraints on intervention possibilities.

Configurational Effects

The independent influence of any particular variable on group or organizational effectiveness is usually small (Hackman, 1987). Instead of varying widely from one another, system features typically cluster in self-reinforcing configurations at the organizational and group levels. For instance, conflict-ridden work teams are likely to (a) be less productive than are teams that handle internal differences successfully; (b) be less cohesive and characterized by lower levels of interpersonal trust; and (c) have members who are less satisfied and less committed to their jobs. Laboratory studies, regression-based analyses of survey data, and other research designs that seek to separate the distinctive contributions of a small number of variables will almost invariably fail to reproduce the tendency toward configuration that actually prevails within organizations.[5]

Timing

The effects of the forces shown in Figure 6.1 depend greatly on the timing of interactions among them. Organizations and groups face distinctive challenges at different phases in their life cycle (Chapter 11); during the development, production, and marketing of new products and services; and during the development and implementation of administrative and technological innovations. The mutual impacts of the forces shown in Figure 6.1 are also likely to be affected by seasons, cycles, and irregular fluctuations in environmental conditions and organizational activities. Individual members of an organization also pass through cycles and phases in their occupational, educational, and organizational careers (Schein, 1971). These career patterns can greatly affect people's efforts, creativity, and responses to organizational rewards and opportunities.

The potential for temporal variations in the context of organizational behavior is well illustrated by the example of symbolic leadership—acts through which managers express the values or aspirations of members of their organization or group. This type of leadership can play a crucial role in transforming a group or organization undergoing a crisis or external threat (Tichy & DeVanna, 1986). But the same types of symbolic acts may have far less impact on organizational effectiveness during periods of stability or managed growth (Mintzberg, 1984). During these periods, the forces of tradition, past precedent, and inertia are more likely to shape organizational development and effectiveness than are isolated acts of leadership.

Contingency

Timing is but one of many contextual and situational forces affecting the relations shown in Figure 6.1. Other important contingencies include the tasks and external conditions facing the organization and its teams, the degree of team and individual autonomy, external cultural and institutional forces, and organizational culture. Although organizational behavior is highly dependent on context, formal models of the contingencies shaping a particular form of behavior (e.g., Fiedler, 1967) are generally too complicated to be useful in diagnosis (Hackman, 1987, 1991).

Indeterminacy

The framework presented here cannot predict or determine the impact of a particular variable or set of variables on other factors in the framework. The framework's indeterminacy stems from the many interactions among its components and variables and from the many contextual and moderating processes affecting organizational behavior. Organizational behavior is also indeterminate, because people act in keeping with their changing feelings and interpretations and in response to their accumulating experience and learning.

Equifinality

All roads do not lead to Rome, but several may. Because there is so much indeterminacy in organizational systems, different practices can produce identical or very similar results. This condition means that work teams or entire organizations can travel different paths toward excellent performance or can display similar signs of decline (see Chapter 11) for many different reasons.

Applying the Framework

The systems framework can help alert consultants and managers to the ways that group behavior is shaped by other system features and, in turn, affects these features. In particular, the multilevel framework helps diagnosticians and decision makers avoid locking their attention exclusively at one level of analysis and thereby overlooking forces at other levels that can help explain the situation of interest to them. For example, the framework encourages users who are accustomed to explaining patterns in terms of employee skills or motives to look beyond these individual-level variables to the group and organizational settings that give rise to the observed individual-level patterns. The framework also alerts people who are accustomed to focusing on formal structures and decisions to the potential impact of group interaction on effectiveness.

Take, for example, the case of the unproductive program-review meetings mentioned at the start of the chapter. Figure 6.1 suggests that the participants' behavior during these meetings might be affected by many factors, including their interpersonal skills, social and occupational gaps among participants (group composition), norms and beliefs prevailing within the group and the organization as a whole, goals and objectives set for participants by the group leader and by higher management, and controls to which the group is subject. The failure of the group to produce valued outputs and its lack of capacity to resolve internal differences, in turn, affect the ways that higher management and other members of the organization view the group and act toward it.

As this example suggests, the framework provides many promising leads for diagnosis of group effectiveness or ineffectiveness. However, investigators need further guidelines to decide which leads to follow. The procedures for specifying the open-systems frame, as discussed in Chapter 2, can provide some of these guidelines. For instance, consultants can examine *fits* among internal processes in groups, as well as alignments between these processes and the environment (Ancona, 1990). Diagnosis can also concentrate on identifying important *gaps* between current and desired levels of team performance in a specific area, such as innovativeness.

The techniques of sharp-image diagnosis can also help guide the diagnosis of team functioning. This approach calls for concentrating diagnosis on critical, ineffective outcomes or on central team challenges. Ineffective outcomes include poor team productivity, dissatisfaction among members, and a climate of distrust. These outcomes might be traced to group processes such as leadership, communications, and conflict.

Among the most critical challenges facing teams are those that are *strategic,* in the sense of directly affecting the organization's ability to obtain and maintain strategic advantage (Chapter 13). Take, for example, the outputs of software design teams. To contribute to strategic advantage during the early stages of design, teams must develop programs capable of handling new functions or improving the performance of existing ones (e.g., voice recognition). But as program development continues, the strategic contribution of innovative programs becomes more dependent on the programs' fit with market requirements—including user friendliness, performance in comparison to competing software, and compatibility with popular software packages and hardware configurations. To meet market requirements, the program development team would have to coordinate its work more fully with marketing, as well as ensure that it produces a technically sophisticated product.

Once major forms of ineffectiveness or team challenges are defined, sharp-image diagnosis looks for forces and causes that are particularly amenable to intervention by clients or consultants. The results of this search for possible intervention points depends on team constraints and contingencies like those discussed above and on the types of interventions that are being considered. At least one generalization about intervention techniques seems to be justified: Intervention is more likely to succeed if it concentrates on shaping the more stable conditions affecting group behavior, rather than focusing on the behavior itself (see the discussion of Hackman's model, below). Support for this generalization appeared in a recent meta-analysis of 131 planned change efforts in North America between 1961 and 1991 (Macy & Izumi, 1993, p. 279). It showed that the interventions that were most effective in improving organizational outcomes (financial, behavioral, and attitudinal) were goal setting and autonomous workgroups.

Rather than stressing stable conditions affecting team behavior, many organizational development interventions sought to bring about change in teams or in entire organizations by training team members in interpersonal and teamwork skills. The expectation was that the retrained members would use their skills to transform interpersonal and intergroup processes within their workgroups. These attempts often failed because the people who underwent off-site training experienced difficulty in transferring their newly learned skills back to the workplace (Katz & Kahn, 1978). One source of this difficulty is the tendency for interaction processes and patterns to emerge spontaneously in group contexts and then to become resistant to efforts by members or managers to change them (see Chapter 9).

Diagnostic practitioners are more likely to discover feasible levers for changing groups if they concentrate on groups undergoing developmental phases that render them more amenable to change. For example, it is easier to shape the behavior of members of a management team during the early stages of the team's operations than after the team has developed accepted routines and norms. Hence, diagnosis and assessment during the planning and startup phases of a group can have a greater impact than can assessments of the operations of well-established groups (Hackman, 1991). Crises and sudden changes in basic operating conditions also provide opportunities for recasting behavior within groups and entire organizations. Managers and consultants can also strive for favorable timing when they intervene at the individual level through programs of retraining. In general, people are more willing and able to change their work patterns and incorporate new skills when they enter an organization or change jobs than after they become well-established in their positions (Schein, 1971).

The process of specifying the focus for diagnosis should also take into account the *contents* of a team's work (Hackman, 1991). For instance, top management teams deal with power, influence, and strategy. Task forces handle ideas and plans. Support teams provide expertise, whereas human service teams deal with people and emotions. In keeping with these differences, teams encounter divergent types of characteristic problems and opportunities. Top management teams enjoy the opportunity to be self-designing but must work without a supportive organizational context. Top management teams also suffer from having loose boundaries and changing participation patterns. Task forces must overcome difficult problems of coordination between disciplines and functions without recourse to existing structures or familiar tasks. Human service groups often struggle with risks of emotional drain and with the need for members to control their emotions.

By way of summary, let us once again consider the possibilities for diagnosing the sources of the ineffective program-review meetings mentioned above. Investigators following the sharp-image approach might start by considering the content of team work. This could lead to design questions, such as whether meetings are the best setting in which to conduct the program-review work, who should participate in these reviews, and what are the desired outputs of the review process. Assuming that the meetings are judged to be necessary, then diagnosis could focus on the forces that strongly affect meeting behavior, are very proximate to this behavior, and are likely to be amenable to intervention. These forces might include the setting of goals for the group by higher management, the way that the group head defines the meeting agenda, and the ways in which the head leads discussions. If the group had developed very entrenched norms governing the nature of its meetings, the diagnosis might conclude that lasting improvements would require changes in group membership or leadership.

Individual and Group Outcomes

As a further step toward applying the framework shown in Figure 6.1, let us now elaborate on each of its main components.

Group Effectiveness

When groups produce readily identifiable and measurable outputs, these outputs can be used to assess group performance. To do so, investigators define the most important goods or services produced by the group and measure their quality and quantity over a given time period. For instance, to assess quantitative outputs among units within state employment security offices, one researcher (Gresov, 1989, p. 441) counted claims processed by intake and processing units, job seekers placed by placement units, and people counseled by employment counseling units. The outputs for administrative, technical, and professional teams with complex tasks are often hard to measure. They include solutions to problems (e.g., how to increase market share), plans (e.g., plan for AIDS education in the schools), tactics, and procedures for coordinating the work of other units. When crucial team outputs are hard to measure, it is risky to base assessments on more readily available measurements. Consider the outputs of surgical teams: Measures of productivity or patient death rates that are not standardized on the severity of the patients' ailments and their overall health make poor substitutes for professional assessments of the quality of the surgical work.

Rather than measuring effectiveness by directly examining outputs, diagnosis can also use the multiple-stakeholder approach developed in Chapter 3. For most teams, the most critical constituencies are team managers and the members of other internal and external teams who provide critical inputs and receive important outputs. Particularly when these other teams are part of the same organization, investigators can ask team members to define the critical standards of effectiveness for the focal unit and to indicate the extent to which the focal unit meets these standards. For example, the data-processing center of a large social welfare agency provides a range of services to different departments and units. To evaluate the performance of the center using the stakeholder approach, the members or heads of each "client" unit receiving data-processing services would be asked to specify the criteria by which these services can be evaluated—for example, precision, timeliness, ease of use, technological sophistication, and costs. Then, the members of these client units would rank the center's ability to fulfill these criteria. The overall effectiveness of the center would be defined in term of its ability to satisfy these multiple internal clients. To focus on stakeholders' views on *in*effectiveness, members of client groups could be asked whether they are dissatisfied with any data-processing services and whether the work of the data-processing center interferes in any way with the clients' ability to carry out their own work.

Process measures of group effectiveness examine the ability of group members to work together at present and in the future. This capability depends on factors such as the level of consensus and conflict within the group; ability of team members to resolve conflicts constructively; quality of work and information flows; interpersonal relations—including cohesion, trust, and communication; and members' capacity to learn from past experiences and to adjust their work patterns accordingly. In this area, as elsewhere, diagnosis can profitably start with concerns about ineffective outcomes. For example, when pay and other working conditions are similar among many groups, high turnover in certain groups may indicate that group members are dissatisfied with team management or with interpersonal relations.

Individual Effectiveness and Its Impacts

Most treatments of individual effectiveness examine output criteria. These include the degree and quality of members' efforts, their degree of initiative, cooperation with other employees, levels of absenteeism, lateness, and commitment to the job. In contrast, 360-degree assessment provides an individual-level analogy of stakeholder assessments of effectiveness (London & Beatty, 1993; Tornow, 1993). This technique involves asking supervisors, subordinates, members of other teams, and clients to assess the effectiveness of specific individuals with whom they work regularly.

The facets of individual behavior and effectiveness that most strongly affect group and organizational behavior and outcomes depend on the group's tasks, goals, and standards. In a surveyors'. unit within a city agency, for example, the members' accuracy and reliability may affect the unit's performance more critically than does the speed with which team members carry out their individual tasks.

Quality of Work Life (QWL) refers to the degree to which employees are satisfied with work, and learn and develop through it (Nadler & Lawler, 1983; Walton, 1975). Well-being refers to the extent to which work promotes physical and mental health and wellness (e.g., Ironson, 1992).

Although QWL and well-being can be treated as desirable ends in themselves (e.g., Davis & Cherns, 1975; "The New Industrial Relations," 1981), their importance for the diagnostic framework presented here lies in their potential for influencing group and organizational effectiveness. Research shows that QWL, as indicated by employee satisfaction with rewards, often reduces turnover and desire to leave the organization (Fisher & Locke, 1992). Under certain conditions, improvements in QWL and employee well-being can also lead to cost savings and higher productivity for work teams and even for entire organizations (Katz, Kochan, & Weber, 1985; Walton, 1975).[6] The effects of very poor QWL are sometimes more evident than the "bottom-line" benefits of QWL improvement. When practices such as downsizing and reengineering undermine job security and weaken beliefs in the fairness of employment practices, employee loyalty can be seriously eroded ("The Downsizing of America," 1996). Instead of working harder, the employees who survive repeated cuts in staff may spend most of their time hunting for another job, playing politics, or just feeling crummy (Leana & Feldman, 1992; "Two Cheers for Loyalty," 1996).

Factors Affecting Group Effectiveness

Individual Factors

Table 6.1 summarizes individual-level factors that can directly or indirectly affect team and organizational effectiveness.[7] The impacts of these factors are contingent on many internal and external conditions. Hence, whenever possible, practitioners should directly investigate the causal impacts of the factors listed in the table, rather than assume that these factors have universal and consistent effects, regardless of circumstances.

The individual characteristics listed in Table 6.1 can directly shape people's motivation to perform a task and their ability to do so. These *human resource inputs* are particularly likely to influence group and organizational effectiveness when members perform tasks that provide high levels of autonomy and discretion. Individual characteristics can also have critical consequences at the group and organizational levels when sizeable groups of employees share the influential characteristics. For example, the rise in educational levels among blue-collar and office workers throughout Europe and North America during the 1960s and 1970s led younger employees to prefer more interesting and challenging work. These pressures, in turn, led managers to redesign jobs and grant more autonomy to workgroups in an attempt to recruit and motivate employees. Despite the influence of such human resource inputs, practitioners and clients should not overestimate their importance. It is sometimes tempting to assume that the problems of a failing program or department could be solved if only the "right" person could be found to run it or the right staff members were chosen. When a unit's problems seem likely to persist even if the "ideal" manager and staff are found, then group and organizational sources of the problem also should be investigated. Practitioners should also consider group and organizational factors when clients cannot readily alter individual factors and human resource inputs—for example, when tenured civil servants cannot be replaced or retrained.

The *job characteristics* listed in Table 6.1 can directly affect employee performance, as well as affect their feelings about work (Baron, 1994; Hackman & Oldham, 1980). Individual motivation and satisfaction can, in turn, affect individual performance, which in turn shapes team effectiveness. However, recent research shows that the effects of motivation on individual performance are much more complex than has often been assumed and depend very much on situational constraints and, of course, individual ability (Kanfer, 1990,

Table 6.1 Key Individual Factors

Human Resource Inputs (Individual Characteristics)

Physical and mental state—health, abilities, job-related traits (e.g., motor coordination, public speaking skills)

Social background and traits—sex, age; ethnic, regional, cultural background

Training and education—formal education, technical training, work experience

Personal values, norms, beliefs, assumptions, attitudes

Individual needs—importance of various types of rewards, job characteristics

Job Characteristics

Pay and benefits

Meaningfulness—task identity, variety, significance (Hackman & Oldham, 1980)

Routineness

Accountability—employee is responsible for important results

Feedback—employee gets feedback for important results

Clarity/ambiguity of responsibilities and assignments; conflict among others' expectations toward role occupant

Access to necessary information and technologies

Physical/psychological stress

Job security

Individual Orientations

Motivation—to work well, remain on job

Rewards experienced:

- Extrinsic: Pay; benefits; security; promotion prospects; peer approval; social status; nonmonetary compensation (e.g., flexible hours, training opportunities); physical conditions; location
- Intrinsic: Job felt to be interesting, challenging; personal growth, learning, feeling of accomplishment

Expectations:

- Link between performance and valued rewards (e.g., promotion depends on good work)
- Consequences of effort, initiative, innovation (e.g., What happens to people who find new ways of doing things?)
- Ability to get things done

Equity—feeling that efforts are fairly rewarded compared to others in organization and to other organizations

Trust—perceived ability to rely on peers and managers and to believe in them

Specific attitudes—satisfaction with administrative procedures (e.g., grievance mechanisms); attitudes toward and assessment of current and proposed projects, changes

---

1992). Consider, for instance, the finding that redesigning jobs to allow greater challenge and group autonomy often enhances work quality while reducing costs (e.g., Eisenhardt & Westcott, 1988; Florida & Kenney, 1991; Griffen, 1991). There is little consistent evidence that this type of job redesign directly motivates employees to perform better (Kelly, 1992). Instead of directly reflecting enhanced intrinsic motivation, the improvements in quality and costs often stem from *structural* changes associated with job redesign. These changes include assigning higher levels of responsibility and account-ability to autonomous employees and setting clear performance targets for them. A further complication in understanding the effects of job redesign on individual and team performance is that the effects of introducing autonomous work teams depend on factors such as the nature of the workforce (e.g., values, training) and the nature of the organization's information and reward systems (Guzzo & Dickson, 1996).

Job performance can also be affected by the specificity and difficulty of goal assignments (Kanfer, 1990, 1992). Goal setting is more likely to enhance performance when people participate in the process or at least understand why they have been assigned particular objectives. In addition, employees are likely to strive to obtain difficult goals only when they have access to the *resources* (skills, information, tools) needed to obtain them.

The third part of Table 6.1 lists *individual orientations*—attitudes, beliefs, and motivational states—that can also affect QWL and performance at the individual and group levels (Cranny, Smith, & Stone, 1992; Goodman, 1977; Lawler, 1977). By examining employees' expectations and understandings of their work situation, consultants may discover explanations for suboptimal team performance. For instance, team output sometimes suffers when team members depend highly on one another and one or two team members perform poorly. Examination of the attitudes of these underperforming members may show that they do not expect their efforts to yield rewards that are important to them.

Diagnoses can also benefit from examining individual attitudes and per-ceptions concerning specific topics and issues being debated within an orga-nization. Consultants might, for example, ask team members how they feel about proposals to create cross-functional teams or to introduce flexible scheduling of work hours. Repeated attitude surveys can also provide feed-back on the operations of particular groups. This information can then con-tribute to the assessment of progress toward a stated goal and can help managers spot problems before they become critical (e.g., Nadler et al., 1976).

Group Factors

Table 6.2 directs attention to group-level factors that can shape individual behavior and influence outcomes at the individual, group, and organizational

Table 6.2 Key Group Factors

Group Composition, Structure, and Technology

Social and occupational composition—Mix of members' characteristics (e.g., Americans versus locals in overseas office); proportions of minorities, genders; divergences of professional training and work experience (e.g., veteran managers versus new MBAs)

Structure—nature, extent of rules, types of work/decision procedures (e.g., judgment, precedent, standard operating procedures); flexibility of task assignments; control procedures (reports, supervision, computer monitoring, peer evaluation); frequency, comprehensiveness of controls (Are all processes or outcomes checked, or just some?), coordination mechanisms

Technology—impacts on group processes (e.g., noise prevents conversation; office layout encourages contact); workflow interdependencies

Group Behavior, Processes, and Culture

Relations among group members—cohesiveness (attachment to group, similarity of views, behavior)

Processes:

- Rewarding: types of behavior rewarded (e.g., conformity vs. individuality); frequency, consistency, process of delivering rewards
- Communication: direction of flows (up, down, across department lines); openness and honesty (Do members share problems or try to look good?)
- Cooperation and conflict—sources, extent, nature, conflict management (collaboration in search of mutually satisfactory solutions, bargaining, forcing solution by superior)
- Decision making (methods, degree of participation) and problem solving (methods, confrontation, avoidance)

Supervisory behavior—supportiveness (encourages learning, provides help, resources); level of participation (shares information and decision making); goal setting and task emphasis (sets clear goals, stresses goal achievement, common purposes); level and nature of performance expectations (e.g., effort, quality expected); style of communication and conflict management

Culture—group identity (language, symbols, rituals); consensus, clarity about goals, values, norms; trust, confidence in peers, managers; beliefs about work and rewards (e.g., getting ahead, risk taking); views on nature of environment, problems, challenges; fit/gap between group norms, beliefs, values and those of management

---

levels. A team's social, educational, and occupational heterogeneity can affect its cohesion, interaction patterns, and performance (Ancona & Caldwell, 1992; Coombs, 1992; Guzzo & Dickson, 1996; Kanter, 1977; Smith et al., 1994). Internally diverse workgroups appear to be able to develop better and more creative solutions to problems than do more homogeneous groups, but the more heterogeneous groups also suffer from lower levels of cohesion and member satisfaction and higher levels of turnover (Milliken & Martins, 1996). The assessment of effects of team heterogeneity, like that of other team features, thus depends greatly on the criterion used. When productivity is important, heterogeneity is often disadvantageous. But when innovativeness and responsiveness to diverse constituencies are prized, heterogeneous teams are likely to be more effective than are homogeneous ones. Yet another criterion for assessing the effects of group composition relates to the impact of heterogeneity on members holding minority status. For example, the proportions of women and ethnic minorities within a group have been shown to affect the pressures that minority members feel toward conformity or overachievement (Kanter, 1977).

Diagnostic studies often trace ineffective behavior to structural and technological factors like those listed in Table 6.2. Sometimes, diagnosis reveals that the reward system encourages one type of behavior, such as individual productivity, while top management continues to hope for some other kind of outcome, such as enhanced teamwork (Kerr, 1995). Assessment of team performance can also lead to unintended consequences when controls do not adequately measure the desired outcomes (Lawler & Rhode, 1976). For example, if long-haul freight crews are evaluated on downtime and damage levels of delivered freight, they may learn to evade time-consuming safety regulations in order to improve their performance ratings.

Many of the factors listed under Group Behavior, Processes, and Culture in Table 6.2 were treated as major determinants of group and organizational effectiveness by traditional organization development consultants (e.g., Beckhard, 1969; Schein, 1988) and by adherents of the human relations model of group processes (e.g., Likert, 1967; McGregor, 1960). According to these researchers and consultants, group and organizational performance and motivation improve when work teams are cooperative and cohesive, communication is honest and multidirectional, group norms support productivity, decision making is participative, and supervision is both task oriented and supportive of individual effort and learning.

In keeping with these assumptions, human relations scholars and consultants developed detailed models of effective organizations, such as Likert's System 4. These models provided the theoretical underpinning for survey feedback interventions aimed at improving supervision and teamwork (Hausser et al., 1975; Taylor & Bowers, 1972). In these interventions, group members are asked to describe organizational climate, supervisory behavior, peer relations, group processes, satisfaction, and perceived group performance. Feedback of these data allow supervisors and other group members to compare themselves to other groups within the organization and to the ideal-typical model of the effective group.

Recent work on supervisory behavior confirms the importance of supervision for group effectiveness but highlights aspects of supervisory behavior that received less attention in the past. Goal setting is one form of supervisory behavior that very consistently leads to objectively higher forms of team effectiveness (O'Leary-Kelly, Martocchio, & Frink, 1994). Work groups that set goals have substantially higher performance levels than do groups that do not set goals. The specificity and clarity of goals also contribute to team performance.

Besides defining the objectives and goals toward which subordinates strive, managers' expectations for subordinates can shape their self-expectations, motivations, and performance (Eden, 1986, 1990; Scott & Bruce, 1994). Through the Pygmalion effect of self-fulfilling prophecy, positive expectations produce motivational and performance gains among team members, whereas negative expectations by supervisors lead to supervisory behavior that blocks subordinate performance. In like manner, studies of transformational leadership (Bass & Avolio, 1990; Sashkin & Burke, 1990; Tichy & DeVanna, 1986) point to the possibility that managers can enhance their own effectiveness and, in some cases, contribute to organizational effectiveness by inspiring subordinates to pursue group or organizational goals, stimulating them intellectually, and helping them achieve higher levels of development and maturity. The transformational leadership style contrasts with the transactional style, which emphasizes management by exception and the provision of rewards in exchange for performance.

On the other hand, studies of group processes other than supervision do not fully support the assumptions and hypotheses contained within the human relations models. In keeping with the human relations assumptions, processual changes such as enhanced participation, communication, and teamwork do often contribute to work satisfaction, QWL, job commitment (Strauss, 1977, 1982), creativity, and innovation (Lawler, 1986). However, enhancing participation and communication within teams does not consistently enhance team performance, as measured by productivity. Furthermore, increasing employee participation does not uniformly improve employee attitudes. Attitudinal improvements following the introduction of quality circles, for example, are much less consistent than would have been expected on the basis of human relations models of motivation (Steel & Jennings, 1992).

Nor have recent drives for total quality management (TQM) and employee involvement produced enduring, organizationwide improvements of the sort implied by the human relations models and anticipated by program advocates (Lawler et al., 1992). Instead, many of the improvements experienced at the start of such programs disappear after a few years (Griffen, 1991). One limitation of participatory interventions, such as quality circles and TQM, is that interventions at the team level cannot overcome the organizationwide effects of polarized labor relations (Katz et al., 1985). Similarly, both labor and middle management may resist implementation of quality circles and other participative programs because they view the programs as a threat to their power or job security. Employee-involvement programs are not likely to overcome quickly the high levels of uncertainty and mistrust produced by repeated cycles of reengineering and downsizing. Given these limitations, practitioners should consider carefully the potential costs of innovations such as TQM and employee-involvement schemes and the barriers to their implementation before recommending them to clients (Lawler, 1986; Shea, 1986).

The last entry in Table 6.2 calls attention to the potential impact on team effectiveness of cultural and subcultural patterns and processes (see Chapter 10). This entry reminds consultants and managers to pay close attention to the shared feelings, perceptions, and interpretations that members of teams or the organization as a whole develop through interaction with one another. Trust among peers, between supervisors and subordinates, and between employees and their organization as a whole is one expression of interpersonal relations that can affect behavior and performance by individuals, teams, and entire organizations (Fox, 1974; Kramer & Tyler, 1995; McAllister, 1995). Trust involves both cognitions and feelings about the extent to which another person can be relied upon, and shares important values and standards (Sitkin & Roth, 1993). People who must work together ·within teams or cooperate with members of external groups can do so effectively only if they trust one another (Dodgson, 1993). Otherwise, they will face difficulties in overcoming setbacks during collaboration and will devote a lot of time and energy to protecting themselves and to monitoring and controlling the behavior of others. High-trust relations should, therefore, reduce organizational transaction costs (Bromiley & Cummings, 1995). Moreover, the degree to which team members trust their supervisor and higher-level managers can affect their identification with organizational objectives, their compliance with administrative procedures, and their willingness to negotiate mutually acceptable resolutions to disagreements and conflicts. Employees who place more trust in their managers also may be more willing to accept changes proposed by management (Smith, 1992).

Other "soft" features of organizational life, such as norms about quality and customer service, can also dramatically shape "hard" outcomes. Group norms and beliefs can enhance or block effort, creativity, innovation, and risk-taking behavior. Attention is also needed to the ways in which administrative activities and organizational structures symbolize particular values or beliefs, such as organizational rationality and efficiency (Bolman & Deal, 1991; Pfeffer, 1981a).

Organizational Factors

Diagnostic studies can profitably explore the effects on group outcomes of the entire range of organizational factors appearing in the top level of Figure 6.1. For instance, patterns of group performance often can be traced to organizational strategies, standards, and goals, all of which help shape the targets that lower-level managers set for subordinates and apply in evaluating them. Team behavior is further shaped by emergent group norms that respond to management's intended and unintended messages about the ways to obtain rewards and avoid sanctions. For instance, when a department chair tells staff members that "we're a publish-or-perish university," faculty members translate that declaration into a simple injunction for newcomers: "Forget about preparing classes and meeting with students. Concentrate on your research!"

Organizational technology and structure shape coordination and control within groups, the division of labor within and between groups, and the tasks assigned to team members. Organizational culture can shape beliefs and assumptions that focus people's attention and channel their interactions. Chief among these are beliefs about the way work gets done, how change occurs, who is powerful, what clients and customers expect, and how external trends and developments affect the organization (Argyris & Schon, 1996; Davis, 1984; Kotter & Heskett, 1992; Schein, 1985; Starbuck et al., 1978).

In addition to the broad types of organizational factors discussed above, diagnosis of individual and group behavior can examine the impact of human resource management activities. These are discussed in Chapter 8.

The sharp-image approach provides one useful way for investigators to decide which features of the open-systems framework shown in Figure 6.1 are most important for diagnosis. Hackman's Action Model provides another promising way to specify the system framework.

Action Model for Group Task Performance

To simplify diagnosis and intervention, Hackman and his colleagues (Hackman, 1987, 1991) developed an action model for group task performance. This model identifies several organizational and group conditions that can serve as *levers* for interventions aimed at helping groups enhance their task performance. Because these conditions provide opportunities for intervention, they can serve both as focal points for diagnosis and as building blocks in the design of new workgroups. The Action Model draws on a synthesis of past research and practice in workgroups, and on its authors' own depth studies of many kinds of groups.[8]

At the center of the model, which is depicted in Figure 6.2, lie three critical group processes that pose the major hurdles to effective group performance:

1. Exertion of enough joint effort to accomplish tasks at acceptable levels of performance
2. Bringing adequate skills and knowledge to bear on the work
3. Using task performance strategies that fit the work and the cultural and organizational setting in which the work is done

Assessment of how well groups handle these critical processes can provide valuable diagnostic information about the groups' capacity for meeting effectiveness targets. However, as suggested earlier, interventions are more likely to enhance group performance when they target the *conditions facilitating the handling of the critical group processes,* rather than attempting to change the processes themselves.

As Figure 6.2 shows, there are four sets of potentially facilitating conditions. These relate to the *organizational context* within which the group operates; *group design and culture; outside help,* such as coaching and consulting received by members; and the availability of material and technical *resources.* Each of these sets of conditions identifies likely causes of ineffective group processes and outcomes and provides potential levers for intervention to improve group functioning and task performance.

Diagnosing Group Functioning and Creating New Groups

Drawing on the Action Model, diagnostic studies of existing groups can examine the degree to which current conditions in each of these four areas

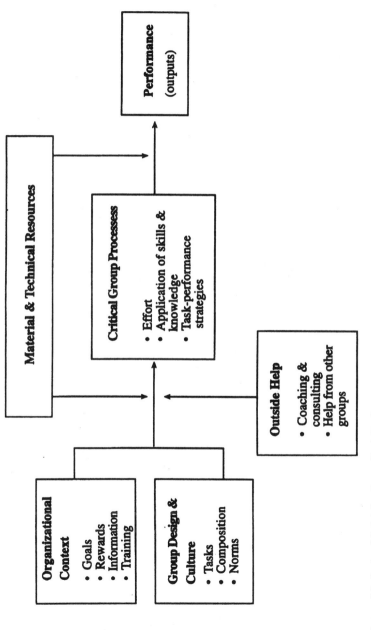

Figure 6.2 Action Model for Group Task Performance

167

facilitate high-level performance or lead to ineffective performance. For example, based substantially on Hackman's model, Denison, Hart, and Kahn (1996) developed and validated a set of diagnostic questionnaire items for members of cross-functional teams. These items ask respondents to report the degree to which their team enjoys supportive facilitating conditions, handles team processes effectively, and obtains desired outcomes.[9]

Another way to use the model in diagnosis is to follow the sharp-image logic, beginning with performance problems and then tracing these signs of ineffectiveness back to difficulties in handling one or more critical group processes. Then, the process difficulties can be followed back to one or more sets of underlying conditions. For instance, a consultant or manager might trace problems of low quality in an industrial workgroup back to a process such as inappropriate quality enhancement strategies, or to members' lack of knowledge about how to use quality assurance techniques. If the quality enhancement strategy is inappropriate, then the solution lies in redesigning the group's task (a facilitating condition) to include appropriate quality assurance techniques, as well as in coaching about the choice and use of these techniques. Suppose, on the other hand, that the group already has an appropriate strategy for quality enhancement, but members lack the skills and knowledge needed to implement the strategy. In that case, the solutions lie in changing other conditions, such as coaching for skill use and development, training programs, or the selection of members who possess appropriate skills.

The Action Model also can serve as a guide to planning and setting up new workgroups. When used in this way, the model points to guiding questions that the people responsible for establishing a new group can raise at each of the main stages in the establishment of a new team or unit. Box 6.1 presents questions for consideration by managers responsible for team formation and operations. These questions can be addressed with or without the help of external consultants.[10] The discussion that follows examines in greater detail the issues referred to in these questions.

Conditions Facilitating Performance

Let us now examine more closely the conditions that can facilitate performance, as shown in Figure 6.2 and as suggested by the questions in Box 6.1. The most critical *task conditions* for groups include defining clear tasks, setting challenging objectives, assigning shared responsibility, and specifying accountability for task performance.[11] In addition, it is important that groups

Box 6.1
Diagnostic Questions for Creating New Workgroups

Stage 1: Preparation

1. What is the main task?

2. What are the critical task demands (e.g., effort, knowledge, and skills; close attention to task performance strategy)?

3. How much authority will the group need, and how much will it be given? Are group members willing and able to operate under these conditions? What are the implications of decisions about who will lead the group (e.g., manager-led vs. self-led) for designing the role of team manager?

4. How advantageous and feasible is it to assign these tasks to a team? What are the benefits and liabilities of assigning them to a group? Will the group get the design and support it needs? How will it operate under likely constraints and limitations on its ideal design and support level?

Stage 2: Planning an Appropriate Design and Supportive Organizational Context

5. How should group tasks be structured?

6. How should the group be composed? Will members have the needed technical and collaborative skills?

7. What feedback channels will be available?

8. What material resources are needed, and can these be obtained? What organizational (nonmaterial) supports are needed and available?

9. How will contacts with other groups and units be designed and negotiated?

Stage 3: Forming and Building the Team

10. How can the team be helped to work together effectively? How will members develop constructive norms and group processes?

11. How will group boundaries be defined?

12. How will members be assigned tasks, and how will they renegotiate their tasks and assignments as they work on them?

(Continued)

Box 6.1 (Continued)

Stage 4: Coaching and Consulting

13. Who will be responsible for helping group members improve their collaborative processes?

14. How can opportunities be given to allow members to renegotiate the group's design and context? Will members participate in and contribute to periodic reviews of group functioning?

15. What process assistance will be provided to promote collaborative processes? How will leaders or coaches help members reduce or eliminate ineffective processes and behavior patterns? How will they help members take advantage of unexploited opportunities? How will members be helped to adjust to changing external conditions and to group development over its life cycle?

16. How can group members be helped to learn from their experiences? Will the organizational context support learning and experimentation?

be as small as possible, because larger groups have more coordination problems. *Compositional features* that contribute to performance focus include the presence of clear boundaries; inclusion of members possessing the needed skills and knowledge—including interpersonal skills; and creation of a good mix of members in terms of training and experience. This mix ensures cross-fertilization and creativity while avoiding insurmountable divergences of opinion and working styles. Finally, groups are more successful when they possess clear and strong *norms* that regulate behavior and ensure coordinated action. It is also important that these norms encourage members to act proactively and to learn from their experiences.

Investigators can develop diagnostic questions based on each of the above facilitants of group processes. For example, diagnosis can assess whether managers set clear, challenging tasks for group members or fall into the trap of telling them to do their best without specifying challenging, operational objectives. Diagnosis can also examine group and individual accountability for tasks in order to be sure that critical tasks are not falling between the cracks. *Responsibility charting* (Galbraith, 1977, p. 171) provides one technique for clarifying which members of a team or unit are assigned responsibility for performing tasks, as well as who is supposed to approve the work, be consulted, and be informed about task activities.

According to the Action Model, four sets of *organizational conditions* frequently influence group functioning. First, higher management can promote performance by defining challenging yet specific *goals* for group performance. Performance is enhanced when management delegates much of the authority for deciding how to attain these goals to the team itself. Second, *reward systems* promote performance by focusing on group performance as opposed to individual performance, and by recognizing and reinforcing good performance. Third, the organization's *information system* can provide access to data and forecasts that both help members formulate their tasks and their performance strategies and provide feedback on performance. Fourth, informal and formal *training systems* can contribute to performance by providing members with the necessary skills and knowledge in advance of task activity and in response to the members' needs.

Along with group leaders, external *coaches and consultants* can help members anticipate or resolve critical coordination problems so that team members learn to collaborate effectively. In addition, coaches can help build commitment to the group and its task. Leaders and coaches also facilitate performance when they help members decide how best to make use of the members' skills and knowledge, how to learn from one another, and how to learn from other groups. Leaders or coaches also help groups avoid performance strategies that are likely to fail, and they can help group members think creatively about new ways to handle their tasks.

To sustain high performance, groups must have timely access to sufficient, high-quality *resources*. Without the needed equipment, funds, or raw material, group outputs will be inferior, even if the group members perform well on all of the process criteria. Furthermore, blocked resources and acute shortages can lead to frustration and even turnover among potential high performers and can thereby erode a group's long-term performance capacity. Resource availability is particularly critical in groups that are undergoing structural change or learning new techniques for handling their tasks. Managers responsible for introducing change sometimes expect performance to improve immediately without investing in the necessary processes of learning, training, and experimentation that occur during change. By singling out material and technical resources as critical variables that intervene between group processes and performance, the Action Model reminds managers and consultants to pay attention to seemingly mundane issues. The model also examines the subtler questions of the availability of needed human resources, knowledge, and information.

Limitations of the Model

The Action Model provides consultants and managers with useful starting points for diagnosing the functioning of groups and for identifying factors helping and harming group performance. Nevertheless, there are several limitations to the model. First, as Hackman and his colleagues note (Hackman, 1991), different types of groups encounter distinctively different types of challenges and difficulties that cannot be included in a general model. These differences shape intragroup processes and may also affect definitions of effectiveness. The distinctive challenge for air traffic controllers, for example, is reliability, whereas a repertory theater group faces problems of maintaining spontaneity and artistic vigor night after night.

Second, by stressing leverage points where managers can readily intervene into team functioning, the model necessarily neglects the "softer" aspects of group interaction, such as mutual expectations and understandings. Yet these can sometimes be crucial to group activity and performance. One way of in-corporating these aspects of small group culture into the model is to recognize that negative spirals of labeling and attribution sometimes can be broken by concrete changes in group design and organizational context rather than by process interventions aimed directly at interpersonal behavior (Hackman, 1991, p. 483).

A third limitation of the model is that it focuses mostly on outputs, which are the more readily measurable and agreed-upon features of group effective-ness.[12] However, the factors affecting the ability of a group to satisfy the requirements of conflicting constituencies may be quite different from those affecting the quality or quantity of performance as measured by a single external observer or client. In particular, the satisfaction of divergent constitu-encies depends substantially on the ability of team leaders and members to handle intergroup political processes. Similarly, the ability of a group to work well together in the future could depend on forces that are quite different from those that determine current performance. Fortunately for diagnosis, the Action Model concentrates on the component of effectiveness that is most commonly used by clients. If consultants and clients want to emphasize one of the other two components of effectiveness, then the diagnostic practitioner will have to develop a more flexible and customized model for assessing the sources of group effectiveness and ineffectiveness.

Fourth, the Action Model, like almost all of the English-language prescrip-tive literature on improving group functioning, reflects the experiences of consultants, researchers, and managers in for-profit businesses within North America. Yet cultural differences in motivational and interaction processes can limit the applicability of North American models to other parts of the world (Hofstede, 1993; Triandis, 1994). Institutional differences within and between countries can also limit the model's applicability. Consider, for example, the model's assumptions that groups will work better when presented with joint objectives and subjected to team, as opposed to individual, rewards. Employees from cultures that stress individual achievement and accountability may regard these arrangements as unjust or unfair and may resist cooperating with them. Team rewards may also fly in the face of long-standing institutional arrangements, such as labor agreements that base pay on an individual's rank, job tenure, and training rather than his or her performance. To date, no models of individual and group performance systematically address the implications of cultural and institutional differences like these.

Fifth, unlike sharp-image diagnosis, the Action Model builds in strong assumptions about the likely signs and causes of ineffectiveness and the best ways to intervene to enhance group performance. Hence, the model can discourage users from attending directly to client concerns and from identifying causes and possible solutions that reflect the organization's distinctive features and the contingencies affecting it.

Conclusion

This chapter examined ways to apply systems-based frameworks and models to the diagnosis and assessment of workgroup behavior. The first part of the chapter presented an analytical framework that calls attention to possible interactions between the individual, group, and organizational levels. Ways to specify the framework in keeping with the approach of sharp-image diagnosis were also discussed. The second part of the chapter critically examined Hackman's Action Model for diagnosing groups and designing new groups. This model's strengths and weaknesses both flow from its bias toward interventions into the organizational, group design, and training conditions that influence group processes and outcomes, rather than into group processes themselves. Chapter 7 continues the examination of diagnosis of design issues, this time focusing on entire organizations and on major units within organizations.

Notes

1. Following current usage (e.g., Guzzo & Dickson, 1996; Guzzo & Salas, 1995), the terms *group* and *team* are used interchangeably in this chapter.

2. Figure 6.1 and the following discussion draw on and extend Lawler, Nadler, and Mirvis (1983, pp. 20-25) and Hackman (1987). In Harrison (1994), an earlier version of the framework is also applied to the diagnosis of individual organizational behavior.

3. In practice, Resource Acquisition and Adaptation criteria of the sort discussed in Chapter 3 are not usually applied to assessments of workgroup effectiveness.

4. Several of these assumptions are discussed in Hackman (1987, 1991).

5. A further problem with many studies in the group dynamics tradition was their reliance on laboratory experiments using ad hoc groups of students (Zander, 1994). There is a legitimate question about whether this body of research can be generalized to groups in real-world organizations.

6. The study by Katz et al. (1985) also shows that higher levels of formal QWL activities, such as quality circles and labor-management committees—as opposed to QWL outcomes such as satisfaction and reduced absenteeism—may reflect the industrial relations climate in a plant, rather than causing that climate or making an independent contribution to productivity.

7. See Harrison (1994) for a review of standardized instruments and other techniques for assessing the variables listed in Tables 6.1 and 6.2.

8. The following presentation of the model reflects both the work of Hackman and his colleagues and our own reading of their work. Some of the original terminology has been adapted to fit the frameworks presented earlier in this chapter and in Chapter 2.

9. Scott, Bishop, and Casino (1997) also sought to operationalize and test the Hackman model, but their study is limited to team process criteria and outcomes.

10. Some of these questions appear in Hackman (1987, pp. 335-337), and some are derived from his discussion.

11. Hackman and his colleagues also stress the importance of task identity, variety, and significance. Research has not shown these features to affect team performance consistently.

12. Hackman (1987) originally referred to all three facets of group effectiveness. Subsequently (Hackman, 1991), he and his colleagues focused mainly on team performance.

Organization Design

The United States Internal Revenue Service introduced personal computers (PCs) to 14,000 of its agents in order to reduce the time spent on processing cases. A subsequent stage of the technological change envisioned an integrated system of PCs that would link the agents in a network and thereby enhance their effectiveness. A year after the PCs were introduced, a survey of 1000 agents showed that the innovation was succeeding in terms of utilization rates and user satisfaction. But the redesign did not produce the desired cost savings. Although most of the agents reported using their computers more than twenty hours a week, only fifteen percent reported that the PCs reduced the time spent on a case. Still, three quarters of the agents thought the computer was an appropriate tool. The explanation for these paradoxical results may lie in side effects of the design change: The agents enjoyed mastering and using the PCs and believed that the PCs enhanced their professional image in the eyes of the taxpayer. (McKersie & Walton, 1991, p. 246)

This case provides a familiar example of the growing trend of organizations to experiment with new organizational designs, many of which rely on computer-based information technologies. Design changes mainly rework the "harder," more visible and manipulable features of organizational structures, technologies, and administrative procedures (e.g., Galbraith et al., 1993; Nadler et al., 1992). Radical design changes, such as reengineering and restructuring through computer networking, offer the prospect—as yet largely unrealized—of dramatic and enduring improvements in productivity and other forms of effectiveness (Davenport, 1993; Hammer & Champy, 1993; Morton, 1991). Some of the most dramatic changes are occurring in manufacturing, where traditional assembly-line production with its Taylorized jobs is giving way to new technologies, such as robotics and computer-assisted design, and to new designs for work organization, including lean production, just-in-time provision of parts, job rotation, and semiautonomous work teams (Clark, McLouglin, Rose, & King, 1988; Osterman, 1994).

Across the globe, organizations are investing billions in such changes and in new technologies with the hope of attaining higher levels of productivity, as well as in efforts to cope with global markets, rising competition, and ever more sophisticated and diverse customer demands. Sometimes, developments like industry deregulation, mergers, and privatization of government-owned firms force design changes on corporate managers. On many other occasions, managers initiate design changes and prefer them to other kinds of planned change because the managers possess more direct authority and control over design features than they do over "soft" organizational features, such as culture, politics, and emergent behavior.

The IRS case points to the often surprising and even paradoxical results of many design projects: Contrary to the expectations of the managers, technical experts, and consultants who take part in design projects, redesigning organizational technologies and structures often fails to produce the sought-for results. Instead, these projects frequently give rise to unanticipated outcomes that reveal unforeseen complexities within organizational systems and the change process.

The first part of this chapter examines the complexity and indeterminacy of design and the benefits of using multiple theoretical frames to reflect this complexity. In contrast, traditional thinking about design failed to reflect its multifaceted nature. Instead, design was viewed through a structural-instrumental frame, which treated design changes as tools for goal attainment (Bolman & Deal, 1991). Beyond this mechanistic side to design, there are systemic, symbolic, negotiated, and political facets, each of which is well described by a distinctive theoretical frame.

Reframing design in terms of these additional perspectives reveals the difficulties of trying to carry out design projects as if they were technical activities in which experts simply choose and apply the best design tools for obtaining clear-cut objectives. Instead, practitioners of design would be advised to treat design projects as diagnostic inquiries into indeterminate and multifaceted process. This approach involves using diagnostic thinking, feedback, and analysis to learn about design and about the focal organization while engaging in a design project. In keeping with this approach, the first part of this chapter introduces a framework for integrating diagnosis and assessment into design projects.

In the second and third parts of the chapter, we examine specific issues bearing on the design of total organizations and of units within organizations. Throughout the chapter, we pay special attention to diagnosing and assessing the uses and effects of new computer-based information technologies.

Contributing to Design Projects

Viewing Design Through Multiple Frames

To understand the complexities of design and possible contributions of diagnosis and follow-up assessments to design projects, let us look at the IRS project described in Case 7.1 through several perspectives—a structural-instrumental, an open-systems, a symbolic-interpretive, a negotiated order, and a political frame. Besides illuminating the design process, this analytical exercise provides an example of some of the benefits of using multiple frames in diagnosis, as discussed in Chapters 1 and 15.

When viewed from a structural-instrumental frame, Case 7.1 seems simply to describe a familiar attempt to apply structural "design tools" to improve productivity.[1] This traditional view suggests two explanations for the failure of the project to obtain its objective—incorrect choice of the structural interventions (PCs and PC networking) or poor planning and implementation of an appropriate choice.

Although design changes guided by structural approaches can produce useful results, this view of design often leads to an incorrect assumption. This assumption is that there is a well-formulated and tested body of knowledge on which experts can draw in order to decide which design tools are best suited to particular objectives and organizational conditions. Unfortunately, no such comprehensive and systematic body of knowledge and expertise exists. Furthermore, given the complexity and indeterminacy of organizational life and the many useful ways to frame organizational problems (Chapter 15), none is likely to be developed.

Instead, as will be seen below, decision makers often choose organization designs for reasons that are unrelated to their instrumental value. Moreover, even when implemented according to plan, design changes frequently produce negative or equivocal results (March & Sproull, 1990; Sproull & Goodman, 1990). The indeterminism of design changes is evident in the failure of many promising design techniques, including the new information technologies (Morton, 1991, pp. 187-200), to consistently deliver their expected benefits.[2] Nor do variations in fundamental design configurations, such as the mix of businesses or services in a corporate portfolio (Galbraith et al., 1993, pp. 15-42; Nayyar, 1992), produce the kind of strong and consistent effects on organizational behavior or performance that the instrumental view of design anticipates (Starbuck & Nystrom, 1986).

Sometimes, enthusiasts of the structural-instrumental view of design fall prey to belief in an optimal design technique, such as quality circles. A management-fashion setting community consisting of business journalists, consultants, management gurus, and business school professors promotes the technique as an all-powerful and universally applicable tool for solving the critical problems facing organizations, industries, and even entire nations. Practicing managers quickly embrace the technique as an instant and quasi-magical solution to their problems (Abrahamson & Fairchild, 1997). Once faith grows in a particular technique, consultants and managers apply it widely whenever organizational improvement is sought.

In contrast to our diagnostic approach and that of most organization development consultants (Burke, Clark, & Koopman, 1984), the enthusiastic backers of a fashionable technique skip over the diagnosis of organizational problems and challenges, ignore other action options, and fail to assess the appropriateness of the technique to the target organization. Another type of uncritical application of design techniques occurs among advocates of whole sets of techniques and ideas that are united by a particular viewpoint and type of discourse, such as that of scientific management (Shenhav, 1995).

This tendency to overlook diagnosis is vividly illustrated by work on business process reengineering (BPR), one of the most radical techniques for structural redesign and, until quite recently, one of the most popular. BPR calls for the restructuring of major functional areas within an organization to enhance the performance of core organizational processes (Hammer, 1990; Hammer & Champy, 1993). BPR thus requires a substantial investment on the part of the organization, often leads to major personnel cuts, and carries high risks. Nevertheless, none of the popular presentations of the technique, BPR handbooks (e.g., Manganelli & Klein, 1994), or research reports on BPR (e.g., Ascari, Rock, & Dutta, 1995) explicitly refer to diagnosis prior to BPR or during the change process. Some BPR practitioners (e.g., Ghani, 1996) do mention techniques for gathering information about the organization prior to BPR, but this quasi-diagnostic stage is hardly implemented in practice (e.g., Grover, Jeong, Kettinger, & Teng, 1995). Even more surprising, analyses of BPR failures (Clemons, Thatcher, & Row, 1995; Grey & Mitev, 1995) overlook the possibility that decision makers failed to conduct an adequate diagnosis of the organization's needs and change options.

In contrast to the mechanistic view of design contained within the structural-instrumental frame, the open-systems frame reveals much of the complexity and indeterminacy to which design projects are subject. As developed in preceding chapters (especially Chapters 2, 4, and 6), this frame provides grounds for diagnosing the nature of organizational ineffectiveness and challenges and for weighing action alternatives *before* locking into BPR or any other system intervention. In the IRS case, such a diagnosis might have helped IRS managers define their organization's problems, challenges, and needs before investing in PCs. Then they could have decided which interventions, if any, could best promote the kinds of effectiveness for which they were aiming. This type of open-systems analysis often rests on an assessment of current fits between system components and on judgments about how design interventions will affect these alignments (e.g., Galbraith, 1977).

The open-systems approach could lead change strategists in the IRS case to compare the likely realignments resulting from introducing PCs and networking to the likely outcomes of other action alternatives. If the IRS managers decided that PC-based redesign was the best option, they would then try to map out the preconditions for creating an effective computer network for IRS agents and would develop a plan to create these conditions prior to and during implementation.

The open-systems frame views technological and design changes as system interventions that can produce effects at levels other than the targeted one and in distant parts of the system that are linked to those undergoing design change. This approach thus alerts design planners to look for possible design side effects, such as those reported in the IRS. Because of the complexities of systems, and because external and organizational contingencies can change rapidly, the course of implementation of design changes and the impacts of a particular intervention are not fully predictable. The open-systems view of design changes thus underlines the vital importance of obtaining frequent feedback on the change process and its consequences.

Further light on organization design and its consequences comes from the interpretive frame—a perspective that highlights the ways that people and groups assign meanings to phenomena and create cultural systems based on shared meanings, beliefs, norms, and values (see Chapter 10). This frame sometimes helps account for surprising consequences of design change, such as the results reported by the IRS agents. According to the IRS agents, the greatest effect of supplying them with PCs was symbolic: PC use—and perhaps even the simple presence of the PCs in the agents' workspace—apparently helped change the agent's image from paper-shuffling clerk to highly skilled and up-to-date professional.

Many new technologies and design innovations possess this capacity to symbolize values such as innnovativeness, competence, and competitiveness (March & Sproull, 1990). Moreover, changes in technology, physical arrangements, control systems, organization charts, and job titles can signify shifts in status, authority, and influence within an organization (Bolman & Deal, 1991). Thus, design changes can lead people to redefine the images they hold of themselves, their organization, and other organizations (Dutton, Dukerich, & Harquail, 1994; Yulevitz, 1997). The meanings and values that people assign to organizational designs can change with the tides of fashion (Mintzberg, 1979) and can vary within and between organizations (Coombs, Knights, & Willmott, 1992; Sproull & Goodman, 1990).

The interpretive frame thus suggests a very different explanation than does the structural frame as to why managers seek to introduce design innovations. By introducing technological and structural changes, managers project the valued traits associated with these innovations. By failing to imitate the innovations, managers risk being labeled uncompetitive or noninnovative. Once organizational designs gain wide acceptance among industry leaders or governmental agencies, adoption of these "correct" and "rational" forms of organization helps ensure the organization's legitimacy and signals its managers' competence (DiMaggio & Powell, 1983; Scott, 1987).

Further insights into the IRS case and the design process in general come from applying two more frames—a negotiations frame (see Chapter 9) and a political frame (Chapters 3 and 5). The application of these frames to the IRS case is speculative, but in many other instances, the frames provide powerful explanations of the origins of design and its effects. The negotiation frame treats administrative structures and practices as emerging in part through informal negotiations among organizational participants. In addition, structural and technological changes create opportunities for members to renegotiate their roles, work relations, and status patterns. Design changes influence, but do not determine, the outcomes of these informal negotiations (Barley, 1986).

When applied to Case 7.1, the negotiation view suggests that IRS agents discovered that the PC strengthened their hand in negotiations with taxpayers. The ability of agents to call up a taxpayer's past records quickly, calculate in an instant all taxes and interest due, and perhaps even display data showing how widely a taxpayer's claimed deductions deviated from IRS norms would all enrich the agents' bargaining tactics and strengthen their position during investigations of taxpayer returns.

The political frame sheds further light on possible reasons why the agents liked their PCs. Equipping agents with PCs heightened their power over taxpayers by providing the agents with a knowledge base and skills that taxpayers lacked. In contrast, consider the power implications of the proposed computer network: Routine participation in an internal network could easily render the agents' work more visible and transparent and thereby subject agents to more intensive surveillance and control by peers and managers. Political analysis thus raises doubts about whether IRS agents will participate enthusiastically in such a network. Moreover, this analysis suggests that the agents may subtly resist network participation if they fear that it will compromise their interests.

The political and negotiation frames thus lead practitioners of diagnosis to attend to the ways that interpersonal and intergroup negotiations and politics shape the choice of organization designs, implementation planning, and the implementation process itself (Pressman & Wildavsky, 1973). Particularly critical are the ways that design choices shape power distributions and other aspects of work that are important to the users of new designs, as well as to their planners (Pfeffer, 1981b).

The political frame further indicates that stakeholders in and around an organization are likely to hold divergent views about the objectives and implications of design projects. Stakeholders will act to promote their own interests before and during the development of such projects, rather than

promote agreed-upon effectiveness outcomes. In some cases, powerful external stakeholders virtually dictate design decisions to an organization that is
dependent on them. For example, firms are often forced to adopt administrative and structural designs that meet the demands or expectations of
dominant suppliers, customers, or regulators (Palmer, Jennings, & Zhou,
1993; Scott, 1987).

There are several ways in which consultants and decision makers can take
political forces into account in considering the feasibility of design interventions and in planning specific design projects. Assessments of the power and
positions of stakeholders, like those provided by stakeholder analysis or force
field analysis (Chapter 5), can guide this type of diagnosis (see also Sankar,
1991). In addition, consultants can sometimes directly assess how key actors
view design objectives and design alternatives (e.g., McDaniel, Thomas,
Ashmos, & Smith, 1987). Under conditions of trust and cooperation, consultants and decision makers can obtain input from divergent stakeholders by
encouraging their active collaboration in diagnosing situations requiring design changes and in developing design interventions (e.g., Thach & Woodman,
1994). Organization development consultants often favor such collaborative
approaches to design (e.g., Kilmann, 1977). However, the feasibility of
involving employees and other stakeholders in design depends on characteristics of the focal organization and the type of design innovations envisioned (Stebbins & Shani, 1989). In many instances, the threat of opposition
to design changes leads top management to impose new designs without consulting potential opponents about the goals or even the means of the redesign
(Dunphy & Stace, 1988, 1993).

As this multiple-frame view of design suggests, the many actors in organization design face a very complex and dynamic field when deciding on and
implementing design projects.[3] To decide whether design projects are feasible
and necessary, change strategists need to be guided by a sound diagnosis of
their organization's needs and the feasibility of alternative change methods.
To cope with the situational factors affecting the planning and implementation
of design projects, change agents and implementors need to pay attention to
interactions among design implementors, recipients (i.e., users), and nonparticipating stakeholders. Furthermore, they need to be aware of the meanings
that these actors assign to technological and administrative innovations. To
increase their capacity to deal with unpredictable developments during design
projects, design planners need frequent feedback on the course of implementation and its consequences. Moreover, change strategists, agents, and imple-

mentors will need to use this feedback to reassess their plans, programs, objectives, and their own understandings of how their organization operates.

Diagnosing and Assessing Design Projects

By treating design projects as an ongoing form of diagnostic inquiry, change strategists and change agents can choose and implement designs that suit the focal organization and help it cope with critical problems or challenges. Frequent assessment of the implementation of new designs can help managers decide to halt or modify unsuccessful design programs and adjust their programs to emerging patterns of use or changing external conditions. Moreover, diagnosis and assessment during design can create opportunities for individual and organizational learning through a process of reflection-in-action (Schon, 1983; see also Chapter 13). In this form of inquiry, managers and consultants surface their own expectations about the likely impacts of design and about the focal organization and then correct or even recast their theories-in-use as they receive feedback throughout the design process.

The flow chart in Figure 7.1 illustrates schematically how diagnostic and assessment studies can contribute to design projects. In the figure and the discussion that follows, the term *assessment* refers to more narrowly focused examinations, whereas *diagnosis* is reserved for the preliminary stage of diagnosing basic problems and challenges. The design projects considered here seek to generate strategic changes within a total organization or major subsystems rather than less fundamental and more incremental changes.[4] Designs aiming at strategic changes include mergers and strategic alliances; major forms of restructuring, such as BPR; creation of entire new lines of activity or major cutbacks; fundamental changes in rules and processes, such as the introduction of TQM programs; and radical technological innovations.

As the first entry in the flow chart suggests, decisions to undertake strategic design changes should flow from a sharp-image diagnosis or some other form of systematic diagnosis of the organization's critical problems and challenges. Given the costs and risks of strategic redesign and the likelihood of side effects, it is more prudent for decision makers to wait to plan major design changes until they are convinced that these changes are necessary and constitute the best possible way to deal with critical challenges or crucial sources of organizational ineffectiveness.

Organizational decline (Chapter 11)—in the sense of a continuing drop in key resource flows—or a serious risk of decline are strong indicators that

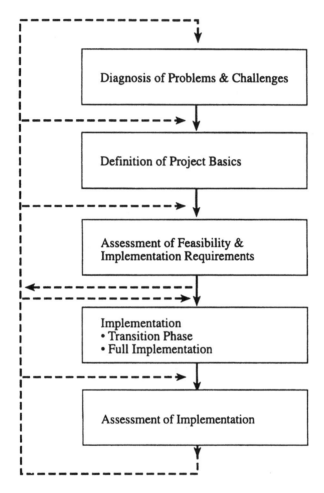

Figure 7.1 Diagnosis and Assessment During Organization Design Projects

fundamental design changes may be needed. Strategic design changes also may be needed when incremental changes have become inadequate or are likely to become so in the near future. Troubleshooting procedures and other system adjustments are inadequate if an organization has fallen into a state of permanent crisis, lurching from one troubleshooting episode to another, or if the short-term solutions to crises create long-lasting havoc in the organization (Sayles, 1979, pp. 160-162). Moreover, organizations may need design change if symptoms of ineffectiveness—such as quality problems, financial losses, operating inefficiencies, and customer dissatisfaction—persist after immediate causes of ineffectiveness have been removed.

By anticipating the need for strategic change, managers and consultants can more readily consider a range of possible strategic moves (see Chapter 13) and can adjust their program for implementing change on the basis of preliminary feedback concerning implementation. In contrast, if managers attempt to make strategic changes only after their organization faces the threats of decline or outright crisis, they will probably have to work within extreme cash and time constraints.

If decision makers conclude that strategic change is necessary and that a particular type of design change appears most appropriate, they take on the role of change strategists and enter the second analytical phase shown in Figure 7.1. Decision making and planning in this phase concentrate on defining the basic parameters of the change project. Chief among these are a systematic description of the design change and its hoped-for outcomes.

For example, take redesigns that are supported by new forms of information technology (IT). IT change can aim for five different levels of organizational change, ranging from streamlining local applications to integration of the entire organization using an IT platform, redesign of basic processes, fundamental restructuring as a network, and redefinitions of strategies to take advantage of possibilities generated by IT (Venkatraman, 1991). The IT innovation described in Case 7.1 aimed initially at the first of these levels and envisioned an initial step toward the second level of change. BPR uses IT to support the third level of change. Restructuring entire organizations as networks or creating networks of suppliers, customers, and producers is feasible but rare. A growing number of organizations are experimenting with these possibilities and are looking for ways to extend or redefine their strategies through IT applications (Daft, 1995).

Another focal issue for consideration in defining the design and its objectives concerns intended impacts on the roles and patterns of influence of major actors in and around the organization and on relations between actors. For example, IT changes in work design can make work more routine and less dependent on operator skills. But IT can also "informate" work by enriching employees' capacity to analyze their activities and then redirect them accordingly (Zuboff, 1988). To take another example, IT-supported innovations can enhance responsiveness to customers by speeding and enhancing data gathering about customer preferences. This use sustains traditional demarcations between customers and employees. On the other hand, IT systems can also blur traditional organizational boundaries by providing customers with the resources for performing operations that were previously handled by staff members (e.g., making bank transactions). Some IT applications even let customers modify products or services to suit their own needs.

Other important design parameters deal with the scope and trajectory of change—including timetables for planning and implementing change in various parts of the organization. Establishing a trajectory involves setting basic targets for each step of the project and deciding on whether to introduce change gradually or all at once.

Another basic decision concerns setting up a project steering committee or task force that will be responsible for planning the project in detail and overseeing its implementation. If change strategists favor involving members of the organization in the design and implementation stages, they may include representatives of employees and other stakeholders on the steering committee. Otherwise, the committee will consist of members of top management and their advisors.

To facilitate reflective inquiry about change, change strategists can map out how they expect the proposed redesign to affect their organization, and they can periodically review their model of the change process in light of feedback obtained during design change. These reviews will help participants see whether their assumptions about the design change and their own organization were, in fact, confirmed during implementation or should be revised in light of these experiences. To map out the expected design process, change strategists and planners need to specify their understanding of the current state of the organization and its environment. Then, they can spell out operational objectives for the project and ways to determine if design changes are attaining these objectives. Next, change strategists need to define the primary units, levels, functions, and operations that are targeted for change.[5] Decision makers should then try to depict the hypothesized links that will lead from specific design changes to attainment of the project's objectives. In other words, how is the design change expected to produce the sought-for results? The answer to this question often is not obvious.

Consider, for example, a program to enhance the productivity of technical staff by providing them with sophisticated work stations. Work stations could boost productivity as a result of several very distinctive changes in work processes (Morton, 1991, pp. 10-12). First, computerization of data-processing tasks could reduce the time that the staff spends on information processing. Second, the productivity gains might come from improvements in knowledge production through the use of techniques such as computer-aided design or expert systems. Third, linkages between workstations could facilitate communication among technical workers by overcoming barriers of time and space. Fourth, productivity could be improved because the workstations provide managers with better ways of monitoring and controlling the performance of technical employees. Careful assessments of project implementation, as opposed to just before-and-after measures of productivity, would indicate the degree to which each type of work transformation took place. This assessment would also provide evidence on the reasons that the workstations led to certain changes in work processes and not to others.

Once they have defined project basics, change strategists, consultants, and members of the project task force can reassess the project's feasibility and assess requirements for its implementation. This is the third phase shown in Figure 7.1. After asessment, as shown in Figure 7.1, change strategists ·and task force members undertake implementation planning to prepare for the project's transition stage and its full implementation.

Assessments of project feasibility can rest in part on examination of the projected fits between the new design and current organizational practices and conditions (Schwartz & Davis, 1981).[6] This type of assessment helps project planners ensure that the organization possesses or can obtain the technical capacity needed to carry out the design project, and that the new design will be aligned adequately with the unique "soft" features of their organization— including its culture, employee attitudes, individual initiatives, informal interactions, and leadership (Zammuto & O'Connor, 1992). Consider, for example, an assessment of fit between IT-supported cross-functional teams and the prevailing organizational culture. This analysis could examine whether staff norms encourage peer cooperation and support or emphasize hierarchical coaching and supervision. The assessment could also investigate whether potential recipients of the planned change view IT-assisted workstations as a sign of progress or a threat to organizational traditions.

An additional assessment issue concerns the organization's capacity to manage the *transition* between the old and the new design and to cope with attendant disruptions to routine operations (Beckhard & Harris, 1977). In some cases, this transition period can take years and can sorely tax the organization's resources. Assessment of this issue examines whether the organization possesses or can readily acquire the human and material resources, technology, and flexibility needed to handle the transition and to adjust to new working arrangements. Similarly, it is important to consider whether actors in the organization's environment will cooperate with the redesign or exploit opportunities to gain advantage over the organization in transition.

Identification of limits on change capacity or of misalignment between the design change and the organizational infrastructure can help project planners choose and plan steps to support the proposed design change. It may be necessary, for example, to recruit, select, and train people with skills and attitudes that fit the new design.

Assessments of project feasibility can also take into account the likely symbolic implications of current and planned designs, as well as their instrumental effects. For instance, a quality program that encourages hospital nurses and members of paramedical occupations to participate on an equal basis with physicians may violate the hospital's traditional status hierarchy and run contrary to the physicians' assumption that they should dominate medical decisions. In a similar fashion, project planners can examine the political feasibility of implementation with the aid of techniques such as stakeholder analysis and force field analysis.

Feasibility studies like these provide change strategists with a more accurate assessment of possible risks and costs of design projects, which can be weighed against expected benefits. Suppose, for example, that top managers of a financial services firm seek to reengineer important customer services in order to attain dramatic improvements in the speed and efficiency of handling these services. Inspired by Hammer's success in reengineering insurance services (Hammer, 1990), the change strategists envision assigning individual managers to handle all the tasks associated with processing customers' credit requests. These tasks are currently dispersed among many functional departments and managers. To reengineer the processing of credit requests, the redesign will provide service managers with computerized decision support systems. To save staff time, the service managers will answer phone calls only after customers have directly provided the computer with relevant data through a combination of voice-recognition inputs and touch-tone entries. The benefits of the redesign for top management are clear: faster service at lower costs. Customers, too, may appreciate any cost savings that are passed along to them, along with the increased speed with which their inquiries are handled.

However, top management can encounter hidden costs in this type of redesign, as well as the more evident costs associated with retraining employees and developing the new service platform. Many employees will lose their jobs through the reengineering process. The downsizing process is likely to create mistrust of management and fear of job loss among remaining employees. As a result, performance levels may drop and staff turnover may rise, with resulting increases in recruitment and training costs. Even more damage may occur because customers will have to deal with a computer before they can talk to a service representative. They may view the new data management system as impersonal and insensitive to their needs. If so, customer loyalty will probably decline, and the firm will be forced to compete mainly on the price of its services rather than on its reputation and quality.

Sometimes, feedback from feasibility assessments like these leads top managers to redefine basic project parameters or even to reevaluate the entire project. More frequently, these interim assessments render implementation planning more realistic and more attentive to nontechnical features of the design change that might otherwise have been overlooked. For example, feedback from political assessments can lead managers to plan steps to mobilize support for design changes and to minimize or overcome resistance (Chapter 5).

As Figure 7.1 indicates, implementation of design projects usually includes a transition stage and a period of full-scale implementation. During transition, the project steering group assigns responsibility for specific aspects of the design change to new and existing teams. Management and its representatives seek to communicate the vision and details of the design change to all levels in the organization. Supportive activities are undertaken, such as human resource programs, to provide project participants with needed skills and training and to create incentives for project participation. New technologies and management systems are purchased, and new operating systems are designed in detail (Davenport, 1993; Heilpern & Nadler, 1992). Pilot programs may also be conducted during the transition period. When feasible, new programs may be implemented alongside existing routines so as to minimize disruptions to ongoing operations. Assessments of the program's progress during the transition stage provide feedback for changing plans and altering programs prior to full implementation. Diagnostic practitioners can contribute to these assessments in many ways. They can, for example, assess how well top management and transition teams are communicating with the people who will ultimately use the new technologies and structures. Assessments can also evaluate progress and outcomes of pilot projects and supportive activities, such as recruitment and training programs.

In addition, practitioners can monitor ways that users modify and interpret design changes through practice, and changes that are occurring in organiza-

Table 7.1 Criteria for Assessing Design Projects

Implementation criteria
- Adherence to schedules
- Rates of use of technological and administrative innovations and new operating procedures
- Degree of use (where discretionary)
- Types of use
- User satisfaction and evaluation

Effectiveness criteria
- Performance in terms of design objectives
- Side effects
- Fit of new design with rest of organization
- Contributions to resource acquisition and adaptation
- User satisfaction and evaluation

---

tional roles and relations in response to the design change. Feedback on these emergent modifications of design innovations and on organizational consequences of redesign can lead managers to alter their original designs or implementation programs. For example, a health maintenance organization (HMO) began to introduce computerized records of medical treatment to streamline record-keeping and improve quality. But HMO managers soon began to propose scanning these records to locate physicians who greatly exceeded the average rates of ordering tests or prescribing medications. Preliminary assessment of the design innovation showed that using computer records to spot high spenders would create resentment among physicians and might lead the physicians to refuse to cooperate with the entire computerization project. In response to feedback about these risks, the HMO managers decided to introduce an incentive system to promote savings in prescription practices. Every physician who prescribed less than the age- adjusted and case-adjusted average was given a bonus consisting of around 20% of the physician's saving on prescription costs.

A variety of criteria can be used to assess the implementation and effectiveness of new design programs. Some of the most commonly used criteria appear in Table 7.1. From a structural-instrumental perspective, implementation is assessed in terms of progress toward full, routine use (McKersie & Walton, 1991, p. 246; Yin, 1981). Assessments can reveal many individual, social, and situational factors that affect people's use of new technologies and other design innovations (Fulk, Schmitz, & Steinfeld, 1990).

Preliminary assessments of project effectiveness usually take a structural approach that stresses the degree of attainment of the project's original objectives—such as improvements in quality, speed, flexibility, revenues, or client satisfaction; or reductions in costs, snags, and complaints. Practitioners can also assess effectiveness in system terms by examining the emerging fit of new designs with system elements that were not changed, such as the culture or the environment, and by assessing the design's contributions to resource acquisition and system adaptation (see Chapter 3, Table 3.1). These system-oriented assessments can also consider unanticipated side effects of design changes. To introduce a stakeholder view of project implementation and effectiveness, the satisfaction criteria listed in Table 7.1 would be applied to all important stakeholders, rather than just to design users (see Chapter 3).

If design changes lead to downsizing, assessment during the transition phase and during full implementation can also examine the very crucial and sensitive area of the management of reductions and relocations of personnel. Assessments of downsizing can examine whether the firm succeeds in retaining highly desirable employees or loses many of them as well. Assessments can also track the attitudes and feelings of the remaining employees. These studies can help management judge the success of its past efforts to ensure cooperation with the transition and help it anticipate problems that may arise from layoffs, relocations, or deskilling of jobs.

The last stage in design projects involves full implementation. During this stage, assessment concentrates on design effectiveness but continues to provide data on implementation. These assessments can provide inputs into managerial decisions about further modifications in the design, additional steps needed to support the change, and future design efforts.

An additional focus for assessment once full implementation has taken place is the degree to which mandated changes have become routine. Routinization refers to the degree to which innovations and changes become accepted organizational practices and become embedded in organizational processes and norms (Yin, 1981). In many instances of planned change, critical new practices do not become routinized. Instead, members revert to their former practices once pressures for change drop off. If, for example, a TQM program mandates involving customers in the design of new products, routinization has taken place only if product development teams are still collaborating with major customers a year or more after the cessation of the TQM campaign. Routinization has failed if team members have returned to their former practice of designing products without customer input and subsequently soliciting customer reactions.

Feedback from assessments of implementation can help change strategists reevaluate their original theories about the likely impacts of design innovations. Sometimes, this type of reevaluation contributes to learning about the organization and its environment and to a reconfiguration of organizational strategy, as well as to a better understanding of specific design innovations. This sort of double-loop learning (Argyris & Schon, 1996) occurred in one hospital-supply firm that underwent an IT-assisted redesign (Morton, 1991, p. 17). In that firm, redesign gave front-line service personnel access to computer data that were generated as a by-product of their work. These data depicted both the service employees' activities and those of their customers. Gradually, the salespeople noticed patterns in their customers' buying behavior. They alerted management to these patterns. The salespeople also suggested converting these data into information that could be sold back to customers to help them regulate their own operations. Management accepted and implemented the idea, thereby discovering a new use for IT and opening up a new line of services. For an organization to take advantage of such by-products of IT redesign, management and front-line operators must share common objectives and trust one another. Moreover, management must be open to feedback from subordinates, clients, and assessment studies, and must move quickly to translate these ideas into practice.

Sometimes, behavioral science practitioners become involved in a design project only during the transition stage, after initial attempts at implementation have proved unsuccessful. At this point in the project, clients usually want detailed feedback on the nature of implementation and advice on ways to improve the process. Consultants can contribute to this type of assessment by looking for social and organizational forces that sometimes lie beneath reports of technical and operational difficulties. Moreover, consultants can help change strategists and planners surface implicit theories and assumptions that are built into new designs. These theories describe the characteristics of the people who will use design innovations, the ways they will use them, and the ways they will be affected by them.

Many new organizational designs founder because of lack of fit between the design and the organization's human resource capabilities. In particular, limited user experience with IT and inadequate training create serious barriers to the implementation of IT-based designs (Morton, 1991, p. 44). In like manner, ineffective implementation often can be traced to poor fit between new designs and the organization's structure, culture, human resource policies, and management processes (Kochan & McKersie, 1992; McKersie & Walton, 1991). If, for example, evaluation systems put a premium on productivity and speed, they can create disincentives for employees to take the time needed to explore possible uses of computerized workstations or to help their peers learn to use the new technology.

Additional implementation barriers include resistance to redesign and the failure of management to generate sufficient support for change. Implementation problems also arise when design planners assume that people will use new techniques in a very specific way, only to discover that the recipients of the design innovations understand and use them differently. Even computer-based control and decision systems can be very vulnerable to user influence. These systems generate many possibilities for users to manipulate information to make themselves or their proposals look particularly good or to make others look bad (Zmud, 1990).

So far, we have considered in general terms how managers can benefit from treating design projects as opportunities for diagnostic inquiry. We have also examined ways to apply diagnostic techniques throughout the process of planning and implementing design changes. To explore further possible contributions of diagnosis and assessment to design change, we now turn to specific design topics, each of which poses distinctive diagnostic issues.

Organization-Level Design

Diagnosis and assessment can profitably concentrate on specific design features and choices at three different points in the diagnostic process. First, as illustrated in Chapters 1, 4, and 6, diagnostic findings on organizational problems and challenges can lead directly to consideration of design changes that might help enhance effectiveness. In considering the best ways to deal with these organizational challenges, decision makers and their consultants often consider design options like the ones illustrated thus far and those discussed in the rest of this chapter. Second, specific design issues can serve as starting points for sharp-image diagnostic studies. For example, a diagnosis might focus on a manager's request for help in designing new structures for coordinating a recently launched interorganizational alliance. Third, sharp-image studies sometimes trace signs of organizational ineffectiveness to design features like the ones discussed here.

Linkages With Other Organizations

In recent years, structural and contractual linkages between organizations have become an increasingly prominent feature of organization-level design. Diagnosis can contribute both to the examination of current linkages between organizations and to decision making about projected interorganizational ties. Before considering these possibilities, let us review some of the most important types of designs for linking organizations, and some of the implications of pursuing these designs (Bluedorn et al., 1994).

When managers seek to reduce operating costs and increase their firm's flexibility within its markets, they may prefer to sign *contracts* with external suppliers of services rather than produce goods and services within their own organization. Autonomous organizations and interest groups can form *temporary networks* when they collaborate over time to act on common problems or objectives (Wood & Gray, 1992, p. 146). More enduring *network ties* result when organizations and individuals develop strong working relations of functional interdependence (Miles & Snow, 1986)—such as long-term relations between authors and publishers; cooperation among small contractors in the building trades (Powell, 1990); and linkages between firms sharing common resources, technologies, and operating styles (Nadler et al., 1992, p. 7). External ties can be formalized in *strategic alliances,* such as joint ventures, industry consortia, licensing arrangements, or acquisitions (Buono, 1991). In the extreme, the partners in an alliance can *merge* to form a single, new firm. More and more organizations are developing strategic alliances as their managers seek to move quickly into international markets and take advantage of the capital, knowledge, or local access offered by alliance partners.

Diagnosis of current and projected linkages often assesses fits between the two organizations and fits among their system subcomponents (e.g., Bluedorn & Lundgren, 1993). The need to achieve system fit between alliance partners depends on the extent to which the alliance requires tight integration of management procedures and cultures (Osborn & Baughn, 1993). *Specialist arrangements*—such as the exchange of a specific form of technology, licensing agreements, and contractual outsourcing of specific tasks—do not typically require the parties to change their administrative practices very much, nor need they shift their current structures, norms, and values. In contrast, *hybrid arrangements*—such as partial ownership arrangements or joint ventures aimed at developing a new set of products or new technologies—require higher levels of integration between the partners. Mergers often require full integration between the partners.

Diagnosis of existing links between organizations sometimes traces ineffective interactions between partners to misalignments between partners' organizational systems or between their system subcomponents. Judgments about whether the two systems are adequately aligned depends on the level of integration required by the strategic alliance. For specialist arrangements, where integration requirements are low, limited fit between the partners' systems is problematic only if it interferes directly with coordination of joint operations. Hybrid arrangements and mergers pose two additional diagnostic issues: First, how good is the fit between the structures and cultures of the partners? Second, if fit is poor, do the managers within one of the organizations have the ability and desire to change their organization to achieve fit (Cartwright & Cooper, 1993)? If not, the alliance is likely to fail.

A similar logic can be applied to diagnostic studies designed to facilitate managerial planning of new alliances. Managers may ask consultants to help them decide whether the anticipated benefits of the creation or retention of external linkages outweigh their disadvantages and potential risks. Or, managers may ask for help in deciding what type of structural linkage will be most appropriate. Many of the business considerations in these decisions fall beyond the province of the behavioral sciences. Still, consultants may help clients weigh the pros and cons of moves like disaggregation and outsourcing (Miles & Snow, 1986). In considering the prospects for strategic alliances, decision makers may wish to bear in mind evidence that organizational diversification into unrelated areas appears to carry greater financial risks than does diversification into related fields (Lubatkin & Chatterjee, 1994). These findings may reflect the fact that mergers between similar organizations provide more opportunities for exploiting synergies of technology, knowledge, and distinctive organizational competencies than do ties between very divergent firms (Lubatkin & Lane, 1996). Links between similar firms also carry lower risks of misalignment between the firm's culture and administrative systems.

When major design changes are being considered, consultants can conduct diagnostic workshops in which clients are asked to review systematically the benefits they seek to achieve by proposed or current alliances, as well as likely risks and costs of such alliances. These issues can also be examined within workshops that examine organization-environment relations more broadly, such as those used in open-systems planning (Chapter 4) and scenario planning (Chapter 13).

Another approach to facilitating planning of interorganizational linkages is to survey or interview members of the many groups of stakeholders that are—or will be—affected by an alliance (Buono & Bowditch, 1990). Feedback from this multiconstituency investigation provides top management with a more complex view of the issues to consider. Interviews and surveys of the people involved in a merger or strategic alliance can explore the alliance's anticipated or current impact on administrative practices, the image and culture of the organizations, and the organizations' members (Buono & Bowditch, 1989). Alliances can affect the members of the organizations in many ways that can ultimately influence the success of the alliance and the overall performance of the partners to the alliance. People involved in a merger or other form of alliance may fear that they will lose their job or organizational standing and therefore may refocus their efforts on their own careers or on finding another job. They may also become embroiled in open and covert bargaining about their roles in the organization. Tension and conflicts may also develop between the staffs of the alliance partners when staff members are used to working in very different ways. If, for example, two very different firms are to undertake a joint venture or merge their operations, the diagnostic investigator can examine whether gaps between the cultures of the firms are likely to disrupt working relations between staff members from each firm. Feedback from the groups affected by a merger or strategic alliance can help top management plan steps that will facilitate the alliance and deal with the plurality of needs, cultural orientations, and interests among the participants in the new venture.

Divisionalization

Divisionalization is another feature of organization-level design that may benefit from diagnostic study. As a rule, organizations that are divisionalized along functional lines (e.g., marketing, engineering, production) are less able to respond to variations in markets and other environmental conditions than are organizations divisionalized in terms of products and services (e.g., life, home, and commercial insurance divisions), or in terms of markets or geographical areas (Mintzberg, 1979). However, there are many variations within types of divisionalization and many opportunities for combining them (Galbraith et al., 1993, pp. 15-42). Practitioners should be wary of generalizing about desirable forms of divisionalization on the basis of current organizational practices (Starbuck & Nystrom, 1986). Apparently, state-of-the-art practices sometimes turn out to be less than optimal or cannot be readily duplicated.

Diagnostic practitioners can assess the adequacy of an organization's current divisional structure by considering two diagnostic questions: Do divisional boundaries group together those people and units that must work together most intensively? Do people work effectively across divisional boundaries? Additional issues are whether the current structure keeps costs to a minimum by avoiding unnecessary duplication of positions and underuse of resources, and whether the structure provides sufficient adaptiveness to variations in markets and other environmental conditions, such as local governmental regulations of products or production processes. Diagnosis of divisional structures needs to consider both technological forces and structural design. Current telecommunication and information technologies offer many opportunities for cooperation across administrative and geographical boundaries. Hence, IT changes can sometimes substitute for structural reorganizations.

An additional diagnostic question concerning the current pattern of divisionalization is whether the current structure allows for structural and operational differentiation between units that face very different types of tasks, technologies, and environments (Lawrence & Lorsch, 1969). To assess whether an organization is sufficiently differentiated, practitioners need to decide whether each division is allowed to adapt its design to fit its own objectives, technology, environment, and personnel. There is too little differentiation if top management imposes organizationwide designs that block divisional effectiveness. There is too much differentiation if divergences in the administrative practices of various divisions create avoidable costs or undermine interdivisional cooperation.

As organizations become highly differentiated, they generally shift from control systems based on monitoring operations and costs to those that monitor results (Mintzberg, 1979). In the extreme, where divisions operate entirely as unrelated businesses, top management may treat each as a separate investment center or strategic business unit (SBU); (Galbraith et al., 1993, pp. 16-17). The shift toward result-oriented controls entails decentralization, a design change that is discussed in detail below in the context of design within divisions. Members of differentiated divisions can also coordinate their operations through lateral techniques, another design feature that is discussed in the section that follows.

Viewing complex organizations as networks of interrelated, semiautonomous units provides one of the most promising ways of diagnosing relations
among decentralized divisions in very large and complex organizations
(Ghoshal & Bartlett, 1990). This approach is most appropriate when multidivisional organizations are composed of SBUs. However, this analytical approach also can be applied to public sector organizations that are divided into
divisions that enjoy substantial budgetary, administrative, and operational
autonomy. By viewing multidivisional organizations as networks, practitioners can pose diagnostic questions about network relations between divisions. These questions are analogous to those raised above concerning relations and links between organizations.

To follow this diagnostic approach, practitioners can treat each SBU as a
semiautonomous organization embedded in an organizational network. Working relations—involving exchanges of products, services, and resources—
then can be traced between the focal SBU and corporate headquarters, between the SBU and other parts of the corporation (the corporate environment),
and between the SBU and external organizations and markets. These relations
will vary in density (extent of exchanges) and in the power that any given
network partner (including corporate headquarters) holds over the subsidiary.
In multinational firms, the division's dependencies and exchanges with its
local (extracorporate) environment are particularly important. These exchanges influence divisional practices and help determine the division's
power vis-à-vis its headquarters.

This network approach to multidivisional organizations allows examination of the benefits and drawbacks for each business unit of current structures
and management processes—such as the mechanisms used by corporate
headquarters to evaluate division performance. Viewing multidivisional firms
in this way also helps practitioners identify the forces facilitating and blocking
cooperation across divisional boundaries—including the boundary between
corporate headquarters and each division.

Network measurement and modeling techniques (Nelson, 1988; Scott,
1991) enable practitioners to gather quantitative data on intraorganizational
relations and allow for comparisons of current relations between divisions and
desired ones (Nelson & Mathews, 1991). Another assessment technique uses
questionnaires to ask people in boundary-spanning roles to report on the
content and quality of their exchanges with members of units both inside and
outside the organization (Van de Ven & Ferry, 1980).

Design Within Divisions and Units

Because divisions and subunits in large organizations vary greatly from one another, many design features can best be examined at these lower organizational levels, rather than at the level of the total organization. Managers often initiate design changes at the divisional or unit levels, even when they intend to diffuse the designs to other divisions or units. The discussion that follows begins with the diagnosis of basic types of designs for coordination and control, two of the most fundamental design problems. Then, we turn to the diagnosis and assessment of design changes based on the new information technologies (IT) and to the application of models of mechanistic and organic design configurations.

Hierarchy Versus Lateral Ties

More and more managers and their consultants face choices between designs based on traditional, hierarchical forms of coordination and control and those based on lateral coordination across organizational boundaries. Lateral ties span administrative boundaries to link the people (including customers) who must cooperate to produce a successful product or service. To choose among competing designs and to assess the fit of existing designs, practitioners need models that help to specify the uses and possible effects of alternative design principles.

One design model (Galbraith, 1977; Tichy, 1983; Tushman & Nadler, 1978), which can contribute to diagnosis, examines the capacity of organizational arrangements to coordinate three types of interdependencies. First are pooled *interdependencies*—where units can work independently of each other (e.g., crews in a home construction firm). According to the model, rules and standard operating procedures usually provide adequate coordination of work based on pooled interdependency. Second are *sequential interdependencies,* where work must flow from one unit to another according to a fixed order and schedule, as it does in assembly-line production or in the procedure for routine admission of hospital patients. To coordinate this type of work, rules and procedures must be supplemented by more detailed planning of the relations between units, closer monitoring of unit outputs, and more supervision from above. Lengthy professional and technical training of staff members also can help ensure uniformity of pooled or sequential operations in settings where direct supervision and the use of many rules are inappropriate or infeasible (Mintzberg, 1979). Neither professional training nor bureaucratic controls provide adequate coordination for work based on the third type, *reciprocal interdependencies.* Here, units or individuals must directly adjust to one another. For example, a television advertising campaign requires close coordination and mutual adjustment among clients; the campaign head; and specialists in design, marketing, and production. Lateral coordination mechanisms, rather than rules and hierarchies, allow for such two-way communication and mutual adjustment and thereby help people handle complex, uncertain, and rapidly changing conditions and tasks. The following list ranks these *lateral mechanisms* from the least to the most complex:

1. Informal linking roles, networks, job rotation
2. Integrator roles
3. Temporary committees and single-purpose task forces
4. Team structures and project groups
5. Matrix structures

Integrator roles, such as project manager or public health coordinator for a municipality, place direct responsibility on the incumbent to coordinate all the functions that contribute to a particular product, service, or process. Matrix structures combine functional and project authority lines in an attempt to cope with uncertain environments and tasks and to obtain the advantages of both forms of organization.

Managers often introduce lateral mechanisms to coordinate the diverse activities associated with producing a particular product or service and to overcome communication barriers between specialized units or tasks. Designs that create a coherent bundle of tasks can also make the work more challenging and satisfying than designs based on narrowly specialized tasks. The need to coordinate ties between organizations also creates pressures for more elaborate lateral links.

Despite their potential benefits, complex lateral mechanisms, such as matrix structures and cross-functional teams, are costly and hard to administer. The dual reporting relations that characterize such structures create ambiguity and stress for employees and complicate the processes of evaluating and rewarding performance. The expansion of communication channels in these complex structures can create too much information, while overlapping responsibilities produce turf battles and a loss of accountability (Bartlett

& Ghoshal, 1990; Davis & Lawrence, 1977). Cross-functional teamwork creates many tensions for members because they suddenly must renegotiate task definitions and responsibilities, group identities and boundaries, and personal payoffs and costs. Team members are challenged to learn how to handle situations like these (Hirschorn & Gilmore, 1992, p. 107):

- Lead, but remain open to criticism.
- Follow, but still challenge superiors.
- Depend on others you don't control.
- Specialize, yet understand others' jobs.
- Defend your interests without undermining the organization or outsiders

Team members may find it hard to cope with these challenges if they are accustomed to tackling problems mainly from a technical or business point of view and are used to traditional reporting relations and job assignments.

Managers and consultants need to remain alert to the difficulties of implementing complex forms of lateral coordination, such as matrix structures. Before recommending such complex forms of restructuring, they would be well advised to consider the prospects for improving coordination through simpler mechanisms, such as informal network ties or the rotation of personnel through roles (Galbraith et al., 1993, p. 117). Managers and consultants can also look for ways to increase subunit autonomy and thereby reduce the need for cross-functional ties.

Diagnosis of current coordination designs can be guided by the model of work interdependencies presented above. In such a diagnosis, people familiar with the work process describe what has to be done to accomplish the work, and they independently describe the mechanisms for coordinating and controlling the work process. The practitioner then uses the model to assess the fit between coordination mechanisms and interdependencies and to guide inquiry into ways to improve poor fits.

A risk in this theory-guided approach to diagnosis is its reliance on generalizations about the work process. Instead, it is often preferable to inquire more directly about the flow of work and information between units (e.g., Rashford & Coghlan, 1994, p. 25; Van de Ven & Ferry, 1980), or even to observe these interactions directly. Then, signs of ineffectiveness can be traced to underlying causes. Interunit coordination is ineffective if members view coordination procedures as clumsy or inadequate, or if interunit contacts are characterized by frequent interruptions, misunderstandings, surprises, or high levels of conflict. If these problems are common, members may not be using existing coordinating mechanisms adequately, or the coordination mechanisms may be inappropriate to the interdependencies between units, to task and environmental complexities, or to the speed at which operations must be performed.

To assess the feasibility of redesigning coordination mechanisms, practitioners can use techniques such as force field analysis (Chapter 5) to assess the strength of forces that would enable or hinder a transition to new forms of coordination. For example, it may be very difficult to create a matrix structure from units that organize their work in fundamentally different ways. Practitioners asked to assess the feasibility of such design changes need to look carefully at the work procedures and administrative practices of each unit. Time use (Ancona & Chong, 1992) is one feature of work organization that merits attention but is often overlooked. Units frequently work at different paces and use different time cycles to organize processes such as production, delivery of services, planning, budgeting, and personnel review. Once established, these time-use patterns are hard to change. Informal relations between units are less likely than are formal ties to disrupt patterns of time use and other deeply entrenched work patterns. Hence, it is generally more feasible for management to encourage informal links between divergent units than to impose new structures on them.

An additional approach to assessing the feasibility of a proposed design is to conduct a stakeholder analysis (Chapter 5)—examining which individuals and subgroups might have a stake in proposed change, their likely reactions to the change, and their power to influence the course of the redesign. Hidden costs of redesign, such as destruction of cohesive workgroups, must also be weighed against the sought-for benefits of the change.

Centralization Versus Decentralization

A design issue that arises at almost all organizational levels concerns the degree of centralization within major organizational units. When power and authority are highly centralized, control over important resources and decisions is concentrated in the higher ranks of the organization. Scholars and consultants have cited many possible benefits of shifting toward a more decentralized distribution of authority and power (Carlisle, 1974; Child, 1977; Kanter, 1983; Khandwalla, 1977; Mills, 1991; but note the complexities cited by Huber, Miller, & Glick, 1991; see also Chapter 5). Chief among these are the following:

- Reduced burden on top management to make decisions and process information
- Cost savings from reduction in administrative levels and paperwork
- Improved information flow and decision quality
- Enhanced ability of middle managers to solve problems on their own
- Flexible and rapid response to local conditions
- Improved morale
- More innovation
- More responsibility for results among lower ranks
- Better management development

Yet decentralization can also produce disadvantages, including those listed here:

- Reduction in top management's ability to forge a unifying strategy and respond quickly to change
- Increased costs for training, compensation, capital equipment, and plant
- Duplication of positions
- Creation of local power centers
- Heightened conflict between units

To diagnose the existing distribution of authority and power, practitioners examine the level at which people are authorized to make decisions in key functional areas and, if possible, actual patterns of decision making and power distribution (Chapters 5 and 9). Once the practitioner has characterized the current degree of decentralization within the focal unit, possible costs and benefits of changes in this pattern can be considered in light of the managers' and the consultants' knowledge of the organization and in light of explicit effectiveness criteria. Practitioners and clients are more likely to favor decentralization when an organization's subunits must be able to respond rapidly and appropriately to local and specialized problems. For example, by giving a single case manager the authority to provide all of the services required by a single, major customer, a firm may ensure coordination of these services and sensitivity to the customer's special needs (Davenport, 1993, pp. 260-265). Responsiveness to local requirements is particularly critical when organizations are very large and are geographically dispersed; environments are very complex, competitive, and changing rapidly; and many tasks cannot be routinized.

Combining Opposing Design Principles

Increasingly, consultants and researchers find that organizations can prosper by simultaneously pursuing what at first glance appear to be opposing
design principles (Cameron & Quinn, 1988). Instead of choosing between
alternatives such as centralization versus decentralization or hierarchical
versus lateral coordination, managers may be able to find ways to enjoy
simultaneously some of the payoffs of both alternatives.

To help decision makers discover such possibilities, practitioners can look
for the simplest designs that provide adequate lateral coordination. Managers
can then incorporate these lateral mechanisms into existing hierarchical
structures. For example, the increasingly popular "mirror-image" structures
make cross-functional ties easier without abandoning functional departments
or creating complicated dual reporting arrangements (Galbraith et al., 1993,
pp. 48-49). In this structure, each functional unit, such as manufacturing or
purchasing, is subdivided into an identical set of product or commodity
groups. For example, an aircraft company's functional units can be subdivided
into wing, tail, and cabin groups. Each functional division within a public
welfare organization can contain units dealing with parallel client groups,
such as retirement-age clients, single parents, and adolescents. In this way,
people working within separate functional groups can readily locate their
counterparts in other units who serve the same clients, contribute to the same
service, or work on the same product.

Adding lateral capacities onto a hierarchical design may often be the only
way that managers can introduce greater lateral control without encountering
overwhelming resistance. Top and middle management, along with other
stakeholders, can lose power or prestige if hierarchical designs are abandoned.
Moreover, hierarchical and routinized forms of control spell order and rationality to many managers and administrators, whereas coordination across
organizational boundaries threatens them with ambiguity and even chaos.
Many firms that have introduced new, cross-functional responsibilities for key
management processes have followed the approach of adding lateral forms
onto existing ones. These firms typically add responsibility for processes such
as customer service or product development onto their managers' existing
responsibilities rather than seek a total structural reorganization along process
lines (Davenport, 1993, pp. 161-162).

New information technologies also offer top management the opportunity
to take advantage of decentralization without abandoning centralized control

(Keen, 1990). Today's information systems allow managers of large firms or divisions to monitor practices and performance of subordinate units while at the same time giving them the authority, resources, and feedback needed to make decisions autonomously. By following this approach, Hewlett-Packard achieved dramatic improvements in purchasing performance while cutting costs and failure rates (Hammer, 1990, p. 110). To allow for responsiveness and service to plants, the firm retained 50 separate purchasing departments that were located within separate manufacturing units. The company added a corporate unit to coordinate and monitor the performance of the local units. The corporate unit gives local units access to a national database on vendors and uses its market power to negotiate lower purchasing costs (Hammer, 1990, p. 110).

In short, instead of striving for design consistency, practitioners and their clients can benefit by combining multiple and even opposing design principles. By doing so, they can sometimes develop arrangements that best fit the changing functional needs of the organization and that respond effectively to the expectations of multiple stakeholders.

Organic Versus Mechanistic Systems

Although competing design principles can coexist effectively, many organizations and subunits develop a coherent pattern or configuration of design features (Miller & Mintzberg, 1983). The well-known model of organic and mechanistic systems can guide the assessment of how well configurations of organizational structure, processes, and culture fit the technology, environment, and personnel characteristics of divisions or entire organizations (Burns & Stalker, 1961; Gresov, 1989; Lawrence & Lorsch, 1969; Tichy, 1983; Tushman & Nadler, 1978). The model can also be applied to smaller organizational units.

The main features of the typology and the conditions under which good fit occurs appear in Table 7.2.[7] Organic systems provide greater information-processing capacity; encourage creativity and innovativeness; and facilitate rapid, flexible responses to change. Organic systems also provide more interesting and challenging work environments than do mechanistic systems. On the other hand, they are more costly and harder to administer. Hence, mechanistic systems usually are more efficient and productive than organic ones in units that perform high-volume, low-variance tasks. Units performing tasks

Table 7.2 Conditions Affecting the Fit of Mechanistic and Organic Systems

System Feature	Mechanistic	Organic
Roles, Responsibilities	Specialized, clearly defined	Diffuse, flexible, change through use
Coordination and Control	Supervision, rules, standard procedures; detailed plans, frequent evaluation based on clear objectives, standards	Consultation among all having related tasks; flexible plans, diffuse, changing goals, evaluation over longer periods
Communication	Top-down emphasis; top management has key outside contacts	Multidirectional, multilevel contacts with outside
Supervision and Leadership	Nonparticipative, one-on-one, loyalty to superiors stressed; position and experience grant authority	Participative, stress on task, team, organization; expertise and knowledge grant authority
Sources of Knowledge	Local, internal	External, professional, cosmopolitan

Fit best when		
Work processes are . . .	Routine (well understood, standardized)	Nonroutine (not well understood or designed for each problem)
Task environment is . . .	Simple, predictable	Complex, unpredictable
External coordination is . . .	Limited	Extensive
Personnel expect . . .	High structuring and routine, control from above	Role flexibility, challenging work, autonomy
Life cycle[a] stage is . . .	Formalization and control	Entrepreneurial or Collectivity
Effectiveness criteria stress . . .	Efficiency; standard, reliable operations; control from top or outside	Creativity, innovation, adaptation, quality of work life, human resource development

a. See Chapter 11.

of this sort usually face fairly predictable external conditions and do not have to carry on extensive contacts with external units.

Organizations that start out as entrepreneurial ventures usually have more organic administrative systems. They may retain these systems as they move into the Collectivity stage in the organizational life cycle, in which group solidarity becomes important, but creativity and innovation continue to be emphasized (see Chapter 11). Administrators introduce more mechanistic systems as their organizations move into a third life cycle stage that stresses formalization, control, and efficiency of operations. If formalization becomes unworkable, organizations may enter a Structural Elaboration stage in which they can differentiate between organic and mechanistic subunits.

To use the model in diagnosis, practitioners assess how organic or mechanistic a division's current administrative system is and how well the current system fits the contingencies and effectiveness criteria listed in the lower half of Table 7.2. Taken as a whole, systems organized along traditional, bureaucratic principles may be judged too mechanistic if they face very unpredictable environments—for example, where customer preferences change rapidly—or must deal with nonroutine tasks—for example, applications of advanced manufacturing techniques (McKersie & Walton, 1991; Zammuto & O'Connor, 1992) or tasks requiring creativity and innovation (Delbecq & Mills, 1985). In particular, a division may need a more organic system if it is unable to cope with the following four types of challenges:

1. Adapt to change and respond rapidly and decisively to threats and opportunities
2. Handle nonroutine tasks in innovative and creative ways
3. Meet employee expectations for creative, challenging work
4. Coordinate relations with other units and organizations.

On the other hand, unless staff development, intrinsic motivation, and employee satisfaction are very critical, divisions that use organic arrangements to deal with predictable environments, limited external dependencies, and routine tasks are probably failing to take advantage of the efficiencies offered by more mechanistic procedures. If a preliminary application of the model suggests that change is needed in either direction, diagnostic practitioners can focus more closely on those design tools that clients can most readily use as levers for moving in the desired direction.

Conclusion

This chapter presented a multidimensional view of organization design that departs substantially from traditional views of design as the systematic application of structural and technological tools to promote organizational improvement. Instead, we stressed that the origins, development, and effects of design projects reflect system interactions, power plays, symbolism and sensemaking, and interpersonal negotiations. These complexities of design explain many of the surprising and even paradoxical outcomes of design projects. Past research and experience in redesign, some of which is synthesized in this chapter, can help consultants and managers become aware of design options and their possible consequences. But there is no cumulative and systematic body of knowledge on how to redesign organizations.

Because of the complexity and indeterminacy of design interventions, consultants and managers can benefit by treating design projects as forms of diagnostic inquiry into change, rather than as technical exercises in choosing and implementing the right technology or structural innovation. If diagnoses are conducted early enough in decision making, they can help decision makers decide whether design change is needed and what types of changes are likely to prove beneficial. Then, assessment and feedback throughout the design process can help change strategists monitor and adjust to unforeseen design effects and to emergent behavior in response to redesign. Even more fundamentally, if decision makers articulate their expectations for design change in advance, feedback can help them test and reassess their basic understandings about the state of their organization, its environment, and about organization design.

Notes

1. Beer (1980) and Mintzberg (1979) list popular design tools.

2. Other findings on the outcomes of design changes are cited in Chapters 1 and 6.

3. The following discussion refers to the roles of stakeholders in planned change, which were discussed in Chapter 5 (see Identifying Stakeholders).

4. See Chapters 2 and 13 on the definition of strategic change.

5. Katz and Kahn (1978) use the objectives, targets, and hypothesized linkages of change projects as bases for comparing behavioral science interventions.

6. Too much emphasis on attaining fit between a proposed change and current conditions may lead analysts to overlook opportunities for mobilizing current resources for "strategic stretch" (see Chapter 13).

7. Table 7.2, which relies in part on Tichy (1983, p. 276), derives from Harrison (1994), which also discusses standardized measures of many of the contingencies and administrative features listed in the table.

8 Human Resource Management

Recognition is growing among managers, consultants, and researchers that the full development of human resource capabilities can contribute significantly to organizational success and can help organizations adapt to rapid technological and environmental change (Becker & Gerhart, 1996; Kochan & McKersie, 1992; Sparrow, Schuler, & Jackson, 1994; Ulrich, 1997). Hence, managers increasingly turn to behavioral science practitioners inside and outside of their organizations for help in assessing current human resource management (HRM) practices and in planning changes in HRM functions.

This chapter presents five highly focused techniques for assessing HRM practices, and it links these techniques to broader diagnostic approaches and issues. Consultants and HR professionals can draw upon these techniques when sharp-image diagnosis or some other form of behavioral science diagnosis points to the need for detailed assessment of particular HRM activities. The techniques can also be used in response to requests from clients for evaluations and assessments of very specific HRM activities, as opposed to broad diagnoses of HRM. Sometimes, these forms of assessment will uncover more general organizational problems or challenges that then become the focus of a sharp-image diagnosis. The techniques presented here can also serve as aids to managerial decision making and can help HR personnel gather evidence about the business and organizational contributions of HRM.

Here are the techniques that are critically examined in this chapter: *Program evaluation* assesses how specific HR programs are implemented and whether they hit clearly defined targets. *Benchmarking* compares current HR practices to those in other organizations. *Strategic HRM* considers the contribution of HR practices to business strategies. *Utility analysis* calculates the dollar costs and benefits of specific HR practices. *Stakeholder assessment* surveys how managers outside the HRM function rate the contributions and services provided by HR personnel.

These techniques can be used to study specific HRM practices and programs from within the broad range of HRM activities, which are defined as activities aimed at shaping the skills, knowledge, attitudes, and behavior of employees. When a diagnosis of the entire range of HRM activities is envisioned, the sharp-image approach, or some other comprehensive diagnostic approach, will be more suitable than the highly focused techniques reviewed here. HRM activities that might be examined using these techniques fall within the areas of staffing, developing, appraising, and rewarding employees. They also include the process of communicating with employees, designing work tasks and relations, managing labor relations, and providing for employee safety and welfare (Fombrun, Tichy, & DeVanna, 1984; Henemen, Schwab, Fossum, & Dyer, 1989). Finally, some techniques, such as stakeholder analysis and benchmarking, can also be applied to the area of change management, which non-HRM managers now view as a crucial HRM competency.[1]

These HR activities can be carried out at three different managerial levels (Fombrun et al., 1984, pp. 42-43). HR assessments can focus on one or more of these levels and on links between them. First, the *strategic level* deals with general policies and goals, and the ties between these activities and top management's strategies and plans. For example, in some firms, top management tries to design reward systems so as to encourage behavior (e.g., risk taking and innovation) that fits the business strategy. Second, the *managerial level* concentrates on processes for obtaining and allocating the resources needed to carry out strategies and promote overall goals. For instance, an HR manager makes decisions about future recruitment and training programs based on plans or instructions received from top management. Third, the *operational level* deals with the day-to-day management of the personnel function. Organizations vary widely in the resources and attention devoted to the major HR activities at each managerial level. Moreover, organizations vary in the roles and organizational functions that are assigned responsibility for HR practices at each level.

The successful introduction of organizational change usually requires special attention to one or more HR practices or to the whole HRM function. The introduction of new information technologies, for example, creates needs for the recruitment or retraining of personnel to ensure that employees have the necessary skills and capabilities (Morton, 1991). Similarly, programs of quality enhancement require support at the managerial and strategic levels in the areas of employee development, compensation, labor relations, and work designs that empower lower-ranking employees (Galbraith et al., 1993; Lawler et al., 1992).

HRM Program Evaluation

The logic of program evaluation (Herman et al., 1987; Rossi & Freeman, 1993) provides several straightforward approaches to assessing new or continuing HR practices at the operational and managerial levels. The types of evaluation activities described here are applicable to well-defined sets of activities that are designed to obtain clearly defined, agreed-upon objectives. Evaluation techniques can guide the assessment of specific HR practices, such as recruiting or selection practices, as well as entire programs of activity, such as programs for quality assurance or employee safety. Program evaluation can tell clients how well their organization performs some HR activity—such as recruiting highly motivated college graduates to their sales force. In some cases, the evaluation can also examine costs of the activity.

Three Types of Evaluation

Evaluation can focus on three distinct areas (Rossi & Freeman, 1993): (a) evaluation of program conceptualization and design, (b) assessment of program impact and efficiency, and (c) monitoring of implementation. Comprehensive evaluations require attention to all three focal areas, but evaluations focusing on just one or two areas also can be very useful.

Box 8.1
Questions About Program Conceptualization and Design

■ What are the program goals?
■ Which specific objectives must be fulfilled to achieve these goals?
■ Which HR activities will promote achievement of these objectives?
■ What types of human, material, and administrative supports are needed to
  support the proposed HR practices?
■ How will the HR practices be introduced?
■ Which employees will be affected by HR activities?
■ Which social and organizational processes are assumed to link HR activities
  to the program's objectives?
■ How will program progress be monitored, and how long will its impact be
  assessed?

Evaluating Program Conceptualization and Design

Evaluations of proposed or current programs can pose basic questions about program design and conceptualization, like the ones shown in Box 8.1. Program goals refer to broad ends, such as improving employee safety. Objectives specify measurable outcomes, such as a 20% reduction in accidents requiring medical attention. HR activities and practices refer to the means to obtain objectives, such as safety workshops. Measures for the performance of these activities can also be specified—for example, participation in the workshop by 90% of employees and receipt of passing grades by 80% of participants in safety assurance exercises.

Sometimes, a straightforward examination of design issues like those listed in Box 8.1 will be sufficient to uncover gaps between program objectives and the activities intended to lead to their achievement. In such instances, the evaluator can suggest ways to close these gaps.

Suppose, for example, that a consultant is asked to help a firm assess whether its management training and development programs will sustain its movement toward transnational operations—a complex, decentralized set of operations in many countries with many strategic alliances to local firms.

Case 8.1 indicates how the consultant could assess current HR needs and the design of current practices:[2]

Case 8.1

The consultant begins by defining the objectives of training and development programs in terms of developing the skills needed by transnational managers. Among these skills are ability to interact simultaneously with people from many cultures, to learn from them, and to treat them as equals. Then, the consultant describes HR practices that would foster these skills. These include formal training activities, on-the-job experiences, and career development among the firm's managers. Current practices are then compared to the ones needed to obtain program objectives. The recommendations would focus on closing gaps between current and desired practices in order to enhance skill development—for example, by increasing multinational participation in training programs and by treating international experience and cultural adaptability as important criteria for career development and promotion.

Preliminary evaluations like this one can uncover basic problems in the conceptualization and design of HR programs. These problems must be resolved if the program is to work successfully. Among the recurring problems is a failure to reach the target population—for example, by establishing sophisticated services for stress counseling that are accessible only to small numbers of employees. Another common problem is reliance on untested or unproven assumptions about the administrative or social processes that link resource allocation to program activities, program activities to program outcomes, and program outcomes to objectives (Nay et al., 1976). For example, health administrators in several nations have proposed to improve the quality of health services by introducing competition among hospitals, clinics, and individual health providers (Organization for Economic Cooperation and Development [OECD], 1992). But this proposal relies on unproven assumptions about the responses of health care providers to competitive forces. In contrast to some of the more optimistic of these assumptions, experience in several countries indicates that public health providers exposed to competition concentrate their efforts on marketing campaigns and on improving highly visible aspects of service quality, such as waiting times, while devoting little attention to improvements in clinical quality that would be invisible to patients and policymakers (Harrison, 1995).

Assessing Program Impact and Efficiency

Impact assessments, which are also known as *summative evaluations,* examine whether HR practices are achieving their objectives by producing specific outcomes. Summative evaluations answer questions like these: Did the introduction of selection interviews reduce turnover among service workers? Did a campaign for accident prevention reduce work accidents? Did programs to train employees to use state-of-the-art office technologies improve employee skills and enhance receptiveness to the new technologies? Did job redesign enhance productivity? Investigators typically derive outcome measures from the program's stated objectives in much the same way that they derive indicators of effectiveness (Chapter 3). This approach provides a direct and apparently unambiguous indication of program success.

To assess program efficiency, outcomes must be compared to program costs. For example, managers might want to assess the efficiency of off-site training sessions versus on-the-job training. To do so, estimates must be made of the costs of each type of training and the value of the outcomes. Where the outcomes are assumed to be identical, only costs need to be compared. In many instances, assessments of program efficiency founder on the difficulty of developing agreed-upon assessments of costs and outcomes. Utility analysis, which is discussed below, provides one well-developed set of techniques that can sometimes produce acceptable dollar estimates of costs and benefits.

Unfortunately, neither provisional evaluations of program design and conceptualization nor evaluations of program outcomes can explain the *causes* of program success or failure. Moreover, impact assessments often show that results were mixed—something well known by the people who planned and executed them. In addition, impact studies are often conducted after organizations have invested much time and money in program design and implementation. Hence, impact studies do not provide decision makers with much guidance concerning how to improve new programs. Nor do impact studies provide clear answers about what actions to take concerning established programs—for example, whether to try to improve the program, redesign it altogether, or abandon it.

Monitoring Program Implementation

To guide decisions like these, evaluation must provide data on the *process* of program implementation, as well as on its outcomes. By following a program from its origins through its entire development, investigators can identify the factors facilitating and hindering implementation. Decision makers can then redesign their programs on the basis of feedback from such implementation studies.

For example, to monitor an in-house program to retrain office workers to use voice mail, work stations, and electronic mail, the evaluator would examine all of the following phases in program planning and implementation: assessment of training needs; formulation of training objectives; allocation of resources to the training program; preparations for training sessions; training procedures; steps to ensure transfer of new skills, such as goal setting; changes in work design to encourage use of the new technologies; and provision of support services for users. Participants in training sessions and their supervisors would be observed or interviewed both during the training sessions and after them. Attention would be paid to issues such as attendance and involvement in the sessions, employee reactions to them, types of learning experiences offered, measures of learning and retention among participants, difficulties of transferring learned skills to the actual work situation, and facilitants and barriers to use of the new technologies within the workplace. These data would be used to account for program outcomes, including employee usage and receptiveness to the new technologies.

Implementation studies document conditions promoting successful implementation, as well as the degree of implementation and measurable program outcomes. *Formative evaluations,* which trace the early development of new programs, can help program planners and change strategists learn from the results of pilot programs or from the transition stage of large-scale program implementation. They can then revise the programs before implementing them fully (see Chapter 7). Findings concerning long-standing programs can help managers decide whether to continue such programs or redesign them.

The monitoring of complex programs can be broken down into stages, subprograms, or processes—such as program design, recruitment, training, implementation, performance assessment, and rewarding. Performance of each stage can be evaluated in terms of the production of specific interim results that are necessary for the program as a whole or for the execution of the next stage. Performance at each stage can also be evaluated in terms of costs and the time taken to complete a particular stage. Investigators and program managers can work together to define the program's stages and to derive measures of the required outcomes for each part.

Monitoring program implementation is more expensive and time consuming than is assessing impacts and costs. But program monitoring is also more likely to help clients pinpoint the sources of program success and failure and make informed decisions about the subsequent administration of the program. The choice to use one or more forms of evaluation must necessarily reflect the objectives of the assessment and the degree to which managers and other clients support it. This choice also depends on the background and skills of the evaluator. Moreover, it reflects a tradeoff between the greater costs and time requirements of the more complex forms of evaluation and their promise of providing richer and more useful findings.

Limitations of Evaluation Research

Despite their differences, all types of HRM evaluation share three limitations. First, by concentrating on short-term programs aimed at specific objectives, evaluations necessarily overlook ongoing HR practices and functions that often serve multiple and conflicting objectives. Hence, the techniques of evaluation do not contribute much to the assessment of the long-term impacts of fundamental HRM functions, such as staffing, employee development, or labor relations. When these enduring HRM functions are the focus of assessment and diagnosis, sharp-image diagnosis will prove more appropriate than will the evaluation techniques just reviewed. Techniques for assessing HRM's strategic contribution, which are discussed later in this chapter, can also contribute to the assessment of HRM's ongoing and long-term contributions.

Second, by concentrating on current administrative practices, the techniques of program evaluation can lead clients and consultants to accept the definition of organizational problems and needs that is built into these programs, rather than challenging these assumptions. In such cases, program evaluation can facilitate the improvement of current practices but is not likely to foster critical evaluation of current performance standards and practices and thereby contribute to double-loop organizational learning (Argyris &

Schon, 1996). For example, assessments of educational programs designed to encourage safe work practices may unwittingly reinforce the common assumption that responsibility for safety lies mainly with workers, rather than being shared with the managers and engineers who design worksites and work practices. In like manner, when HR personnel invest a lot of energy in evaluating the results of quality assurance programs, they may unwittingly strengthen the largely unsubstantiated assumption that quality improvements routinely produce dramatic improvements in organizational competitiveness (Harari, 1993; Steel & Jennings, 1992).[3]

By assessing the impact of all of an organization's HR practices on a broad range of effectiveness measures, consultants and managers can help clients question the assumptions built in to HR practices. Stakeholder assessments of HRM, which are discussed below, can also facilitate a more critical approach to current HR practices.

Third, program evaluation does not address the broader diagnostic issue of whether the organization as a whole or its HRM staff engage in the HR practices that can best contribute to organizational effectiveness or reduce critical forms of ineffectiveness. For example, even the most rigorous evaluation of an employee-involvement program will not indicate whether the program enhanced the firm's competitive position;[4] nor will such an evaluation necessarily help decision makers decide whether their energies might be better invested in other areas, such as enhancing teamwork with strategic partners. The assessment methods discussed in the rest of this chapter offer partial solutions to these limitations of program evaluation.

Benchmarking

General managers and HRM specialists often question whether their organization is developing the HR programs and practices that are most critical to success. One way to answer this question is through benchmarking (Glanz & Dailey, 1992; Hill, Mann, & Wearing, 1996). This technique involves measurement of a key HRM practice, followed by a comparison between practices in the focal organization and the best practices of other organizations in order to target areas for improvement. In very large organizations, such as multinationals, practices from other units within the same organization can be used as internal benchmarks. Benchmarking had its origins in investigations by one firm of another firm's practices in functional areas, such as production or distribution, in which the second firm has an outstanding reputation (Tucker, Zivan, & Camp, 1987).

Benchmarking can help HR managers decide which current practices should be encouraged and which new practices initiated. HR practitioners can also use benchmarking to help legitimate and justify investment in particular HR practices.

Nonsystematic HRM Benchmarking

Nonsystematic HRM benchmarking is a common practice, but it is very risky. Informal surveys of competitors' activities may yield information on programs that seem to contribute to success in the competing firm. Conferences and symposia that highlight successful HR activities encourage nonsystematic benchmarking, as does the granting of awards for outstanding managerial practices. Books and articles in academic journals and the business press also encourage managers to compare their activities to those of successful companies and to adopt the practices found in those companies. Management bestsellers can make benchmarking seem easy by formulating sets of management principles for self-assessment and recommendations for action. Blackburn and Rosen (1993) recently applied this approach directly to the HR practices associated with TQM. They interviewed HR professionals in the eight firms that had won the coveted Malcolm Baldrige National Quality Award. Based on these interviews and on company documents, the authors list a set of ideal HR practices that can serve as a benchmark for other firms.

Comparisons with other firms can stimulate members of an organization to evaluate their own practices carefully and can suggest alternative paths of action that deserve careful consideration. But nonsystematic benchmarking does not provide consistently valid assessments of HRM activities. The successes of many firms cited for distinction are often short-lived. The Wallace company filed for bankruptcy just 2 years after winning the Baldrige Award (Hill, 1993), and several of the companies cited by Peters and Waterman (1982) for excellence ran into financial difficulties shortly after the book's publication. Furthermore, the contribution of HR practices to success is often unclear and hard to determine. For example, interpretations vary as to whether the efforts to introduce TQM and win the Baldrige Award contributed to the decline at Wallace or enhanced the firm's ability to manage decline (Hill, 1993). Sometimes, the adoption of a popular HR practice by a successful firm is less a cause of success than a sign that its members can afford to indulge in the latest managerial fashions (Abrahamson, 1991).

A further difficulty with benchmarking derives from the risks of relying on generalizations from the experience of a very limited number of companies and on generalizations from one industry or nation to another.[5] Many reports on HR practices in highly successful organizations play down hard-to-replicate features of the organization that facilitated implementation of the HR practice or directly propelled organizational success. These features may include the organization's history; its market and financial positions; its managers' skills, experience, and personalities; its institutional and cultural environments; and its systems of politics and labor relations.

Research Supporting Systematic Benchmarking

Two major projects have sought to overcome these limitations by gathering data on large numbers of organizations. They illustrate both the promise and the limitations of systematic benchmarking. The Human Resource Competencies of the 1990s project (Ulrich, Brockbank, & Yeung, 1989; Ulrich, Yeung, Brockbank, & Lake, 1993) examined HRM in 250 large, diversified, U.S.-based firms. This study showed clear variations among industries in HR practices at both the operational and strategic levels. The authors concluded that industry conditions determined the ways that HR practices should be delivered (Ulrich et al., 1989, p. 331). The "Best International HRM Practices" project is a multicountry, multiresearcher effort to determine best practices in both domestic and globally oriented firms (Von Glinow, 1993). Preliminary data from this study show wide variations in HRM practice that reflect each country's economic profiles and culture (see also Sparrow et al., 1994).

The greatest contribution of these studies is their documentation of wide variations in HR practices between countries, between industries, and under varying organizational contingencies. These findings suggest that comparisons of HR practices should be made within countries and within industries or sectors. Attempts to copy practices from other countries or even from other sectors within a single country may not be successful. The studies also suggest that systematic attention to HRM may indeed contribute to a company's financial success.

Unfortunately, these ambitious studies so far provide only limited opportunities for benchmarking by individual firms. The schemes used for surveying and reporting HR practices are so general that little detail is obtained on many of the concrete HR activities of interest to practicing managers. Managers and HRM consultants may eventually be able to use the international data to determine whether a particular firm relies more or less on interviews as a selection device or stresses training for teamwork more or less than do other firms. But HR managers will not learn from the data whether other firms are using specific techniques of interest, such as cafeteria benefits, particular types of employee assistance programs, or new techniques for providing employee feedback to supervisors. Nor will they be able to find systematic data on the effects of these practices within their industry.[6]

Prospects for Benchmarking

At its best, benchmarking can help managers identify HR practices that contribute to organizational performance and effectiveness. HR professionals can also use benchmarking to cultivate credibility within their own organization (Ulrich et al., 1989). In addition to facilitating assessment of current programs, benchmarking can aid decision making about changes in HR practices. But benchmarking serves these ends best when data are available on the contribution of the specific HR practices in question to organizational success. Until recently, hard evidence about the contribution of HRM to success was quite limited, and the available empirical studies suffered from methodological limitations (Block, Kleiner, Roomkin, & Salsburg, 1987). Recent research (Huselid, 1995) shows that a small set of high-performance work practices can reduce turnover, enhance productivity, and thereby contribute to corporate financial performance. Moreover, effective strategic HR practices—including teamwork, employee participation, productivity incentives, and quality assurance—have been shown to contribute to the financial performance of firms (Huselid, Jackson, & Schuler, 1997). However, no evidence is yet available concerning the appropriateness of specific HR practices to the distinctive conditions prevailing at the level of individual firms.

Benchmarking is most applicable to HR practices that can readily be copied from one organization to another. But only organizations that have a high capacity and readiness for change and can undertake sustained implementation programs are likely to succeed at introducing major design innovations, such as TQM. Transplanting HR practices from one nation to another or from a given institutional, industrial, or sectoral setting to another also requires careful planning and assessment of the ways that contextual forces affect the HR practice (Adler & Jelinek, 1986; Chimezie & Osigweh, 1989; Fottler, 1981).

Finally, HR practitioners and consultants who wish to use benchmarking as an assessment technique should bear in mind that many of today's large and famous organizations are currently struggling with major challenges to their continued success or are likely to encounter such challenges in the near future. Managers who uncritically adopt the practices prevailing in other organizations run the risk of copying practices that do not currently contribute to organizational adaptiveness and flexibility and may actually hinder success. As two veteran researchers of organizational design have correctly observed, practices like benchmarking may encourage imitation of the wrong organizations:

> Indiscriminate empirical studies are much more likely to reveal practices which are threatening survival than practices which are fostering survival, much more likely to observe transient characteristics than stable characteristics, much more likely to find practices which dissatisfy some stakeholders than practices which satisfy everyone, and much more likely to find characteristics which are generating social problems than characteristics which are solving social problems. If some organizations are worth imitating, they are peculiar organizations that have to be chosen carefully from the general population. . . . Well designed organizations would differ from most current organizations. . . . Such organizations would probably be seen as suspect deviants by their environments—which appreciate conformity to societal norms and values. (Starbuck & Nystrom, 1986, pp. 8-9)

Assessing HRM's Strategic Contribution

HR practices can run smoothly and achieve their stated objectives at the operational and managerial levels without contributing much to overall organizational success. However, recent research and theory indicate that HRM systems can directly affect a firm's financial performance and its sustained competitive advantage (Becker & Gerhart, 1996; Huselid, 1995). HR practices contribute most directly to competitive advantage and to performance when they elicit behavior that is consistent with the firm's strategy and with its environmental contingencies (Huselid & Becker, 1997; Huselid et al., 1997).

The strategic HRM approach leads to direct assessments of whether HRM helps the organization obtain its strategic goals, thereby contributing to competitive advantage (Fombrun et al., 1984; Lengnick-Hall & Lengnick-Hall, 1988). The strategic approach to HRM can also support decision making and planning about ways to use HR practices to obtain strategic advantage and ways to enhance fit between HRM and competitive strategy. Strategic HRM can concentrate on either the total organization or the managerial and operational levels of HRM, where organizational strategies are translated into actual practice.

Organizational Level

Organizational-level assessments of the strategic contribution of HRM can start by assessing the fits among HRM activities and between HRM and the other system components—such as environment, strategy, technology, and structure (Jackson & Schuler, 1995; see also Chapter 2). It is also possible to examine fits between HR policies and practices at different structural levels (Millman, Von Glinow, & Nathan, 1991). To assess fits, the investigator defines the HRM inputs called for by current strategies and then examines the extent to which HRM supplies the needed inputs. This approach guided the investigation proposed in Case 8.1. To take another example, if the organizational strategy of a firm calls for competition on service quality, fit assessment would examine the degree to which staffing, development, compensation, and work design support service excellence. Later in this section, we will show how to extend organizational-level assessments like these to the functional level.

HRM fits can also be assessed with the aid of life cycle models (Chapter 11). An organization's strategy and its system components undergo major shifts as the organization moves through the life cycle. These changes create new demands on the HRM function (Baird & Meshulam, 1988; Fombrum et al., 1984, pp. 35-41). For example, an organization that is structured along functional lines can usually rely on HR practices that encourage functional orientations and departmental goals. As the firm moves toward diversified operations, its HR practices need to foster cross-functional skills and orientation toward the goals of the corporation as a whole. Many practices in areas such as staffing, training, and rewarding may have to be reorganized to shift managers' loyalties from their own departments or divisions to the organization as a whole.

It is possible to develop detailed models of HRM requirements at each stage of the life cycle and then assess the extent to which actual practices fulfill these requirements (Baird & Meshulam, 1988). Although informative, these models can become quite abstract and are generally more normative than descriptive in nature. Moreover, these life cycle models can overstate the case for achieving fit. Their most important contribution to HRM assessment is to sensitize consultants and practitioners to possible effects of life cycle developments on the functional requirements for HRM.

In HRM, as in other areas of system functioning (see Chapter 2), tight fit among system components can reduce flexibility—in the sense of ability to adapt quickly to changing internal and external conditions (Becker & Gerhart, 1996; Lengnick-Hall & Lengnick-Hall, 1988; Millman et al., 1991). HRM enhances flexibility when it encourages members to monitor their environment carefully and critically and to exercise initiative and creativity in responding to the environment. HRM can also promote organizational flexibility by ensuring that staff members have the capacity for adaptive behavior and by encouraging the development of a broad set of skills that applies to diverse and rapidly changing conditions.

When organizations press toward tight integration among HRM practices and fit between HRM and other organizational features, they often cut back HRM activities that facilitate adaptiveness. These include staff development programs that build a wide range of skills, innovative work designs, and reward and appraisal systems that foster innovation and creativity. The trade-off between fit and flexibility can be especially serious when tight fits are sought between HRM practices at corporate headquarters and those engaged in by foreign subsidiaries (Millman et al., 1991) or semiautonomous strategic business units within divisionalized firms.

Achieving tight fit between HRM, strategy, and structure appears to be most appropriate in organizations that anticipate long-term operations in current markets and environmental sectors, and that stress operational control and cost efficiency. These concerns are more characteristic of organizations in the Formalization and Control stage of the life cycle (Chapter 11) than for firms in the earlier Entrepreneurial and Collectivity stages (Millman et al., 1991). But even in the Formalization stage, organizations need to encourage innovation and flexibility at the same time that they drive toward coordination and control. Organizations in the Elaboration stage typically operate in very dynamic and diversified environments. These conditions require both flexibility and the integration of diverse operations (Millman et al., 1991).

Sometimes, HRM can serve as a tool for creating new sources of competitive advantage, rather than simply supporting current business strategies

(Schuler & MacMillan, 1984). For example, for many years, IBM trained programmers in its customer firms as a way of cementing the links between those firms and IBM. Organizations can also achieve competitive advantage if they use HRM to differentiate products and services from those of other firms, or to cut costs and introduce operating efficiencies. Because most firms do not use HRM proactively to foster competitive advantage, consideration of this possibility is more important as an aid to managerial decision making and planning decisions than as a guide to assessment.

Functional Level

To guide assessment and decision making at the managerial and operational levels of HRM, consultants and practitioners need to define and assess the links between organizational strategies and specific HRM activities. Strategic Performance Measurement and Management (Schneier, Shaw, & Beatty, 1991), a technique originally designed to facilitate strategy implementation, can be adapted to guide the assessment of these links in the strategy-HRM chain. Figure 8.1 shows how the technique can be used for assessment purposes.

To start, top managers must agree on a few critical success factors (CSFs) and core competencies. CSFs and core competencies make explicit what the organization must do to succeed. They reflect current and anticipated conditions within the organization and its environment and the competitive strategies used by the organization (see Chapter 13). Take the case of a mail-order retailing firm that competes primarily by differentiating its services from those of its competitors. This firm's CSFs could include maintaining outstanding customer relations, guaranteeing smooth distribution channels, and targeting merchandise to customer tastes. Additional CSFs for this firm would include capabilities required for continued profitability, such as the ability to locate low-cost suppliers of quality merchandise.

After CSFs have been defined, consultants and clients need to define the specific HR activities needed to achieve CSF objectives. If excellent service is a CSF, then HR practices that support service must be defined and assessed. At the operational level, these practices include supervisory behavior that ensures attention to customer inquiries and complaints. At the managerial level, service can be fostered through appraisal and reward systems that provide incentives for excellent service. Consultants and clients can then

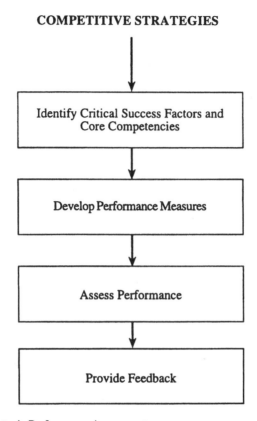

COMPETITIVE STRATEGIES

Identify Critical Success Factors and Core Competencies

Develop Performance Measures

Assess Performance

Provide Feedback

Figure 8.1 Strategic Performance Assessment

specify performance measures for the desired operations at the individual, workgroup, and unit levels. With the aid of these measures, diagnosticians can judge how well operational- and managerial-level HRM contributes to the CSFs.

Strategic performance measurement also requires assessment of fits between the practices designed to promote achievement of CSF objectives and other system elements, including technology, culture, and organizational structure. For example, a firm will face difficulties in using bonuses to encourage customer service if pay has traditionally depended mainly on seniority and prior training, and if the organizational culture discourages competition among employees. Once these assessments have been completed, the findings can provide feedback to decision makers responsible for taking the actions needed to enhance the organization's competitive advantage.

Applying the Strategic HRM Framework

The strategic HRM framework can help consultants, HR professionals, and line managers assess the contributions of current HR practices to an organization's strategic success and can serve as a valuable framework for managerial decision making and planning. However, this approach neglects the possibility that HRM, like other functions, can contribute actively to strategy formation, rather than simply reflecting strategic mandates from top management. In many organizations, strategies emerge through interactions among divergent functions and units, rather than being systematically formulated and imposed by top management. In such cases, matching HR practices to current strategies will not be sufficient to contribute to the development of competitive strategies. Instead, the human resource function can contribute to strategic advantage by picking up weak signals of important developments within the organization's environment—such as changes in labor market or regulatory conditions—and making others in the organization aware of these developments (Bamberger & Phillips, 1991).

More generally, none of the applications of the strategic HRM approach directly assesses the adequacy of the current organizational strategy. Instead, analyses of HRM's strategic contributions accept as given the strategic priorities and directions that have been defined by top management. An additional drawback of the strategic HRM approach is that it does not confront conceptual and practical problems that are inherent in the concepts of organizational strategy—such as the political, organizational, and cognitive constraints on rational decision making (Eisenhardt & Zbaracki, 1992; Harrison & Phillips, 1991); the tendencies toward emergent, incremental, post hoc, and even anarchic strategy formation (Quinn, 1980; Weick, 1985); and the ability of organizations to pursue ambiguous and conflicting strategies at the same time (Cameron & Quinn, 1988). Such ambiguities and conflicts will create difficulties when the investigator seeks to operationalize and measure the activities that support current strategies. Tracing the links between overall strategies and HR practices and assessing fits between HRM and strategy will prove particularly difficult in not-for-profit organizations. There is often limited agreement within these organizations on goals and strategies. Moreover, it is very hard to create adequate measures of the obtainment of strategic objectives for many public sector organizations (Fottler, 1987; Kanter & Summers, 1987).

Utility Analysis

Decision makers who receive diagnostic feedback or seek to plan HR changes often want data on the cost-effectiveness of proposed actions. Similarly, consultants and HR practitioners sometimes seek to assess the immediate contribution of particular HR activities to business operations without having to diagnose the entire HR function or having to examine HR's strategic contributions. These assessments of the impact of HRM practices on business expenditures or revenues can help make top management more aware of the contributions of HRM to business success (Schlesinger & Heskett, 1991).

Quantitative assessments of HRM's business contribution require estimates of the dollar costs and benefits of specific HR practices (Fitz-Enz, 1984). Costs are usually easier to estimate than are benefits. For example, the costs of hiring a new staff member can be computed by adding the costs for all HR activities related to recruiting, selecting, and training new recruits, divided by the number of recruits handled (Fitz-Enz, 1980).

Estimating HR benefits, as opposed to costs, is trickier but not impossible. Studies based on utility analysis (UA) provide several formulas for calculating the dollar benefits (after costs) of a particular HR practice, such as the use of a selection test or a training program (Boudreau, 1991). UA models have been used mainly in research on the benefits of selection practices, and to a lesser degree on placement and classification practices. Applications to training programs have also been attempted. In principle, UA can also be applied to many other HR practices and can be adapted for broader assessment purposes or as aids to decision making.[7]

Applying Utility Analysis

The UA formula that is most applicable to assessing HR practices is the Brogden-Cornback-Glaser (BCG) model (Boudreau, 1991, pp. 636-639). To illustrate the application of this model, suppose that the HR staff in a firm wants to assess the benefits of continuing to use a particular selection practice, such as a pen-and-pencil test of math abilities. The BCG model shows how to estimate the incremental benefit in dollars of using the results of this test, as

Table 8.1 One-Cohort Entry-Level Selection Utility Decision

Cost-Benefit Information	Entry-Level Computer Programmers
Current employment	4,404
Number separating	618
Number selected (N_s)	618
Average tenure in years (T)	9.69
Test information	
Number of applicants (N_{app})	1,236
Testing cost/applicant	$10
Total test cost (C)	$12,360
Average test score ($\overline{Z}_x$)	.80 SD
Validity ($r_{x,y}$)	.76
SD_y (per person-year)	$10,413

Utility Computation

Quantity = Average tenure × applicants selected
= 9.69 years × 618 applicants
= 5,988 person-years
Quality = Average test score × test validity × SD_y
= .80 × .76 × $10,413
= $6,331 per person-year
Utility   = (Quantity × quality) – cost
= (5,988 person-years × $6,331 per person-year)– $12,360
= $37.9 million

SOURCE: Boudreau (1988).

opposed to selecting applicants without using the test. Once we have estimated the expected benefits of using the test for any given applicant, its costs per applicant can be subtracted to obtain a measure of its net benefit.

Table 8.1 applies this model to assessing the benefits of using a selection test for 618 entry-level computer programmers employed by the U.S. government. It is assumed, based on past data, that the programmers will stay on the job an average of 9.69 years. The entry for validity in the table reflects the quality of the selection test—measured in terms of its ability to predict to performance criteria (such as supervisors' ratings) that are assumed to be highly correlated with job performance. The standard deviation term in the table estimates the dollar value of a one-standard-deviation difference in job performance among the applicant population. This term thus estimates the dollar utility obtained by reducing variation through improved selection. These improvements can result from cost savings, generation of more or higher-priced services, or increased productivity. The estimated utility of employing the selection test is the expected quantity improvement times the quality of the estimate, minus the cost of testing.

The utility estimates obtained from formulas like those used in Table 8.1 remain positive even when much less optimistic assumptions are made about the payoff of using a particular test or about its ability to predict performance. Suppose that we estimate that the test examined in the table has very low predictive ability (r_{xy} = .1 instead of .76), and we assume that the payoffs of reducing variations in employee performance are also limited (SD = $100 per year rather than $10,413, as estimated in Table 8.1). Rerunning the calculations in Table 8.1 shows that there will still be an expected utility of $35,544 from using the test.

UA models can also be manipulated to identify the *break-even points* for particular HR practices. A major advantage of calculating break-even points is that investigators do not have to commit themselves to estimates of the actual payoffs of the HR practice. To justify continued use of the practice, they need to assume only that the payoffs exceed the figures produced by the break-even calculation.

UA models can be made more precise by including estimates for hidden costs, such as service costs associated with higher volumes of corporate activity, and taxes on expected benefits from HR practices. Selection models can also be made more sophisticated by taking into account the movement of recruits through the organization and their turnover patterns. These models can aid decisions concerning HR practices affecting recruitment, internal organizational movement, and separation from the organization, as well as selection. As computer applications become more sophisticated, HR managers and consultants may find these more complex models useful for applications to assessment and decision making. However, the added complexity and sophistication of the UA formulas could make UA results harder to interpret and explain, and could discourage many potential users.

The Utility of Utility Analysis

In conclusion, let us note some of the possible benefits and disadvantages (or costs) of using UA as an assessment technique. First, as the above illustration shows, UA can provide HR practitioners and other decision makers with dramatic, quantitative evidence of the bottom-line payoffs of routine HR practices. UA studies of selection tests have typically estimated major dollar benefits. These results hold up even under far less optimistic estimates than those used in the original studies. Moreover, the estimated benefits far exceed the break-even level (Boudreau, 1991, p. 664).

Second, UA can serve as a useful aid to HR decision making. Practitioners can use it to compare the anticipated utility of alternative HR practices, or to decide whether a proposed practice is likely to yield enough dollar benefits to offset its costs. The very process of thinking systematically about the costs and benefits of HR practices may also improve decision making, even if it does not yield unambiguous results.

Despite these benefits, consultants and diagnostic practitioners should note three major disadvantages of UA. First, UA requires reliance on many untested assumptions, which often raise doubts about the validity or applicability of the estimates. For example, to estimate the dollar payoffs of improved selection, the analysts have to decide which aspects of performance are likely to be affected. But there is no agreed-upon procedure for estimating the impacts of selection on quality and quantity of work, work costs, and the price that can be obtained for services or products sold. Nor is there any widely accepted measure of job performance differences on any scale, let alone dollars (Boudreau, 1991, p. 660)! Calculating break-even values for the parameters in the models can reduce the severity of the problem of estimating model parameters but does not eliminate it.

Second, as with most rational decision approaches, UA assumes that the people participating in HRM decisions can agree about complicated empirical and value issues. In practice, HR managers often face complex decisions in which they must weigh noncomparable and unmeasurable factors, such as legal constraints and the fit between an HR practice and the organization's personnel and culture, as well as estimated dollar costs and benefits. Third, reliance on UA as an assessment or decision technique can lead consultants and managers to overlook important but virtually unquantifiable features of HRM—such as the effects of training programs on organizational learning, or the relations between reward systems and innovation. Fourth, the very sophistication of the UA techniques may restrict the ability of HR practitioners or consultants to apply them to a wide range of practices and to diffuse their results to a broad range of clients. Because of these difficulties, UA has thus far remained the province of a small group of researchers. Still, the growing pressure on HR managers to provide hard evidence of HRM effectiveness can gradually lead to the diffusion of the UA approach.

Stakeholder Assessment

The multiple stakeholder approach to effectiveness (Tsui, 1990; see also Chapter 3) points to the need for examining how HR practices are assessed by internal stakeholders who receive HR services or are affected by them. Stakeholder assessment can help managers and consultants deal systematically with the conflicting expectations to which HR professionals are subject, as well as with the very wide range of services provided by HR units. Stakeholder assessment is based on the assumption that HR practices are diverse and are meant to satisfy many different units and groups within the focal organization. Hence, HR practices must be assessed in terms of multiple criteria, rather than a single criterion. Moreover, HRM is assumed to include many important services—such as ensuring conformity to equal opportunity legislation or advising employees about retirement options—that do not have clear, measurable benefits and cannot be readily linked to the organization's guiding strategies and goals. Instead, the importance and effectiveness of these operations must be judged by the members of the organization who have a stake in them.

To conduct a stakeholder assessment of an HR unit, consultants and managers can carry out the following five activities: (a) identify stakeholders, (b) specify HR services or outputs received by stakeholders, (c) survey stakeholders concerning HR outputs, (d) analyze findings, and (e) provide feedback.

Stakeholders can be identified in two ways. The first method involves asking the managers of the HR unit to list the groups with which their unit interacts as it carries out its activities (Tsui, 1990). This method has the advantage of determining the unique groups that are most relevant to the HR unit's everyday operations, but it may overlook more distant services and stakeholders, such as the union's work committee or the organization's top management. This method is best suited for assessments aimed at providing HR practitioners with feedback about their work. The second method for identifying stakeholders involves asking organizational members to specify *all* of the units that regularly receive services from the HR unit or provide parallel services, such as training in computer skills. To this set may be added the manager to whom the head of HR reports. This second method is preferable when the assessment data will be fed back to top management, rather than to members of the HR unit. These data will help top management see how key power holders and members of competing units evaluate the HR unit.

Once the stakeholders have been identified, the heads or representatives of stakeholder groups are asked to list critical services or outputs of the HR unit. The respondents can then be asked to rate how well the HR unit provides the most important of these services. In addition, the respondents can be asked to rate the overall effectiveness of the HR unit (Tsui, 1990, p. 469). Data analysis focuses on the degree to which current forms of HRM meet the expectations of divergent stakeholders. The analysis can look for points of agreement and disagreement among stakeholders and for HR services or outputs that are regarded as particularly problematic by more than one type of stakeholder. Feedback can provide overall effectiveness ratings, and it can also pinpoint types of services or outputs to which stakeholders assign very positive or negative ratings.

Stakeholder assessment can also be used to diagnose diffuse HR functions, such as training or employee safety, that are not the sole responsibility of a particular HR unit. In this case, the investigator asks clients to name all of the groups that have a stake in the function being studied. The consultant might include additional stakeholding groups after conducting a prestudy of the functional area. The respondents are then asked to rate the contribution of these workgroups to the HR function and to rate how effectively the function is performed in their organization.[8]

Stakeholder assessments inject awareness of the political character of organizations into the assessment of functions such as HRM. Moreover, this type of analysis can help HR professionals locate those groups and individuals who are particularly dissatisfied with their HR services and activities. Very negative ratings of HR operations can encourage decision makers to examine the sources of these ratings and can serve as inputs into a sharp-image diagnosis of the HR function.

Despite its contributions, the stakeholder approach also possesses significant limitations. In particular, stakeholder assessments are necessarily subjective. They also do not assess the impact of HRM on important organizational states, such as competitiveness and flexibility. Hence, stakeholder assessments that report high levels of consensus about HRM and satisfaction with this function run the risk of overstating the contribution of HRM to organizational effectiveness, whereas assessments that uncover discord and dissatisfaction may underestimate HRM's contributions to the organization as a system.

Conclusion

With the exception of stakeholder assessments, the models examined in this chapter treat HR practices mainly as managerial tools. Hence, they treat HR practices as more readily designable and controllable and as less emergent than they are in practice. Moreover, program evaluation, stakeholder analysis, and utility analysis all share a serious limitation: They do not encourage users to view current HR practices in a broad, strategic context, nor to compare these practices to those prevailing elsewhere. The narrow focus of these techniques may produce the unintended effect of encouraging both analysts and recipients of feedback to accept current practices as given, rather than raising questions about the desirability of current practices and about the assumptions and standards that are built into them.

Despite these similarities, each of the assessment techniques examined here stresses a different assessment criterion. Program evaluation concentrates on the attainment of stated or derived HRM objectives and the degree of HR program implementation. Utility analysis looks at dollar costs and benefits of HR activities, whereas strategic HRM introduces an open-systems perspective by examining links between HRM and organizational strategy. Benchmarking compares current practices to those presumed to contribute to success in other organizations. In contrast, by using a political frame, stakeholder assessment stresses that HRM, like all organizational functions, must simultaneously meet the needs and expectations of divergent groups and individuals.

The techniques examined in this chapter pay limited attention to the contribution of HRM to internal system states that are sometimes taken as indicators of effectiveness. These include interpersonal relations, smooth workflow, internal consensus, and cooperation (Chapters 3 and 6). Yet HR practitioners trained in the behavioral sciences have historically placed great emphasis on fostering these internal system states. The neglect of these system states and the stress on HRM as a management tool reflect the pressures to which HR professionals have been subject in the past two decades to contribute to business success. Consultants and managers who wish to supplement assessments aimed at bottom-line results with attention to internal system states can draw on the model provided in Chapter 6, along with the procedure for assessing system fits discussed in Chapter 2.

None of the approaches reviewed adequately illuminates the symbolic functions of HR practices. Yet HR activities play an important role in shaping organizational culture. For example, employee-involvement programs rely on and sometimes foster optimistic assumptions about the willingness and ability of rank-and-file employees to contribute to their organization. These basic assumptions contrast dramatically with the assumptions about employees implicit in traditional forms of work design. In addition, HR activities shape the image of an organization held by both employees and outsiders. Even when popular HR practices do not alter performance, their adoption can help an organization demonstrate its progressiveness and can project management's dedication to values such as employee welfare or customer satisfaction.

In short, the techniques reviewed here can provide useful supplements to diagnosis but cannot serve as substitutes for it. Nor do the techniques embody a comprehensive view of the development and effects of HRM. In particular, more attention is needed to ways that HR activities become embedded in the contexts of emergent organizational behavior and in organizational cultures and subcultures. These contexts are explored more thoroughly in the next two chapters.

Notes

1. See Chapter 1, Note 1.

2. This illustration is derived from a report by Adler and Bartholomew (1992) of a study of the human resource programs in 50 North American firms. The study assessed the degree to which these programs contribute to the development of the competencies required for managers in transnational firms.

3. Limited evidence that quality programs may affect competitiveness appears in research conducted by Lawler et al. (1992, p. 108). Executives in manufacturing firms reported that total quality practices enhanced productivity, quality, and customer service, whereas executives in service firms reported that these practices contributed to competitiveness, profitability, and quality of work outcomes. Only perceived impacts were studied.

4. In fact, research indicates that employee-involvement programs often contribute to employee satisfaction but less frequently make noticeable contributions to bottom-line outcomes, such as productivity, which in turn affects competitiveness (Steel & Jennings, 1992).

5. In contrast to the intuitive generalizations that prevail in the business press and in many academic publications, the statistical technique of meta-analysis (Hunter, Schmidt, & Jackson, 1982) does provide a basis for making valid inferences from the findings of multiple research studies, each of which investigated only one firm or a small number of firms.

6. Ulrich and his colleagues (1989, 1993) do report that particular HR practices were linked to the firm's perceived competence, which in turn is correlated with its financial performance.

7. The following discussion draws on Boudreau's (1991) comprehensive survey of UA. We stress the applications of UA research to assessment and adopt a more critical view of the approach than does Boudreau.

8. Stakeholder analysis has also been used to obtain ratings of the performance of individual HR professionals (Ulrich et al., 1995).

Emergent Behavior and Workforce Diversity

Diagnosis frequently requires both a broad overview of the client organization and close-up examination of behavior, interpretations, and informal structures that emerge gradually, rather than being designed and set in place by managerial fiat. Emergent behavior and members' interpretations of internal and external developments shape the organizational context in which organizational problems and challenges must be diagnosed and confronted. Furthermore, practitioners of sharp-image diagnosis often discover that these "soft" organizational features lie behind difficulties in implementing design programs, or lead to other forms of organizational ineffectiveness, such as gaps between current and desired levels of performance.

This chapter and the next provide practitioners of diagnosis and organizational decision makers with frames for examining emergent forms of behavior and interpretation, and with methods for investigating them. The first part of this chapter focuses on the diagnosis of gaps between emergent behavior and official mandates. The second part examines how emergent behavior is shaped by workforce diversity. In response to growing concern about the management of diversity, this discussion provides guidelines and a diagnostic framework for assessing group and organizational effects of diversity. Particular attention is given to the gendering of organizations, because emergent behavior typically reflects gender relations and is affected by them, and because gender relations are of increasing concern to managers and other organizational stakeholders.

A fine-grained examination of everyday actions within an organization can draw in part on the open-systems frame and models elaborated in previous chapters. However, the assessment of emergent behavior and structures requires more attention than the systems models provide to *patterns of interaction and interpretation* among members of the focal organization. To attain the needed focus, this chapter and the next draw on several theoretical frames that help sensitize consultants and managers to the development and influence of emergent organizational action. These partly overlapping frames include the *political frame,* which was introduced in Chapters 3 and 5; a *negotiation frame,* which treats administrative structures and practices as emerging in part through negotiations among organizational participants (Strauss, Schatzman, Ehrlich, Boeker, & Sabshin, 1963); and an *interpretive frame,* which stresses the impacts of the meanings that members assign to events within and outside the organization. Although these perspectives help sensitize observers to important features of organizational life, none has been formalized into systematic models that can serve as diagnostic guides.

We have used the interpretive frame in previous chapters without fully spelling out the ideas embodied in it. To develop the frame here, we draw on the perspective of *symbolic interaction* (Charon, 1995; Farberman & Perinbanayagam, 1985). This perspective assumes that the interpretations that people make of other people's behavior, organizational arrangements, and external conditions shape their own behavior and ultimately influence the behavior of others as well. The dependence of organized activity on these processes of sensemaking (Weick, 1979) introduces uncertainties and dynamics into organizational functioning that are not well depicted by the open-systems, structural, or political frames. Sensemaking within organizations produces particularly tangible consequences when shared interpretations crystallize into organizational cultures and subcultures (Chapter 10).

Gaps Between Emergent Behavior
and Official Mandates

Diagnosis can profit from examining gaps between officially mandated behavior and processes and those that emerge and prevail in practice (Chapter
2). These gaps develop because members redefine organizational instructions,
procedures, and rules through interpretation and negotiation. These processes
can gradually lead to the emergence of working arrangements that diverge
radically from official descriptions of organizational practices and from
official norms about how people should act.

Gaps between official mandates and actual practice partly reflect the effects
of symbolic interaction among people at work. To work together, organizational members must develop expectations about the people with whom they
come into contact. Gradually, these members adjust their expectations about
how other actors will behave in response to their own *interpretations* of the
other actors' behavior (Morrione, 1985; Silverman, 1970). Individual and
joint actions flow from these adjusted expectations. To illustrate these processes, suppose that Ms. Jones, a new group supervisor in a large firm, arrives
10 to 15 minutes late for work on several occasions. Jones's superior, Ms.
Hunt, interprets these instances of lateness as resulting from poor motivation.
Once she has developed this explanation for Jones's behavior, Hunt will
probably attribute Jones's future latenesses to the same cause and will use her
implicit theory to explain other forms of unsatisfactory behavior by Jones.
Hunt will thus begin to treat Jones quite differently than she would have had
she initially attributed Jones's lateness to some other cause, such as transit
strikes or difficulties in obtaining adequate child care. Jones, too, interprets
Hunt's (presumed) thoughts and actions. Then Jones acts in keeping with this
interpretation. For instance, Jones might conclude that her boss, who has no
children, lacks tolerance for workers with small children and regards family
obligations as a barrier to achievement at work. This interpretation might lead
Jones to look for another job or to become resigned to the "facts" that her boss
is biased against her and that her chances for promotion are limited.

Interactions also evolve through implicit and explicit negotiations between
individuals and groups over the terms of their relations. Sometimes, these
negotiations become very visible because they involve many parties and are
subject to formal procedures. Negotiations of work grievances by unions are

one common example. More frequently, negotiation plays a part in everyday interaction and talk and is hard to discern. Take the emergent relations between Ms. Jones and Ms. Hunt. Suppose that when Jones was first reprimanded for being late, she replied that she would make up the lost work at lunch time. This response contains an attempt to renegotiate some of the terms of Jones's employment, and perhaps those of other group members. Jones implied by her proposal that she was entitled to some discretion in the organization of work time, as long as her performance was not affected. Her boss, Ms. Hunt, could have accepted or rejected this suggestion. If Hunt accepted the proposal, the conversation would have led to a barely noticeable redefinition of Jones's work hours and responsibilities. Noticing the shift, other people in the office might also have sought to negotiate for greater flexibility in their working arrangements. Had they done so successfully, a new set of practices and expectations about work would have emerged within the office.

As this example suggests, the processes of interpretation and negotiation can gradually produce outcomes that become routinized. Of particular importance for organizational operations are the routinization of emergent structures of communication and work relations (Brass & Burkhardt, 1993; Ibarra, 1993). These are the "informal structures" or "grapevines" on which people rely to find out what is really going on in their organization. People also rely on emergent structures to bypass hierarchical reporting arrangements and control mechanisms in order to get work done faster or promote their own interests at work.

Although emergent behavior and relations can become very stable and predictable, they can also change rapidly. Changes or uncertainties in the set of interacting people, in work conditions, tasks, technologies, and administrative rules and procedures all provide opportunities for renegotiation of working relations (Barley, 1986; Maines & Charlton, 1985; Strauss et al., 1963). Emergent behavior patterns can also undergo change if influential group members start behaving differently or develop new perceptions of their own actions, others' actions, and organizational conditions. The processes of mutual interpretation and negotiation in organizations thus introduce complex and dynamic forces into work relations, and sometimes into the operation of the organization as a whole. These microprocesses are more likely to produce organizationwide effects during the early stages in an organization's life cycle and during other periods when organizational routines are disrupted and ambiguity is high, such as crises or major design changes (House et al., 1995).

Focusing on Emergent Practices

What benefits can analysis of emergent practices bring to diagnosis and consultation? First, this type of analysis focuses attention on the implementation of programs of planned change, rather than on their formulation (see Chapters 7 and 13). Specialists who do not work on the shop floor, top managers, directors, and other external policymakers often arrive at their decisions and formulate plans and programs without much contact with the people responsible for implementation. In contrast, investigators who look at organizations as fields for negotiation and reinterpretation expect to find gaps between decisions made far from the units or levels that are ultimately responsible for implementation. Once decision makers recognize that negotiation and reinterpretation cannot be "engineered out" of the implementation process, they are more likely to value feedback on implementation. Assessments conducted during implementation can provide data on valuable innovations and alterations introduced by recipients of planned change, as well as expose problems and difficulties requiring attention. By conducting assessments during the early phases of implementation, management can deal with developments that will become harder and more expensive to remedy as implementation progresses.

The advantages of conducting formative evaluations throughout implementation, rather than waiting until programs have been up and running for several years, can be seen in the divergent approaches adopted in Sweden and Britain toward design changes in the countries' national health systems (Harrison, 1995). In both countries, politicians designed and introduced far-reaching reforms during the early 1990s. These reforms subjected public service providers to competition and to payments that reflected patient choices and preferences. In Sweden, the politicians who formulated the reforms supported prompt follow-up studies of the reform process. These assessments showed many unanticipated developments. Among them was a rapid increase in total hospital costs resulting from the physicians' (over)enthusiastic response to incentives for departmental productivity. Recognition of unanticipated developments like these led the politicians to redesign program features that were raising costs and threatening to destabilize the entire health system. In contrast, the British politicians and change agents who pushed for reform resisted calls for evaluation, claiming that the reforms had not yet had time to prove themselves. The result has been a change process that seems to be running out of control and is producing many unanticipated and undesired outcomes.

A second benefit of focusing on emergent behavior is that emergent patterns can help explain ineffective outcomes, such as declining customer satisfaction, that form focal points for sharp-image consultation. By focusing on gaps between official and emergent behavior, consultants can uncover sources of ineffectiveness and point to issues requiring managerial attention. Clients can, in turn, reduce gaps between official and emergent practices by creating incentives for desired behavior and by tightening controls over ongoing practices. Clients can also reduce gaps by redefining their expectations and more closely matching managerial mandates to emergent realities.

Gaps between official mandates and emergent behavior can occur in almost any aspect of organizational operations. Some gaps reflect effects of political behavior, such as those discussed in Chapter 5. Here are additional types of emergent behavior that make appropriate targets for gap analysis. Gaps between these types of emergent behavior and official mandates can substantially affect both group- and organization-level outcomes:

- Operative goals and priorities
- Personal ties and networks
- Working definitions of roles and functional responsibilities
- Informal leadership
- Actual work techniques and procedures
- Informal reward systems, including beliefs and norms about rewards
- Routines for dealing with clients, customers, and other outsiders

To assess operative goals and priorities and compare them to officially stated ones, diagnosticians can examine budgets and other forms of allocating financial resources. Other clues to operative priorities appear in salary scales for positions and units and in allocations of resources to particular projects and functions. Gap analysis can also compare techniques and practices that people actually use to get work done to practices that appear in the rule books or are taught by trainers. For example, some sophisticated information technologies, such as expert systems and computer networking technologies, can be applied to a wide range of tasks and used in a variety of different ways. These emergent uses for new technologies can diverge greatly from those envisioned by the people who designed and implemented them. A related topic centers on the actual standards that employees and their supervisors use to judge the quality of their work, as compared to mandated standards.

The delivery of rewards and sanctions in practice forms yet another important facet of emergent behavior for comparison to official declarations and structures. Employee behavior is greatly influenced by shared perceptions about emergent reward contingencies—such as beliefs about what to do to survive an upcoming cut, or what it "really" takes to get ahead. In addition to the types of emergent behavior listed above, diagnostic practitioners can also examine gaps between official and emergent practices in areas like learning (Argyris & Schon, 1996); conflict management (Greenlagh, 1986; Pondy, 1967; Walton & Dutton, 1969); decision making (e.g., Hickson, Butler, Cray, Mallory, & Wilson, 1986; March & Weissinger-Baylon, 1986); organizational control (Lawler & Rhode, 1976); and the monitoring of organizational environments (Starbuck et al., 1978).

A third benefit of diagnosing emergent behavior lies in the contribution of this type of analysis to the choice of steps toward organizational improvement. By understanding how an organization's "informal system" operates, consultants can help clients plan actions to fit emergent norms and patterns or to restructure them. This type of analysis can build on and extend diagnostic techniques for assessing the political forces affecting planned change (Chapter 5). In particular, consultants can alert clients to instances of very poor fit between planned managerial actions and prevailing norms and practices. For instance, workers are likely to ignore new safety regulations if these regulations require them to use procedures or equipment that will slow down the work and thereby reduce their earnings. By aligning safety regulations with actual reward systems and work practices, or by restructuring reward systems, management can increase the chances of compliance with the regulations.

Collecting Data on Emergent Behavior

Practitioners of diagnosis can enrich their understanding of emergent practices by triangulating their data-gathering techniques, using multiple measures, and seeking information from people with divergent roles and viewpoints. Documents and declarations about a firm that are meant for broad distribution can provide useful insights into the image of the firm that the authors seek to project to the public. But these statements cannot serve as guides to emergent organizational practices (e.g., Case 5.2). Managers may, for example, report that they frequently consult with their subordinates before reaching important decisions. But subordinates' own reports and other data sources on decision making, such as records of memberships in crucial committees, may not confirm this idealized picture.

The richest data on emergent practices usually come from direct observations, intensive interviews, or analyses of existing organizational records. If respondents are especially cooperative and candid, data on ongoing social and working relations can also be obtained using sociometric questionnaires. Respondents to these questionnaires name people or positions with whom they work closely or have frequent contact (Brass & Burkhardt, 1993; Moch, Feather, & Fitzgibbons, 1983; Tichy et al., 1980). The patterns of one-way and mutual choice between respondents can then be analyzed to provide maps of relations or simple statistical analyses of network ties (Nelson, 1988). Alternatively, investigators can incorporate questions about group leadership and work relations into open interviews.

Open or semistructured interviews elicit the most useful and valid data when respondents provide explicit descriptions of how they act in a range of work situations, rather than giving generalizations or expressing attitudes. To obtain data about the actual division of labor within a project group, for example, researchers can ask team members to describe what each person did during the design of a project. The researchers then draw conclusions after examining patterns and variations across a set of episodes or interviews. This procedure is more likely to yield valid results than is asking members to generalize about whether "responsibilities are clear" in the group or asking perceptual questions (e.g., "Are task assignments flexible enough to allow for unforeseen circumstances?").

A useful technique for focusing questions explicitly on behavior is to ask respondents to describe in detail how they dealt with critical incidents (Flanagan, 1954)—specific episodes that concretely illustrate the type of behavior under study. For example, to study the use and consequences of different types of influence techniques, Schilit and Locke (1982) asked respondents to describe in detail one successful and one unsuccessful attempt to influence their supervisors at work. In a similar vein, investigators seeking information on emergent norms and channels of communication can ask about cases where subordinates had bad news for their unit or organization. What, if anything, did subordinates say or do? If they told their supervisors or others higher up in the organization, how did these people deal with the discrediting information (Argyris & Schon, 1996)?

Another fruitful strategy for examining emergent practices is to gather data from interviews and organizational records concerning the whole path along which a service, product, client, or idea moves through an organization. To study hospital coordination mechanisms, for example, investigators can trace the entire course of treatment of representative hospital patients from reception to release. To study decision making and working relations in an industrial firm, they can gather retrospective data on the development of a new product from its earliest design stages through routine production.

An advantage of direct observations and of the analysis of existing data is that much information may be obtained unobtrusively (Webb, Campbell, Schwartz, & Sechrest, 1966) without interfering with people's behavior or influencing it. For example, by observing attendance at meetings or by checking records, practitioners might discover that a project that is officially assigned high priority is being neglected by senior staff members. Although such observational data can be very informative, their reliability may be low, and they are usually hard to quantify. Unless observations are quite intensive, the data obtained from them usually must be compared to results obtained from other techniques. Having considered broad issues relating to diagnosing emergent behavior, let us now focus on a diagnostic topic of considerable current relevance—the impact of workforce diversity on emergent processes in groups and organizations.

Workforce Diversity

During the past few decades, workforces throughout North America and Europe have grown far more diverse, and there is little sign of an end to the trend. Racial and ethnic minorities, immigrants and their native-born children, women, teenagers, older employees, and people with physical or medical disabilities are moving from the margins of the labor force toward the mainstream (Naisbit & Aburdene, 1990, pp. 228-256). In many businesses, public services, and governmental agencies, women and members of minority groups already form the majority of the workforce. Organizational mergers and the expansion of businesses across national boundaries are also bringing together employees who differ greatly from one another in their national, cultural, educational, and occupational backgrounds.

As the workforce has become increasingly diverse, and members of minorities and other social subgroups have become more assertive, relations among employees from different backgrounds have caught the attention of managers, policymakers, subgroup members, and human resource consultants (Cheng, 1996; Jamieson & O'Mara, 1991). Workforce diversity sometimes gives rise to new organizational problems or tensions. As new types of employees enter workplaces, they may challenge patterns of emergent behavior that were once taken for granted (e.g., conducting business after hours in all-white, male-dominated settings, such as bars and golf courses). Workforce diversification can also create organizational challenges and burdens when new recruits have higher rates of substance abuse, limited fluency in the dominant language, or less familiarity with work techniques and practices than do veteran employees. Furthermore, minorities within organizations can become involved in controversies and conflicts if they drive hard for changes in organizational practices and policies that are opposed by other subgroups (e.g., Von Glinow, 1996).

At the same time, diversity is creating new organizational possibilities. Employees from previously underrepresented social groups and backgrounds can bring new insights into markets and can suggest new ways of doing business.

Sometimes, managers turn to internal and external consultants for help in diagnosing problems or conflicts that are directly related to diversity, or for assessments of human resource programs aimed at promoting or managing workforce diversity. In addition, diagnostic practitioners may need to examine workforce diversity in order to diagnose its effects on emergent practices or to help clients decide on appropriate steps for organizational improvement.

Observable Differences Versus Underlying Differences

In examinations of workforce diversity, it is useful to distinguish three types of characteristics on which employees can differ from one another. These characteristics are ranked here from those that are most visible to those that are hardest to see and measure:

1. *Subgroup characteristics:* Readily observable characteristics, such as race, gender, age, ethnicity, and physical characteristics
2. *Background:* Less readily observable, but still easily measured differences in education; job and group tenure; work experience (including occupation, function, and industry); social class; religious and voluntary affiliations; regional background; and national origin

3. *Underlying individual attributes:* Underlying skills, knowledge, values, beliefs, preferences, work style, and personal orientations (e.g., assertiveness, tolerance of criticism, willingness to take risks, willingness to help others at work)

Although an employee's background characteristics are not immediately visible, supervisors usually know them, and peers can gradually discern them.[1] Subgroup and background characteristics provide categories that people use when making attributions about each other. These characteristics also provide reference points for the formation of individual and group identity at work and for the importing of social identities from outside the organization. For instance, veteran employees may attribute both negative and positive traits to workers belonging to a particular ethnic or national group, saying, for example, that people in this group are hard workers but do not help their fellow workers out of jams. People who are categorized according to a particular ascriptive or acquired trait, in turn, often form a distinctive sense of identity that revolves around this trait and further distances them from other employees.

Diversity in subgroup characteristics and in individual background attributes within a workgroup or organization can alert practitioners of diagnosis to the possibility that individual members of the focal group will diverge on important underlying attributes. Moreover, diversity is likely to affect interpersonal and intergroup behavior.

Nevertheless, practitioners of diagnosis cannot reasonably assume that all members of a particular subgroup or all employees with similar backgrounds think and feel the same way. Even though they differ in gender or social background, employees in similar situations often share similar orientations and act in similar ways. When variations in attitudes and behavior do occur, they can follow lines of rank or functional specialization just as readily as those of social identity or background. For example, much of the research on gender has reported small, although noteworthy, differences in work behavior and attitudes between genders and among divergent subgroups (Epstein, 1988). Recent studies that control carefully for other background variables, such as educational level, job tenure, and pay, show few, if any, differences between the genders in work attitudes and reactions (Lefkowitz, 1994). In short, observable categories, such as race or gender, do not determine individual orientations and behavior. Hence, it is not possible to predict how particular employees from minority subgroups will act at work or how members of dominant groups will react to employees who differ from them (Nkomo, 1992; Stone & Colella, 1996).

Instead, work interactions among people from different backgrounds depend on the underlying skills and orientations of the people, the norms and
managerial practices affecting cooperation with people from different backgrounds, and the understandings and expectations that emerge as people work
together. Furthermore, there is good reason to expect that relations will change
gradually among socially diverse work teams. One possibility is that the team
members will gradually adjust to divergence in their peers' work styles,
personal preferences, and orientations. If this adjustment occurs, then differences in interaction patterns between socially diverse and homogeneous
workgroups will gradually disappear (Watson, Kumar, & Michaelsen, 1993).
Another possibility is that newly created, diverse teams will not remain
diverse. Instead, as many studies of distinctions in race, gender, and age
indicate, dominant members of a group (e.g., white males) often resist diversification and consciously or unconsciously push people from other subgroups
out of the group (Milliken & Martins, 1996). Unfolding patterns of interaction
like these will, in turn, affect group and organizational outcomes in ways that
are complex and not yet well understood (Milliken & Martins, 1996; Smith
et al., 1994).

How Do People From Diverse
Backgrounds Work Together?

Growth in workforce diversity creates a serious challenge for practitioners
of diagnosis, as well as for managers: As workforces become more diverse, it
becomes harder to assume that people will work together in the same ways
that they did just a few years ago. Moreover, increasing workforce diversity
seems likely to lead to many unanticipated consequences. For instance, if
veteran employees now encounter new recruits who differ from them in
observable features, such as gender or race, the veterans may be much less apt
to socialize informally with the newcomers. If the more senior employees feel
uncomfortable in informal interaction with people from different backgrounds, then the veterans may consciously or unconsciously curtail conversations with new recruits by the coffee machine or refrain from inviting them
to after-hours visits to bars or restaurants. Interactions in these informal
settings provide occasions for socializing new recruits into accepted norms
and work practices. A subtle change in these interaction patterns can thus
reduce the continuity of organizational practices and can place a greater
burden on formal mechanisms for training and socializing new employees.

Faced with diverse workforces, managers sometimes have to revise practices that have produced acceptable results among white, male, middle-class American managers. Many of these practices are not universally applicable (Chimezie & Osigweh, 1989) and can have very different effects at lower levels in the organization, among employees from divergent socioeconomic and cultural backgrounds (see Chapter 10), and among female managers.

The impact of workforce diversity on managerial practice is well illustrated by the question of how employers can best provide fringe benefits to their employees. Married employees with large families and nonworking spouses are more likely than single employees to value traditional fringe benefits, such as pension plans and comprehensive medical insurance, whereas single employees might prefer other benefits, such as vacation leave. In response to the growing diversity in the social characteristics and preferences of their employees, nearly one third of the largest firms in America now offer flexible, "cafeteria" benefit packages (Lawler, 1990, p. 217).

Gendering

Interactions at work surrounding gender differences are important in their own right and also illustrate the implications for diagnosis of interactions within socially diverse workplaces. In examining emergent behavior, diagnostic practitioners need to pay attention to patterns of gendering, because so much emergent behavior is gendered and because gender inequality is so rooted in emergent interaction patterns (Ridgeway, 1997).

Organizational life is gendered in the sense that it defines relations between men and women, as well as expectations for each gender, and it is patterned in ways that reflect socially accepted distinctions between men and women. Gendering shows up in organizational patterns of advantage and disadvantage; power and control; interaction, group, and individual identities; and shared beliefs and meanings (Mills & Tancred, 1992).

One of the most important expressions of gendering is the common practice of assigning men and women to different types of jobs that offer different types of rewards and prospects for advancement. Gradually, it becomes taken for granted that men are "better suited" for some jobs and women for others. In practice, until very recently, this arrangement often led to the preservation of management-track jobs for men and the shunting of female applicants into dead-end clerical, service, and production jobs that were limited in power and influence (Kanter, 1977). Not surprisingly, people in dead-end jobs lose interest in their work and show little initiative. The predominance of women in jobs like these and their failure to show initiative can readily reinforce the stereotype that women are "unsuited" for managerial positions. In the past two decades, many organizations in the United States have opened managerial positions to women. Research suggests that women have made major gains in their access to managerial career paths. However, they apparently are not getting equal chances to demonstrate their managerial capabilities and to acquire valuable experience by receiving high-responsibility and high-stakes assignments (Ohlott, Ruderman, & McCauley, 1994).

The process of gendering occurs within the context of the social norms and beliefs about gender that occur in the society at large (Hearn & Parkin, 1983; Mills, 1988) and the focal organization. Thus, practitioners will have to interpret the nature of gender patterns and prospects for change in such patterns in light of developments in the client organization's environment.

Consultants need to pay attention to patterns of gendering if they are to make valid inferences about organizational behavior. Suppose, for example, that a manager plans a design change that will delegate more authority to staff members. The manager asks a consultant to assess whether staff members are indeed likely to show greater initiative in response to this change. The consultant observes staff members during team meetings in an effort to obtain some indication of the members' willingness and ability to act autonomously. Unfortunately, observations of female staff members in meetings may lead to invalid conclusions. Many studies in the United States have shown that women talk less than men in mixed-gender groups and are more likely to praise and agree with others, thus performing a group maintenance function (Colwill, 1982, p. 143). An observer who failed to recognize that meeting behavior is gendered might incorrectly infer from these observations that women on the staff are less willing or able than their male colleagues to take advantage of delegated authority and to take initiative at work.

The gendering of interaction styles can also affect consultant-client inter-actions during diagnoses and during other types of consultation. When a consultant works with a member of the client organization of the opposite gender, the consultant needs to consider ways in which this interaction may be affected by the person's expectations about working relations between men and women. These expectations are illustrated in the following fictional episode, which, unfortunately, is quite true-to-life:

Case 9.1

Shortly after completing her MBA, Robin Jenkin took a job with a prestigious management consulting firm. One of her first assignments required interviewing and working closely with Martin Furst, an important marketing executive. Furst was introduced to Jenkin by Tom Santis, Director of Human Resources. Mr. Furst gave Ms. Jenkin a long look and remarked that Ms. Jenkin's good looks might distract him from the task at hand. Then he wondered out loud whether Ms. Jenkin's boss gets distracted by her as well. To avoid offering a sharp reply to this putdown, Jenkin reminded herself that these wisecracks might reflect deeply entrenched gender expectations within the firm and that Furst might be only dimly aware of how offensive he was being. She uttered a silent vow to carry out her assignment like a professional and thus to show Furst that his stereotypes were way off course.

Gender expectations can also affect clients' reactions to a consultant's behavior. For instance, in many male-dominated firms, a macho style of interaction prevails among managers, who pride themselves on being aggressive, hard driving, and results oriented. Male managers who are used to behaving this way expect other men to do the same, but they expect women to be more passive and cooperative. These managers are likely to regard with dismay male consultants who use a client-centered and nondirective consulting style, which provides feedback without making specific recommendations for action. Male consultants who act this way are likely to be branded as "wishy-washy" or "effeminate," and to be viewed as unlikely to deliver decisive solutions to the tough issues facing the firm. On the other hand, women consultants who adopt a very directive consulting style run the risk of being viewed as too pushy to work effectively with the management team.

A further implication of gendering relates to the planning of organizational change. In considering steps toward change, diagnostic practitioners should consider the possibility that managerial and consultant interventions are more likely to encounter resistance if they try to alter gendered organizational roles—by putting men or women into nontraditional roles, shifting power and status relations between men and women, or by breaking up single-sex workgroups. When such interventions are planned, clients and consultants need to estimate the extent of potential resistance and to consider whether resistance can be overcome through leadership by supervisors, individual coaching, training in interpersonal relations, or team building.

We have examined gender distinctions because of their centrality in emergent behavior and because they are paradigmatic of the ways that social differences can affect interaction within organizations. In summary, Box 9.1 presents questions that consultants and managers can ask about any focal organization or unit to determine the extent to which interactions build in taken-for-granted expectations about gender. These questions can help practitioners of diagnosis identify gendering processes and assess managerial efforts to reduce gender inequalities. Analogous questions can be raised about distinctions of race, ethnicity, national origin, education, and other observable subgroup and background characteristics.[2]

Assessing the Effects of Diversity

Practitioners of diagnosis can contribute to the ability of a client organization to manage gender differences and other forms of workforce diversity and to benefit from diversity. To contribute to these ends, diagnosticians can help clients assess current consequences of diversity and can provide guidelines for thinking about anticipated changes in workforce composition. To further these ends, Figure 9.1 presents a framework that distinguishes among the three types of diversity described above and separates short- and long-term effects. This framework does not specify or predict relations among the elements shown because the effects of workgroup diversity are not well understood. However, the frame can help practitioners of diagnosis and their clients become aware of possible outcomes and recognize them more quickly.

As Figure 9.1 shows, diversity in subgroup and background characteristics can lead to both direct and indirect short-term consequences. The indirect consequences depend on the degree of normative and cognitive homogeneity that emerges in workgroups and the organization as a whole (see Milliken & Martins, 1996, for a literature review). Research in the United States points to several possible direct consequences of diversity on affective relations in groups. These include reduced mutual attraction and cohesion among group members and lower levels of individual satisfaction, commitment, and iden-

Box 9.12
Assessing the Effects of Gendering

- How does gender affect a person's experience on the job?
- Does the organization reproduce gender roles and relations that prevail in the society at large?
- Is gender built into the definition of a manager and into other tasks and functions?
- Is there a "glass ceiling" beyond which women are not promoted?
- Do people in the organization often refer to gender when they explain why people act the way they do?
- How does the gender composition of groups affect interactions within and between groups?
- Are gender relations linked up with distinctions concerning race and ethnicity or with other subgroup and background characteristics?
- How do gender distinctions affect the power and influence of individual employees and of entire categories of employees?
- Does the organization meet current legal standards for hiring, placing, and promoting men and women equally and/or for affirmative action toward women?
- Do managerial initiatives reinforce gendering or help overcome it?

tification with the workgroup. As a result, individuals working in diverse settings often have higher levels of absenteeism and turnover.

Diversity can also lead to direct symbolic consequences for the team or organization.[3] Organizations and units with more diverse staffs may better meet community or legal standards for treatment of women or minorities. More generally, organizations or units that recruit more diverse staffs can present themselves as pursuing progressive human resource policies and as promoting multiculturalism. In addition, diversity may enhance the image of the organization in the eyes of women and minority group members and can contribute to employees' feelings of empowerment.

Indirect cognitive effects of diversity include the emergence of a wider range of perspectives and ideas during interaction, which in turn can enhance innovation. Other cognitive effects relate to the perceptions that subgroup members develop about their treatment by others (e.g., perceptions that others are prejudiced or uncaring). There may also be indirect affective consequences

252

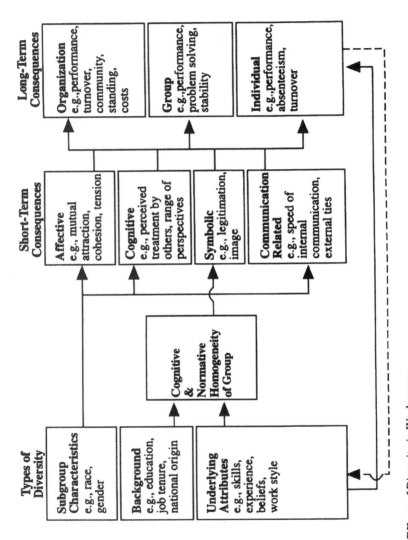

Figure 9.1 Effects of Diversity in Workgroups

SOURCE: Milliken and Martins (1996), p. 418. Adapted by permission.

of diversity. For example, subordinates who are different from their super-visors in characteristics such as age sometimes experience more role ambigu-ity than do those who are similar to the supervisor. Differences on underlying attributes can also contribute to tension and conflict within and between groups. Diversity can also have indirect consequences for communication processes. Work teams with greater staff diversity are likely to take longer to make decisions because of the divergence in members' opinions and working styles. On the other hand, when group members have diverse skills, they may more readily carry on communications with external teams and individuals.

The long-term organizational, group, and individual outcomes shown at the right of Figure 9.1 depend on the intervening, short-term effects of diversity. For instance, by affecting cohesion and commitment, diversity can increase turnover in workgroups and in the organization as a whole. Training costs can also rise if an organization recruits individuals who lack required skills or if it invests in programs designed to enhance interpersonal and intergroup relations. Team and organizational outcomes that depend on a rich flow of ideas can be enhanced by diversity in the backgrounds and underlying attributes of team members. But routine decisions and task performance can take longer in diverse teams.

Diagnostic investigators can use the frame shown in Figure 9.1 as a guide to investigating specific links between diversity and important group or organizational states or outcomes. If, for example, turnover is important to the focal organization, human resource managers or consultants can track data on employee tenure or use employee surveys that measure the person's desire to find another job. In large organizations, groups that vary in composition can be compared on process and outcome measures (see Chapter 6).

To assess how group composition, participants' subgroup characteristics, and participants' backgrounds affect individual and group outcomes, other possible explanations for outcome differences must first be eliminated. In particular, investigators need to consider the possibility that the ability of team members to work together reflects leadership, informal norms, attitudes toward minorities, and mutual expectations among group members. When underlying individual attributes become particularly important to a diagnosis, it is best to measure them directly rather than try to deduce them from observable employee characteristics. Suppose, for instance, that employees from one ethnic group seem to be ignoring a work quality initiative, whereas other employees participate actively. Rather than trying to deduce an explanation from the employees' background characteristics, investigators should talk directly with the employees and seek to determine how they view the project and the forces shaping their involvement in it.

In applying the frame shown in Figure 9.1, it is important to note that the individual consequences of diversity are likely to be quite different for majority and minority members of an organization. For instance, one study found that increased group heterogeneity had stronger negative effects on the levels of psychological attachment felt by white employees toward their group and organization than was the case for nonwhite employees. This same differential effect reduced affect among men more than it did among women (Tsui, Egan, & O'Reilly, 1992). It is also important to recognize that organizational or task changes designed to support diversity can carry advantages for some types of employees while creating disadvantages for others (Stone & Colella, 1996).

Diversity and Diagnosis

In summary, practitioners of diagnosis can help clients deal with workforce diversity in at least three ways. First, they can help clients and other members of the focal organization determine whether stereotypical treatment of men or women or of members of social categories limits the organization's ability to take full advantage of its human resources. If, for example, female clerical workers or minority group members are prejudged to possess limited management potential, the firm is unnecessarily narrowing the pool from which it recruits its managers.

Second, practitioners of diagnosis can help clients and other group members understand how relations among people from different backgrounds become interwoven with other forms of emergent behavior that affect group effectiveness. Interactions between members from distinctive subgroups or backgrounds can shape each of the critical group processes and the conditions affecting those processes, as shown in Figure 6.2 and discussed in Chapter 6 (e.g., Smith et al., 1994). Interracial tensions, for example, can affect the quality of group decision making or the willingness of group members to cooperate with one another. The examination of interactions between genders and among social subgroups can thus help consultants and clients identify forces that lead to or reinforce ineffective group behavior.

Third, awareness of employees' underlying orientations can help clients and consultants judge the applicability of specific managerial and consulting practices and of proposed organizational interventions. During planned change, clients and consultants need to decide which practices are likely to suit the client organization and its distinctive workforce, rather than unselectively importing practices from one setting to another. Managers can alter their practices to fit actual work styles and cultural orientations, or they can take measures to change workforce traits or behavior—for example, through training or new control procedures.

Fourth, consultants can help clients assess how well their organization is coping with current changes in workforce composition, and they can help managers plan steps to deal with anticipated changes (e.g., Walker & Bechet, 1994). Many, but not all, of these steps will focus on human resource management (Cox, 1991; Jamieson & O'Mara, 1991). For instance, if a firm anticipates growth in service personnel who are not fluent in the local language, human resource managers could plan to increase linguistic training for new recruits or to translate training materials into the recruits' own language. Alternatively, technologies or work processes could be redesigned to make job performance less dependent on language skills.

The frame shown in Figure 9.1 can also provide a guide to preparing for changes in workforce composition. Consultants and clients can begin by identifying changes in the employee traits shown on the left side of the figure and can then consider likely short- and long-term effects of these changes. The clients can then decide on appropriate steps to support the move toward diversity, along with any actions needed to avoid anticipated negative effects.

Consultants can contribute to choices about appropriate steps for handling diversity by contributing behavioral science knowledge concerning the likely effectiveness of specific types of programs. They might point out, for example, that short-term training programs for reducing prejudice or changing attitudes toward minorities do not ordinarily produce lasting results (Katz & Kahn, 1978; Stone & Colella, 1996). In fact, recent efforts to train employees to value diversity have apparently produced considerable confusion and hostility (Nemetz & Christensen, 1996). On the other hand, training programs aimed at improving concrete job skills are more likely to achieve their objectives. If programs for coping with diversity have already been introduced, diagnostic practitioners can help evaluate the programs and assess their utility (Chapter 8). In like manner, assessments of the implementation of programs for managing diversity will help consultants and clients refine their understanding of the effects of diversity and can guide management's responses to emergent developments.

Conclusion

This chapter encouraged practitioners of diagnosis to look closely at patterns of emergent behavior within client organizations and suggested several theoretical frames that can assist in such fine-grained examinations. These include the political, negotiation, and interpretive frames. Emergent behavior patterns help define the organizational context in which problems must be diagnosed and confronted. Moreover, in practice, behavior shapes an organization's capacity for change and its interactions with its environment. Assessments of gaps between emergent practices and officially mandated ones can help diagnostic practitioners account for organizational ineffectiveness and an organization's capacity to handle critical challenges. Examination of emergent behavior can also contribute to assessments of the implementation of design changes and of other types of planned change.

Interactions within socially diverse workforces form a possible diagnostic focus that is growing in organizational and managerial importance. We illustrated the importance of workplace diversity for diagnosis by looking at gendering and gender relations in organizations. Then, we provided a framework for the assessment of the consequence of workforce diversity for workgroups and for entire organizations. Continuing this chapter's focus on internal diversity and interpretive behavior, Chapter 10 examines the implications of organizational culture for diagnosis and assessment.

Notes

1. Hence, unlike Milliken and Martins (1996), we have distinguished background characteristics from underlying individual attributes.

2. In fact, most of these questions were adopted from a list of "Asked and Unasked Questions About Race" (Nkomo, 1992, Table 1, p. 506).

3. Milliken and Martins (1996) discuss only the symbolic consequences of diversity for individual employees.

10 Organizational Culture

As used in diagnosis, culture usually refers to shared norms, values, beliefs, and assumptions concerning organizational affairs. These shared orientations take shape and change through processes of interpretation like those described in the preceding chapter. Cultural orientations and emergent behavior are tightly intertwined with one another. Emergent behavior often reflects members' underlying cultural orientations. Routine conversations, for example, express and reinforce shared cognitions and feelings through metaphors and symbols—such as descriptions of an organization as a jungle or battleground. Emergent behavior, in turn, gradually shapes organizational cultures. For example, when downsizing intensifies insecurity and competition among surviving employees, new rules of the game emerge that erode norms supporting organizational commitment and altruistic behavior (Cascio, 1993): As they struggle to survive, members gradually stop expecting one another to take time out to help new recruits get adjusted or to sacrifice personal needs to company priorities.

Like organizational politics and emergent behavior, organizational culture can have a major impact on organizational effectiveness, characteristic problems and sources of ineffectiveness, an organization's need for change, and the feasibility of alternative routes toward improvement. Culture also affects interactions between consultants and clients and among members of the client organization during diagnosis, consultation, and planned change.

Over the past decade and a half, a complex and often bewildering body of research and theorizing developed about organizational culture and its consequences (for reviews, see Martin, 1992; Schultz & Hatch, 1996; Smircich, 1983; Trice & Beyer, 1993). Rather than producing a single model or a consistent analytical frame, this work has yielded several different ways of investigating and understanding interpretive processes and patterns within organizations. Unfortunately, many culture researchers have ignored the implications of their work for managers and consultants. Yet these diverse approaches to culture can help alert practitioners of diagnosis and managers to distinctive features of culture and to divergent ways of assessing cultural orientations.

The first part of this chapter explores the implications for diagnosis of four useful perspectives on culture.[1] These perspectives focus on culture as a source of organizational *integration,* cultural *differentiation* within organizations, *ambiguity* of cultural forms, and the *institutional function* of culture—gaining legitimacy in the society at large. All four of these perspectives draw on the interpretive frame described in the preceding chapter. In addition, the integration and institutional perspectives incorporate open-systems views of culture and stress its organizational functions. The discussion that follows criticizes attempts to treat culture primarily as a stable and widely shared feature of open systems. The second part of the chapter examines ways to diagnose culture and take account of its impacts on consulting and management practice. The chapter concludes with a critical review of techniques for gathering diagnostic data on organizational culture.

Framing Culture

As noted in Chapter 9, cultural orientations emerge within an organization as members interact with one another and with people outside the organization and try to make sense out of these interactions. Through a process of reality construction (Berger & Luckman, 1967), interpretations gradually become shared and taken for granted by many people in the organization. Apparently stable meanings, norms, and values must be reconfirmed through interaction and implicit negotiations among actors.

Members of complex organizations and external stakeholders come from diverse backgrounds, have divergent personal priorities and outlooks, work in different roles and organizational settings, and experience organizational and social change from their own distinctive standpoints. Hence, consultants and managers cannot safely assume that everyone within an organization interprets events or symbols in the same way or shares the same norms, values, and beliefs. Nor can it be assumed that particular cultural manifestations, such as office decor or company stories, provide valid indications of underlying cultural features, such as cognitions and values. Instead, the degree of sharing and consistency of cultural forms and orientations needs to be investigated in each focal organization.

Differences among members of an organization and among organizational stakeholders lead to recurrent negotiations about the meaning and value of organizational states and outcomes. Much of this negotiation is implicit and may not even be recognized as such by those engaged in it. The more powerful members of an organization, and in particular, top managers, exercise more influence over the construction of organizational culture, but their attempts to shape cultural orientations rarely go uncontested.

This view of culture as negotiated and socially constructed takes a pessimistic view of the possibilities for planned, top-down culture change: Many actors engage in negotiations about cultural values and meanings, and at least some are strong enough to resist attempts by management to impose cultural orientations on them. On the other hand, situations do arise in which managers or other actors can decisively influence the way members of an organization define problems or set priorities. The power of top managers to influence the development of cultural orientations derives from their influence on organization design, and in particular from their dominance of decisions concerning human resource functions, such as staffing and controlling performance. Top managers also shape culture by setting agendas for decision making and strategy formation.

Layers of Culture

As shown in Figure 10.1, the diverse elements within an organizational culture can be thought of as a set of layers. The upper layers of organizational culture are the most visible, both to observers and to members of the focal organization. Visible, cultural artifacts include dress patterns, physical arrangements, and organizational logos. Behavior patterns include jargon and

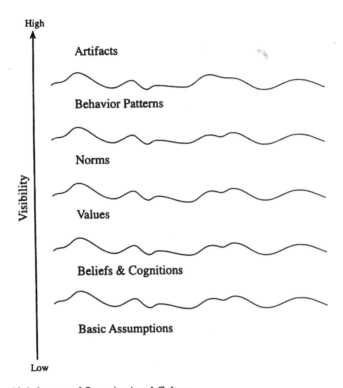

Figure 10.1 Layers of Organizational Culture

patterns of speech, stories, work routines, and organizational rituals and ceremonies. These two upper layers of culture form particularly significant parts of an organizational culture when they express underlying norms, values, beliefs, perceptions, or assumptions. However, visible manifestations of culture often relate only loosely to the less visible aspects of culture, which appear in the lower layers of Figure 10.1. Take, for example, an annual company dinner in honor of retiring employees. This ceremony might symbolize that members of the company highly value the contributions of all employees and respect them as individuals. On the other hand, the retirement dinner could be an empty ritual that most participants feel is a big waste of time and that is out of phase with members' underlying values and everyday practices.

Diagnoses of organizational culture use familiar concepts, such as norms, values, and beliefs, that derive from the sociology and anthropology of entire societies or major subcultures. The application of such concepts is convenient and often illuminating. However, consultants and managers need to be careful to preserve the original complexity implied by these concepts, rather than turning them into caricatures or abstract types that are very distant from the organization's actual web of cultural orientations. For instance, formal mission statements are interesting and potentially important cultural artifacts. But these brief documents, framed and publicized by top managers, cannot possibly capture the broad range of beliefs and values within the whole corporation. Nor is it likely that one or two abstract descriptors can adequately characterize the cultural climate of an entire organization. Thus, caution is warranted before describing an organization in ideal-typical terms like "quality culture" (Cameron et al., 1991), "learning organization" (Wick & Leon, 1995), or "high-involvement organization" (Lawler, 1986).

The two lowest layers in Figure 10.1 point to cognitive elements within organizational culture. Because shared cognitions can directly shape organizational strategy formation (Chapter 13) and other critical aspects of organizational behavior, they deserve close attention in diagnosis. Cognitive orientations within organizations take at least four different forms (Sackmann, 1992):

Dictionary knowledge involves assumptions about the "what" of situations, such as What is a problem? What is effectiveness? or What is a source of status? These assumptions show up in labels and definitions that members routinely use in referring to events in and around the organization. For example, when staff in a university hospital use terms such as "frustrating," "depressing," "vegetables," or "gorks" to refer to elderly stroke patients, their choice of terms points to their assumption that these patients are beyond hope of recovery and should be moved elsewhere for nursing care (Hoffman, 1974).

Directory knowledge entails assumptions about how common practices work, and about causal relations—such as assumptions about the causes of individual or organizational success, and about influence processes within the organization. This knowledge provides "theories in use" (Argyris & Schon, 1996) that shape the way that people deal with challenges and problems and handle critical organizational processes, such as strategy formation.

Recipe knowledge contains prescriptions about how to improve or remedy processes and outcomes at individual, group, and organizational levels. Hence, recipes can be embedded in articulated beliefs and can express norms and values. Recipes include lessons learned from the past—such as "You should have gone ahead without waiting for authorization"—and guides for the future—"From now on, don't request authorization. Just act as needed!"

Axiomatic knowledge refers to basic assumptions about the nature of things and why events occur (Schein, 1985). It includes assumptions about human nature, the environment, individual and organizational capacities for change, and the ability of the organization to influence its environment.

These four types of cognitions are grounded in the deepest, least visible layers of culture. Nevertheless, they can show up in more visible cultural features. For example, during conversations, formal presentations, and interviews, members of an organization often state at least some of their beliefs about how things work in and around the organization (directory and axiomatic knowledge). Interviews, observations, and formal questionnaires about organizational beliefs (Bernstein & Burke, 1989) can also yield clues to directory knowledge about managerial practices, norms, the paths through which work flows, rules for compensation, the location and behavior of important actors in the environment, and the kinds of data that are obtainable on the environment (Daft & Weick, 1984). In like manner, members' statements about how things ought to be done and their judgments of themselves rest on recipe knowledge. Dictionary and directory knowledge show up in an organization's cultural artifacts, including its jargon, popular metaphors, myths, and mission statement (Larwood, 1992). Dictionary and directory knowledge are also expressed in recurrent patterns of behavior, including both work routines and more obviously symbolic events, such as ceremonies and rites (Trice & Beyer, 1984).

Here is an illustration of the ways in which everyday behavior, which might be encountered during a diagnostic study, expresses underlying cognitions. Physicians in an outpatient clinic complain that patients fail to follow medication regimes as instructed. This complaint suggests an underlying set of causal assumptions (directory knowledge) that assigns patients, rather than caregivers, the responsibility for administering their medications and blames patients for any deviations from the prescribed regime. Moreover, the complaint is often accompanied by normative suggestions (recipe knowledge) that the problem can be solved by teaching patients how important it is to conform strictly to their physicians' instructions. Some colleagues and laypeople challenge these cognitions. They note that physicians sometimes rattle off the required procedures without giving patients or family members time to write them down and without instructing them to do so. What is more, patients sometimes encounter objective difficulties in conforming to conflicting instructions received from several different physicians. Physicians who assume that the patient is to blame for failing to take medicines as directed will probably reject such suggestions as implausible or downright impertinent.

As this example suggests, organizational cognitions that become widely accepted and taken for granted within an organization can crystallize into consistent ways of understanding events. These consistent cognitive configurations have been described as frames; theories in use; interpretations (Daft & Weick, 1984); schemas (Bartunek, 1984; Bartunek & Moch, 1987); cognitive maps (Huff & Schwenk, 1990); and thought worlds (Dougherty, 1992). Once people become accustomed to using a particular schema to understand their organization and its environment, they find it difficult to give up automatic use of this taken-for-granted schema. Yet organizational learning and fundamental strategic reorientations (Chapter 13) depend on people "switching gears" into a mode of active and critical thinking (Louis & Sutton, 1991). This active cognitive mode can lead to the revision of existing schemata and to the adoption of new schemata.

Culture Versus Climate

Many applied researchers and consultants treat organizational norms and practices as expressions of organizational climate, rather than culture. Climate refers to members' *perceptions* of organizational features such as decision making, leadership, and norms about work. In the past few years, many applied and academic studies of culture have used standardized questionnaires and cultural inventories (see Denison, 1996; O'Reilly, Chatman, & Caldwell, 1991; Rousseau, 1990a), which rely on members' perceptions and reports of cultural features, and thus closely resemble the instruments originally developed for climate studies. These instruments contribute to the search for universal dimensions of culture. These dimensions can focus on norms, such as support for innovation (Case 10.2), and on broader value distinctions, such as uncertainty avoidance, power distance, individualism versus collectivism, and masculinity versus femininity (Hofstede, 1980). Standardized instruments can also measure typical behavior patterns, such as employee-oriented versus job-oriented practices and tight control versus loose control over work (Hofstede, Neuijen, Ohayv, & Sanders, 1990). Standardized instruments are particularly popular among organizational consultants and researchers who favor positivistic models of organizational behavior. In contrast, advocates of more inductive and qualitative methods for studying culture draw their inspiration from the interpretive and humanistic perspectives common in fields such as anthropology, phenomenology, and symbolic interactionism, and in literary and cultural studies.

Despite the growing overlap between cultural and climate studies and possibilities for cross-fertilization between them, there are important differences between culture and climate (Denison, 1996; Rousseau, 1990a). In our view, these differences contain significant implications for practitioners of diagnosis. Climate studies mainly reveal shared features of the upper, more visible layers of culture. Hence, they can help illuminate broad cultural differences between organizations or between national cultures. In contrast, inductive and interpretive studies are more suited to exploring the depths and complexities of organizational culture within a single organization or in a limited number of cases. These qualitative studies help reveal the pluralities and ambiguities of cultural orientations.

The view of culture presented in this chapter rests mainly on an interpretive, social-constructionist frame derived from symbolic interaction. From this viewpoint, cultures are embedded in peoples' emergent practices and interpretations, rather than forming an objective set of conditions to which people react. Cultures constantly evolve as the people who create and use them negotiate with one another and try to make sense out of ambiguous situations (Weick, 1979). These interpretive processes lead members of organizations and even of subunits within organizations to develop unique cultural configurations that cannot be summarized adequately in terms of a few universal dimensions. The interpretive frame further leads to the recognition that many important cultural elements are hard to discern and measure, and therefore are not amenable to questionnaire study. Moreover, the contested and negotiated nature of culture makes it quite resistant to managerial attempts to introduce change from above.

In contrast to the interpretive approach to culture, climate studies and some quantitative studies of culture treat people as separate from the social context in which they act (Denison, 1996). This approach draws on the research of Kurt Lewin and other social psychologists who adopted a positivistic approach to studying group dynamics. From this viewpoint, people work within a climate, but they do not create it. Instead, top managers create the climate. Climate researchers use questionnaires to assess participants' thoughts, feelings, and reported behavior—features that may or may not reflect deep cultural phenomena. Investigators of climate often examine links between features of organizational or group climates, such as authoritarian decision making, and the motivations, attitudes, and behavior of those subject to the climate (Chapter 6). This approach to climate is atemporal and nonevolutionary. The creation of climate is not examined, and managerial action is treated as the main mechanism for climate change.

Diagnostic studies in the climate tradition often seek to generate recognition of the need for change and motivation to make change by reporting gaps between the current climate and the desired one. Consultants who seek to study culture using the standardized instruments and underlying assumptions of climate research need to be aware of the limitations of this approach and should be prepared to supplement standardized measures with qualitative information gathered through interviews and through interaction with members of the client organization (e.g., Schein, 1985).

Integration, Differentiation, Fragmentation

At present, three distinctive perspectives compete with one another within the research literature on organizational culture (Frost et al., 1991; Martin, 1992). These three perspectives are at least partially complementary (see Martin & Frost, 1996). Moreover, each can make a distinctive contribution to diagnosis. The *integration perspective* regards organizational culture as consisting of widely shared norms, values, beliefs, and assumptions. Consultants and academic researchers using this approach usually assume high consistency between cultural manifestations at different levels (e.g., between artifacts and norms) and among manifestations at the same level (e.g., between norms about decision making and those governing communication between ranks). This perspective also contains the strong assumption that top managers can change culture from above by manipulating symbols and influential design features, such as rewards and job assignments (e.g., Kerr & Slocum, 1987). The assumption that top managers play a decisive role in creating and shaping culture shows up in the title of one of the most influential books articulating the integration approach—*Organizational Culture and Leadership* (Schein, 1985).

The integration perspective enjoyed wide circulation in the business and academic press (e.g., Peters & Waterman, 1982) and in management training programs. This approach promised consultants and managers a way to identify a small number of cultural traits or dimensions that could dramatically affect organizational performance and effectiveness. To measure these traits, researchers and consultants developed standard questionnaire instruments like those described above. Consultants using the integration perspective counseled managers to reduce misalignments among cultural orientations and between culture and other system features. They further pointed to ways that top managers could mold effective cultures through organization redesign and by personal example. Critics of the integration perspective have uncovered many limitations to this functional perspective. Many of these limitations are captured by the differentiation and fragmentation perspectives discussed below. Other problems with the integration view are discussed later in this chapter.

Instead of cultural consensus and consistency, the *differentiation perspective* points to inconsistency in cultural orientations between subcultures and consensus within them. Organizational subcultures often emerge within functions or subunits—such as marketing and production (e.g., Cooke & Rousseau, 1988; Sackmann, 1992). Subcultural divergence also commonly occurs between ranks within organizations. Occupational groups, such as hospital physicians or social workers, can also form distinctive organizational subcultures (Gregory, 1983). Organizational subcultures draw on cultural traits that people bring to the organization from their own personal, professional, and cultural backgrounds, as well as on internal sources of differentiation (Adler & Jelinek, 1986).

Investigators using the differentiation perspective do not expect to find fit or consistency between the layers of culture or between culture's many expressions. Instead, these investigators often discover gaps among cultural features. For example, a consultant or researcher who adopted the differentiation approach might find that mistrust and rivalry between departments lurked just below the placid surface of a company picnic. From this standpoint, the CEO's declaration that the firm is one big, happy family merely diverts attention from fundamental sources of cultural difference and tension.

Although most differentiation studies are academic in nature, they contain crucial implications for consultants and managers. The differentiation view suggests that managers can rarely expect to forge a genuinely consensual culture. Instead, the success of managerial or consultant interventions depends on the development of dialogue and cooperation between members of divergent subcultures. Interaction between members of these groups often rests on narrow agreements about working arrangements, rather than on deep and broad consensus about values and cognitions. Successful product design, for example, depends on the ability of management to create collaborative contexts that bring together and take advantage of the distinctive contributions and divergent approaches of people filling technical, field, manufacturing, and planning functions (Dougherty, 1992).

The differentiation perspective warns diagnostic practitioners and managers that external appearances of unity and consensus can be deceiving. In particular, interviews with organizational spokespeople or reliance on questionnaires containing standardized measures of culture (e.g., Case 10.2) and diagnostic interventions aiming to achieve consensus (e.g., Case 10.4) are likely to mask subcultural differences within complex organizations. The differentiation perspective also suggests that top-down cultural change is hard to accomplish. Members of powerful subgroups are likely to reinterpret mandates from above in keeping with their own norms and understandings, which diverge substantially from the assumptions, norms, and values of top management.

Even within subgroups, the *fragmentation perspective* finds little clarity or consensus about the meaning and importance of cultural components. Instead, fragmentation studies emphasize divergence among individual interpretations of cultural elements and point to inconsistencies among cultural manifestations. Different people in and around an organization are thus shown to assign different meanings to the same event or symbol. Moreover, the fragmentation approach reveals cognitions, values, and norms to be negotiated and situational, rather than consistent across situations. As situations change, even the same person assigns different meanings to events and evokes different values and norms.

Consider, for instance, the meanings that Mr. Black, the head of a product development team in a high-technology firm, assigns to the professional activities of Dr. Yin, a computer systems researcher. When Yin skips an important meeting of the product development team in order to present a paper at a professional conference, Black criticizes Yin's disloyalty to the team and to the company. But just a few weeks later, when trying to justify a raise for Yin, Black cites Yin's conference presentations as evidence that Yin is a nationally known researcher whom the company must make every effort to retain. The fragmentation view treats both assessments of the meaning of Yin's conference presentations as anchored in distinctive situations, rather than assuming that one assessment is true and the other was fabricated to fit the situation.

Like the differentiation view, the fragmentation perspective casts doubt on the ability of managers to forge consensual cultures. The fragmentation approach places greater stress than either of the other two perspectives on the continual flux of cultural meanings and orientations as a result of negotiation, reinterpretation, and changing circumstances. This flow of meaning sometimes creates opportunities for managers, for members of other subgroups, and even for consultants to influence norms or definitions of the situation. For instance, by providing data about external threats to an organization's survival, a consultant can sometimes help deeply divided subgroups redefine their adversaries (e.g., foreign competitors instead of other groups within the firm) and forge common goals, such as entering new markets to ensure survival. From this theoretical perspective, opportunities for dramatically reshaping cultural orientations are assumed to be quite rare. They occur most often during periods of crisis or life cycle transition (Chapter 11). Between such episodes of dramatic and rapid change, cultural orientations change slowly. Management and other subgroups in and around the organization struggle for dominance over the process of interpretation without any group consistently exercising control over the sensemaking process.

Both the fragmentation and differentiation perspectives remind consultants and their clients that cultural change occurs mainly through gradual processes of negotiation and reinterpretation, rather than through programs of planned change. By identifying forces and processes leading to cultural change, practitioners of diagnosis can help clients understand likely cultural trends in their organizations. Once managers recognize the prevailing drift of change, they may decide to wait for culture to evolve naturally, rather than trying to steer its development in a particular direction (e.g., Case 10.3).

Despite the divergence of these three perspectives, practitioners of diagnosis can derive analytical frameworks from each of them that can contribute to the diagnosis of any client organization (Martin & Frost, 1996): The integrative perspective leads analysts to search for consensual orientations; the differentiation perspective points toward subcultural differences; the fragmentation perspective leads toward exploration of ambiguity in cultural meanings and orientations and toward the processes by which people negotiate and interpret the nature of organizational life.

When applied to complex organizations, the integration perspective highlights agreements about very abstract and fundamental assumptions, such as those dealing with basic organizational processes and with causal relations. Cultural divergence over more operational issues can rest on these consensual foundations. This pattern of simultaneous differentiation and integration occurred in one medium-sized conglomerate studied by Sackmann (1992). In that firm, members of all divisions and functional subgroups shared common assumptions about the underlying processes by which innovations and changes were accomplished. At the same time, people in separate functional areas formed distinctive subcultures, each of which defined the most important innovations and changes that had occurred in the company in terms of distinctive types of events and focal areas. Within one division, there were marketing people who believed that success at innovation turned on acquiring new customers and market niches. In contrast, other managers within the same division saw innovation as depending on the coordination of projects and on fostering the exchange of ideas among people from different functions.

Just as the integration perspective can discern consensus within complex, highly differentiated organizations, the differentiation perspective can focus attention on subgroup differences within organizations enjoying high levels of cultural integration. Finally, the fragmentation perspective attunes us to instances of cultural ambiguity, disagreement, and negotiation, even when these elements lie deep within hard-to-observe patterns of emergent behavior.

It is important for diagnostic practitioners to apply these multiple analytical perspectives to their investigations of organizational culture, because members of client organizations, and consultants themselves, often become used to using a single "home perspective" on culture. This home perspective is an unquestioned theory-in-use that assumes that organization cultures are integrated, differentiated, or fragmented (Martin & Frost, 1996). Home perspectives form part of an organizational culture but do not provide an adequate description of that culture. In universities, for instance, professors of anthropology, who are used to discerning subtle differences among cultures and subcultures, might view universitywide affairs through a home perspective that highlights the many sources of cultural differentiation among faculty. Yet outside observers can discern areas of agreement among faculty despite their differences—for example, shared values supporting empirical inquiry, norms regarding academic publication, and widespread beliefs about the processes of learning and teaching.

Although all three perspectives can apply to any organization, diagnostic investigators can also usefully characterize organizations as more or less consensual, divided into clear subcultures, or fragmented (Schein, 1994). This characterization can have practical implications for diagnosis. For example, it can help consultants and managers determine which organizations are most appropriate for benchmarking (Chapter 8) or for other forms of comparison. Consulting interventions and managerial practices that work well in organizations characterized by high levels of cultural consensus frequently prove less applicable to organizations with highly fragmented and negotiated cultures, like those found in many professional organizations (e.g., Passmore, Petee, & Bastian, 1986).

In summary, diagnostic practitioners can benefit from initially applying all three perspectives on organizational culture to a focal organization and then seeking the perspective(s) that best describes the focal organization.[2] This approach parallels Morgan's (1986, pp. 329-331) proposal that organizational analysis can best proceed through two phases. In the first phase, the analyst seeks the insights of multiple perspectives, whereas in the second, critical evaluation phase, the analyst decides which insights are most useful and seeks to integrate them into "the most effective story line" (p. 329).[3]

Organizational Culture and Legitimacy

Unlike the three perspectives just reviewed, all of which examine intraorganizational aspects of culture, *institutional theories* of organization (Scott, 1987) call attention to cultural links between organizations and their environments. According to this approach, many practices and symbols are adopted or retained by organizations because powerful actors within the organizations' environment view these cultural elements as correct and appropriate. In some cases, members of an organization import external cultural orientations as part of their personal beliefs and values and take them so much for granted that they are not even aware that they possess them. For example, teachers and school administrators in much of the western world take for granted that children should do their own work and should be judged on individual performance. The educators build these individualistic assumptions into many aspects of curriculum and instruction in the classroom. The legitimacy of the school system is thus enhanced by its embodiment of assumptions and values prevailing within the surrounding society. Although this process of expressing external beliefs and values enhances legitimacy, it does not necessarily contribute to other aspects of organizational effectiveness. For example, the stress within schools on individual learning and competition does not help prepare young people to work effectively in teams or learn to cooperate with their neighbors and fellow citizens.

Another form of external influence on culture takes place when managers copy long-established structures and practices that prevail widely in their field or industry or are practiced by industry leaders (DiMaggio & Powell, 1983). Adoption of these practices helps the firm gain legitimacy among government regulators, other agencies that license or approve organizational practices (e.g., funding agencies), external stakeholders, the public at large, and its own members (e.g., Deephouse, 1996). Adoption of new and fashionable forms of management practice can also help legitimate an organization. These practices send signals to stakeholders that the firm is innovative and is committed to the rational pursuit of organizational improvement. In most instances, the links between the adopted practices and organizational effectiveness go untested. External legitimation is particularly critical to organizations that operate primarily within *institutional environments,* which are dominated by supervisory and standard-setting bodies. Unlike technical environments, in which buyers reward the production of goods and services, institutional environments reward the use of correct structures and processes (Scott, 1992). The rules and requirements elaborated by regulatory and norm-enforcing bodies eventually become part of the organizational cultures of institutionalized organizations. Institutional actors, such as governmental and professional agencies, exercise powerful influences over schools, medical organizations, legal organizations, governmental bodies, and welfare agencies. But banks, utilities, and many other types of firms that operate within strong technical environments can also be subject to institutional pressures simultaneously. In recent years, for example, firms in the United States have been subject to strong institutional pressures to adopt affirmative action practices in hiring and to introduce procedures designed to enhance workers' occupational safety.

The cultural orientations that organizations adopt in response to institutional pressure grant them legitimacy and entitle them to funding and other forms of support. Adoption of the expected cultural forms also helps buffer institutionalized organizations from intervention by clients and by regulators (Meyer & Rowan, 1977). Once the "proper" structures and processes are in place, people outside the organization assume that internal operations will run smoothly. External stakeholders then exercise minimal control over the organization's daily operations, unless violations of fundamental expectations become patently obvious, as when surgeons amputate the wrong limbs or teachers physically abuse schoolchildren.

Practitioners of diagnosis can incorporate the insights of institutional theories by examining the ways that cultural features shape an organization's reputation, legitimacy, and interactions with its environment. It is particularly important to consider the symbolic meaning of organizational structures and administrative processes in the eyes of both external stakeholders and group members (Bolman & Deal, 1991). Some practices fill both instrumental and symbolic functions, whereas others contribute to legitimation or organizational prestige without making any direct contribution to performance. Elaborate cycles of planning and budgeting can, for example, symbolize that decision making is rational and goal oriented, even when these activities do not directly enhance efficiency or contribute to obtaining short-term managerial objectives. When practices are found to fill primarily symbolic functions, clients may seek to eliminate or reduce them. On the other hand, before doing so, they need to weigh carefully the contributions of these practices to the organization's culture and to the legitimacy and reputation of the organization.

So far, we have seen how research and theorizing on organizational culture can enrich the analytical frames that consultants and their clients use to diagnose and understand culture. Let us now examine more directly the techniques for diagnosing culture and assessing the feasibility of planned cultural change.

Diagnosing Culture

Culture in Sharp-Image Diagnosis

We advocate focusing diagnosis directly on forces underlying symptoms, problems, and challenges of concern to clients. If this sharp-image approach is followed, cultural orientations and links between culture and other system features will be among the range of possible explanations considered during diagnosis. If diagnosis brings cultural sources of challenges or problems to the surface, consultants and clients will then assess the feasibility of interventions that could alter cultural orientations. Thus, our approach contrasts with that of consultants who decide, without conducting a thorough diagnosis, that a particular organizational feature, such as culture or design, explains organizational problems and contains solutions to them.

Practitioners who follow a sharp-image diagnostic begin to examine cultural features in depth only after preliminary analysis points to their impact on ineffectiveness or on an organization's ability to meet specific challenges, such as entry into global operations (see Case 8.1). Case 10.1 illustrates how this type of diagnosis can lead to analysis of organizational culture.[4]

Case 10.1

Executives in a rapidly growing electronics firm complained that it was hard to convince the firm's technical experts to take on managerial positions. Preliminary investigations pointed to a gap between the needs for staffing top management positions and the employees' career patterns. In addition, there was a gap between the expectations of top management and their employees' underlying assumptions about work and careers. This finding led the investigator to look closely at cultural orientations and at fits between culture and human resource practices. The investigator gathered data on these focal areas using a clinical approach, which merged data gathering and feedback. Besides conducting semistructured interviews with members and observing their interactions, he actively fed back to them his developing understanding of the nature of their culture. Then, he incorporated their reactions to the feedback into a grounded model of the organization's culture and its emergent behavior patterns. His model focused in particular on divergence among top executives' assumptions about work and rewards and the assumptions held by members of two recognized subgroups—technical experts and middle managers.

The model pointed to gaps between the subcultures of the two subgroups in the following cultural orientations: assumptions about organizational and subunit goals and about how to accomplish these ends; assumptions about rewards—how people can best serve their own interests and whether people are treated equally; and assumptions about managerial roles. Gaps in these assumptions blocked the recruitment of technicians into top management positions and threatened to undermine the ability of technicians and managers to work together to bring state-of-the-art projects to market.

According to the investigator, technicians aim for product innovation and believe that creating state-of-the-art products will produce organizational success. Middle managers, on the other hand, aim for growth, revenue flows, and market share and believe these can best be achieved by marketing and by improving existing products, rather than through product innovation. The technicians favor loose organizational arrangements, whereas middle managers believe in the benefits of clear managerial structures based on delegation, response to customer preferences, and meeting deadlines. Most importantly, the technicians assume that they can get ahead by doing outstanding technical work, whereas the middle managers are beginning to doubt their prospects for promotion. Furthermore, the middle managers doubt the managerial competence of top executives. Top management reinforces many of the assumptions of the technical subculture by limiting their praise for middle management, restricting their attention to purely managerial issues, and defining technicians as "the real marketers" in the company. Moreover, top managers have sometimes passed over middle managers and recruited executives from outside the firm.

After receiving this diagnostic feedback, top managers examined ways to close the cultural gaps between middle managers and technicians. The diagnosis led top managers to reorient their promotion policies in order to avoid passing over middle managers and to encourage technicians to enter top management positions. The top managers also sought to bridge the gap between engineers and middle managers by structurally integrating members of both groups into teams assigned to areas such as customer service.

This case illustrates two important situations in which cultural orientations can lead to ineffective outcomes: gaps between subcultures that block cooperation between members of these subcultures, and gaps and misalignments between cultural orientations and organizational requirements in areas such as human resource management.

Cultural orientations can also lead to ineffectiveness when managers share assumptions that encourage misinterpretations of critical environmental or technological developments (Kotter & Heskett, 1992; Starbuck et al., 1978; Weitzel & Jonsson, 1989). One common form of maladaptive belief is the "not-made-here" view, which leads people to overlook good ideas originating outside of their own organization. Managers of large and thriving organizations are particularly at risk of falling into this "success trap" (Nadler et al., 1995, p. 10). Their rejection of "foreign" ideas in part reflects their assumption that approaches and techniques associated with past successes within their organization will also lead to success in the future. This assumption, in turn, gains credibility through a common error in causal reasoning—assuming a causal linkage between a preceding event (such as a marketing campaign) and some subsequent development (such as a rise in sales).

Culture can also block effectiveness and produce ineffectiveness when cultural orientations do not provide sufficient support for managerial strategies and programs. This type of lack of fit is particularly common during organizational transitions and periods of restructuring. For example, professional managers who take charge of a formerly family-run business may encounter ways of organizing and commitments to particular services and markets that clash with the new managers' conceptions of how to run the business. In instances like these, lack of consensus about the firm's mission, long-term goals, and basic operating norms can sap its ability to make the strategic transition successfully.

Before concluding that lack of agreement among members concerning cultural orientations creates fundamental sources of weakness and ineffectiveness, investigators should recall that subcultural diversity, internal pluralism, and lack of consensus within organizations can also contribute to organizational adaptation and flexibility (Meyerson & Lewis, 1992). Divergent norms, values, and cognitions provide soil for innovation and for criticism of current organizational practices. Divergence and dissent may thereby pave the way for organizational learning and adaptation. Particularly during periods of rapid external change or organizational crisis, organizational members who depart from accepted wisdom can help their colleagues and supervisors develop new ways of defining problems and coping with challenges.

Diagnosing Culture's Contributions to Effectiveness

Rather than seeking to uncover the most important or accessible sources of organizational ineffectiveness and effectiveness, some consultants chose to start their diagnoses by focusing squarely on organizational culture and on ways to help clients manage or "engineer" culture (Kunda, 1992; Martin & Frost, 1996). Most diagnoses that aim to support the management of culture concentrate on the three highest layers of culture shown in Figure 10.1. Practitioners of diagnosis look for clues to underlying values in organizational artifacts (Layer 1) and in behavior patterns (Layer 2), such as budget allocations and managerial presentations to employees and clients. Behavior patterns are particularly central to this type of diagnosis because top managers can more readily make design changes that reshape these patterns than they can influence deeper cultural orientation. Moreover, many managers and consultants assume that redesigning human resource systems and other administrative features will ultimately reshape employees' cultural orientations as well. Less often do managers try to influence subordinates' cultural orientations directly by modeling and symbolizing the kinds of orientations they seek to foster. For instance, managers can tell stories, perpetuate organizational myths, and take part in organizational ceremonies and rites that are presumed to strengthen particular values and beliefs (Trice & Beyer, 1993).

If consultants and their clients regard this type of cultural management as both appropriate and useful, consultants can carry out diagnoses aimed at identifying managerial steps for enhancing organizational effectiveness. Once consultants and clients have defined criteria for effectiveness, the diagnostic investigator tries to determine which existing cultural artifacts and behavior patterns reinforce effectiveness.

Consider, for example, organizations in which highly reliable, error-free performance literally becomes a life-and-death issue. Research on aircraft carriers indicates that continuous performance reliability and safety depend on a state of "collective mind"—a cognitive and affective configuration entailing intense levels of mutual attentiveness, constant mindfulness of critical work processes, tight interactions among crew members, and high levels of mutual trust among the personnel on the carrier deck and between them and the pilots (Weick & Roberts, 1993). If preliminary diagnosis of the culture of an aircraft carrier sustained the foregoing characterization, the diagnostic investigator could then seek to discover those ceremonies, symbols, forms of supervision and control, and structures that promote shared heedfulness and responsibility among all those involved in launching and landing the planes. It might be found, for example, that these orientations were reinforced by distinction awards and by promotions based on service to the work unit and to the entire carrier crew, as opposed to individual achievements.[5] If so, to enhance effectiveness, these solidarity-reinforcing practices need to be sustained and strengthened. In like manner, commanding officers need to be careful not to introduce ideas or practices stressing individual differences and needs, because these practices might unintentionally disrupt the delicate fabric of relations on the carriers.

As the preceding illustration suggests, consultants can approach the management of culture inductively. First, they seek to identify cultural forms and underlying norms, values, and beliefs that contribute to effectiveness within the focal organization. Then, they ask what can be done to strengthen or maintain these cultural features and to avoid disrupting desired cultural patterns.

Another approach is more deductive: Consultants who follow it concentrate on cultural patterns that were shown to shape effectiveness in past research, consulting, and management practice. The main emphasis is on practices that management can readily alter. If, for instance, effectiveness is defined in terms of employee motivation and commitment, then diagnosis can concentrate on managerial practices that have been shown in the past to affect these psychological outcomes. These include using symbols in ways that convey to the employee that the company depends on the individual's contributions. The popular practice of nominating "employees of the month" and of publicizing their contributions to the firm is one way to communicate this message. Practices like these are most likely to achieve their end when they occur in tandem with other expressions of inclusion, such as the sharing of information via a company newsletter and the deployment of employees in semiautonomous teams. On the other hand, isolated efforts to symbolize employee involvement are not likely to bear fruit if they do not coincide with the implicit messages conveyed by managerial actions in crucial areas such as decision making, training, promotions, hiring, and firing.

Another area for diagnosis of this type concerns cultural artifacts and practices that foster organizational learning and innovation (Chapter 13). In particular, diagnosis can examine patterns of behavior that lead to norms and beliefs encouraging members of the organization to seek to improve current practices and to review and challenge current standards and policies in light of external challenges and their own values. Consider, for example, the ways that managers deal with information about the performance of their unit and the organization as a whole (Wick & Leon, 1995). When managers hoard this information, they communicate their resistance to input from below and from their peers and thereby discourage learning. When managers share this performance information with subordinates and also act upon suggestions for improvement, they enhance norms supporting learning and foster beliefs that participation in improvement and change is possible. Unfortunately, many organizations disseminate reams of data about inputs and outputs (costs, sales, services rendered, earnings) without providing comparison points and other guides to interpreting the data. Furthermore, managers often ignore requests for clarification of the data or calls for action in response to the accumulating evidence. In these cases, dissemination of performance data becomes an empty ritual that can generate frustration and cynicism among the recipients of the data, rather than reinforcing norms and cognitions that support learning.

Similarly, when top and middle managers are confronted by subordinates during meetings and other interactions, the managers' responses can either discourage or sustain norms supporting learning. Defensive reactions to suggestions or to requests to investigate problems give a clear message that managers expect conformity and discourage critical thinking. On the other hand, honest and nondefensive reactions reinforce norms of learning and commitment to improvement. Organizational routines, such as periodic reviews and self-study activities, can contribute to a pro-learning orientation, provided that participants view these activities as genuine and as capable of producing recommendations that will indeed be implemented.

The idea of promoting cultural orientations that support effectiveness appeals to both managers and consultants. However, before recommending managerial steps to encourage such positive cultural orientations, consultants need to recall that the empirical evidence for culture's direct and independent contributions to effectiveness is still very limited. A small but growing body of research and reports by consultants does show that cultural orientations can affect organizational processes and outcomes, including financial performance, that are particularly important to consultants and managers (Cameron & Freeman, 1991; Denison & Mishra, 1995; Rousseau, 1990a, 1990b; Sashkin & Burke, 1990; Sheridan, 1992; Yeung, Brockbank, & Ulrich, 1991).[6] However, these studies also demonstrate that the relations between culture and effectiveness are far more complex than originally thought.

For example, strong organizational cultures (Sathe, 1985)—ones that contain clear and well-ordered orientations that are widely shared and very influential—do not universally contribute to performance and other dimensions of effectiveness. Instead, strong cultures contribute to performance when they support an appropriate organizational strategy. But strong cultures can reduce effectiveness when they reinforce orientations that block organizational learning and adaptation to environmental change (Kotter & Heskett, 1992; see also Cameron, 1994). In addition, organizations with strong cultures and high levels of employee commitment appear to generate higher employee expectations, which can breed higher levels of discontent than can those occurring in organizations with weaker cultures (Baron & Cook, 1992).

Analyzing Cultural Gaps and Fits

Investigators who focus directly on the management of organizational culture often look for gaps between current and desired cultural states, assess fits among cultural manifestations, and examine fits between culture and other system features. Diagnosis of fits was introduced in Chapter 2 and was discussed in depth in Chapter 8. Hence, we will concentrate here on diagnosis of culture gaps.

Consultants sometimes choose to investigate culture gaps in areas that have been found to be important in prior research and consultation. It is also possible to choose features for gap analysis that respond to problems presented by clients. Both approaches to gap analysis require a standard of comparison for assessing the size of gaps and their implications. This standard can refer to past conditions, other parts of the focal organization, conditions in some other organization, or some abstract standard of desired cultural orientations. To examine predefined cultural features, consultants usually rely on standardized culture inventories or models. The following case (based on Kilmann, 1985; Kilmann & Saxton, 1981) depicts comparisons between actual and desired norms, as assessed by standardized instruments.

Case 10.2

Members of the focal organization are asked to characterize the actual and desired workgroup norms that prevail within their workgroups. According to the consultants, closing gaps between actual and desired norms will improve organizational performance. The norms are assessed through closed-ended items contained in a standardized questionnaire, the Kilmann-Saxton Culture Gap Survey (Kilmann & Saxton, 1981). The questions are designed to yield four scales covering norms about task support, task innovation, social relationships (e.g., communication and teamwork), and personal freedom. Gaps between actual and desired norms are then calculated arithmetically. Next, the consultants conduct workshops in which they help surface normative gaps and encourage participants to define new norms that will close gaps. Finally, participants look for ways to reinforce these normative changes.

To justify using an instrument like the one just described, consultants must assume that the cultural features targeted by the instrument are indeed the most relevant features for diagnosis and intervention. Moreover, they must assume that the instrument provides a valid assessment of the relevant features. In evaluating these assumptions, consultants should note that the design and use of standardized instruments like these rules out the possibility that members disagree about the meanings of norms or even about the terminology used in the questionnaire. In like manner, no allowance is made for subcultural differences within or between workgroups. Yet another problem with the approach described in Case 10.2 and with many standardized cultural inventories is that workshop participants may be unable to bring about normative change in the targeted areas, even if they can accurately identify areas of gaps between current and desired norms. These drawbacks should be considered along with the questions raised earlier in this chapter about the applicability of climate-type measures to the assessment of culture. At the least, it would seem advisable for diagnostic practitioners to conduct a preliminary investigation of their own in order to decide whether the Kilman-Saxton survey or any other standard instrument accurately reflects important cultural orientations within the focal organization and whether the measured orientations are indeed the most central to diagnosis and action planning.

Whenever diagnosis uncovers gaps, diagnostic practitioners and clients face two additional issues: Will reducing these gaps enhance effectiveness or reduce ineffectiveness? Is closing the gap feasible? Gaps between current and ideal cultural standards need not reflect organizational malfunctions. Instead, the gaps can simply reflect the ability of people to imagine a more ideal organizational state. There is no guarantee and little empirical evidence that movement toward that ideal state necessarily enhances organizational performance and other forms of effectiveness. Changes in articulated norms or beliefs often have little impact unless they are accompanied by meaningful changes in other areas. For example, changes in the normative climate concerning innovation will be insufficient to sustain technological breakthroughs unless fundamental changes in organizational strategy, resource allocation, organizational structure, and human resource management accompany the cultural change.[7]

Analogous issues arise when consultants diagnose fits among cultural features or between culture and other system features. Misalignments among cultural artifacts, behavior patterns, and norms can reflect ambiguities and patterns of subcultural differentiation that are common in most complex organizations and do not harm effectiveness. In fact, research indicates that the internal consistency of an organization's culture affects organizational performance less than does the *content* of the culture (Cameron & Freeman, 1991; Huselid, 1995; Kotter & Heskett, 1992).

Sometimes, cultural ambiguity and misalignments can even be beneficial to an organization. Ambiguity about the meaning of slogans, evaluation standards, and rules can allow people having very divergent views and preferences to work together without undue tension and conflict. Conflict would be rampant if people who disagree fundamentally could not take refuge in different interpretations of their joint tasks, priorities, and evaluative criteria (Astley & Zammuto, 1992; Meyerson & Lewis, 1992). Consider, for instance, ambiguities and downright inconsistencies in the meanings assigned to that central symbol of the educational process—the grade. What would happen if parents, teachers, pupils, administrators, and school boards all agreed on precisely what grades meant and how to interpret them, and if grades were all based on identical criteria and were universally valid and reliable within and across classrooms and schools? Many conflicts would come to the fore that currently remain safely buried under the ambiguous and multiple meanings that educational stakeholders assign to those all-important numbers.

In short, it is possible to apply the diagnostic procedures described in Chapter 2 to culture so as to uncover gaps, poor fits, and even critical interdependencies among cultural features and between culture and other system features. However, these investigations of fits and gaps may draw attention to conditions that may have little bearing on organizational effectiveness or ineffectiveness. Because the links between culture and organizational performance are so complex, adopting a sharp-image approach to diagnosis appears preferable to using diagnostic techniques that commit the investigator to cultural assessments. Moreover, when planned or unplanned organizational changes do lead to significant cultural changes, diagnostic practitioners and their clients can gain an understanding of these changes and of ways to deal with them by engaging in diagnostic inquiry throughout the change process (see Chapter 7).

Assessing the Feasibility of Culture Change

No matter what approach they take to diagnosing culture, consultants need to assess carefully the feasibility of interventions aimed at changing culture. In particular, consultants and clients need to be aware of serious barriers to planning and implementing major changes or transformations in an organization's culture and subcultures (Adler & Jelinek, 1986; Martin & Frost, 1996).

Culture change is difficult to accomplish for many reasons. First, well-established, widely shared beliefs, values, and norms are very resistant to managed change. Second, culture-change programs often clash with members' interests and political alignments. Third, the managerial and consulting techniques for generating change in cultural orientations are not well understood, and the effectiveness of popular techniques for changing culture, such as training programs, has not been demonstrated widely. Fourth, interventions aimed at changing culture often produce unintended and undesirable results. In particular, programs of major organizational and cultural change can unintentionally undermine existing cultural patterns that contribute to effectiveness, such as norms supporting employee commitment. Fifth, a successful program of culture change requires major commitments of organizational resources and can take a very long time—as long as 5 to 15 years by some estimates (Bluedorn & Lundgren, 1993). During such a long time period, the requirements for change in culture and in other organizational features can shift several times, so that trying to change culture becomes like trying to hit a moving target. Sixth, serious ethical questions arise when management attempts to control or manipulate its employees' basic values and beliefs. In light of the difficulties and uncertainties surrounding attempts to manage major culture change, it is not surprising that many contemporary consultants and researchers no longer share the enthusiasm for planned culture change that was so widespread during the 1980s (e.g., Davis, 1984; Kilmann et al., 1988; Kilmann et al., 1985; Tichy, 1983; Trice & Beyer, 1993; Uttal, 1983).

In contrast to major culture changes, managed culture change of an incremental nature may prove more feasible. To assess the feasibility of either type of change, diagnostic practitioners can use the same techniques that they apply to assessing the feasibility of design changes and other strategic changes (Chapter 7). These techniques include assessing political support and resistance to proposed interventions (Chapter 5). Backing by top management is particularly crucial for major culture change, because cultural transformations are typically driven by top leadership and require simultaneous transformations of most system elements (Kilmann et al., 1988; Schein, 1985). Feasibility assessments can also cover the availability of needed resources and the capacity of human resource management and other functions to facilitate both the transition stage and full implementation (Chapter 7). To assess feasibility, consultants and change strategists can also compare the anticipated costs and risks of change to anticipated benefits.

Besides considering issues that are common to any change program, planners of culture change also need to take into account the extent to which proposed changes in culture are compatible with cultural orientations that will not undergo change. In addition, it is important to judge whether the organization's cultural and institutional environment is likely to support proposed changes. The more that planned changes depart from prevailing cultural orientations within the organization and its environment, the more difficult and risky planned change becomes. Radical culture changes cannot build on norms, values, and beliefs that are accepted by members. Moreover, radical transformations of culture risk disrupting cultural orientations that provide for organizational continuity and contribute to effectiveness, such as norms of mutual assistance and values supporting employee commitment to the organization.

Case 10.3 (based on Bourgeois & Jemison, 1982) provides an illustration of a diagnosis of culture that directly considered the feasibility of managed culture change.

Case 10.3

Consultants to the top management of an Indonesian subsidiary of a North American firm asked participants in a weeklong strategic planning session to devote a day to analyzing their corporation's culture. During individual analyses, small-group discussions, and a plenary meeting, participants developed a series of descriptions of the culture. They were then asked to look at the synchrony, or match, between these cultural elements and trends they had identified in their environment. They performed a parallel analysis for fit between cultural traits and proposed strategic changes. Once the participants had identified potential matches and mismatches, they ranked the strength of the cultural features they had identified and targeted features that were potential constraints on strategic change. Finally, they considered whether to attempt to change these constraining features or to try to work within the constraints imposed by them. The strongest mismatch identified by the executives involved what they described as the "please-the-boss" culture. The executives viewed this orientation as a characteristically Indonesian pattern that encouraged subordinates to hide unpleasant or discrepant information from their bosses. The result was that decision quality suffered.

When the participants examined the feasibility of action alternatives for reducing the poor fit between this cultural element and the requirements of accurate and rapid decision making, they decided not to attempt to intervene in the culture. Their decision reflected their view that the please-the-boss mentality had carried over from the colonial period but would gradually disappear among managers who had grown up after independence. Hence, as a new generation of managers joined the firm, the norm would become less widespread and influential within the organizational culture. The participants in the strategy session decided that changing the norm through direct intervention would take almost as much time as waiting for the recruitment of a new generation of managers. Therefore, they preferred to devote their energies to other action alternatives and to accept the presence of the please-the-boss norm as a constraint on strategic planning and action.

In this case, diagnosis of organizational culture took place within a formal strategic planning session, rather than in a separate diagnostic study, and the diagnosis relied exclusively on an integrative perspective on culture. Nevertheless, the case clearly illustrates the importance of considering the feasibility of attempts to intervene directly into organizational culture.

Because of the costs and risks, managers are understandably hesitant to undertake broad programs of culture change and may even refrain from introducing modest steps to change specific cultural orientations. Instead of trying to intervene in a well-established organizational culture, managers sometimes seek to introduce new cultural orientations by setting up new units or organizations and allowing them freedom to develop a distinctive organizational culture (Trice & Beyer, 1993). Large manufacturing organizations, for example, can set up separate companies or semiautonomous divisions charged with a mission of developing new products. By creating small and nearly independent units or organizations for this purpose, the managers in the parent company hope to provide conditions that will support the emergence of an innovative and entrepreneurial culture, as opposed to the bureaucratic and risk-averse one that characterizes the parent company.

Because of the difficulties of implementing major culture change, most fundamental changes in organizational culture occur without much guidance or planning. Instead, they emerge in response to basic changes in organization design or strategy, many of which follow organizational crises and changes in leadership or ownership (Kilmann et al., 1988; Tichy & DeVanna, 1986).

Culture as Context

Culture deserves the attention of consultants and managers, even if they do not view it as a primary source of organizational ineffectiveness and effectiveness or as a target for intervention and planned change. Like emergent behavior, cultural patterns within organizations and in their environments influence the context in which consultants and their clients carry out their work.

Understanding organizational and national cultures can thus help consultants manage the consulting process in ways that fit dominant cultural orientations within the client organization (Zeira & Avedisian, 1989). For example, if members of a client organization do not trust one another and are unwilling to discuss problems openly, diagnostic practitioners face barriers to involving members in diagnosis and sharing diagnostic feedback with a broad spectrum of members. In organizations characterized by limited interpersonal trust and openness, it would probably be more appropriate for consultants to take primary responsibility for diagnosis and to give feedback to a limited number of clients.

Cultural orientations play a particularly important role in shaping clients' expectations about the techniques and contents of diagnosis and consultation. If diagnostic procedures do not meet client expectations, clients are likely to be dissatisfied with the project and the consultant, and they are unlikely to act on diagnostic feedback. One particularly salient issue involves clients' dispositions toward positivistic diagnostic studies, as opposed to more interpretive and interactive ones. People trained in quantitative fields, such as accounting, marketing, finance, and engineering, often prefer to receive feedback in objective-looking, quantitative formats. Moreover, they often expect consultants to take the role of outside experts, rather than that of facilitators of learning and change. Clients who favor positivistic diagnosis are liable to regard collaborative diagnostic techniques as unscientific and may resist feedback based on qualitative and impressionistic data. In contrast, clients with strong humanistic orientations, such as those articulated by many social workers and members of other helping professions, are more likely to want to be involved in diagnosis and may prefer open-ended feedback. People with humanistic orientations are liable to view purely quantitative summaries of diagnostic findings as attempts to reduce their feelings and views to "a bunch of numbers."

The national cultures in which organizations are embedded can also shape client expectations for diagnosis and intervention. Diagnostic practitioners need to take note of national cultural differences in order to choose appropriate diagnostic techniques and to help their clients discover appropriate routes toward organizational improvement.

For instance, consultants working outside of North America may face difficulties in applying organization development techniques that assume distinctively North American cultural orientations, such as the value of open communication across hierarchical ranks and the importance of frank discussion of conflicts. Techniques based on these orientations may turn out to be inappropriate to cultures like those of Latin America, in which very different values prevail (Jaeger, 1986).

In like manner, recent studies point to many ways in which national culture influences the applicability of managerial techniques and interventions. These studies raise doubts as to whether management ideas and techniques that were originally developed in North America apply to very different cultural settings (Boyacigiller & Adler, 1991; Hofstede, 1993). One investigation found both compatibilities and incompatibilities between American managerial techniques and the norms held by workers in Russia's largest textile factory (Janssens, Brett, & Smith, 1995). The techniques of behavioral management (making social rewards contingent on functional behavior) and of extrinsic rewards (providing performance-contingent material rewards) produced dramatic short-term improvements in productivity, apparently because these techniques were largely compatible with norms and values among the Russian factory workers. But productivity declined when applied researchers introduced a participative management technique. This technique required workers to meet with an applied researcher without their supervisor to discuss ways to enrich their jobs. This technique violated norms of loyalty to peers and supervisors, as well as norms restricting the sharing of information about work with outsiders.

In preparing action recommendations, consultants, clients, and members of the client organization who support change need to examine their own cognitive perspectives and biases, as well as cultural orientations within the focal organization (Armenakis & Bedeian, 1992). It is particularly important for advocates of change to examine gaps between their own assumptions and those held by members of the client organization. Consultants and other change agents often introduce perspectives and schemata that diverge from and challenge those that members take for granted (Bartunek et al., 1992). Particularly where major changes are envisioned, consultants and their clients need to consider carefully how to avoid conflicts between their own cognitive schemata and those of the people responsible for implementing change. Planners of change may be better able to find ways to reduce cognitive conflicts during implementation if they anticipate the cognitive processes that accompany exposure to new ways of thinking and acting. For example, consultants and other change agents can prepare for the likelihood that people who have just adopted a new schema are more likely to expect the schema to be followed exactly than are people who have gained further experience using the new schema.

In weighing the effects of cultural contexts on diagnosis and action, consultants need to take into account important subcultural divisions within the client organization. One useful approach to diagnosing organizations containing deep subcultural divisions involves having members of the organization create a project steering committee which includes representatives of major subgroups. This committee takes responsibility for defining goals for diagnosis and action that are acceptable to members of all subgroups, planning mutually agreed-upon interventions, and supervising project intervention (e.g., Kolodny & Sternberg, 1986; Shirom, 1983). Even if consultants do not use techniques that explicitly recognize the existence of subcultural differentiation, they would be well advised to take such differentiation into account in selecting diagnostic techniques and interventions. For instance, when dealing with very pluralistic organizations, consultants would avoid techniques such as open-systems planning (Chapter 4), which require participants to reach consensus on fundamental values and goals before engaging in action planning.

When client organizations contain deep subcultural divisions, consultants can help clients anticipate and accept divergence in the ways that members of the major subcultures react to proposals for change and to managerial innovations. By taking subcultural differences into account, managers can adopt more flexible and pluralistic change programs. At best, these programs will reflect the diverse needs and orientations of major subgroups. At the least, the programs will define common tasks and coordination mechanisms without forcing everyone to conform to a single set of norms and values. In deeply divided organizations, consultants can also help members of divergent subgroups learn to understand and accept cultural differences and to work more effectively under conditions of cultural differentiation.

Data-Gathering Techniques

Diagnosing culture poses difficult methodological issues that are closely related to the complexities of framing culture that were discussed in the first part of this chapter. The following discussion aims to clarify these methodological issues while providing guidance about the selection of data-gathering techniques.

Practitioners of diagnosis gain their first impressions of organizational culture during the scouting phase of diagnosis and obtain further information as they gather additional data on the organization and on the concerns presented by clients. In many cases, consultants explore and surface cultural orientations as they examine patterns of emergent behavior (Chapter 9). Interviews on emergent behavior are likely to be most informative about the most visible layers of culture, but actual organizational practices may also be found to reflect underlying norms, values, and interpretations.

Intensive Qualitative Methods

When culture becomes a central concern for diagnosis, investigators can include questions about cultural features in general diagnostic interviews (Harrison, 1994), or they can conduct entire interviews that focus on cultural manifestations and underlying cultural features. Interviews can ask directly about culture—for example, by inquiring as to norms about productivity or about relations between ranks. More fruitful are indirect questions from whch investigators make inferences about underlying orientations. For example, an investigator might ask informants to describe whether it "pays to stick your neck out or take risks around here," and then make inferences from responses about underlying assumptions and interpretations. Similarly, practitioners of diagnosis can analyze the cultural orientations that lie beneath respondents' answers to many questions that are not directly related to culture. For example, consultants may ask individual respondents or groups to give accounts of organizational successes and failures (Argyris & Schon, 1996, pp. 53-64). In analyzing such accounts and preparing feedback, the consultant pays close attention to assumptions and behavior that members take for granted. In a similar fashion, investigators can look at the values and cognitive frames that respondents take for granted when describing challenges and problems facing their organization. Are challenges defined in terms of political threats and constraints, opportunities for proactive managerial action, unpredictable and insurmountable developments, or some other frame? Diagnostic practitioners can also tease out assumptions and value positions implied by respondents' descriptions of ostensibly objective phenomena—including internal and external work relations; work processes and techniques; and the history and development of major projects, organizational units, or the entire organization (e.g., Dougherty, 1992; Leach, 1979; Sackmann, 1992).

Interview data can be supplemented by observations of cultural artifacts and behavior patterns, including both emergent behavior and repeated and formalized behavior, such as that which occurs in meetings and organizational rites and ceremonies (Trice & Beyer, 1984, 1993). By triangulating data from multiple sources, investigators considerably enhance the credibility and validity of their inferences.

This type of qualitative research on culture draws heavily on the inductive, empirically grounded techniques of ethnography and qualitative field research. Traditionally, these studies had academic goals and produced elegant portraits of an organization's distinctive cultural patterns and those of its subcultures (e.g., Kunda, 1992; Pettigrew, 1985; Van Maanen, 1979). As the foregoing discussion of sharp-image diagnoses of culture suggests, practitioners of diagnosis can also use qualitative techniques to uncover distinctive cultural configurations that lead to organizational ineffectiveness in a particular client organization.

In applying qualitative techniques, some consultants take a clinical approach (e.g., Case 10.1), in which interaction and collaboration between consultants and members of the client organization contribute directly to analysis of cultural orientations (Bartunek & Louis, 1996). One useful clinical procedure involves observing and interviewing participants, providing them with feedback on preliminary findings, and then working with clients individually or in small groups to develop a characterization of their own organizational culture (Schein, 1985). After several cycles of this sort, an agreed-upon, well-grounded understanding of the organizational culture may emerge. The clinical approach can succeed only if clients are both willing and able to take an active role in examining themselves and their own organization. These preconditions are likely to be absent when interpersonal tensions and conflicts run high and when clients expect the consultant to act as an independent expert.

Both the clinical and the broad ethnographic approaches are very time-consuming and require the deployment of highly skilled investigators. Focusing qualitative work on presented problems and specific sources of ineffectiveness can reduce these time investments considerably.

Workshops

Some consultants have proposed using workshops to bring out cultural features, either as part of a clinical study of an organization or as a separate diagnostic intervention aimed at facilitating change (e.g., Case 10.3). Workshops are usually designed to generate qualitative data about culture more rapidly than are other qualitative approaches and to involve members of the organization directly in the diagnostic process. Workshops on culture are often intended to build consensus and teamwork within a management group. Workshops also may be designed to produce data and understandings that can feed into programs of planning or change. Case 10.4 (based on Lundberg, 1990) illustrates these processes:

Case 10.4

The nine top executives of a medium-size manufacturing firm met with the head of training/organization development and with an external organization development consultant in a day-long workshop. The workshop was intended to socialize new executives into the firm's culture, enhance relationships among them, and provide the basis for a round of strategic planning that was to follow. After an explanation of the nature of organizational culture, the external consultant led participants in an examination of common cultural artifacts, such as shared language, dress, and rituals (e.g., Monday lunch—weekly, catered working lunch for the executive team). Then, the team sought to generate and choose among brief statements that captured shared norms, values, and basic beliefs. These statements were responses to questions like "What's really valued around here?" "What does [the firm] really stand for?" that the consultant posed to the group of participants. At the end of the session, several statements characterizing each cultural feature had been agreed upon.

Workshops like these may indeed help consultants and participants understand their organization's culture more quickly than would be possible using intensive qualitative methods. Moreover, the workshops can help to direct participants' attention to cultural orientations containing immediate action implications. But culture workshops can succeed only if participants trust one another and communicate openly. Moreover, if workshops like these are to promote effective strategy formation or action planning, workshop participants need to possess the power, ability, and readiness to assess and implement action proposals.

Before undertaking such workshops, practitioners should consider several potential drawbacks. First, by concentrating on culture, workshops like the one described in Case 10.4 may divert participants from diagnosing major noncultural sources of organizational effectiveness or ineffectiveness. Second, the search for shared cultural features may encourage participants to assume that cultural cohesion and normative conformity are both desirable and obtainable. Thus, participants may be discouraged from airing fundamental differences of value and belief and diverted from considering possible benefits of cultural pluralism and ambiguity. Third, workshops may not yield valid cultural data. Validity can be undermined by pressures to group conformity, the participants' inability to think reflectively about their own culture, and the exclusion of representatives of divergent organizational subcultures and subgroups. Fourth, these workshops are unlikely to generate clear implications for action. Many forces besides culture constrain decision making and administrative action. Hence, participants are unlikely to be able to base action planning directly on their cultural diagnosis.

Culture Inventories

In an attempt to overcome the methodological limitations of qualitative research and to promote rigorous research on organizational culture, scholars and consultants developed standardized instruments for assessing particular culture features.[8] Most of these instruments consist of inventories of statements or terms describing the norms and values prevailing within an organization. Respondents sort the statements or react to them using Likert scales.

Among the most extensively tested and validated instruments are two designed to measure the cultural variations identified in the Competing Values model (Denison & Spreitzer, 1991; Zammuto & Krakower, 1991). According to this model, organizational values and assumptions vary along two main dimensions: focus on internal maintenance versus focus on external, competitive position; and emphasis on stability, control, and order versus emphasis on change and flexibility.[9] In keeping with these variations, organizations stress different combinations of means and ends (e.g., use of planning and goal setting as a means to goal attainment versus reliance on individual and team adaptability). Cross-tabulating the two dimensions creates a typology of ideal types: the team (or clan), the adhocracy, the hierarchy, and the firm

(Denison & Spreitzer, 1991).[10] The first and most widely used Competing Values instrument (Quinn & Spreitzer, 1991; Zammuto & Krakower, 1991) presents respondents with a set of characteristics describing the four ideal-typical organizations. This instrument forces respondents to decide which type their organization most closely resembles and then aggregates individual choices. The result is a holistic profile of organizational culture that is not suited to correlation-based statistical analyses (Quinn & Spreitzer, 1991).

The second Competing Values instrument produces independent measures of the same organizational dimensions (Quinn & Spreitzer, 1991). These instruments have been used in research on a wide range of organizations, including businesses and universities in the United States (e.g., Cameron & Freeman, 1991). Measures based on the Competing Values instruments correlate with organizational productivity, effectiveness, and organizational practices, such as human resource management practices (Yeung et al., 1991).[11]

An advantage of standardized instruments for measuring culture is that they allow practitioners to start the diagnosis with a predefined set of potentially influential norms or values. When the topics for diagnosis have been studied widely in previous research, such standardized instruments can provide valuable data. Cultural inventories can facilitate comparisons between subgroups and between entire organizations, as well as comparisons over time. In addition, some of the instruments, such as the Competing Values instruments, operationalize theoretical models of direct diagnostic relevance. Unfortunately, there are serious drawbacks to relying on the current set of quantitative inventories (Martin & Frost, 1966; Rousseau, 1990a). Only a limited number of studies document the impact of culture on group and organizational effectiveness. Another problem is that most standard instruments are designed, administered, and analyzed in ways that assume and portray cultural integration, rather than differentiation or ambiguity. Yet close attention to the distributions reported in quantitative studies reveals wide divergences in reported norms and values among units, levels, and functions within the same organization.

Because standardized instruments stress cultural features that prevail across many organizations, these measures do not help investigators discover poorly understood patterns and cultural effects or those that are unique to a particular organization or to a subculture within it. Moreover, questionnaire studies of necessity neglect the situations and organizational contexts that shape the meanings that people assign to symbols and actions. By concentrating on cultural patterns that can be readily described by members, these inventories tap into the upper layers of culture, rather than illuminate hidden or unarticulated beliefs and assumptions. In addition, there is a risk that respondents to questionnaires will prefer organizationally or socially desirable responses to frank revelations. The use of standardized instruments also prevents the investigator from learning about the terms, concepts, and frames that participants use when they describe their organization in their own words. Yet when subject to careful analysis, the metaphors and terms that people use to describe their organization, along with their selective emphases and omissions, can provide valuable clues to their underlying cultural orientations (e.g., Larwood, 1992; Marshak, 1993).

Conclusion

As they rode the wave of popularity in the 1980s, management consultants specializing in culture change declared confidently that "soft is hard"—that culture and other ill-defined and difficult-to-assess features of organizational life can decisively affect bottom-line results. More than 10 years later, few would deny that possibility. Nor would many consultants ignore the impacts of culture on the consulting process and on the formation and implementation of managerial decisions. Nevertheless, it is time to admit that the very characteristics that make culture and emergent behavior important for diagnosis and for management render them hard to assess and resistant to planned change.

This chapter examined ways that practitioners of diagnosis can understand and diagnose these "messy" and management-resistant features of culture in order to provide useful feedback to clients about culture as context for action and object of change. The diagnostic implications of four theoretical perspectives on culture were explored, along with specific diagnostic techniques and data-gathering methods. In light of the difficulties of directly managing or altering culture, we stressed the importance of assessing the feasibility of interventions aimed at culture change and the importance of considering ways to influence culture indirectly rather than through direct interventions.

Acknowledging the difficulties of diagnosing and changing culture seems preferable to trying to force culture in all its complexity and ambiguity into a narrow, functionalist mold. That effort promotes too simple a view of the nature of culture and too casual an approach to trying to manage cultural change. To put it another way, consultants and managers need to recognize that organizational culture is not just another design feature that can be rearranged by management fiat. Organizations do not really *have* cultures, they *are* cultures. And cultures are usually multifaceted, ambiguous, and hard to manage. When organizational cultures do become very cohesive, influential, and subject to managerial control, organizational members run the risk of becoming ill-equipped to consider alternative points of view and to adapt to rapid external change.

Many of the risks associated with diagnosing and managing culture can be avoided if practitioners of diagnosis follow the sharp-image path. In sharp-image diagnosis, the investigator begins to examine cultural orientations in depth only when these orientations appear to account for major ineffective outcomes or to bear directly on pivotal organizational challenges. Even in these instances, diagnosis includes consideration of alternative or complementary sources of ineffectiveness or effectiveness and carefully weighs the likely usefulness and feasibility of action alternatives. When clients directly intervene to change culture, or when culture is to be altered as a consequence of other types of planned change, consultants and their clients can benefit by treating the change project as a form of diagnostic inquiry into change. This approach can help generate opportunities for learning about the organization's culture and about culture change throughout the change project.

This chapter concludes the second part of the book, in which we examined the diagnosis and assessment of focal areas that are important in many organizations and situations. Part 3 extends the applications of sharp-image diagnosis and often forms of diagnosis to macro-organizational functions and conditions that can be crucial to managers, policymakers, and other clients of diagnosis. The topics covered include labor relations, business strategy, the dynamics of organizational growth and decline, and the performance of entire organizational sectors. Surprisingly, these important areas have not received the attention due them in past treatments of organizational diagnosis and assessment (e.g., Howard et al., 1994).

Notes

1. We limit ourselves to examining modern, as opposed to postmodern, analyses of culture. However, as Martin and Frost (1996) suggest, even postmodernism contains insights of value to practicing managers and consultants. To date, few postmodernists have presented their ideas in ways that make them clear and useful for nonspecialists.

2. In contrast, Martin and Frost (1996) view it as a "misunderstanding to conclude that a particular organization has a culture that is best characterized by one of the three perspectives" (p. 610).

3. Ways to combine perspectives and entire theoretical frames are discussed in further detail in Chapter 15.

4. Our presentation of this case restructures findings and interpretations from Wilkins (1983) into a sequence that fits our diagnostic approach. Wilkins does not appear to have used this type of approach in his original analysis.

5. Weick and Roberts (1993) suggest that this is indeed the case, but they do not seek to account systematically for the sources of collective mind on the carriers.

6. Huselid (1995) does not deal explicitly with culture in his important analysis of the impacts of high-performance human resource practices on turnover, productivity, and financial performance. However, several of the practices considered (e.g., quality assurance programs, information sharing with employees) are characteristic of organizations having cultures supporting high employee involvement in the work process (Lawler, 1986; Lawler et al., 1992). See also Becker and Gerhart (1996).

7. See Contributing to Innovation and Organizational Learning in Chapter 13.

8. For examples, see the references in the section on Culture Versus Climate, earlier in this chapter.

9. In their original formulation, Quinn and his colleague (Quinn, 1988; Quinn & Rohrbaugh, 1983) referred to a third dimension, stress on means versus ends. This dimension appears in many formulations of the Competing Values model, but not in the applications of the model to culture study, which are cited here.

10. Cameron and Freeman (1991) and Zammuto and Krakower (1991) label these four types the clan, the adhocracy, the hierarchy, and the market. Quinn and Spreitzer (1991) describe these types respectively as possessing group, developmental, hierarchical, and rational cultures.

11. In addition to its use as a basis for assessing culture, the Competing Values model has been applied to the study of organizational configurations, effectiveness, life cycles, and leadership roles. See Buenger, Daft, Conlon, and Austin (1996) for references to this literature.

PART III APPLICATIONS

Diagnosis Across the Organizational Life Cycle

M ust mature organizations decline and fail, much as people and other organisms grow old and die? Can managers revitalize their firms before organizational hardening of the arteries sets in? Can organizations adapt gradually and continuously to external developments, or must they periodically undergo major upheavals and transformations? Questions like these have occupied consultants and managers for decades. They reflect the popularity of life cycle (LC) models borrowed from biological studies of living systems. This chapter examines three LC models that contribute to the analysis of the dynamics of organizations as open systems. These models can help managers and consultants diagnose the distinctive developmental requirements and problems that arise during an organization's life cycle and consider alternatives for coping with these challenges.

Do Organizations Go Through Life Cycle Stages?

Classic LC models, which are surveyed in Quinn and Cameron (1983), typically envision an orderly passage of organizations from a *birth* or *start-up* stage into a period of *growth* and then on to *maturation*. After maturation, most LC models describe a stage of *revitalization* or *elaboration*. Some models (reviewed by Miller & Friesen, 1984a) include a stage of *decline*, which can lead to organizational *death*. Authors who use LC models as a guide to management practice usually assume that managers and consultants can intervene to avert undesirable LC developments, revitalize them, and even bring about full-scale organizational transformations (Adizes, 1988; Greiner, 1972; Kanter et al., 1992; Tichy & DeVanna, 1986). Consultants and managers can benefit from using LC models, but they should exercise caution and care in applying these models to specific organizations. In particular, users should be skeptical of models that posit a single, typical LC path—whether or not these models assume that managers can alter this path.

The greatest contribution of LC models is that they help diagnosticians and managers see how an organization's future practices and performance depend partly on its past development. LC models also show how the characteristic challenges and problems facing an organization shift as the organization develops. For instance, young firms still under the tight personal control of their founders face different types of coordination problems than do mature firms with professional managers, well-established hierarchies, and elaborate formal operating systems (Flamholtz, 1986).

In contrast to these potential contributions, LC models that posit inevitable, sequential movement from one LC stage to another can be misleading (Whetten, 1987). Here is a listing of documented findings about change processes that do not fit well with the picture of orderly, sequential change contained in most LC models: Young and small organizations face greater risks of dissolution than do older and larger ones (Singh, Tucker, & House, 1986). At all stages, both successful performance and failure can lead to disappearance through buyouts and mergers. Decline can occur at any stage in an organization's development, not just after it has become old and top-heavy with administration (Miller & Friesen, 1984a). Organizational change and transitions create risks of organizational failure, even when the changes promote adaptation to external change (Amburgery, Kelly, & Barnett, 1993; but compare Haverman, 1992, p. 55).

Many organizations do not move sequentially through a typical LC sequence (Miller & Friesen, 1984a; Mintzberg & Westley, 1992). Instead, some organizations retain a single constellation of strategy, structure, and behavior more or less indefinitely, rather than passing from one constellation to another (Meyer & Zucker, 1989). Other organizations gradually and continuously evolve (Eisenhardt & Tabrizi, 1995), and some oscillate between periods of convergence around distinctive strategies and periods of divergence and experimentation (Mintzberg & McHugh, 1985). Organizations can also move backwards in the LC sequence by downsizing and adopting simpler structures. With these caveats in mind, let us turn to a research-based model of LC processes that has crucial yet largely unrecognized implications for the diagnosis and management of strategic change.

Momentum Versus Periodic Upheavals

Punctuated Equilibrium

Many organizations go through long periods of momentum (Miller & Friesen, 1984b) that are disturbed by periodic shocks or upheavals.[1] During the 30 years after World War II, Volkswagenwerk closely followed a pattern like this (Mintzberg & Westley, 1992). After a period of strategic stability, the firm met market resistance in the 1950s. Piecemeal adaptations without basic changes in strategy were enough to preserve stability until the mid-1960s. At that point, the company went through an upheaval that led to a search for a fundamentally new design of bodies and engines. The new design and marketing strategy provided the basis for a dramatic turnaround.

The punctuated equilibrium model captures the main features of this LC pattern (Romanelli & Tushman, 1994; Tushman & Romanelli, 1985). According to this model, during periods of momentum, the organization's system elements remain fairly stable and are reasonably well aligned with one another. Moreover, these system elements converge into a discernible pattern or configuration (Gersick, 1991; Miller & Mintzberg, 1983). Minor adjustments do occur during periods of momentum, and there may be some poor fits and loose coupling (Chapter 2). But the forces for organizational inertia (Hannan & Freeman, 1984) remain strong enough to overcome pressures for fundamental strategic change.

Eventually, organizational upheaval upsets the momentum. Within organizations, power struggles, executive succession and other personnel changes, and mounting pressures to improve performance can trigger these upheavals. Environmental turbulence can also upset organizational momentum. In particular, sudden technological breakthroughs, market shifts, and new governmental regulations can precipitate upheaval (Anderson & Tushman, 1990; Romanelli & Tushman, 1994; Tushman & Romanelli, 1985).

Organizational upheavals, or transformations, involve major changes in all or most of the major internal system components discussed in Chapter 2, in power distribution, and in organizational strategies.[2] Transformations like these pose many risks to an organization and often lead to decline or failure. Nevertheless, research suggests that short bursts of discontinuous organizational change are more likely to lead to successful transformations in major system components and features than will small changes in limited system domains (Romanelli & Tushman, 1994).

Envisioning and Planning Change

Consultants and managers can draw on the punctuated equilibrium model to facilitate diagnosis and constructive decision making about two of the most momentous issues facing an organization's dominant coalition: (a) Do current or foreseeable trends in environment, technology, or leadership create challenges that necessitate a major transformation because they cannot be met adequately through incremental adjustments and the use of short-term coping tactics? and (b) If transformation is necessary, should radical changes be attempted within a short time period, or should the organization undertake longer-term programs that encompass coordinated yet incremental moves?

Managerial experience, consultant expertise, academic knowledge—none of these provides a solid guide to steering an organization into the future. Instead, these moves are fraught with uncertainty and with unintended consequences. Hence, judgments about the nature of environmental and technological threats or opportunities, and decisions about how to deal with these challenges, fall within the province and responsibility of an organization's directors, owners, and top managers. In consequence, the diagnoses that can inform these judgments can be carried out most appropriately through the participation of top managers and other change strategists in collaborative diagnostic techniques such as open-systems planning (Chapter 4) or scenario planning (Chapter 13). Alternatively, a consultant might conduct a diagnosis focused on these issues and develop action recommendations, which then serve as inputs into independent strategic decision making by members of the dominant coalition.

The first question posed at the start of this section asks whether or not the organization can ride out current challenges without having to undergo fundamental reorganizations. Decision makers who try to ride out external or internal challenges to accepted ways of organizing and working make the least difficult and least costly moves that may respond adequately to changing conditions. The still-limited research base for the punctuated equilibrium model suggests that most organizations ride out change most of the time. Managers following this approach can, for example, simply ignore downturns in demand and other external challenges in the hope that they are temporary. Similarly, they can ignore or try to suppress power struggles and conflicts that reflect external challenges. Managers can also cope with challenges by employing short-term coping tactics, such as temporarily hiring additional staff or laying off employees. They can also symbolize concern with adaptation without making commitments to concerted action—by studying developments without acting on them, engaging in public relations campaigns, or introducing superficial improvements in service or production without fundamentally reorganizing core processes. Finally, managers can take steps toward adaptation to new challenges that do not require major reorganizations. For example, they can improve or extend products or services without entering into entirely new lines of activity.

Trying to ride out change or cope with it on a piecemeal basis poses fewer risks and generally requires less effort in the short run. But in the long run, this response to external and internal challenges may hold great risks.

Practitioners of diagnosis and decision makers can use three analytical techniques to help them judge whether the focal organization can reasonably follow a conservative approach to coping with current and anticipated challenges. First, diagnosticians can use gap analysis (Chapter 2) to assess past outcomes of tactics for riding out challenges and to judge the likely consequences of relying on these tactics in the future. To start, the consultant and any other participants in the diagnosis identify important gaps between current performance and performance expectations by powerful stakeholders, including owners, funding agencies, and customers. The participants in the diagnosis then judge whether coping tactics helped narrow this gap in the past, and whether they are likely to do so in the future. For instance, members of a financial services company facing a downturn in new business could evaluate the effects of past advertising campaigns in order to judge whether launching another such campaign would be likely to help close the gap between current services and customer responses to those services. If the answer is negative, then a meaningful change in the services offered is probably needed.

A second way to decide whether coping moves will be sufficient to handle challenges is to assess current and anticipated fits among the organization's system components and the environment. If the organization is judged to be seriously misaligned, or if such misalignments are expected in the near future, then small adjustments to current operations are not likely to be sufficient to help the organization cope with expected challenges and threats. Instead, a fundamental reorganization may be necessary.

Consider a firm based in a midwestern American city that flourished for decades by building close, personal ties between the firm's managers and their local suppliers, banks, and customers. College graduates from prominent local families received management positions in the firm and represented it in negotiations with external actors. These managers received technical backing from assistants, who were recruited from outside the area. The firm's managers and their external colleagues viewed each other as friends and neighbors and often conducted their business at backyard barbecues and on the golf course. Most of the business in and outside the firm was conducted orally, with only brief written summaries being made, as required by law. Now the firm is about to be acquired by a national corporation that relies heavily on written communication, quantitative control systems, and portfolio management (Hedley, 1977). The strategies, management processes, and cultures of the national and local firms are radically out of alignment with each other. It seems very unlikely that these misalignments can be handled adequately through incremental moves, such as retraining managers in the local firm or making minor alterations in the firm's control systems. Instead, major changes in strategy, personnel, power distribution, controls, and technology are likely to follow the acquisition, as are other changes in structure and culture.

A third means of judging whether fundamental change is necessary is to use the techniques discussed in the last part of this chapter to assess whether external threats and organizational responses presage organizational decline. If decline has begun or is expected, then more than short-term adjustments or coping techniques are needed to reverse this course of events. Instead, radical reorganization is probably called for, despite the risks involved.

Suppose that decision makers reach the conclusion that they must embark on a radical reorganization of their organization. The second question posed at the outset of this discussion asks whether radical changes should be attempted within a short time period, say a year or two, or whether a set of well-integrated, incremental moves should be preferred. The former approach might be thought of as involving bold strokes, whereas the latter requires a long march toward change, which could extend over several years or more (Kanter et al., 1992, pp. 492-495). Bold strokes are short-term strategic moves with immediate, noticeable, and restricted impacts. They include reassigning resources to develop new technologies or products, closing plants, selling parts of the firm, or negotiating a strategic alliance with another organization. A set of coordinated bold strokes can provide the basis for a major program of organizational transformation.

Practitioners of diagnosis can help decision makers weigh the pros and cons of each approach to organizational transformation. Managers can only contemplate long marches if their organization does not face immediate threats to its survival and has not entered into a trajectory of decline. If time is of the essence, only bold strokes can be considered. At first glance, if time constraints permit a choice, the long march seems to be preferable. It allows management the time needed to diagnose challenges, plan changes in design and strategy, ensure that other system components sustain these changes, implement programs in stages, and assess program implementation (Chapters 7 and 13). Furthermore, this approach allows for preserving continuity with past operations and holds out the prospect of avoiding disruption of constructive features of the current organizational configuration.

Unfortunately, close examination reveals many drawbacks to the long-march approach to change that go beyond those cognitive constraints that limit the effectiveness of any type of planned change. Long marches are particularly hard to accomplish because they require the investment of much time and money and the coordination of many different operations and procedures over a period of years. Furthermore, the sought-for transformation requires the cooperation, participation, and commitment of people from many levels of the organization. These types of involvement cannot be mandated and executed from just one level of management. Moreover, as complex change programs unfold, they are likely to encounter resistance by affected stakeholders.

Perhaps the fatal flaw in attempts to plan integrated, long-term steps toward transformation is that the environmental, technological, and strategic contingencies that shaped the original program for transformation are likely to change before the program has been fully implemented. These changes in critical contingencies will, in turn, require management to revise its plans and to recoordinate the complex moves on which the overall transformation depends. Under conditions of rapid environmental and technological change, coordinating long marches thus becomes a very taxing and daunting challenge for top management.

Bold strokes can produce clear, short-term results and sometimes can produce radical, meaningful change in a short period of time—before further external changes occur and before stakeholders can mobilize to resist change. Moreover, a well-integrated series of bold strokes that recasts fundamental design features can gradually and indirectly lead to changes in organizational culture or even in strategy. For example, a series of cutbacks and outsourcing decisions can trim functions in a highly integrated firm to such a degree that the firm is transformed into one with a narrow functional specialization. The transformed firm becomes much more closely linked to the market for crucial products and services than was its predecessor.

Despite their promise, bold strokes often do not achieve the fundamental transformations that change strategists hoped for (Romanelli & Tushman, 1994). One reason is that uncoordinated moves within a single system component, such as structure, do not usually trigger changes in other basic features, such as culture or behavior patterns. In particular, unless major changes occur in human resource processes and in control systems, taken-for-granted assumptions and routine ways of working may survive structural change and other bold strokes.

Bold strokes may also fail because they destroy continuities with the past and thus destabilize an organization's current operations. For instance, cuts in personnel and in entire management levels or functions can make it hard for members of an organization to draw on past experience and accumulated expertise. Instead, they must reinvent and redevelop procedures that were once routine. In a similar fashion, radical changes can undermine loyalties that linked employees, suppliers, and other parties to the organization and helped ensure smooth operating conditions.

Whether managers opt for coping tactics, bold strokes, or long marches, they need to diagnose carefully the challenges and threats to which they wish to respond. Such a diagnosis will include a careful assessment of the feasibility and likely impact of proposed moves (Chapter 7). In making these assessments, diagnosticians and their clients can consider the time frame in which moves must be made; sources of leadership, support, and resistance to change; resources and capacity for change; coordination and fit between system elements undergoing change; and operational problems with implementing change. Assessments during implementation can help enhance the chances of successful implementation. Feedback can encourage managers who are responsible for change to adopt a reflective approach, through which they learn about their organization and the change process as change unfolds. Thus, they can reassess both their programs and their own implicit models and understandings in light of feedback on implementation.

The punctuated equilibrium model helps remind consultants and managers that organizations typically enjoy long periods of moderate stability and system equilibrium during which small-scale improvements and extensions of current operations are sufficient to maintain or even enhance effectiveness. Only the most radical disjunctions between organization, environment, and technology necessitate major organizational transformations. This model thus serves as a corrective to claims that the environments in which modern organizations operate have become so turbulent and chaotic that managers must give up on conventional management practices and resign themselves to engaging in permanent, radical change (e.g., Vaill, 1989). Although valuable, the punctuated equilibrium model does not appear to be universally applicable. Some organizations seem to operate indefinitely without undergoing upheaval and reorganization. The punctuated equilibrium model also suffers from its abstractness. The model reviewed next uses somewhat less abstract categories to capture the changes that organizations undergo as they grow and adapt to changing conditions.

Diagnosis During Life Cycle Stages

Stages of Growth Model

Here is one synthesis of the many models of stages of organizational growth and development, which can serve as a guide to diagnosis (Bartunek & Louis, 1988; Cameron & Whetten, 1983; Quinn & Cameron, 1983). This model specifies four developmental stages:

Entrepreneurial stage: A powerful entrepreneur or founder initiates and coordinates activities. Roles and structures are loosely defined. Without much formal planning or coordination, resources are marshalled and an environmental niche is discovered. Many ideas and proposals circulate, and risk taking is encouraged.

Collectivity stage: Structure and communication remain informal. Teamwork becomes important, but coordination remains centered on the leader/founder. There is a strong sense of mission and group identity. Commitment remains high, and members often work long hours. Innovativeness and creativity continue to be emphasized.

Formalization and Control stage: As rules and procedures become formalized and agreed upon, stable structures and operating procedures emerge. The culture becomes more conservative as management stresses stability and efficiency rather than innovation and risk taking.

Structural Elaboration stage: The structure becomes more complex and may be decentralized as the organization expands its domains, adapts to internal and external developments, and undergoes renewal.

Many successful businesses follow a developmental path similar to the one described by this model (Miller & Friesen, 1984b; Scott, 1971). In doing so, they undergo one or more transformations like those described by the Punctuated Equilibrium model. Although the stages-of-growth model fits the experience of many organizations, we must overcome three limitations in the model in order to make it broadly applicable. First, as the next part of this chapter shows, organizations can undergo decline, not just growth. Second, organizations do not inevitably move forward from one stage to the next. They may shift back to a previous stage as they develop new products, services, and markets, or as they reorganize their operations.

Third, and particularly important for diagnosis, divisions or subunits within one complex organization can be located in separate stages of development. Functional subsystems may have been established at different times and may have developed along different LC paths. Even functionally parallel units may be located at different stages. Suppose a multidivision firm acquires a small private business that is in the Collectivity stage. To preserve the flexibility and team spirit of the new acquisition, corporate headquarters may define the new unit as an autonomous strategic business unit (SBU). This new SBU can remain in the Collectivity stage even though other SBUs within the organization have moved into the Formalization and Control stage, and the organization as a whole is in the Elaboration stage.

Contributions to Diagnosis

The stages-of-growth model can contribute to diagnostic studies by orienting practitioners to four sets of important issues that are affected by LC development: First, a unit's LC stage shapes the main system requirements facing that unit and the characteristic problems that arise in handling these requirements. LC developments thus help define relevant diagnostic issues and focal areas. Second, the LC stage influences the types of effectiveness criteria that are most strongly emphasized within an organization (Quinn & Cameron, 1983). During the Entrepreneurial stage, effectiveness is usually judged in terms of acquiring resources, establishing an environmental niche, and maintaining innovativeness. These criteria continue to be important during the Collectivity stage, but considerations of internal solidarity and human relations now come to the fore. During the Formalization and Control stage, powerful stakeholders are likely to emphasize criteria related to efficiency, stability, and organizational control. Criteria such as adaptation and system fit (Table 3.1) become especially critical as the unit or organization moves toward the Structural Elaboration stage.

Third, the LC stage can affect the appropriateness of particular managerial and consultant interventions. Consider interventions that clarify reporting relations and job definitions.[3] These interventions suit many organizations that are moving toward the Formalization and Control stage. Further growth and restructuring can require additional clarifications of formal structural features, such as job titles and hierarchical relations. But as an organization matures, further elaborations of hierarchical controls and reporting relations carry an increasing risk of blocking communication flows and stifling innovation and creativity.

Fourth, the LC stage can affect issues of consulting process, such as relations between practitioners of diagnosis and their supporters and sponsors. For example, in an organization's Entrepreneurial stage, it may be appropriate for the founder of the organization to serve as the sole client for diagnosis and for other forms of consultation. But suppose that this organization enters the Collectivity stage and encounters serious problems in building an effective management team. Then, consultants and founders may need to define all members of the management team as clients so as to promote team building. As the organization grows and becomes more complex, the differences between units and stakeholder groups become more pronounced. Hence, more complex definitions of the client that reflect stakeholder diversity can become appropriate. A steering committee made up of representatives of stakeholding groups can fill this type of client role. Alternatively, the manager who is directly responsible for implementing the study's findings can serve as its chief client.

More generally, LC developments shape internal political processes (Gray & Ariss, 1985; Mintzberg, 1984) and thereby influence the types of diagnostic and consulting practices that are likely to be effective (Harrison, 1991). Client-centered diagnosis and traditional organization development practices, such as team building and participative planning for change, require mutual trust and openness among participants and between consultants and the members of the client organization. These supportive conditions are more likely to occur when organizations are growing steadily. Growth provides slack resources that management may deploy without threatening vested interests. Growth also increases the chances that changes can benefit most groups rather than benefiting some people at the expense of others. In contrast, relations often become more politicized and conflict ridden during transitions between LC stages or when growth lags and stagnation or decline sets in. During transitions, when the future prospects for the organization are uncertain, proposals for diagnosis and change are likely to arouse fears and conflicts concerning possible losses of jobs, power, status, and funds. In some cases, skillful consultants may help members of a client organization overcome divergences of interests and define common goals and needs. They may thereby facilitate compromise and bargaining among participants, who represent divergent interest groups, such as management and labor.

Locating the Focal Organization Within the Life Cycle

To define the location of a focal organization within the LC, diagnostic practitioners can follow three basic guidelines:

1. *Focus on relevant subunits.* When organizations are small and simply organized, it is possible to locate the entire organization at a particular stage. When working with complex organizations, it is preferable to focus just on the units that are the target of the diagnosis. For example, suppose that a consultant conducts a sharp-image diagnosis that focuses on the quality of administrative services, such as billing and records management, provided by a large hospital. The hospital as a whole may be in the Elaboration stage, having developed a differentiated structure to cope with a complex mix of patients, tasks, and employees. But the hospital's central administrative bureaucracy, which is most important for the diagnosis, has probably remained in the Formalization and Control stage.

2. *Concentrate on structural and administrative features to determine the LC stage.* Organizations in each of the four stages differ in the formalization

and elaboration of their structures, as well as in other features, such as their emphasis on effectiveness criteria, and their norms and values. Differences in formal structures and administrative procedures are listed first in the capsule definitions of the LC stages given above. These features are easier to observe and isolate and are more definitive of each stage than are the other features of the LC stages. Formal structural features are also more clear-cut than are quantitative indicators of LC development, which are treated next.

3. *Define and measure quantitative indicators of LC growth.* Growth and decline are often defined in terms of changes in an organization's major resource flows, such as revenues from sales and services or budgetary allocations. Less frequently, other indicators are added of the size of operations and levels of .performance. Studies that establish LC location by growth rates (e.g., Miller & Friesen, 1984a, p. 1166) usually anticipate a curvilinear pattern. Growth is highest during the first two stages; levels off, but remains positive during the Formalization and Control stage; and rises once the Elaboration stage has been entered successfully. Stagnant or declining annual figures signal the inability of for-profit organizations to accomplish the LC transitions and may herald decline.

Where appropriate, additional measures can be developed to track the organization's productivity, competitive position, and financial performance. In selecting indicators of growth, practitioners must take into account their appropriateness to the particular organization and its current stage in the life cycle. For instance, once they reach the Collectivity stage, many not-for-profit organizations and even some private firms (Churchill & Lewis, 1983) can survive and even prosper without further growth. Hence, if clients and stakeholders do not define effectiveness in terms of growth, practitioners of diagnosis should not exaggerate the importance of growth indicators. The discussion of decline that follows considers additional aspects of the measurement and interpretation of quantitative LC indicators.

Diagnosis Across the Life Cycle

After identifying a focal unit's LC stage, practitioners can address opportunities and problems that are particularly characteristic and critical at that stage. The organization's treatment of characteristic LC requirements and problems can affect its future development and pave the way to further growth or decline. Sometimes, clients will directly approach consultants for help in making LC transitions. In other cases, the clients present immediate concerns that reflect system requirements that are characteristic of a particular LC stage or of transitions between stages. In the latter case, through sharp-image diagnosis, the practitioner can discern the LC dynamics that underline presented problems or symptoms of ineffectiveness.

Table 11.1 lists some of the most characteristic system requirements for each LC stage and gives questions to guide diagnosis of how well the focal unit or organization meets these developmental needs. Each diagnostic question refers to several organizational functions, such as the capacity to monitor internal and external developments and to take action on them. Failure to meet the functional requirements that are characteristic of a particular LC stage is hypothesized to be a common source of ineffectiveness during that stage. For example, during the Formalization stage, problems of poor quality and high costs often come to the fore. These problems frequently can be traced to deficiencies in formal administrative and operating systems or to emergent practices or cultural orientations that work against quality and cost savings. Practitioners will have to develop clear definitions and appropriate assessment methods for those requirements and system features that preliminary study shows lead to ineffectiveness or harm the focal organization's capacity to meet important challenges.

Many of the requirements listed in Table 11.1 for a particular stage arise at an earlier stage, but in that stage, they do not seriously affect crucial organizational processes or outcomes. For example, the need to establish reliable operating systems, which is noted under the Collectivity stage, already arises during the Entrepreneurial stage. But during the Entrepreneurial stage, operations are usually modest enough to be amenable to personal control by the founder and a few other top managers (Mintzberg, 1979). Once operations broaden greatly, personal supervision and provisional controls begin to break down or produce ineffective outcomes, such as client dissatisfaction or work delays.

In summary, the stages-of-growth model helps orient diagnostic practitioners and organizational decision makers to the problems and challenges that often become acute during particular stages in the organizational life cycle and to the system requirements underlying these problems. In addition, this model draws attention to LC contingencies affecting the impacts and appropriateness of interventions by managers or consultants.

Table 11.1 Developmental Requirements and Diagnostic Issues Across the Life Cycle

ENTREPRENEURIAL STAGE

Acquiring Resources

Are key resources available—capital, staff, know-how, technology, authorizations?

Finding the Right Niche

Has the founder discovered or created an underserviced market niche? Do the organization's products and services meet market needs and standards?

Fostering Innovation and Flexibility Without Chaos

Do management procedures support innovation, creativity, and rapid response to new challenges?

How successful is the founder or head of the organization at generating commitment to his or her vision and goals? Does the founder effectively coordinate internal operations and relations?

COLLECTIVITY STAGE

Coordinating

Do communication and decision-making processes enable members to cope with rapid growth and changing external conditions?

Do operating procedures ensure a reliable flow of services and products?

Promoting Cohesion

Is the staff operating well as a team? Is it cohesive, high in morale, and guided by common goals and culture?

Developing Human Resources

Do the rewards offered and the opportunities for individual development fit the needs and capabilities of employees? Are employees developing managerial skills and other skills that will be needed as the company grows?

FORMALIZATION STAGE

Shifting to Professional Management

Has the organization succeeded in shifting responsibility for major functional areas from the founder (or the founding group) to trained and experienced managers?

Monitoring the Environment and Internal Operations

Do mechanisms for scanning internal and external conditions identify major opportunities and threats to organizational viability? Is the organization capable of acting on this information?

Managing External Relations

How effectively does the organization cope with external constraints and conflicting external demands? Does the management actively shape external conditions and choose favorable environmental sectors in which to operate?

Holding Down Costs and Ensuring Quality

Do formal operating and management procedures ensure quality and efficiency? Do emergent behavior patterns and culture also contribute to quality and efficiency?

Achieving Coordination and Control Without Rigidity

Do administrative structures and procedures grant managers the autonomy they need to do their best work? Do rewards, norms, and values support innovativeness, creativity, and initiative?

(Continued)

TABLE 11.1 Continued

ELABORATION STAGE

Adapting to Change
   Is the organization improving its current products and services to meet market demand?

Developing New Products and Services
   Is the organization diversifying its products and services so as to exploit its distinctive competencies in new markets or environmental sectors?

Integrating Divergent Units and Functions
   Have structures emerged that appropriately reflect the divergent markets and tasks facing the organization? Is there sufficient coordination between differentiated units? Does top management have adequate control over operations within divisions or subunits?

Managing Transitions
   Has the management developed appropriate goals and plans for further transitions—such as renewal, cutbacks, turnaround—that the organization must undergo? Does the organization have the capacity to carry out these transitions?

Organizational Decline

The last LC model for examination can guide diagnosis of the forces that drive organizations into decline and consideration of ways to cope with or avoid decline. The following example serves to illustrate the problems of defining and diagnosing decline:

> After its founding in 1936, the Israel Philharmonic Orchestra (IPO) gradually earned an international reputation and attracted a long list of dedicated subscribers to its local concert series. During the 1950s and 1960s, the IPO served at home and abroad as a shining symbol of Israel's national revival. By the 1990s, the IPO had lost its unique role and reputation. Today, major cultural events often feature other orchestras from Israel and Europe. IPO subscriptions no longer sell out. Instead, the IPO competes for audiences and subscribers with several other popular orchestras and with a flourishing new opera company. What is more, the New Israel Opera and other newly founded bodies are successfully competing with the IPO for public funding. Critics attack the IPO musical director for lacking imagination in his choice of repertoire, failing to attract top conductors and soloists, and neglecting local composers and artists (Ben Zeev, 1993). Is the IPO declining? Or has it simply entered a period of maturity and stability that followed years of spectacular growth and success?

Clear definitions and models of decline can help consultants and managers diagnose why many organizations, like the IPO, seem unable to live up to their past achievements. These analytical guidelines can help analysts decide whether an organization is declining and, if so, can guide diagnosis of sources of decline, its extent, and possibilities for managerial action.

Sources of Decline

Decline is best defined as an involuntary downturn in the flow of resources to an organization or as a drop in organizational performance (Cameron et al., 1987). By this criterion, the IPO is declining if its overall revenues from subscriptions, donations, and public subsidies have fallen off over the past few years. But as the IPO example suggests, decline can also contain a second, more subjective dimension—decline of the image of the organization in the eyes of its influential exchange partners (Sutton, 1990). These partners are individuals and groups that can ultimately affect the organization's right to operate (e.g., by licensing or granting special operating privileges) or determine the flow of resources to it (e.g., by making budget allocations). In terms of this subjective dimension, the IPO is declining if its image has become tarnished in the eyes of potential subscribers, critics, private patrons of the arts, and the politicians and public servants who decide on its subsidies.

Declines in resource flows often can be traced to a shrinking or shifting resource base within the environmental sector or niche in which an organization operates (Cameron et al., 1987; Cameron, Sutton, & Whetten, 1988; Zammuto & Cameron, 1985). These changes in the level and types of demand within a niche affect all the organizations operating there. The level of demand for products or services within the niche may drop as a result of demographic changes, decisions by external organizations that affect prices or subsidies, and changing consumer tastes. If this type of environmental change were affecting the IPO, then the drop in IPO subscribers could be traced to trends such as the aging of the population and fading interest in classical music among younger people.

Shifts also occur in the types of products and services demanded within an environmental niche. This type of change would be occurring in the IPO case if total subscriptions for classical music have not declined in Israel, but classical music subscribers increasingly prefer tickets that cost less than those offered by the IPO or prefer chamber music to performances by full-scale symphony orchestras.

Changes in an organization's operating niche can occur gradually or suddenly (Zammuto & Cameron, 1985). Shifts in demographics, taste, and market forces usually produce gradual erosion or dissolution of a niche. On the other hand, sudden drops or shifts in demand or environmental support can stem from economic and political upheavals; social crises such as scandals and whistle-blowing episodes; and technical, natural, medical, and military disasters (Pearson & Mitroff, 1993). Pivotal events—such as the passage of a law, the enactment of a regulation, court decisions, management succession, product recalls, or dramatic innovations by competitors—can also lead to sudden changes in demand.

In contrast to declines affecting all organizations in an environmental niche, one or more organizations can experience decline while operating in a stable or growing niche. In this instance, actions by the declining organization are more likely to be directly responsible for the drop in resource flows. Suppose, for example, that analysis shows that the subscription sales of competing orchestras in Israel are rising, whereas those of the IPO are falling. In that case, the IPO's problems cannot be attributed just to trends within the national classical music market. Instead, they are likely to stem from unique organizational characteristics and from organizational actions that can be identified through careful diagnostic study.

Temporary Downturn or Long-Term Decline?

Assessment of the depth and persistence of decline, along with careful analysis of its sources, can make a major contribution to managerial decision making. If managers can distinguish between temporary and enduring downturns, they can better decide which types of action are needed. In particular, as the Punctuated Equilibrium model suggests, managers need to decide whether to take only limited defensive actions, so as to ride out the downturn, or to engage in more intensive and extensive remedial actions.

If the downturn is enduring, the organization's resource flows will continue to drop unless top management takes effective remedial action that produces both short-term relief and long-term strategic change. In some cases, these strategic changes will contribute to full-scale organizational transformations like those described by the Punctuated Equilibrium model. Left unchecked, the downward spiral of decline can eventually lead to organizational crisis, in which the organization lacks the funds needed to continue daily operations or faces legal, political, or normative threats to its right to operate (Weitzel & Jonsson, 1989).

Early detection of both temporary and enduring declines can greatly ease the burden on management. Early warning may help managers avert the need for drastic emergency measures to halt cash-flow crises or restore confidence in their organization. Moreover, when managers have more time to cope with a downturn, they can experiment with alternative ways of handling external challenges and can more carefully plan and implement recovery programs or even full-scale transformations, should these be judged necessary.

Examining Trend Data

Trend data that are carefully gathered and analyzed can help diagnostic practitioners assess the depth and extent of decline. But these data rarely generate results that are unambiguous, and they cannot predict the future. Different indicators can tell different stories, and people can interpret statistical patterns in keeping with their own perceptions about what is happening within the focal organization. An additional problem is that the people who generate or transmit trend data sometimes seek to gloss over evidence of poor performance or declining revenues. Analysts therefore need to be sure that their trend data are valid. Whenever possible, it is advisable to triangulate the measures of expansion, contraction, and performance, as well as the sources of these data. Data on organizational performance can be compared to data on output flows, and reports by management can be compared to assessments by external stakeholders and independent evaluators.

Indicators of growth and decline can be chosen in much the same way that effectiveness criteria are selected (Chapter 3). Investigators usually start their analysis by examining trends on indicators that powerful clients and stakeholders regard as most critical. For instance, assessments of growth and decline among publicly held companies often examine return on investment rather than ordinary revenue measures because investors rely on this indicator to judge a firm's performance. Budgetary allocations often give the best indication of the extent to which public sector organizations or subunits continue to enjoy political and financial support.

Interorganizational comparisons can supplement assessments of temporal developments within a single organization. For instance, analysts can compare the growth or performance of a focal organization to industrywide or sectoral trends or to other comparable organizations within the industry. Suppose that IPO subscriptions dropped by 10% during the past decade. If total classical music subscriptions rose or remained stable during the decade, then the 10%

drop may indeed signal management failure. But if the total number of subscriptions dropped by 30% during the decade, then the IPO has successfully increased its share of a declining market.

Practitioners can also look for evidence of long-term growth prospects. For instance, a consultant to the IPO might look for indicators that the orchestra was successfully attracting and retaining first-time subscribers, on the assumption that satisfied new subscribers will produce enduring revenue flows, help the organization retain its public standing, and may even recruit additional subscribers and supporters. In a similar fashion, consultants to industrial firms sometimes examine trends in patents granted or in expenditures for research and development on the rather strong assumption that new product development predicts future sales and profits.

Warning Signals

Qualitative data can supplement quantitative trend data and can sometimes provide warning of decline before it shows up in statistical trends. Here is a list of possible early warning signals that were drawn from studies of declining organizations (D'Aveni & MacMillian, 1990; Nystrom & Starbuck, 1984; Starbuck et al., 1978; Weitzel & Jonsson, 1989; Whetten, 1987):

- Deteriorating image in eyes of customers, funding agencies, public
- Failure to diagnose and respond to client and customer dissatisfaction
- Failure to track environmental developments and plan responses
- Current strategies, resource commitments, and management procedures rule out innovation and experimentation
- Ignoring actions taken by other comparable organizations to deal with eroding or shifting demand
- Lack of attention to coming pivotal events—such as elections, court decisions
- No contingency plans for upheavals, disasters, crises
- Denial of external threats, risks, erosion, shift of demand
- Overconfidence, feelings of invulnerability

Most of these warning signals point to failures of management to pay close attention to external developments and to respond to negative feedback from the environment. Managers sometimes ignore or deny external threats and temporary downturns because their organization's past successes seem to guarantee a rosy future. Furthermore, the very strategies and policies that contributed to past successes can block innovation, experimentation, and adaptation to changing external conditions. The emergence of vested interests that benefit from the status quo and resist change can further intensify this "dilemma of success" (Kanter et al., 1992, p. 45).

Evidence of warning signs of decline can supplement statistical evidence of decline or help decision makers and consultants anticipate it. The risk of decline rises when more of these signs occur or when they are particularly acute. Downturns in revenue and performance may have already begun. If not, unless external conditions improve or management takes remedial actions, downturns are likely to follow.

Stages of Decline

Another way to judge whether an organization faces a temporary downturn or one that threatens the organization's survival is to examine whether the organization is passing through the following five stages of decline (Weitzel & Jonsson, 1989, 1991):

1. *Blinded stage.* Decline begins. Decision makers ignore negative evidence and pressures for change.
2. *Inaction stage.* Decline is noticeable. Managers acknowledge internal and external problems but hesitate to act to correct the situation.
3. *Faulty Action stage.* Objective indicators of decline multiply. Internal differences and poor information lead managers to take quick, stopgap measures. Managers fail to make plans for reorganization and long-term recovery or are unable to implement them.
4. *Crisis stage.* Last chance for reversal. Slow erosion results if the environment is tolerant. Otherwise, rapid loss of resources occurs, and confidence of external stakeholders drops quickly.
5. *Dissolution.* Decline is irreversible. It is rapid in unforgiving environments and slow in forgiving ones.

According to this model, organizations may be suddenly thrust into crisis because of catastrophic events, or they may gradually move toward crisis as they pass through the three preliminary stages.

To apply the stages-of-decline model, diagnostic practitioners and organizational decision makers need to decide first whether available data point to organizational decline. If the data do indicate decline but management denies this possibility, the organization may be in the first, Blinded stage of decline.

If management acknowledges the evidence of decline but is unable or unwilling to act on it, then the organization is in the second, Inaction stage. The organization has entered the third, Faulty Action stage when there are many objective signs of decline, but management still resists systematic diagnosis and remedial action. During this stage, management prefers low-cost steps that promise to bring rapid improvements in revenues or performance and temporarily fend off external criticism.

The implication of the above model is that decline can be reversed at any stage in its development except the last. Support for this optimistic assumption is found in empirical studies showing that organizational decline often stimulates adaptation and strategic changes capable of producing rapid organizational transformations (McKinley, 1993; Romanelli & Tushman, 1994). However, the longer management delays systematic and comprehensive remedial action, the greater the risk that decline will lead to crisis and dissolution (D'Aveni & MacMillian, 1990). Bold strokes by management provide little help if they are poorly planned and produce only superficial change. Instead, they can waste vital resources and harm current operations rather than bring relief from decline (Cameron et al., 1991). Managers can help avoid moving into the advanced stages of decline by developing systems for scanning and evaluating conditions that can affect their long-term viability, as well as by acting promptly and decisively on the data generated by these scanning systems.

Although the decline model suggests that managers can successfully halt decline, it also shows that the interests, beliefs, and commitments of incumbent managers frequently block effective remedial action. Managers who are closely associated with past ways of thinking and organizing often fail to sense the need for change or lack the will or power to introduce bold moves. Furthermore, during crisis and decline, incumbent managers can lose the trust of corporate directors and the subordinates who must carry out needed changes. Hence, recovery from decline and other types of strategic change are often accompanied by or triggered by executive succession (Griner, Mayers, & McKiernan, 1988; Romanelli & Tushman, 1994; Tushman & Romanelli, 1985).

Management During Decline

In addition to helping decision makers recognize enduring and dangerous downturns, practitioners of diagnosis can also help them decide on remedial responses to decline. By providing feedback on appropriate action possibilities, consultants encourage managers to prefer adaptive responses to crisis and decline over the very common, but very risky, alternative of rigidity and inaction (McKinley, 1993).

To decide on appropriate actions, consultants and clients need to distinguish between three types of actions: (a) actions needed to provide short-term relief from crises and threats, (b) bold strokes that involve strategic moves toward recovery, and (c) steps to deal with the internal consequences of decline. The discussion that follows concentrates on the second and third types of actions.

Assessing Responses to Decline

Recovery from decline depends on appropriate organizational actions, favorable external conditions, and luck. Hence, no model can specify responses to decline that will invariably produce recovery. The literature on turnaround and recovery strategies (Stewart, 1984; Whitney, 1987) can inform managerial decision making but cannot show managers just how to pull their organization out of decline. Nor will diagnostic feedback yield specific, sure-fire techniques for managing decline. But sharp-image diagnosis of the forces underlying symptoms of decline can help managers understand the sources of decline and decide on remedial actions that best fit their organization's current challenges and capacities.

Research on decline does suggest that the strategies developed in response to decline are more likely to succeed if they fit the nature and sources of decline, as described above (Zammuto & Cameron, 1985). Consider the link between the sources of decline and the time available to managers for coping with change. Gradual erosions or shifts in an organization's environmental niche typically provide managers with more lead time prior to action. When managers discern environmental trends early, they gain months or even years to cope with declining or changing demand for their products and services. They can develop and implement strategies aimed at increasing their shares of contracting markets, or they can gradually diversify into new but related areas of activity. Organizations facing gradual erosion of their niche can also take steps to defend their role in that niche, such as generating political or economic coalitions that support their activities.

In contrast, when managers face sudden environmental downturns or fail to anticipate gradual environmental changes, the managers are forced to cut back promptly on current activities or to turn to the government for emergency support. Managers may also try to move their organization rapidly into new areas of activity, but they will have very little time to plan and implement these moves.

The option of moving into new fields of activity is often not available to public sector organizations. These organizations frequently operate under charters that narrowly define the range of products or services they can provide and limit their revenue sources. Public administrators who are subject to constraints like these have limited options for strategic change. If they recognize early that demand or resources are declining, they can lobby for additional support and introduce efficiencies through cutbacks and through the consolidation of operations on core activities. If public managers fail to recognize these trends toward decline, they can face serious operating crises.

Practitioners can assess the feasibility and likely consequences of alternative strategies for coping with change. To do so, they can examine the political implications of proposed changes (Chapter 5). They can also assess the fits between proposed changes and internal organizational features, as well as organization-environment fits (Chapters 2, 4, 7, 8, and 13).

Internal Consequences of Decline

Diagnostic practitioners can also help managers in declining organizations cope with the internal consequences of organizational decline. When organizations undergo decline, processes can occur within them that produce further harm to current operations and block recovery programs. These processes include increased conflict, secrecy, rigidity in thinking and analyzing problems, centralization, formalization, scapegoating, and conservatism (McKinley, 1993). Declining organizations also experience decreases in morale, innovation, participation, trust in management, and long-term planning (Cameron et al., 1987; Roberts, 1986; Sutton, 1990; Whetten, 1987). Downsizing, which is a common response to downturns, usually intensifies these undesirable outcomes (Cameron et al., 1991). Because of its dysfunctional outcomes, downsizing often does not yield the expected improvements in productivity, cost savings, and smoother operations (Cascio, 1993).

These findings suggest that practitioners of diagnosis can fill two important roles within organizations undergoing decline. First, they can help managers of declining organizations monitor the internal effects of decline and assess the internal effects of programs for combating decline, such as downsizing or the creation of strategic alignments. Second, diagnostic practitioners can help managers explore ways to reduce the negative internal effects of decline and of remedial responses to it.

During decline, perhaps more than at any other stage in the life cycle, diagnostic studies can provide managers with feedback that they might otherwise fail to obtain. Emotions often run high during decline, and interpersonal relations can become polarized and politicized (Gray & Ariss, 1985; Greenlagh, 1982; Krantz, 1985). Managers are often swept up in the internal turmoil created by decline. Hence, during decline, managers are more likely to have difficulty diagnosing and managing internal tensions and conflicts without the aid of consultants.

Resource declines can lead managers to tighten mechanistic administrative systems in ways that weaken the organization's internal flexibility, innovativeness, and adaptation to changing external conditions—features that could contribute to recovery (Whetten, 1987). Resource declines threaten the managers' jobs, careers, and organizational authority, and they also pose threats to employees. As a result, the managers of declining organizations often become increasingly dependent on familiar administrative procedures and seek to intensify and formalize organizational controls (Sutton, 1990). This tendency toward conservatism and rigidity blocks the flow of information from the environment, just as it blocks internal communication and information gathering. Diagnostic feedback can highlight resultant misalignments between rigid administrative practices and rapidly changing external conditions. Feedback of this sort can help managers avoid or modify administrative moves that can harm their organization's capacity for recovery.

Practitioners can also provide their clients with feedback on the effectiveness of specific steps taken to deal with decline. In particular, practitioners can gather data on the degree to which members of an organization view the steps taken to combat decline as decisive, well thought out, and fair. Subordinates appear to be more likely to accept recovery programs that seem equitable and that reduce doubts about the survival of the organization (Sutton, 1990; Whetten, 1987). Still, even well-conceived and well-communicated recovery programs are likely to threaten many employees and other stakeholders and to heighten anxiety among those who survive initial cutbacks and reorganizations. Managers of recovering organizations may, therefore, continue to face high levels of anxiety and mistrust among their workforce. These developments create a need for careful diagnosis of the political forces sustaining and resisting anticipated steps toward recovery (Chapter 5).

Conclusion

The diverse models presented in this chapter carry a single message for practitioners of diagnosis and their clients: Organizational change often follows developmental paths of growth and decay. Rather than being inevitable and irreversible, movement along these paths depends on powerful external and internal forces, as well as on managerial responses to these forces. These forces produce discontinuous shifts from one organizational state to another.

Although there are no fail-safe techniques for coping with current and anticipated environmental threats and challenges, LC models can help consultants and their clients confront fundamental challenges to organizational stability and survival. In particular, these models can help managers decide when major strategic changes and even full-scale transformations are required to sustain LC shifts or to ward off crisis and decline.

More generally, LC models point to developmental contingencies affecting the nature of system requirements, organizational problems, and appropriate solutions to them. By incorporating a dynamic perspective into the open-systems frame, these models show users how system needs and problems vary across the life cycle and how solutions that fit one LC stage may be inappropriate for others.

Notes

1. Miller and Friesen (1984b) describe the fundamental reorganizations that result from such upheavals as quantum change. Mintzberg and Westley (1992) refer to periodic bumps. Gersick (1991) contrasts long periods of equilibrium with brief periods of revolutionary upheaval.

2. Tushman and Romanelli (1985) identified five domains that are critical to organizational activities and survival: power distribution, strategy, structure, control systems, and culture. In their scheme, technology and environment drive changes in the other domains.

3. See, for example, the discussion of responsibility charting in Harrison (1994, p. 85) and Galbraith (1977, p. 171).

Labor Relations

Action researchers, consultants, and practitioners are often interested in making planned changes in workplace labor relations in order to improve their effectiveness. A prerequisite of such planned changes is a valid diagnosis of the labor relations system (LRS) in question. This chapter presents a diagnostic model constructed for this task. This model is an application of the sharp-image diagnostic approach to the LRS. It elaborates and applies the open-systems frame, as presented in Chapter 2, and also incorporates elements of the political frame, including stakeholder analysis (Chapter 5).

In many industrialized countries, planned changes in workplace labor relations have been introduced at a progressively increasing rate during the past two decades (Macy & Izumi, 1993). Staff experts in human resources, organization development consultants, mediators, and action researchers may all become involved in providing guidance on restructuring LRSs. This group of professionals is the potential user of the diagnostic model of labor relations presented in this chapter.

In Chapter 5, we pointed to the impact of political forces in determining the success of planned change efforts. Labor relations deserve close attention as one of the most important arenas in organizational politics. In many instances, management-labor relations directly influence the success of interventions by consultants and managers. In addition, labor relations sometimes emerge as a focal topic for sharp-image diagnoses.

For simplicity's sake, the diagnostic model of an LRS was developed in the context of a public sector organization that has some autonomy in handling its labor relations affairs. Following a brief introduction that explains some of our central assumptions, the chapter provides a conceptualization of the constructs of effectiveness and ineffectiveness in an LRS. Then, each of the major components of an LRS is described, and a set of guidelines are given for diagnosing labor relations. The application of several of these diagnostic guidelines is illustrated in the next section of the chapter. The conclusion discusses some advantages and limitations of the proposed diagnostic model.

Several key terms used in this chapter need to be defined. The term *labor relations* is used as an equivalent to union-management relations. It covers, among other things, interactions between representatives of employees and of management, both of whom are referred to as participants. These interactions are goal oriented in that they aim to resolve employment-related issues that arise in relations among participants and/or among their respective constituencies. Labor relations also refers to the institutional framework within which these interactions take place and to their immediate antecedents and consequences in a work organization. The relevant domain for the application of the proposed model is that of pluralistic political systems of advanced industrialized countries in which unions operate independently of political parties and of the state.

The present chapter develops a diagnostic model in the context of unionized work settings in the public sector. In these settings, management bargains with the representatives of a local union. The choice of a public sector organizational unit was intentional, because in this sector, in most advanced, industrialized countries, union density and collective bargaining coverage have held steady or grown during the past two decades relative to other sectors of the economy (Chaison & Rose, 1991).

Several simplifying assumptions are made in the presentation of the model: (a) that only one local union is involved in the organization or focal unit; (b) that participants are authorized to sign a local, supplementary collective bargaining agreement covering certain local conditions (e.g., a productivity agreement)—that is, the organizational unit involved is semiautonomous in its labor relations; and (c) that the bargaining relations are quite well established. These simplifying assumptions may be relaxed and the diagnostic model applied to other contexts, but at the cost of increased complexity of the model's components.

In their attempts to make sense of interactions among LRS participants, labor relations researchers and practitioners use sets of ideas that help them to describe and explain these events. When these sets of ideas are organized in a systematic fashion, with each element in a set related via propositions or statements to the other elements, researchers refer to them as theories (Bacharach, 1989). Labor relations consultants and applied researchers also use theories, but these are often implicit theories-in-use that are based on experience, intuition, and conventional wisdom. Many of these theories-in-use are naive and oversimplified. Experienced researchers use their understanding of the logic of inquiry and their knowledge of empirical conditions to build models of labor relations realities. However, past models of LRSs often suffered from ignoring important outcomes of an LRS, being static rather than dynamic, being of limited applicability, and being unable to guide subsequent empirical inquiries.[1] Moreover, none of these past models was constructed with diagnostic use in mind. Would-be diagnosticians could hardly be guided by these frameworks, because crucial facets of the LRS were largely missing. Therefore, it was necessary to construct a new diagnostic model.

Effectiveness and Ineffectiveness in Labor Relations Systems

The application of organizational behavior theories and organization development diagnostic strategies to LRSs necessitates a working definition of what constitutes an effective LRS. This is necessary because, as pointed out in Chapter 3, diagnostic studies often precede planned changes intended to enhance the effectiveness of work organizations. Thus, in organization development, improving organizational effectiveness is the criterion. The effectiveness of an LRS, however, has often been defined as a multidimensional construct.

The multiple stakeholder approach to organizational effectiveness (Chapter 3) is the one guiding our conceptualization of effectiveness in the context of an LRS. This approach stipulates that organizations comprise multiple constituents who have both convergent and divergent interests. These interests are typically many and varied. The organization serves as a vehicle for their coordination and integration.

The stakeholder view of effectiveness is an especially appropriate theoretical point of departure to conceptualize an LRS. In it, the two primary constituencies are labor and management. Their representatives, the system participants, interact continuously to resolve labor relations problems or issues. In addition, several secondary constituencies may be identified, such as the national union with whom the local is affiliated. Each of the primary participants on whom the chapter focuses has a set of interests, goals, or needs satisfiable primarily through certain behaviors of the other participant and its constituency. This argument can be illustrated by observing the panel of outcomes in Figure 12.1 below. For example, union representatives (Participant A) have an interest in enhancing the employment security of employees. This can be achieved if Participant B and its constituency, namely management, guard and support this interest through management's everyday behavior. In a similar manner, Participant B has an interest in provision of services uninterrupted by work stoppages or sanctions. This interest is likely to be achieved if Participant A and its constituency behave accordingly.

Theoretically, an LRS's effectiveness may be defined as the extent to which the relevant sets of interests of labor and management are optimally satisfied, thus maximizing their capacity and willingness to achieve bilaterally controlled outcomes, such as mutual trust and quality of work life. In practice, this definition gives rise to very difficult conceptual and measurement problems, discussed in Chapter 3 in the context of the operationalization of organizational effectiveness.

Each of the participants may have many interests, and effectiveness in satisfying one interest of Participant A may be inversely related to effectiveness in satisfying another interest of Participant B. In Chapter 5, some of the vexing problems that consultants face in justifying their diagnostic project to stakeholders having nonoverlapping interests were discussed, and some solutions were offered. This consulting dilemma often occurs in working with LRSs. For example, management's interest in flexibility in assigning workers to jobs may conflict with workers' interests in job security, in continuing residence in a particular town, and in satisfying work. The very notion of what are relevant interests is dependent upon a participant's perceptual schema at a point in time, and the other participant may resist defining particular interests as legitimate and subject to resolution within the LRS. Clearly, then, interests are subjectively defined by each participant. Assessment of their "optimal" satisfaction often involves value-laden judgments.

These conceptual and methodological problems, discussed in the organizational effectiveness literature, are further complicated by the fact that there is continuous interaction and mutual dependence between the overall effectiveness of the organization (or the firm) and that of its LRS (Schneider, 1985, p. 597). Because of the difficulties associated with the conceptualization of interests and their operational measurement, we shall instead refer to *outcomes* of an LRS. This term has the advantage of adhering to the system terminology provided in Chapter 2. In a subsequent section of this chapter, several clusters of such outcomes, related to the participants' interest, are described.

To avoid the difficulties of defining and measuring the effectiveness of an LRS, we propose to follow the procedure recommended for sharp-image diagnosis in Chapters 1 and 3: Focus on ineffectiveness rather than effectiveness. This emphasis on ineffectiveness fits the realities of labor relations in public sector organizations in most advanced economies—a reality of job retrenchments, client complaints about poor service, work stoppages, and attacks on public ownership.

To determine the views of representatives of labor and management on ineffectiveness, diagnostic practitioners can use interview techniques like those described in Chapter 3. Interviewees can be asked which outcomes of the LRS are unsatisfactory for them, which outcomes would be satisfactory, and what can be done to improve the current situation. Research described at the end of this chapter showed that when asked questions like these, labor and management representatives identified very similar sets of ineffective outcomes. This interview procedure yields two lists of ineffective outcomes, one for each of the two participants, along with evidence of gaps between the present, unsatisfactory state and a preferred future state of affairs. An alternative and more demanding methodology for examining the positions of participants, that of stakeholder analysis, is provided in Chapter 5. This technique is more demanding because it requires consultants to gather data on each stakeholder's power, predisposition to act, and potential impact on each issue at stake.

Diagnostic Guidelines

All of the diagnostic guidelines presented here reflect the techniques of sharp-image diagnosis presented in Chapter 1 and the diagnostic procedures described in Chapter 2. The first diagnostic guideline flows directly from the above discussion of ineffectiveness:

1. *Regard frequently mentioned ineffective characteristics as the major outcomes to be explained in your diagnosis. Represent ineffective outcomes in terms of gaps between the present state of affairs and a preferred state.*

The necessary information may be gathered from LRS participants and a representative sample of their constituencies (hereafter referred to as respondents, in the sense of interviewees from whom diagnostic data have been gathered). When fed back to participants at the end of the diagnostic process, the above gaps should represent information gathered from both sets of participants and organized in a broader diagnostic framework.

It is also possible to identify ineffective outcomes by examining organizational records (e.g., data on lateness, turnover, work stoppages) rather than relying on perceptual data. Using organizational records as a source of data inevitably raises the problem of gauging the extent to which an outcome is indeed ineffective. As explained in Chapter 3, several standards of comparison are available, including normative judgments, past performance, or comparisons to other systems. This problem is frequently encountered in the area of evaluation research, and there are several useful guides on the merits and disadvantages of each of the above standards (e.g., Patton, 1986).

The diagnostic model for an LRS, in keeping with the sharp-image diagnostic approach, is embedded in an open-systems frame. Therefore, important axioms in the general systems approach (Ashmos & Huber, 1987) apply to the LRS. A first axiom is that all LRSs have certain common properties, including the interaction of participants to resolve employment-related issues or problems using power resources. A second axiom is that all LRSs consist of component units, or subsystems, coupled in particular relationships (Miller, 1978; see, e.g., Figure 12.2). The caution offered to readers in Chapter 2 should be emphasized: Namely, the open-systems approach does not provide an explanatory theory. More appropriately, it should be viewed as a heuristic device that is applicable to all social systems and is highly useful for the purpose of describing properties of a specific class of systems, classifying its components, and outlining its major interactions. Thus, it does provide a solid basis for further theorizing, for example, in formulating guides to diagnosing and explaining ineffective outcomes in LRSs.

There were several reasons why the open-systems approach was used as a conceptual stepping-stone in the diagnosis of labor relations. First, it is perhaps the most widely used foundation for theorizing in organizational behavior and organization development. Second, it is particularly suitable for analyzing labor relations because it presupposes multidirectionality of inter-actions, a prominent feature of LRSs. Third, it helps diagnostic practitioners focus on relevant behavioral criteria of ineffectiveness and on antecedents of ineffectiveness, as opposed to criteria that are formal or structural in nature. Fourth, the open-systems approach promotes and sustains a present-oriented, interactive, and holistic view of reality, in contrast with past-oriented expla-nations of labor relations (e.g., Chaison & Rose, 1991).

A note of caution is warranted here. The term *system* has been used abundantly in labor relations theories ever since the appearance of Dunlop's (1958) *Industrial Relations System.* However, Dunlop and those who sub-sequently refined and elaborated his work were influenced by the structuralist-functionalist school of thought in sociology, associated with Talcott Parsons, and not by the general systems approach. Furthermore, some of the major weaknesses of the structural-functional school—namely, the overemphasis on institutional structure and the difficulty of accommodating dynamic processes and conflicts (Buckley, 1967)—are evident in the thinking of Dunlop and his followers. For all those reasons, such loose usages of systems terminology were avoided here.

To apply the open-systems framework to labor relations, would-be diag-nosticians require a conceptual road map with an agreed meaning for each of the map's signposts, namely, each of the system's components. This road map is provided in Figure 12.1.

In the following sections, each of the main components of an LRS will be represented as a distinct subsystem, as shown in Figure 12.1. The second diagnostic guideline stems directly from the above reasoning:

> 2. *Always present the results of your diagnosis in terms of all other system compo-nents that are related to the identified ineffective outcomes. An overall system perspective must be provided to those who receive diagnostic feedback.*

The clients of the diagnostic effort should be able to think about ineffective outcomes in terms of the set of interrelated subsystems that produce them. When they contemplate any intervention or corrective action, they should be

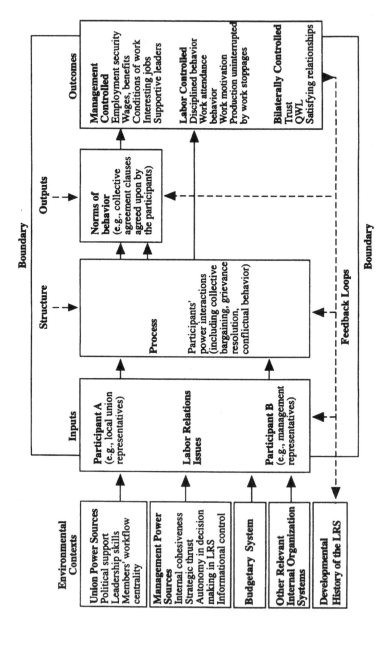

Figure 12.1 Components of the Labor Relations System of a Public Sector Organization
SOURCE: Shirom (1993). Copyright 1993 by JAI Press. Adapted by permission.

able to conceptualize its implications for all interacting components of the LRS. To illustrate, if poor service quality is defined as an ineffective outcome, and if a new vision of excelling in quality of service is introduced into the LRS as a desired outcome, an intervention in one component (e.g., changing the collective bargaining agreement) would necessarily imply changes in several other components (e.g., establishing a feedback system providing system input from customers).

Each of the panels in Figure 12.1 represents a basic component of the LRS, to be discussed below, starting from the outcomes and going left. For some components (but not all), a specific diagnostic guideline was formulated.

Outcomes

Outcomes of an LRS were previously described as actual changes in behaviors of the participants and/or their respective constituencies. The overriding social legitimacy of an LRS stems from its producing behavioral changes that are exported to the system's environments. The outcomes are also fed back to other system components via communication channels that give the system its dynamic and ever-changing quality. In Figure 12.1, outcomes are linked with system processes. Outcomes may result from system processes, as when consultations regarding a technological change lead to an effective introduction of change. This effective introduction, in turn, may raise employees' level of motivation and may also enhance the overall quality of work life in the organization. Yet another path leading to the outcomes is represented in Figure 12.1 by an arrow that leads from outputs, such as formal wage agreements, to outcomes. This arrow relates to the participants and/or their constituencies behaving in accordance with their respective contractual obligations. For example, when management pays each employee the overtime wage rate, as prescribed in the collective agreement, the management-controlled outcome is mediated by the wage agreement.

Outcomes may be classified using a variety of criteria. They can represent changes in management's behavior, such as the provision of safe and interesting jobs; in employees' behavior, such as changes in their work attendance or length of breaks; or in both constituencies' behavior, such as an agreement to change required working hours. Changes may be one time (e.g., annual bonus) or continuing (e.g., maintenance of work discipline), and they may relate to a variety of work units (e.g., individuals, groups, departments). Outcomes may be either tangible (e.g., wages) or intangible (e.g., climate of trust in the system); and they may be formally specified by the collective agreement (e.g., working conditions) or not (e.g., rights and duties of labor representatives). Therefore, the outcomes of an LRS are multidimensional and multilevel in nature.

The outcomes are considered multilevel because they may include individual-level outcomes, such as the satisfaction of the personal need of management's spokesperson to achieve or to gain power; group-level outcomes, such as the satisfaction of desires for job autonomy and control among a group of skilled craftsmen; and organization-level outcomes, such as labor productivity or efficiency. In Figure 12.1, three categories of outcomes were identified. The first includes rewards and inducements controlled by management. The second includes contributions of employees to their employing organization, contributions that are mostly controlled by them in conjunction with their representatives. Examples of behaviors in this category include low rates of product damage and absenteeism, and relative absence of workdays lost due to collective stoppages. The third category of outcomes refers to jointly controlled outcomes that may be regarded as those exported by an LRS to the organizational climate or culture, and includes variables such as mutual trust, satisfaction from relations, and the quality of work life.

The location of the outcomes box in Figure 12.1 on the system's boundary indicates that outcomes are influenced to a certain extent by other work-organization systems, as well as by the system's environments. For example, employees' work attendance is substantially affected by the processes and outputs of the LRS under consideration, but attendance is also influenced by other work-organization systems, including technological health hazards and environmental conditions within the employee's communities and families (Nicholson, 1977).

The outcomes described in Figure 12.1 are for illustrative purposes only, and the list provided is certainly not an exhaustive one. Also, the distinction between outcomes controlled by management and labor signify only relative (rather than absolute) control. Each supervisor, for example, has a significant impact over the work motivation of employees in his or her group. Past studies (e.g., Biasatti & Martin, 1979; Kochan, 1980) considered only a subset of possible outcomes, such as the quality of labor relations. To reiterate an earlier guideline, the focus should be on ineffective outcomes. Because ineffective outcomes are specific to an LRS under consideration, an exhaustive list of possible outcomes is not necessary for the diagnosis. This focus leads to the following third guideline:

3. *Explain ineffective outcomes in terms of other system components. Investigate, as possible causes, system processes, structures, inputs, environments, and feedback loops, as well as interactions among system components.*

The above guideline means that the diagnostic process moves from right to left on Figure 12.1, regarding each system component as if it was caused by the one to the left of it. Our stress on assessing and explaining effectiveness appears in several well-known diagnostic models, including those of Weisbord and Porras, which were discussed in Chapter 4. Similarly, most studies of strikes and other forms of industrial conflict seek to explain these ineffective outcomes in terms of the industrial system's processes and structures (see Kochan, 1980).

As noted in Chapter 2, the notion of fit among system components is a widely accepted diagnostic principle and is incorporated in several diagnostic models in the literature. An optimal fit between the contributions of organizational members and inducements provided to them by the organization was postulated in organization theory classics to be necessary for the organization's long-range survival (March & Simon, 1958; Thompson, 1967, p. 106). The participants in an LRS are parties in an exchange relationship in which they have different sets of interests. Each participant can satisfy its own interests by contributing to the satisfaction of the other participant's interests. This mutual dependence between participants underlies every bargaining process. This suggests that each participant derives a utility from helping the other, and in this limited sense, their interests are aligned. Diagnosticians should always keep in mind that during feedback sessions, the fruits of their work will be scrutinized by multiple organization constituencies with divergent and often conflicting interests, including the participants. Integrating the above theoretical themes in the diagnostic model, the following guideline was derived:

4. *Seek to identify misfits between the clusters of outcomes and between ineffective outcomes and other system components.*

The conceptual framework proposed here invokes the concept of misfit for two major purposes: (a) to explore hypothesized relations between the first two categories of outcomes (i.e., rewards vs. contributions), and (b) to identify specific linkages among ineffective outcomes and other system components.

This diagnostic guideline should be applied with care. Not every form of temporary tension or every gap in the system is a persistent misfit, and fit should not be equated with harmony. Yet another reservation concerning indiscriminate use of this diagnostic guideline is that sometimes, poor fit does not necessarily mean that the system is ineffective. As an illustration, consider the case of two separate organizational entities established by the participants: a collective bargaining committee and a joint labor-management quality improvement team. These two groups were designed to be loosely coupled. They pursue different objectives, are staffed by different representatives from each party, schedule meetings at different times and places, and use different decision-making processes. Lack of overlap between the two bodies allows the system to reduce interference between them. Given the above circumstances, a diagnostician should not rush to conclude that the lack of fit between two of this system's structures necessarily represents a source of ineffectiveness. Instead, the investigator should see whether an identified misfit is related to specific ineffective outcomes. Bearing the above caveats in mind, identified misfits still provide diagnosticians with powerful tools of analysis. Following the admonition of Fry and Smith (1987), diagnosis of poor fits among system components should help clients understand the reasons for ineffective outcomes. By presenting to the clients misfits among outcomes in the feedback sessions, the diagnostician may explicitly recognize possible divergences among the participants' interests, but the emphasis is on the overacting system's perspective that interrelates them. Still, diagnosticians must be constantly sensitive to ongoing power struggles occurring in the political arenas in which they operate (Cobb, 1984, 1986).

Outputs

The formal, mostly written, norms of behavior in a system are depicted in Figure 12.1 as LRS outputs. Outputs are presented as a distinct system component because several theories of labor relations "systems" (especially Dunlop, 1958) regarded outputs as the final product of labor relations.

Processes

A system's processes include power interactions involving the participants that are related to labor relations issues (as defined below). A power interaction refers to a participant's inclination or predisposition to use power, actual acts of influence (i.e., attempts to change the other participant's position), and the results of the act of influence (i.e., agreement or resolution of a labor relations issue). Whenever agreement on a labor relations issue culminates in a written document defining the participants' future contractual relations—such as a collective bargaining agreement or grievance proceedings—the document becomes part of the system's outputs. Written documents produced by third parties, such as arbitrators' decisions, also become outputs. Most other agreements belong to the psychological contract (Rousseau, 1997) that exists between participants, that is, to the informal, unstructured, and highly fluid expectations that each partner maintains toward the other. Whenever processes are highly structured, take place periodically, and result in a written agreement that becomes part of the outputs, the processes are referred to as collective bargaining processes.

The view of systems processes as consisting of power interactions is rooted in the political frame discussed in Chapters 3 and 5. If organizations are arenas of political conflict, as Bacharach and Lawler (1980) posited, then diagnosis of LRSs needs to assess the interactions between participants in the system. Following Bacharach and Lawler, it is proposed that power interactions can meaningfully be studied only on an issue-by-issue basis. There is compelling evidence that problem solving in organizations is organized around problem categories or issues in the LRS (Smith, 1995; Wofford, 1994). The choice of an issue affects the orientations of the participants and the power resources used by them (Goodstadt & Kipnis, 1970; Greening & Gray, 1994). A participant's predisposition to use power in relation to an issue (PPI) appears central to diagnosis. As Black (1983) has demonstrated, militancy over a specific issue is an important dimension of attitudinal militancy of trade union leaders. The term *predisposition* is used here as synonymous to an orientation, but it connotes a closer proximity of the attitudinal component to actual behavior, or a behavioral intention. A PPI probably reflects past experience with past solutions to the same or similar issues. PPI probably also reflects the perceived importance of the issue under consideration (see Walton & McKersie, 1965).

PPIs are regarded as determining, to a considerable extent, the course of acts of influence that follow them (Cobb, 1984). On the basis of this set of arguments, the following fifth guideline was formulated:

5. *Assess each participant's predisposition to use power in relation to each significant labor relations issue (PPI) that arises.*

An example of how measurement of PPIs was actually carried out was provided by Shirom (1980). The range of issues arising in a sample of LRSs in the public sector was identified by content analysis of processes. Expert judges were used to cull similar items into meaningful issues. Respondents were then requested to use a "power thermometer" to indicate the amount of power they were inclined to use on a given issue in order to persuade the other participant. For each participant, a mean PPI score was calculated for every issue. Having completed this measurement task, the diagnostician can arrange the issues in order of increasing PPIs and draw a graph to connect them. Such a graph, drawn for each of the participants, has many potential diagnostic applications, discussed elsewhere (Shirom, 1993). For instance, it can be used to identify issues that can potentially be resolved by integrative bargaining (Walton & McKersie, 1965) or through participative modes of problem solving, as well as issues that are high on their conflict potential. The scope or range of issues dealt with in the LRS in question can be compared with others. Procedures for dealing with each set of issues may be compared.[2] Each of the varying arrangements established by the participants to deal with specific issues may have explanatory power relative to an ineffective outcome. Restrictions on the scope or range of issues dealt with by any given LRS may signify restricted autonomy of one or both participants. Fragmented decision-making authority is a well-known feature of public sector labor relations (Kochan, 1980).

The above discussion leads to yet another diagnostic guideline:

6. *Whenever a set of issues can be related to ineffective outcomes, examine processual characteristics known to affect these issues.*

Often, groups of issues can be directly related to a specific ineffective outcome or outcomes. The literature on bargaining behavior provides evidence indicating that certain communication patterns between participants, and also within each participating group, would be closely associated with the type and quality of resolution of certain sets of issues (Walton & McKersie, 1965). Thus, several empirical studies (Peterson & Tracy, 1976, 1977) have identified certain processual predictors of successful problem solving in labor negotiations. These predictors include availability of information on the issues, willingness of each participant to share information on the issues and explore its solution without commitment, frequency of interaction between participants, effective working relationships within participant teams, and ability of either participant to clarify the issues to the other participant. Knowledge of these more effective communication patterns should assist diagnostic practitioners in focusing on specific antecedents of ineffective outcomes. Lack of variance on PPIs for a participant is highly important diagnostic information, as is discussed below.

Structure

A system's structure consists of all forms of institutionalized behavior—that is, relatively stable, patterned, and recurring interactions. Accepted practices and customs—such as those formalized as negotiation procedures outlined in a collective bargaining agreement, or as grievance committees, or as joint safety committees—are examples of elements of a system's structure. Labor laws (e.g., minimum wage laws) and relevant higher-tier collective agreements (e.g., an industry-level, cost-of-living agreement signed by an upper echelon of the participants' organizations) are also elements of structure.

The participants' organizations, namely, the local union and the relevant employer association, are conceived as environmental contexts affecting system inputs. For example, even though a local union may occasionally deal with disputes between its members, these disputes become labor relations issues only when the other participant (i.e., the representatives of management) insists that the issues be resolved bilaterally. Partial overlap between the participants' organizations and a system's structure occurs frequently, as illustrated by a joint bargaining committee that is constituted in a way that merely extends the top leadership structure of the existing organizations of the participants.

In diagnosing the structure of an LRS, it is important to assess the extent to which there exists a general, pervasive orientation of one participant to others, regardless of the issue involved. Such pervasive orientations were discussed in several attempts to construct topologies of workplace labor relations (see Kitay & Marchington, 1996, for a review). A basic unwillingness to accept the legitimacy of the other participant is treated here as a structural characteristic of a system because it implies a certain view of the world that is deeply ingrained and that finds expression in almost all processes (Kochan, 1980, pp. 183-191).[3] To illustrate, if management harbors an anti-union ideology, the participant representing management may develop a strategy of fierce and aggressive resistance to the union participant on any issue. Similarly, ideologically rooted, innate aggressiveness may lead the union participant to adopt militant policies toward management without

regard to the subjects being discussed. It is instructive to note that a participant's lack of awareness and lack of respect of positions and needs of the other
participant was found to be predictive of low-quality labor relations (Biasatti
& Martin, 1979). This leads to the following proposed guideline:

> 7. *Pay special attention to the existence of a basic labor relations strategy that
> denies the legitimacy of the other participant, because this strategy is apt to have
> a pervasive influence on ineffective outcomes within the LRS.*

Inputs

In the specification of LRS inputs, a diagnostician should be able to offer
a definition of the set of participants in it, the sources of energy provided for
LRS processes, and the forms that this energy takes. In the preceding sections,
the participants in the system were defined as those directly representing labor
and management. This is a reasonable working definition for most systems.
However, in some public sector LRSs, the participants would have to include
other actors, including arbitrators and officers of the union not directly
involved in the system's processes. A useful approach to the identification of
powerful players was suggested by Cobb (1986). This approach, which
emphasizes looking for formal and informal wielders of power, as well as
powerful coalitions and networks within each of the two constituencies, may
be incorporated into the diagnosis of LRS inputs.

Yet another difficult definitional problem concerns the subject matter of
the participants' interactions in an LRS. What is actually being transformed
by labor relations processes? Shirom (1994) proposed that participants in an
LRS raise and resolve labor relations issues or problems. This conceptual
approach is congruent with the open-systems approach. A labor relations issue
may be defined as information that concerns a state of disorganization that
has occurred inside the system or, more plausibly, in its environments. This
information is brought into the system by a participant. To be processed in the
system, an issue must involve an aspect of relations between employees and
management. That is, one of the participants must perceive the issue as one
that should necessarily be resolved by the system's processes. In the United
States, a minimal set of issues would include mandatory subject matters for
bargaining, wages, hours, and other terms and conditions of employment. All
nonmandatory labor relations issues, such as adjustment to recent technological changes, would also be included in the system's inputs.

It is noteworthy that labor relations researchers hardly, if ever, investigate the whole range of issues involved in any LRS. Studies typically cover a subset of specific issues (e.g., wages or disciplinary procedures) or a novel issue, such as individualized working hours or cash bonuses for efficiency proposals. It would be advisable for a diagnostician to cull issues into issue sets. This can be done by using the criterion of the extent to which the environmental resources of the participants are potentially committed to pursuing issues in a set. Because this criterion will ultimately be reflected in an issue's PPI, issues with similar PPI scores can be grouped as an issue set. A range of such issue sets was suggested by Shirom (1980). Issue sets are important because mobilization of power resources is ultimately tied to issues and their characteristics. Expert power, for example, is highly relevant for the resolution of safety issues but relatively unimportant with respect to the resolution of disciplinary issues. This discussion invokes the following guideline:

8. *Arrange issues in relevant groupings (or clusters).*

Environments

The environments of an LRS were regarded, in most past applications, as a cluster of heterogeneous variables interconnected with the focal system under consideration. This approach may be illustrated by Poole's (1986) detailed description of environmental conditions. In one block of variables, similarly located relative to the block of industrial relations processes, Poole included social, political, technological, legal, and demographic structures, as well as economic and legal policies, political ideologies, and cultural values. Thus viewed, environmental variables appear as a hodgepodge of miscellaneous influences on an LRS.

In contrast, following the open-systems approach, environments can be arranged, in reference to a focal system, by an organizing theoretical principle, such as the relative proximity of the constraints represented by each environmental context to an LRS. In Figure 12.1, this procedure is illustrated with reference to those environmental contexts that are most closely interconnected with the LRS under consideration.

Other environmental contexts, which are not described in Figure 12.1, may include economic, legal, political, sociodemographic, and sociocultural contexts. These more remote environmental contexts are hypothesized to interact with the LRS primarily via the environmental contexts depicted in Figure 12.1.

The links among variables in the environmental contexts considered here and the inputs into the LRS may be exemplified by reference to the link between the budgetary systems and inputs. Changes in the budget allocated to an organization (or, in for-profit organizations, changes in the economic performance and profitability of the firm) ultimately affect the behavior of the participants. Thus, an increase in the budget allocated to a unit may create a perception of slack, increase aspiration levels among union representatives, and eventually may be reflected in new issues that need to be resolved. A mirror image of such a development may happen when the budgetary axe falls and curtails the organization's allocated budget. Again, new issues, such as redistribution of available work among employees, blocking of retrenchments, or finding new sources of income among clients may come to the fore. In general, it could be predicted that any substantial change in the economic resources available to an organization will lead to the emergence of new issues, with a high potential for conflict (Low, 1991).

In the panel of environmental contexts in Figure 12.1, two clusters of variables are prominently represented: union and management power sources. As was noted, system inputs involve energy or power. The reciprocal acts of influence by means of which the participants try to resolve labor relations issues, namely system processes, invariably involve the use of power. Following Pruitt (1981, pp. 87-88), power resources are defined as self-perceived and relational. The finding that equality of power among participants is conducive to higher quality of work life (Biasatti & Martin, 1979) is of relevance here. In the same vein, studies of mediators' behaviors concluded that they encourage a problem-solving approach by participants during collective bargaining negotiations by influencing participants to adopt a perception of power equality with respect to the other participant (Pruitt, 1981, pp. 204-205).

From the above arguments, the following guideline may be derived:

9. *Assess the balance of power resources between participants, because severe imbalance can lead to many ineffective outcomes.*

Having established the need to assess the balance of power resources, it is necessary to develop a method to gauge the relative power of the participants. Classification systems of sources of power and guides as to their measurement have often appeared in the research literature, and there are initial adaptations of the above to the context of an LRS (Shirom, 1994). An especially detailed guide for the assessment of power resources was developed by Cobb (1986).

The discussion of stakeholder analysis in Chapter 5 also included a taxonomy of power resources and indications of how to assess them (see Table 5.1).

Boundaries

The openness of the LRS allows for a continuous exchange across the boundaries between it and its environment. This exchange is essential for the system's viability. The LRS both affects and is affected by its environment. Katz and Kahn (1978, pp. 65-66) suggested that boundaries are the demarcation lines for the determination of appropriate system activity, new members, and other inputs. In accordance with this approach, issues which by mutual consent or by legal decree are considered nonbargainable (e.g., management's pricing and marketing policies, or the local union's procedure for the election of new officers) may be used as boundary markers. The boundary condition applies also to the process by which outsiders enter and become participants in an LRS. This usually requires formal notification and approval procedures. Past studies in labor relations hardly dealt with the delineation of a system's boundaries. The concept of boundaries is of importance to the diagnostician because it emphasizes the dynamic and shifting nature of any system. Labor relations systems tend to be contemporaneous, dealing with live issues, and hence their boundaries tend to shrink and expand.

Feedback Loops

Characteristics of information feedback are crucial in determining the performance of an LRS. A system's structure, processes, inputs, and time delays interact with information feedback to determine how successful a system is in terms of its outcomes. Feedback loops endow the system with its dynamic quality: They provide "circular causal chains" (Buckley, 1967). For instance, it is well established that feedback about the nature of interdependencies among system outcomes is an important determinant of integrative collective bargaining (Walton & McKersie, 1965).

For an LRS, several feedback loops may be suggested, each playing a different role in terms of the system's self-regulation and endogenous change (see Figure 12.1). For instance, employees who develop high workplace commitment tend to influence their union representatives to adopt less militant bargaining postures (see Kitay & Marchington, 1996), which represents a feedback loop between a system's outcomes and processes. In the diagnostic model, feedback processes may serve as a pillar of support for the planned intervention. Also, absence of feedback may provide a clue as to the causes of an ineffective outcome.

Applying the Diagnostic Model

To facilitate future applications of the diagnostic model, Figure 12.2 presents a map of the nine guidelines described thus far, each embedded in the system component to which it refers. Application of the diagnostic model cannot be carried out in a vacuum but must be an essential part of a diagnostic project, as described in Chapters 1 to 5. Such a project would necessarily include several other components and ingredients besides those dealt with in this chapter. They include managing interpersonal and intergroup relations among the diagnosticians and the participants in an LRS, data-gathering methods, feedback of results to the participants and their constituencies, and criteria for evaluating the diagnosis.

Rather than illustrating a full-fledged diagnosis, the study reported here shows how Guidelines 1, 2, 3, and 6 can be applied in research. This study also exemplifies applications of some of the theoretical arguments presented above. Only the segments of the study relevant to these objectives are presented here.

The study sought to relate certain characteristics of LRS processes to the level of bilaterally controlled outcomes, and especially to the level of trust between the participants and their overall satisfaction from their relations. The study's findings are pertinent to the diagnostic model primarily because the sample was preselected to represent work organizations that were high and low on these outcome variables. Therefore, it was possible to compare the relations of processual characteristics to effective versus ineffective outcomes.

This study was designed to investigate systematic differences between effective and ineffective LRSs. Effectiveness was defined in terms of a cluster of outcomes defined by the participants. The factors explaining effectiveness and ineffectiveness in LRSs were expected to be qualitatively different. It was expected that in those firms diagnosed as having highly effective LRSs, the most powerful set of predictors of effective outcomes would be structural, particularly having to do with procedural consistency and extent of institutionalization in the system. In contrast, in firms having highly ineffective

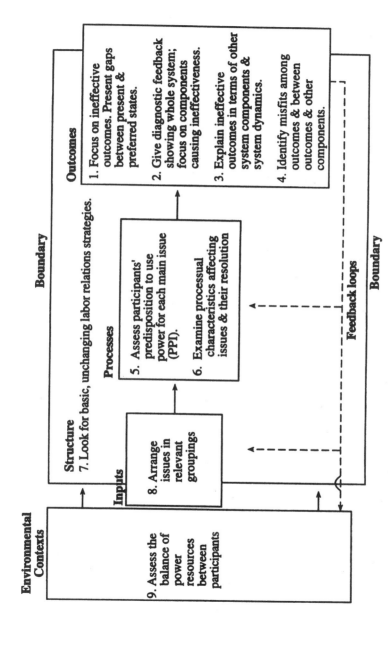

Figure 12.2 Model for Diagnosing Labor Relations

NOTE: Numbered statements refer to guidelines for constructing the model (see text).

345

LRSs, the most powerful set of predictors of these outcomes was expected to be processual, particularly having to do with the communication process between participants and the extent of flexibility of the participant representing management (see Kaminka, 1983).

To identify workplaces having effective and ineffective outcomes, we turned to a large group of informants drawn from the national "roof" organizations of labor unions and employers, and from the Department of Labor Relations of the Ministry of Labor. Each informant was asked to prepare a matched-pair list of work organizations known to be highly effective and ineffective. Effectiveness was operationalized primarily in terms of mutual trust and extent of satisfaction with management-labor relations (see Figure 12.1). The informants were asked to match the pairs on the attributes of size, economic branch, and type of ownership (private versus other forms of ownership). Frequently mentioned pairs were selected for the initial sample. Entrance into ineffective systems proved to be very difficult. The researchers were able to gain access to 15 effective and only eight ineffective systems, each of which corresponded to a different work organization. In each organization, employees in the two "worst" departments (in the eight ineffective systems) and the two "best" departments (in the 15 effective systems), as judged by key participants in each of the systems, were selected for the final sample. Data were collected through personal interviews with the participants and through questionnaires distributed to samples of employees in the best and worst departments. Effective and ineffective systems were represented in the final sample by 314 and 151 respondents, respectively. Difficulties encountered during the data collection undermined strict comparability between the effective and ineffective systems.

Overall, the findings were supportive of the hypothesized importance of process-related variables in explaining ineffective outcomes in labor relations. Results pertaining to the subsample of workplaces with effective LRSs were less conclusive. In the context of the diagnostic model and its third and sixth guidelines, it is noteworthy that inflexibility in dealing with labor relations issues on the part of management, as well as short-circuited communication channels between the participants, were found to distinguish workplaces with ineffective labor relations outcomes. Process-related predictors were found to be important explanatory factors of the level of ineffectiveness among the ineffective systems. Tentatively, the results of this study could be used to argue that entirely different interventions are needed to deal with the improvement of effective LRSs and the improvement of ineffective LRSs, respectively. This conclusion supports a key guideline of the diagnostic model, which directed diagnosticians to focus on ineffective outcomes in LRSs.

Future Development of the Model

The purpose of this chapter was to present an initial set of guidelines for diagnosing LRSs. The development of a sharp-image model for this purpose drew on concepts and analytic frameworks from the area of labor relations. The main section of this chapter presented a series of diagnostic guidelines for each of the major components of an LRS. These guidelines were formulated to be of help in the diagnosis of a system's outcomes, processes, structure, inputs, and environments. It is recommended to apply the diagnostic guidelines sequentially, starting with ineffective outcomes and going backward toward the features shown on the left side of Figure 12.2. In the chapter's final section, a partial application of the model was provided.

It was suggested that the proposed diagnostic model has the capacity to generate highly useful knowledge, and that it is likely to enhance the validity of any diagnostic effort aimed at LRSs. It is further contended that the model represents a meaningful advancement in translating concepts and ideas from organization behavior and organization development into diagnostic applications in the area of labor relations. For labor relations consultants, mediators, and other practitioners, the model has the potential of increasing the effectiveness of planned changes in LRSs.

Despite its potential uses, the model has clear limitations and shortcomings. By noting these, we can outline useful directions for further developments and applications of the model. Before doing so, we should note that this chapter has only examined the framing and explanation of ineffectiveness in LRSs. A full-blown diagnostic project would involve system entry, interactions with participants, data gathering, and feedback—none of which was discussed here.

What, then, are some of the limitations of the proposed diagnostic model? For didactic purposes, the diagnostic procedures were presented in a distinct sequence. This description suffers from the typical problem of linear, progressive models of diagnosis. In actual applications, the model, the diagnostic phases, and the relevant guidelines will overlap, combine, and shift location during diagnosis. Another possible limitation of the diagnostic model is its focus on negative features of the client system, that is, the exclusive emphasis on LRS ineffectiveness. It should be noted, however, that negative information (e.g., diagnostic gaps such as those resulting from the application of the first diagnostic guidelines) has been found to be more conducive to planned change efforts in organization development (Cameron, 1984).

Another limitation is that some parameters in the model remained underspecified. Generally speaking, diagnosis should give preference to long-term forms of LRS ineffectiveness. As Cameron (1984) indicated, short-term ineffectiveness is sometimes tolerated in order to obtain long-term effectiveness. However, for lack of empirical studies or appropriate theoretical rationale, the whole issue of time frame was left for future elaboration. Yet another limitation points to an avenue for future research. This concerns interrelations among the LRS, the organization at large, and other systems affecting the organization, such as technological and legal systems (see Kitay & Marchington, 1996, p. 1279).

In an effort to not complicate the model further, we left unspecified the important subsystem of labor relations climate or culture, which includes participants' basic values, beliefs, and underlying assumptions (e.g., Biasatti & Martin, 1979). Future elaborations of the model should give more prominence to cultural characteristics, such as disbelief in the legitimacy of unions. As noted in Chapter 10, cultural features of organizations can often lead to ineffective system outcomes.

Still another theoretical path to be followed in future work concerns the sources of the participants' power resources. From what sources do these power resources stem? How are they mobilized, and what explains differences in their use? The conversion of potential bargaining power to actual power has been the subject of theoretical investigations (e.g., Bacharach & Lawler, 1980) and could profitably be examined within the model.

Notes

1. For references to previous research on LRSs, see Shirom (1993, 1994).
2. Categorization of issues and development of issue sets is discussed below, under Inputs.
3. Strictly speaking, orientations like these are cultural features. For simplicity, we preferred not to introduce yet another analytical category into an already complex diagnostic model.

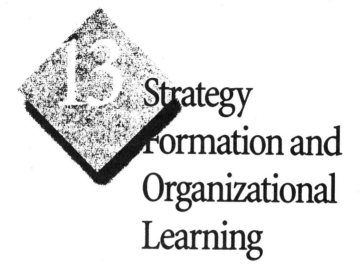

13 Strategy Formation and Organizational Learning

Top managers and their advisors in businesses and not-for-profit organizations devote much of their energy to making decisions and formulating actions that are strategic, in the sense of allocating substantial resources and influencing their organization's position in its competitive environment. Top decision makers also work hard to mold these decisions into integrated strategies and to explain their strategies to organizational stakeholders. Many decision makers and consultants make serious efforts to improve the *contents* of strategic decisions—for example, by applying sophisticated techniques for deciding where to invest, how to compete, and how to market new products.

However, managers and consultants often put less effort into enhancing the *processes* of strategic decision making and implementation—perhaps because they underestimate the crucial effects of such processes and assume that wise decisions will, in the end, be implemented. During implementation, processual forces often reshape strategic plans, or else they block implementation altogether. Interactions among members of the organization and learning from experience shape the initial formation of many strategies, as well as their implementation. Furthermore, many successful strategies emerge more through these processes of interaction than through formal processes of top-down decision making and planning. When strategies develop in an emergent fashion, decisions and planning do not necessarily proceed sequentially through a lengthy chain of steps in formal planning, like the ones shown below in Figure 13.2. Instead, steps can be skipped and repeated, and their order can be altered. For example, strategic decision models assume that problem identification and definition lead to a search for solutions. Yet in many cases, existing "solutions," such as available staff members, technology, or capital investments, drive problem identification and definition. Moreover, managers can make strategic choices without clearly defining strategic problems and issues. Research shows that such deviations from the ideal-typical rational decision process can produce results that are equally as good or bad as those stemming from formal planning (Harrison & Phillips, 1991). In light of the many variations in strategy formation, decision makers and consultants need to pay close attention to the processes through which strategies form, as well as to their contents.

Two types of diagnostic models can help managers develop successful strategies: models identifying conditions affecting the appropriateness and feasibility of particular strategy formation *processes,* and models that guide choices about the *contents* of strategies. The first part of this chapter presents a contingency model of strategy formation processes. It can help consultants and managers decide when strategy can best be made *deliberately* through formal planning processes and when it must be allowed to *emerge* gradually. The second and third parts of the chapter address content and processual issues relating to deliberate and emergent strategy development, respectively. The fourth section treats ways that diagnosis can contribute to the development of two enduring sources of strategic advantage—innovativeness and organizational learning.

Our proposals for diagnosing strategy formation and implementation combine insights from several theoretical frames that were discussed in earlier chapters. The treatment of deliberate strategy formation applies the open-systems frame and the structural frame, which views organizations as tools for goal attainment. To add realism to the diagnosis of implementation processes, we also draw on the political and negotiation frames. The examination of emergent strategies also makes use of the interpretive frame. This frame helps us examine how leaders can craft strategies by defining strategic directions or visions that shape the ways that members of an organization and external actors view organizational challenges, capacities, and actions. A combination of these frames also contributes to our proposals for diagnosing the conditions contributing to innovation and organizational learning.

Contingency Model of Strategic Decision Processes

Managers and consultants need a simple model to help them decide which types of strategic decision processes are most appropriate for an organization or for a major unit within an organization. Surveys of the literature on strategy formation point to three main possibilities:[1]

1. *Deliberate strategy formation*, which involves systematic, formal, and top-down decision making and planning
2. *Crafting strategy*, in which top managers seek to steer and guide strategic developments that are at least partly decentralized and emergent
3. *Reactive decision making*, in which an organization does not develop a coherent strategy

Deliberate Strategy Formulation

Textbooks on business strategy, popular articles and books on strategic planning, and management training programs often urge managers to aim for the ideal of top-down, rational-comprehensive planning. To approach this ideal, managers must define and diagnose problems explicitly, conduct extended searches for solutions, systematically weigh and select alternative solutions, develop detailed strategic plans, translate those plans into comprehensive operating plans, monitor implementation, and make strategic and operational adjustments as needed. Decision processes approximating this ideal can be termed *planful.* Planful decision techniques often quantify as many of these steps as possible. Inputs to the planning process can come from techniques such as market and operations research, financial accounting, cost-benefit analysis, and portfolio management.

Although most of these planning techniques were originally developed for private firms, they have also been applied to not-for-profit organizations. For governmental organizations in the United States, the Planning, Programming, and Budgeting System (PPBS) provided a parallel to strategic planning (Wildavsky, 1979b). Additional adaptations of the deliberate planning model have been developed for social agencies and other not-for-profit organizations (Bryson, 1988; Burkhart & Reuss, 1993). Case 13.1 describes one suggested application of deliberate strategic planning techniques within Britain's National Health Services. It was proposed by a leading consultant on quality improvement in the health sector (Ovretveit, 1992).

Case 13.1

Managers of service units need to formulate a clear service strategy that can drive and guide quality-enhancement efforts. This strategy will define target clients, client needs, and the types of services to be offered for each target group. Decisions concerning these strategic choices are to flow from an analysis of ways in which the organization can differentiate its services within the market in order to obtain competitive advantage over other providers. To develop the service strategy, members of each unit can conduct a traditional SWOT analysis—assessing the unit's strengths and weaknesses in light of environmental opportunities and threats. The management of the unit then decides, on the basis of resource availability, which subservices to develop, which to reduce, and which to contract out. Then, the managers formulate overall business and marketing plans for the organization that contain packages specifying the design for each subservice and a plan for its development. The business and marketing plans spell out the basis for controlling and assessing these services, timetables for implementation, landmarks, responsibilities, and procedures for review and reassessment.

Once enormously popular, deliberate strategic planning like that proposed in Case 13.1 has undergone attacks during the past two decades by managers, consultants, and researchers (Mintzberg, 1994). Much of this criticism centers on the failure of formal planning procedures to produce strategies that are aggressive or proactive in content. These terms refer to the extent to which decision makers anticipate changes in their environments and try to shape these environments, rather than just react to external pressures and developments. Managers who act aggressively look for opportunities contained within external developments, rather than viewing them as threats or constraints. Aggressive managers actively seek new markets for existing products and forge alliances with other organizations. They also develop new products and services and seek to generate demand for them.

Why do deliberate planning processes yield few aggressive strategies? The explanation lies in the techniques of formal planning, which encourage participants to plan actions that closely resemble past activities. The search for systematic, quantifiable measures of inputs and expected outputs from the planning process often leads participants in the planning process to focus on present or highly predictable environmental developments and thereby overlook newly emerging opportunities, which can be understood and assessed only intuitively. The stress in planning to obtain good fit between the requirements and constraints of the environment and the current or projected capacities and resources of the organization blocks planners' ability to react flexibly and opportunistically to unanticipated external changes. Unanticipated changes can undermine current plans and render current strategies obsolete, but such changes can also present nimble managers with opportunities to expand current operations, develop new ones, and forge new ties with other firms. Rather than encouraging exploration of these possibilities, strategic planning frequently leads managers to underestimate their ability to stretch their organization's current capacities to achieve new objectives or to take bold steps toward reshaping their competitive environments (D'Aveni, 1994; Hamel & Prahalad, 1994).

These criticisms find support in research showing that firms using formal planning procedures are not consistently more successful than are firms without formal planning at fostering innovation or developing and executing aggressive strategies. Instead, the evidence points to considerable tension between planfulness and aggressiveness (Harrison & Phillips, 1991; Mintzberg, 1994). Nor is there consistent evidence that formal planning contributes to profitability or to other measures of economic success (Mintzberg, 1994; but compare Capon, Farley, & Hulbert, 1994).

Perhaps the most famous strategic decision technique that failed to deliver the promised financial and managerial benefits was portfolio theory (e.g., Hedley, 1977)—a way to generate models for acquiring and managing diversified businesses. In fact, reliance on portfolio theory often proved counterproductive from the standpoint of financial outcomes (Lubatkin & Chatterjee,

1994). One problem with portfolio models was that they focused most of the strategists' attention on current features of the businesses owned by the firm and those considered for acquisition, rather than on future opportunities for developing ongoing businesses and expanding into new areas (Lubatkin & Lane, 1996).

Disenchantment with deliberate planning techniques and programs also stemmed from the failure of these techniques to help top managers in large American firms cope with powerful and sudden environmental jolts. These external shocks began with the oil price shocks and stagflation of the 1970s and then gave way to spiraling technological changes, deregulation, globalization, and conditions of "hypercompetition" (D'Aveni, 1994) in some markets.

Perhaps even more damaging was the fact that large organizations often encountered serious problems in implementing the elaborate plans they produced. During the late 1980s, disillusion with lack of implementation of formal plans became particularly acute in the public sector. In many cases, governmental organizations failed to implement their elaborate plans for large-scale change (Pressman & Wildavsky, 1973). In both the private and public sectors, many obstacles can block, delay, or divert the implementation of articulated strategies. These include the separation of planning experts from the implementation process and even from the top levels of line management, opposition by powerful stakeholders, difficulties of making strategic goals operational and measurable, and reinterpretation of programs by the people who are ultimately responsible for their implementation.[2]

Emergent and Crafted Strategies

Rather than being deliberately formulated, most strategies emerge through interaction among many actors in and around an organization and through an iterative process of learning through experience. Managers can sometimes guide or *craft* these emergent strategies without fully determining their course. These crafted, "umbrella" strategies (Mintzberg, 1994, p. 25) describe broad strategic targets and directions but allow details to emerge gradually and experimentally under the umbrella. Decision makers concentrate more on formulating a vision of the future and on preparing the grounds for integrating diverse organizational activities than on developing formal plans for resource allocation to subunits or establishing elaborate systems of internal control. Unlike deliberate strategies, emergent strategies sometimes can be very aggressive. Solo entrepreneurs and heads of development teams can stress innovation, opportunistic decision making, and intuition while showing little concern for formal planning exercises.

Top managers in some successful firms reveal a talent for directing the emergence of corporate strategy, even when they cannot fully determine it. Through this crafting process, which has also been described as logical incrementalism (Quinn, 1977, 1980), top decision makers decide on the direction in which they want to guide their organization. By deftly managing their organization's political system and using systematic planning techniques in a supportive, guiding role, these executives move their firms in the planned-for direction. At the same time, they remain open to unforeseen opportunities and constraints and depart from plans in order to handle these contingencies. Like Quinn, Hamel and Prahalad argue that executives in large firms can craft overall strategy by developing a clear definition of their firms' *core competencies* and by creating a shared sense of direction that guides interactions among units and expansion into new areas of activity (Hamel & Prahalad, 1994; Prahalad & Hamel, 1990).

Managers throughout the organization take part in this open-ended search for new opportunities to exploit their firm's core competencies. The approach to strategy formation articulated by Hamel and Prahalad may help executives introduce new energy into their organization and foster cooperation and synergy across functional lines or between strategic business units. However, their concept of core competencies has proved difficult to operationalize and work with ("How to Identify," 1994). Like Quinn, Hamel and Prahalad generalize from a limited sample of successful firms. Moreover, their most dramatic examples are drawn from high-technology fields. It remains to be seen whether the managers of other large and complex organizations, operating in a wide range of domains within both the private and public sectors, can obtain the kinds of results promised by the advocates of crafting strategy.

Reactive Decision Making

In many firms and public organizations, top managers possess neither a strategic plan nor a strategic vision. Their organizations simply "muddle through" (Lindbloom, 1959)—reacting in an ad hoc fashion to internal and external developments. Managers adopt this reactive stance when they face conflicting demands by powerful stakeholders in and around their organization and when regulation and other forms of external control drain away organizational autonomy. Under these nearly paralytic circumstances (Butler, Astley, Hickson, Mallory, & Wilson, 1977-1978), managers can best make changes through incremental steps that do not attract too much attention or ignite opposition.

When managers facing severe constraints seek to bring about major organizational change, they can most reasonably proceed by quietly building coalitions and mustering resources in support of their program and announcing plans for action only when material and political support are assured. Another possibility is for managers to maintain "business as usual" until a crisis develops (or is engineered). The atmosphere of crisis provides the managers with opportunities to urge former opponents of change to abandon their opposition to change and to cooperate with managerial proposals to save the organization.

Contingencies of Strategy Formation

Before consultants and managers seek to enhance an organization's current style of strategic decision making or advocate the adoption of a new type of strategy formation, they need to diagnose the appropriateness of prevailing decision styles to current organizational conditions and system features. For example, the management of a highly diversified conglomerate seeking to expand into new areas might appropriately articulate an integrative vision for the firm as a whole, as a supplement to current financial planning techniques. On the other hand, such a vision will not be of much use to managers of a resource-poor, public sector organization who face pressing problems and are subject to powerful political constraints.

Table 13.1 provides a model that summarizes the major conditions favoring deliberate, crafted, and reactive strategy formation.[3] The first row in Table 13.1 indicates that a decision style that fits a well-understood and clearly defined strategic task, such as the acquisition and divestment of financial assets, may be poorly suited for dealing with an ill-defined, poorly understood task, such as planning for new product development or forging strategic alliances with other organizations. In keeping with the preceding discussion, the table shows that managers can most appropriately employ the techniques of systematic, deliberate strategy formation when the managers define decision problems as familiar and fairly well-understood. The solutions to well-understood problems can, in turn, be broken down into detailed operating plans. Table 13.1 also shows that deliberate strategy formation is more feasible

Table 13.1 Contingency Model of Strategy Formation

	Strategy Type		
Condition	*Deliberate*	*Crafted*	*Reactive*
Task familiarity and clarity	High-moderate	Moderate-low	Moderate-low
Environmental predictability	High-moderate	Moderate	Low
Resources	High-moderate	Moderate-low	Low
Organizational autonomy	High-moderate	High-moderate	Low
Top management's power and expertise	High	Moderate	Low
Organizational state	Momentum	Upheaval	Varies
Size	Large	Varies	Varies
Age	Mature	Varies	Mature-old
Structure[a]	Machine bureaucracy, Divisionalized	Divisionalized, Adhocracy, Simple	Machine, Professional bureaucracy

a. See Mintzberg (1979).

when an organization operates in at least a moderately predictable environment and enjoys substantial resource flows and high levels of autonomy. In addition, to implement deliberate strategies in a nonparticipative, top-down fashion, top leaders need a lot of internal power and political support.

The item in Table 13.1 labeled Organizational State refers to the distinction between long periods of organizational momentum and the briefer intervals of upheaval and significant change (Chapter 11). Many organizations enjoy years of relative stability between those intervals, during which pressure for change becomes intense. The periods of momentum between upheavals create conditions in which deliberate strategy formation works adequately, at least in some decision domains (Mintzberg, 1987). During periods of momentum, organizations can achieve fairly good fits (equilibrium) between their internal structures, external conditions, and their strategies. These fits can contribute to effectiveness when change is not rapid. On the other hand, tight fit between system elements can become an obstacle when change becomes discontinuous (Nadler et al., 1995).

The deliberate strategies that are pursued during periods of momentum and system equilibrium are more likely to be conservative and reactive than proactive and forward-looking. The justification for continuing to rely on traditional, deliberative processes of strategy formation is that the more improvisational and iterative styles of crafting strategy are risky and difficult to use. Arguments that most contemporary organizations face "permanent white water" (Vaill, 1989) or continuous "hypercompetition" (D'Aveni, 1994) can exaggerate the degree of turbulence and external threat facing many firms and public sector organizations. These sweeping judgments may encourage managers to undertake new initiatives that are costly, risky, and unnecessary.

During periods of rapid external change and uncertainty, deliberate strategy formation becomes impractical: It fails to help managers hit the moving targets created by rapid environmental and technological change. To survive and prosper during such upheavals, organizations may have to undergo radical, even frame-breaking change (Nadler, 1988). These quantum leaps cannot be designed through reliance on the techniques of deliberate strategy formation. Unless managers seize the initiative and begin to craft their organization's new strategies, they will be forced into a reactive position.

To craft strategy successfully, top managers must enjoy substantial autonomy from external regulation and control and at least a moderate flow of resources. Otherwise, their decision making will be pushed toward the reactive mode. Moreover, to craft strategy, managers require substantial internal power in order to mobilize internal backing for their vision and to shape the organization's structures and processes in support of that vision (see Supporting the Crafting of Strategy, below). In addition, top managers must possess or have access to the expertise required to initiate change and form strategy. These conditions sometimes prevail in large organizations, but they are more common in small- and medium-size firms that have simple or adhocratic structures.

In organizations where expertise is widely diffused, tasks are poorly understood, and innovation and creativity are primary goals, the distinction between periods of momentum and upheaval becomes less critical. In adhocracies and professional organizations, for example, strategies emerge throughout the organizational life cycle (Mintzberg, 1979). Nevertheless, even loosely coupled adhocracies and professional organizations contain islands of order and predictability (Weick, 1985). Enough agreement among participants, decision-maker autonomy, and presumed task clarity exist within these islands of order to support relaxed versions of deliberate strategy formation. Consider, for example, members of a university department or faculty who finally overcome their differences and agree that they need to revamp their undergraduate curriculum. After much negotiation, the faculty members ultimately get a mandate from higher administrative levels to go ahead. At this point, the curriculum planners can reasonably follow the old-fashioned, systematic decision process through diagnosis, search, choice, planning, implementation, and follow-up. The curriculum planners have temporarily retrieved their decision-making processes from the proverbial "garbage can," which is full of divergent, largely unrelated goals, means, actors, and decision opportunities. At least for a while, the planners can follow the route of bounded rationality.

When internal and external stakeholders can impose their own priorities and agendas on an organization, top managers face serious obstacles to implementing top-down plans and crafting strategy. Public sector and voluntary organizations are particularly vulnerable to resource constraints and to conflicting demands by funding bodies, regulators, community groups, unions, and external stakeholders. However, managers of private firms in many sectors also face growing external constraints on their decisions. Under these circumstances, strategic decisions are particularly likely to be conservative and reactive.

Perhaps the best that consultants can do for clients facing such extreme constraints is to try to help their clients make decisions incrementally or find ways to build up their political support and their organization's resource base. For example, the charters of some resource-poor, public service organizations forbid or limit selling services on the private market and taking other steps to develop new sources of cash flow. Nevertheless, if the heads of an organization facing such constraints can cultivate new sources of political support and legitimation, the organization may win new degrees of strategic freedom. The managers can then extend their operations beyond their original mandates and search for new sources of revenue.

The model shown in Table 13.1 can help managers and consultants decide when deliberate and crafted approaches to strategy formation are likely to prove workable. Nevertheless, in today's world of changing markets, technologies, and governmental policies, radical jolts and upheavals may lurk just around the corner. Hence, managers need to exercise caution before deeply committing their organization to formal planning processes.

As is suggested by investigations of organizational life cycles (Chapter 11), today's top managers can benefit by preparing themselves and their employees to face uncertainty and discontinuity, even as they manage for stability (Mintzberg, 1987). Managers can both continue to operate in terms of current strategies and simultaneously assume that these strategies will require revision within a couple of years. In a similar fashion, they can safely assume that product life cycles will grow shorter. Thus, managers can prepare themselves mentally for the possible need to make radical changes without undercutting currently successful operations (Handy, 1995, p. 57).

Supporting Deliberate Strategies

Diagnostic models and techniques can support both deliberate and crafted decisions. The discussion that follows examines ways in which diagnosis can facilitate the formation and implementation of deliberate strategies.

Formulating Strategy

The search for competitive advantage forms the cornerstone of deliberate strategy formation (Andrews, 1980; Porter, 1985). According to this approach, to find ways to obtain advantage over competitors, managers and their advisors examine the threats and opportunities presented by the business environment and look for those distinctive organizational competencies that can give the firm an edge over competitors. SWOT analysis is one technique for searching for an optimal fit between organization and environment (see Chapter 2).

Figure 13.1 provides a schematic summary of this type of analysis, as envisioned by Andrews and others. Potentially important forces in the general environment include political, economic, social, and technological developments at local, regional, national, and international levels. These forces can shape many crucial conditions in the close environment, including demand for products or services; support and legitimation of organizational actions; flows of human and material resources; and costs, work processes, and other operating conditions. Behavioral science consultants can sometimes make an important contribution to the analysis of external developments by pointing to potential impacts of hard-to-measure but nevertheless influential developments in fields such as social issues, culture, and politics. The procedures presented in Chapters 2 and 4 can help managers and consultants conduct this type of analysis of the general environment.

The most critical part of a firm's task (or close) environment is the business and industrial conditions that shape competition. Technical analytical tools (e.g., Porter, 1980, 1985) are typically used to analyze the competitive environment of firms. However, the general diagnostic models presented in

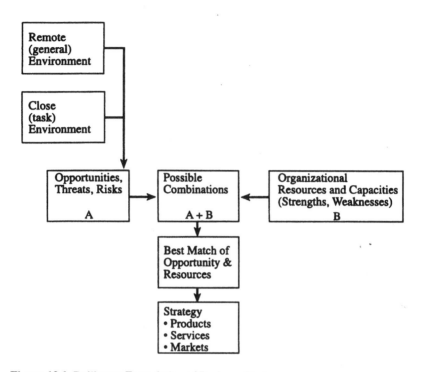

Figure 13.1 Deliberate Formulation of Business Strategy

Chapters 2 and 4 can guide the analysis of other features of the firm's task environment. These models can also structure an analysis of the close environment of not-for-profit organizations.

Practitioners of diagnosis can also help decision makers in a client organization identify their organization's strengths and weaknesses, as well as its resource base. By comparing organizational strengths to environmental opportunities, decision makers can identify distinctive competencies. It is important to scan financial, managerial, technical, knowledge, and political capabilities, along with competencies in functional areas, such as human resource management or marketing. Functional areas in which industrial firms can develop distinctive competencies include technology and the development, design, production, and distribution of products (Fiegenbaum et al., 1996; Porter, 1985). In particular, consultants and their clients need to look beyond current activities as they search for underlying organizational capabilities, including capacities for innovation and learning, that can be translated into new products and services.

Organizational resources and capacities can also constrain development or exploitation of distinctive competencies and prevent organizations from taking advantage of market opportunities. In addition to identifying current strengths and weaknesses, the assessment should consider prospects for increasing organizational capabilities and overcoming weaknesses. For example, possible strategic contributions of training and other human resource management functions can be examined (Chapter 8). Once the assessment of internal and external conditions is complete, managers and consultants can seek the best match between external opportunities and organizational resources and capacities. Identification of this match leads to choices about business strategy and, in particular, to decisions concerning the desired mix of products, services, and markets; ways to compete on costs; and ways to differentiate products by attributes, such as quality and accessibility (Porter, 1985).

The search for a match between organizational capacities and external opportunities moves beyond the examination of demand for current products and services or for alternative outputs. Instead, the decision centers on discovering additional profitable products or services that the organization can provide at lower cost or higher quality than its competitors. Suppose, for example, that an architectural firm currently concentrates on designing factories and warehouses for industrial firms. Even though this type of service provides most of the firm's income, the firm faces stiff competition in this niche. In contrast, the firm may possess a distinctive competence in the design of retirement facilities—an activity that currently provides only a small fraction of the firm's income but promises to be very profitable. Recognition of this distinctive competence can lead to a redirection of more of the firm's activities into this previously neglected market niche.

Consultants can contribute to decisions about the contents of competitive strategies through the use of either client-centered or consultant-centered techniques. Consultant-centered studies are often performed by experts in fields such as marketing, industry analysis, and business strategy. The results of these studies then serve as inputs into strategic decision making by top managers. In contrast, consultants can also lead decision makers in client-centered diagnoses of strategic challenges and possible sources of competitive advantage using techniques such as open-systems planning (Chapter 4) and scenario planning (e.g., Case 13.2 below). The advantage of these collaborative techniques is that participation in analyses of external conditions and of organizational competencies enhances the likelihood that participants will accept and agree with these analyses and will become committed to the strategies emerging from them. On the other hand, participants in strategic planning may lack the expertise necessary to analyze external and internal conditions. Moreover, participants from divergent professional and functional backgrounds often disagree about the nature of crucial conditions and about appropriate ways of dealing with them.

Assessing and Guiding Strategic Processes

In addition to enhancing the content of deliberate strategies, many of the diagnostic procedures, models, and approaches developed in earlier chapters can help enhance the processes by which deliberate strategies are formulated and implemented. Figure 13.2 presents these processes schematically as a series of phases.[4] In practice, strategy formation often does not move through these phases sequentially. Activities relating to one or more stages can be repeated or omitted altogether.

For each phase shown in Figure 13.2, diagnostic practitioners can assess current practices in terms of the three diagnostic procedures presented in Chapter 2—fit assessment, identification of system gaps, and diagnosis of interdependencies. At its most general, fit assessment deals with the degree to which a proposed or current strategy fits other organizational features. One influential formation of this approach, known as the 7-S framework (Waterman et al., 1980), counsels concentrating on fits between an organization's strategy, structure, operating and administrative processes, basic vision and goals, culture, human resources, and distinctive organizational capacities and skills.[5] According to this approach, formal changes in strategy and structure will boost organizational effectiveness only if these changes are supported by compatible changes in other, primarily "soft" features of the organizational system, such as the working style of top management, formal and informal administrative procedures, overarching goals, and members' attitudes and norms (see also Bluedorn & Lundgren, 1993; Bourgeois & Jemison, 1982).

At a less abstract level, fit analysis focuses on alignment among the units and functions that must work together to perform one or more of the phases shown in Figure 13.2 (e.g., Chapter 8, Assessing HRM's Strategic Contribution). It is also possible to assess alignment between plans developed in separate steps during the overall process of strategy formation and implementation. For example, investigators might examine the consistency between the strategic choices developed and selected in the second and third steps shown

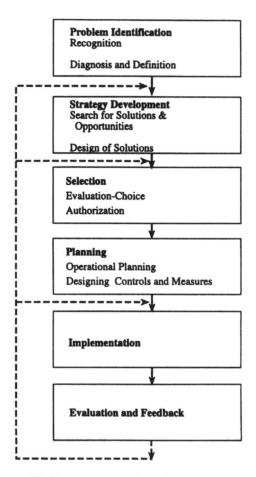

Figure 13.2 Phases of Deliberate Strategy Formation

in Figure 13.2 and the operational plans developed during the fourth step. Diagnostic questions concerning this interface include the following: Do the controls built into the operational plans measure the strategic outcomes of greatest importance? Does the reward system reinforce behavior that is crucial to the attainment of strategic goals?[6]

Diagnosis of the management of interdependencies can focus directly on interactions and coordinating arrangements that must emerge for the strategic process to succeed. These arrangements include conditions for effective problem identification and search, including the functioning of a cohesive yet self-critical management team. Other crucial conditions relate to the management of interdependencies during planning and implementation. Because strategic programs require the coordination of many separate units and actors, integrating mechanisms, such as project teams, must be put in place to bridge the gaps between people in separate functions, organizational levels, and locations.

For each phase in Figure 13.2 and for the process as a whole, gap analysis can contrast current outcomes or practices to desired ones. Consultants can define desired outcomes or ask top managers and the people responsible for implementing strategy to do so. To be genuinely useful, gap analysis cannot reasonably turn on simplistic comparisons between present activities and those depicted in the ideal-typical model of comprehensive, rational decision making. Nor can consultants and clients safely assume that the client organization should copy the strategic practices employed by successful organizations in the same industry or sector (see Chapter 8, Benchmarking). Instead, desired practices can best be defined as activities that are very likely to lead to important outcomes for the focal organization, such as more aggressive strategies or greater organizational involvement by divergent stakeholders.

Besides examining gaps, interdependencies, and fits during strategy formation, practitioners of diagnosis can contribute in many other ways to the deliberate formation and implementation of programs of strategic change. Some of these possibilities were illustrated in the discussion of diagnosis of design programs in Chapter 7. Here, we concentrate on additional diagnostic approaches that can contribute to managerial attempts to craft strategy, as well as to deliberate strategy formation.

Implicit choices during the earliest phases of strategy formation—problem definition, diagnosis, and the search for solutions—can determine all subsequent phases of the strategy formation and can radically affect chances for developing and implementing successful programs. Yet these early choices are among the least well defined and least formalized parts of deliberate strategy formation. Moreover, these choices are often neglected in discussions of strategy making.

The underlying cognitive maps or schemata used by decision makers can greatly affect the ways they think about strategic issues and make strategic decisions (see Chapter 10 and Schwenk, 1995, for a research survey). Managers undertake proactive strategies when they believe that their organization has both the need and the capacity to test, learn from, and even change its environment. In the absence of such beliefs, managers react passively to information and demands coming from their environment (Daft & Weick, 1984). For example, managers may attribute organizational failures to uncontrollable external events, such as changes in governmental regulation, rather than assuming that the cause of failure lies in the organization's ability to anticipate and cope with such changes. The causal maps developed by managers also shape the substantive focus of their strategic decisions, as well as its aggressiveness. For example, decision makers in some industrial firms seem to assume that clients react to price and appearance of products but pay little attention to quality or service. Reliance on cognitive models or schemata directs energy toward particular actions, such as cost reduction, at the expense of others, such as improvement of service. Furthermore, cognitions like these sensitize members of an organization to particular kinds of information about the environment and internal operations, while making them insensitive to other types of information.

By using qualitative research methods such as open interviewing, content analysis, or group workshops, consultants can gather information on the mental maps and implicit theories that members of the client organization employ during these formative phases of decision making. If consultants discern that the implicit models or theories in use reduce the range of strategic options considered or otherwise harm learning and decision making, the consultants can provide feedback on these implicit models and their effects. Feedback of this sort can encourage the adoption of broader or more complex approaches to the issues at hand and can encourage clients to reduce their reliance on interpretive frames that block organizational learning and adaptation (Argyris & Schon, 1996).

Another way to diagnose managerial cognitions is to examine the targets or reference points that decision makers use in evaluating strategic choices (Fiegenbaum et al., 1996). A growing body of knowledge about cognition and decision making indicates that decision makers who view their firm as performing below its strategic reference points are more likely to engage in risk-taking behavior than are those who see their firm as operating above its reference points. Managers operating above their targets tend to be risk averse (Fiegenbaum, 1990). Reference points can refer to internal functional capabilities, such as innovativeness, quality, and speed; to external relations, such as competitive standing, customer ratings, or stakeholder satisfaction; or to the firm's past or future practices. Managers of more effective firms are hypothesized to set reference points above current performance in all three domains and to revise reference points frequently as they focus on new challenges and opportunities. In contrast, firms that use a narrow range of reference points are expected to perform less well. The managers in these firms fail to develop a strategic vision capable of helping them discern new opportunities, deal with multiple constituencies, and react flexibly to change. Examination of strategic reference points may thus help diagnostic practitioners account for the nature of current strategies and provide a model for giving feedback that can enhance strategic decision making.

Another fruitful area for diagnosis and feedback concerns the range and quality of the formal and interpersonal information sources on which decision makers rely. The choice of both formal and interpersonal information channels shapes and is shaped by managerial understandings of the nature of their organization and their work and by their assumptions about available action alternatives. Take the question of whether public administrators consider contracting services to the private sector as a way of increasing organizational flexibility and efficiency. Whether the administrators consider this option depends on their assumptions about the efficiency of public and private sector organizations, their political ideologies, and their exposure to information sources on outsourcing to private contractors.

During problem identification and strategy development, managers in large, complex organizations sometimes rely heavily on a very limited band of information sources. Diagnostic studies can assess the extent to which managers run this risk or expose themselves to contrary and alternative ways of framing and solving problems. For instance, analysis of the managers' interaction networks (Scott, 1991) can show whether managers in one functional area routinely discuss problems with managers from different functions. In like manner, interactions with customers and suppliers can be assessed. Interviews can further highlight the extent to which managers consider alternatives to the solutions eventually adopted and actively weigh possible drawbacks of the favored solution.

Diagnostic studies can also help clients confront the decisive effects that organizational politics can have on strategy formation and implementation (see Eisenhardt & Zbaracki, 1992, for a research review). Recognizing that implementation requires the cooperation of divergent internal and external stakeholders, consultants can help clients assess the likelihood that groups affected by a broad strategic thrust or by a specific strategic move will cooperate with the move or oppose it. Techniques for identifying key stakeholders and assessing their capacity for threat or cooperation with managers were treated in Chapter 5.

Approaches like stakeholder analysis provide clients with inputs into decisions that can reinforce or revise power alignments in and around an organization. Consultants differ in their willingness to take an active role in such highly politicized decisions. The appropriateness and feasibility of consultant involvement in organizational politics also turn on the nature of the consulting contract, the types of challenges facing the organization, and conditions within the client organization (Harrison, 1991).

Supporting Emerging Strategies

Diagnostic models, techniques, and approaches can contribute to the formation of both emergent and deliberate strategies. The discussion that follows first examines potential contributions of diagnosis to decisions about the *contents* of emergent organizational strategies and then turns to contributions to the *processes* of emergent strategy formation.

Rethinking Competitive Advantage

Emergent strategies, like deliberately formulated ones, contribute to organizational success when they help an organization mobilize its distinctive competencies to gain competitive advantage in the environment. However, to gain and sustain strategic advantage in rapidly changing environments under conditions of uncertainty, managers must depart from traditional ways of thinking about the core concepts of distinctive competency and competitive advantage.

To foster aggressive, emergent strategies, managers and their advisors concentrate on enhancing their organization's environmental position in the *future,* rather than concentrating on current or past positions and conditions, as does most formal strategic planning.[7] Rather than analyzing SWOTs at present or a year or two down the line, decision makers facing uncertainty and rapid change need to analyze and work toward possible organizational and environmental developments that are 5 to 10 years away. In addition, participants in strategic thinking need to anticipate possible discontinuities in external threats and opportunities. They also need to expect change in internal strengths, rather than assuming that current conditions will continue unabated. To develop this type of proactive orientation, firm managers need to scan their environments for nontraditional competitors and to alter or abandon their own established products and services *before* their competitors begin to undermine the firm's competitive advantage (Lawler & Galbraith, 1994). Perhaps most importantly, decision makers must challenge their own operating assumptions and interpretive frames in order to avoid falling into the trap of assuming that past successes ensure future ones (see Smircich & Stubbart, 1985, and Organizational Learning, below).

One way for decision makers to locate environmental discontinuities is to identify long-term trends in areas to which most organizations in the environment have failed to respond (e.g., demographics, social norms and practices, or technology development). For example, top and middle management in many public and private service organizations have not yet examined ways to redirect or develop their services in light of the long-term trend toward the aging of the population and toward enhanced physical and intellectual capacities among many retirees. Organizations that initiate programs quickly in response to trends like these may gain an advantage over those that respond more slowly.

Consultants can help members of an organization think systematically about the future by showing them how to develop simulations of possible developments and organizational actions (Senge, 1990), such as scenarios of possible futures for their organization's operating environment (Mason, 1994; Thomas, 1994a). Scenario planning is a form of diagnostic intervention in which consultants help members of top management or of a cross-functional strategic planning team create several scenarios of possible future developments in relevant industries. Participants then examine possible organizational strategies for dealing with these alternative futures and contrast them to likely outcomes if the organization continues on its current course. Then, participants seek to forge a robust strategy that will be advantageous across the range of possible future developments.

The following case illustrates how the scenario planning technique was used in one finance and insurance company in the United States (Thomas, 1994b):

Case 13.2

Top management at OPM Finance and Insurance (fictitious name) undertook scenario planning in an effort to enhance their ability to manage future environmental uncertainties. OPM faced rapidly changing markets as a result of deregulation, globalization of markets, and rapid technological change in telecommunications and information processing. OPM managers saw these changes as creating new competition and new products. Members of an external consulting firm specializing in strategic planning interviewed managers and conducted workshops in order to construct five plausible but very different scenarios of developments in OPM's business environment during the next decade. Each scenario included details on macroeconomic conditions, such as employment and interest rates, that fit the assumptions used in that scenario. Then, senior management examined the scenarios in a series of workshops, treating each scenario as if it described real-life events. In these sessions, the participants tested current corporate strategies against projected developments and sought to forge alternative goals and strategies to deal with each projected future. The participants then sought to define robust goals and strategies that would work well no matter which future evolved. The managers developed a set of robust core strategies concerning new services and marketing approaches. However, they did not reach consensus in other areas. Instead, participants began to question what business their firm was in and what role they wanted in this business. To date, the managers continue to use scenario-derived insights to test and amend their strategies for marketing and services. OPM has also introduced scenario planning at other organizational levels for use more as a learning tool than as a planning exercise.

In developing images of organizational futures and examining strategic options, participants in strategic decisions need to be careful not to jump on the bandwagon of already faddish ideas. Even if these ideas are excellent, their very popularity makes them risky as ways to gain advantage over other firms. For instance, firms that are currently striving to take advantage of the commercial possibilities for reaching potential customers through the World Wide Web may discover that the niches within this developing marketplace that suit them best are already overcrowded by early arrivals. If that is the case, the late arrivals must either react to the threats created by their competitors in this emerging market or seek out new sources of advantage within or outside of the Web.

Many sketches of the future and tentative strategic initiatives that emerge within the middle or upper ranks of an organization will turn out to be incorrect, but some may be accurate and rewarding. When proposals for strategic changes turn on the development of new products, services, or programs, the potential benefits of the proposals can be partly evaluated by constructing and testing prototypes, market testing, or running experimental programs. Top management can then seek to craft guiding umbrella strategies from these initiatives. They can learn lessons from unsuccessful experiments and can expand experimental programs that demonstrated high potential for contributing to management's overall strategic vision.

In firms that develop aggressive, emergent strategies, the assessment of proposed strategic moves concentrates on ways that the organization can stretch its resources and capacities to meet new strategic objectives, rather than checking whether proposed strategies fit current capacities (Hamel & Prahalad, 1994). Too much concern with fits between current capacities and proposed strategy can lead participants in strategy formation to underestimate their ability to obtain additional resources or to mobilize current resources in new ways. By stretching current capacities, organizations can achieve a more ambitious and aggressive strategic thrust than could be achieved by relying on traditional strategic planning techniques.

To facilitate strategic stretch, consultants and decision makers need to consider ways in which the organization can leverage current resources to move toward targets that would otherwise be beyond reach. Practitioners of diagnosis can also help both internal entrepreneurs and top managers explore ways that the organization or unit might obtain additional resources from within or outside the organization.

In particular, top managers and their advisors can consider the possibilities that an overarching strategic vision may motivate people to work harder and may open up previously unrealized possibilities for cooperation and cross-fertilization between disparate functional units. For instance, high-technology firms may benefit from concentrating development efforts on a range of products, all of which draw on one distinctive technological innovation, such as a super-fast computer chip. Similarly, members of separate university departments can enhance their ability to obtain grants and attract talented staff and students by cooperating to develop expertise in a major interdisciplinary field like biotechnology or environmental studies. In organizations where expertise is highly diffused, such as universities and hospitals, consultants can help members of separate units discover and explore such possibilities for cooperation. Moreover, consultants can help top administrators craft strategies for integrative, interdisciplinary development by providing them with data on the current interests, aspirations, and plans of potential contributors to such cooperative undertakings.

Consultants can further contribute to the crafting of emergent strategies by helping top management create a structural platform that can support and facilitate pursuit of the organization's strategic thrust (Hamel & Prahalad, 1994; see also Nadler et al., 1992; Nadler et al., 1995). Although top managers cannot develop a detailed operating plan for managing unforeseeable initiatives and innovations or for taking advantage of emerging opportunities, the managers can establish structural conditions that will support a range of innovations and strategic initiatives, all of which fall within management's overall strategic direction.

For instance, if interunit cooperation is critical to strategic development, then management needs to foster technical and organizational conditions that support and even encourage such cooperation. These conditions include computer networks that make cross-boundary communication easier and more effective; material incentives and promotion channels that encourage innovation and cooperation across boundaries; and structural links, such as product managers and teams, that can coordinate interunit activities (see the section on Innovativeness, below, and Ashkenas, Ulrich, Jick, & Kerr, 1995).

Behavioral science consultants can support the construction of such a structural platform by helping clients decide on desired features and by assessing the degree to which the organization already possesses the required structural and system features. For instance, decentralization of authority and resource allocation are necessary to empower experts who are dispersed throughout the organization to initiate strategic initiatives. Previous chapters examined ways to assess the prevalence of structural and political conditions like these and to follow through on attempts to implement strategic design changes (Chapters 5 and 7). The following discussion examines additional ways that diagnosis can support strategy formation. Here, the emphasis is on potential diagnostic contributions to the *processes* of emergent strategy formation, as opposed to the contents of these strategies.

Supporting the Crafting of Strategy

The creation of new ideas, techniques, and proposals for action forms an even more critical stage in the formation of emerging and crafted strategies than it does in deliberate strategy formation. Strategic initiatives can come from a broad range of experts, middle managers, and top managers. The survival and development of new ideas depends on interaction among these diverse actors.

Diagnostic investigators can assess an organization's capacity for creative strategy formation by examining the sources of information and ideas considered by potential contributors to emergent strategies. In addition, consultants can investigate the range and kinds of images and models used by these actors. It is also possible to trace the fate of a set of new ideas and proposals from their initial creation through top management's responses to them. Studies of idea generation and development will provide evidence of the degree to which the organization's managerial culture supports and encourages innovative and critical thinking.

In like manner, consultants can follow the processes through which top management seeks to craft organizational strategy. Such a study would assess the degree to which top management coalesces into a cohesive leadership team capable of formulating and implementing a strategic vision. A further assessment issue concerns the extent to which this team communicates its vision to key actors throughout the organization and mobilizes their support for it (Kotter, 1995). Because crafted strategies often call for the reallocation of organizational priorities, they grant opportunities for some units and individuals but threaten others. Hence, data from stakeholder analyses on potential support and opposition to strategic moves form important inputs to managers seeking to craft strategy, as well as to those who would plan strategy deliberately.

If top management develops a structural platform to support its strategy, diagnostic consultants can provide feedback on the implementation of these new structures and assess the degree to which they facilitate work within and between critical organizational units. The specific questions that will guide such a diagnosis will depend on the nature of the platform that is envisioned. For instance, if management seeks to encourage and foster cooperation across units and organizational boundaries, then diagnosis can concentrate on the types and quality of working relations that emerge between relevant units (e.g., see Van de Ven & Ferry, 1980, and Chapter 6).

Assessment of the quality of communication up and down the organizational hierarchy is particularly central to diagnoses of crafted strategy formation. To craft strategy successfully, top management must do more than communicate its vision and programs to people responsible for implementation. Management must also be open to and actively support bottom-up proposals and ideas coming from internal entrepreneurs and from people who work closely with clients, suppliers, and other external groups. Other structural features that can shape the formation and implementation of crafted strategies include recruitment, training, and reward patterns; feedback and assessment mechanisms; and patterns of internal financial support for the development of innovations.

Another focus for diagnosis concerns aggressive actions through which members of an organization redefine and shape their own environment in keeping with their strategic objectives, rather than simply adapting to what seems to be "out there" (Smircich & Stubbart, 1985). Diagnostic investigators can help clients judge the feasibility of such aggressive moves and can follow up on their realization. For example, a firm seeking to expand high-tech operations in a region lacking in suitable personnel may enter into partnerships with nearby educational organizations to train people in the skills that the firm's employees will need in the future. In this case, behavioral science consultants can help the firm develop criteria for evaluating this project and can provide feedback on its progress. In like manner, members of an organization can sometimes forge alliances with powerful political or business partners who help them shape critical external conditions. Periodic analyses of the positions and behavior of such key partners and stakeholders can facilitate the development of vital interorganizational alliances like these.

In the final analysis, managers at all ranks can only generate successful emergent strategies if they can consistently foster organizational innovation and learning. The next section examines potential contributions of diagnosis to these crucial processes.

Contributing to Innovation and Organizational Learning

Firms that compete by developing and marketing new products and services can create an enduring source of competitive advantage by building in high capabilities for technological innovation. Similarly, all types of organizations that face recurring environmental and technological challenges can enhance competitive advantage by developing the capacity for fundamental organizational learning (Nadler et al., 1995). This learning capacity can sustain frequent reassessments of strategic alternatives and programs and can pave the way to practically continuous systemic change.

Innovativeness

Innovation refers to inventing or importing technologies, products, services, or administrative practices that are new to the organization (see Rogers, 1995, for a literature survey). Innovativeness contributes to adaptation in all types of firms, but it becomes a matter of life and death in industries where competitive advantage stems from developing and selling new products. Some large American firms appear to be able to foster continuous technological innovation despite barriers presented by size, complexity, hierarchy, and formalization.

Research on these innovative firms provides the basis for a model that can guide assessments of an organization's capacities for innovation and can point to ways that managers can enhance innovativeness. Four factors help large firms develop and sustain technological innovativeness (Delbecq & Mills, 1985; Kanter, 1983; Klein & Sorra, 1996; Pennings & Harianto, 1992; Purser & Passmore, 1992; Quinn, 1985):

1. *Strategic thinking and decision making.* Top management is committed to innovation and views change opportunistically. The dominant coalition develops a qualitative vision or guiding strategy that extends beyond numerical targets and measures (e.g., to be leaders in commercial applications of biotechnology). Top management retains a strong market orientation and develops close ties with external organizations, such as customers or partners in strategic alliances. Interactive learning draws on multiple external sources of information and technology.

2. *Resource allocation.* Top management generously provides internal capital for promising new ideas. It simultaneously supports several competing approaches to product development and chooses among them only after the production of prototypes. In support of the strategic vision, management invests in long-term actions within and across divisions.

3. *Human resource management.* Efforts are made to attract highly skilled and creative people and to provide them with opportunities for professional growth and autonomy. Innovators and implementors of innovations receive training, technical support, financial incentives, and other rewards.

4. *Structure.* The firms maintain fairly flat organizational structures based on small teams (six or seven key people), as well as divisions of no more than 400 people. Much development work occurs in semi-independent, loosely structured, interdisciplinary project teams (e.g., skunk works, pilot projects). These teams are free of most administrative constraints and emulate the work style and climate found in small firms during the entrepreneurial or collectivity stages of the organizational life cycle (Chapter 11). Integrating mechanisms, such as projects,

task forces, horizontal links between units, and informal networks bridge boundaries between technical and marketing staff and between other disciplinary and functional groups. Strategic alliances (e.g., licenses, joint ventures) with other firms provide access to new technologies and facilitate risk sharing.

The features just described support other types of organizational innovation, as well as technological innovation (Kanter, 1983). Innovation in areas such as marketing, services, and administration depends heavily on the empowerment of people who can develop and promote new ideas—no matter where they are located in the organizational hierarchy. Like technical innovation, administrative innovation depends on the emergence of structures and processes—such as communication, technical and logistical support, management norms, and rewards—that support these innovations. Long-term internal funding plays a smaller role in nontechnical innovations than it does in those focused on advanced technologies.

Diagnostic practitioners who want to assess a focal organization in terms of this model can develop measures of each feature and then gather data on the strength and distribution of the feature. Standardized measures of some of the features are available and can be applied to entire organizations or to selected subunits. For example, the Kilmann-Saxton Culture Gap Survey (Kilmann & Saxton, 1981; see also Case 10.2) contains questions about teamwork, communication flows, and norms supporting innovation.

Organizational Learning

Unfortunately, the introduction of many technical and administrative innovations in an organization does not ensure that innovation will occur repeatedly and that innovations that are implemented will contribute to organizational effectiveness. Nor does innovation ensure intensive or extensive organizational learning. Organizational learning turns on the ability of people, groups, and organizations to modify the ways they currently think about and deal with problems and challenges. For individual and group learning to become truly organizational, members' learning experiences need to be encoded in routines—rules, procedures, ways of thinking, conventions, strategies, and technologies—that guide future behavior (Levitt & March, 1988). At its most modest, *type one* or single-loop learning (Argyris & Schon, 1996) involves finding ways to improve current practices, as judged by current standards and norms. This level of learning can produce dramatic improvements, such as cost savings, but does not generate the ability to make future improvements in the system. Instead, type one learning results only in first-order change, which reinforces the frames, or schemata, through which participants interpret their organization and its environment (Argyris & Schon, 1996; Bartunek & Moch, 1987).

In contrast, during *type two* or double-loop learning, members review and challenge standards, policies, and procedures in light of external changes and their own underlying values. In this fashion, members learn to learn. For instance, they may build continuous quality-improvement techniques into their operations or conduct routine reviews of strategies, goals, and operating targets. Type two learning thus yields second-order change, in which participants consciously modify their schemata in a particular direction. *Type three* learning, the most far-reaching and rarest form of learning, breaks current frames and yields fundamental changes in the organization's guiding vision or approach and in fundamental assumptions about work and organizing (Nadler, 1988). At its most optimal, type three learning does not just substitute one way of looking at the organization for another. Instead, it produces third-order change through which participants become aware of their own interpretive schemata and prepare to change these schemata as needed (Bartunek and Moch, 1987).

The organizational features that support innovation also contribute to learning. However, additional cultural and structural conditions are necessary for type two and type three learning that are not needed for innovation (Argyris & Schon, 1996; Morgan, 1986; Purser & Passmore, 1992; Senge, 1990; Smircich & Stubbart, 1985; Useem & Kochan, 1992; Walton, 1995). These conditions typically cluster into a configuration. The absence of one or more of the needed cultural or structural conditions can block higher levels of organizational learning, even when some facilitating conditions are present (Hedberg, 1980).

Structural conditions that support organizational learning extend and deepen structural features that contribute to innovation. Type two learning requires the creation of conditions and processes through which people get valid information, initiate actions, and see and learn from the results of their actions (Argyris & Schon, 1996). To sustain learning-oriented norms and reduce defensiveness among managers and subordinates, higher-level managers seek to decentralize authority and introduce norms and reward systems that effectively empower managers to make decisions, take risks, and learn from their experiences.

Managers can also promote learning by enriching the mix of inputs to decision making. Assessments of stakeholder perceptions of organizational effectiveness (Chapter 3) can thereby make a crucial contribution to organizational learning and viability (Lawler & Galbraith, 1994). To facilitate environmental scanning, learning, and assessment, organization designers create permeable boundaries that allow for the spanning of vertical, horizontal, organization-environment, and geographical boundaries (Ashkenas et al., 1995). Thus, they build structural links that make possible cooperation and information sharing across boundaries. Moreover, they periodically reconfigure these structures to ensure responsiveness to customers, products, processes, locales, and suppliers (Lawler & Galbraith, 1994).

In addition, organizations foster diversity by bringing together people from divergent occupational, educational, and organizational backgrounds, including some "wild geese" (Lawler & Galbraith, 1994, p. 15), who can be counted on to say the "unsayable." Thus, human resource diversity can lead members to consider a broader range of strategic and operational possibilities and can enhance creativity in decision making (Chapter 9). However, managers who seek to foster diversity also face difficulties in coordinating the work of people accustomed to very different styles of working and thinking (Useem & Kochan, 1992; Walton, 1995).

In brief, the following structural conditions can facilitate organizational learning:

- Permeable boundaries in and around the organization
- Teams, integrating roles, and other linking mechanisms
- Close ties to customers, suppliers, and strategic partners
- Decentralized decision making that effectively empowers organizational participants
- Multichannel information flows
- Recruitment of diverse personnel and development of procedures for exposing members to diverse viewpoints
- Rewards and incentives for addressing and solving recurring problems and challenges

Although these structural conditions facilitate learning, they are not sufficient to sustain systematic type two learning. Cross-boundary ties and other new organizational designs will contribute to learning only if the organizational culture fosters openness to new ideas and genuine sharing of information across boundaries, and if the reward system sustains these prolearning norms and values (Useem & Kochan, 1992). For instance, sales managers who routinely meet with important customers may nevertheless develop attitudes and mental frames that lead them to discount or deny the importance of the customers' criticisms and suggestions.

Ironically, successful organizations often develop cultural conditions that block learning by making members unwilling or unable to examine past and current practices critically (Chapters 10 and 11). In like manner, an organization may fall into a competency trap (Levitt & March, 1988) in which favorable experience with a particular procedure or technology leads members to accumulate ever more experience with that technology. As they specialize their skills, members unintentionally deprive themselves of sufficient experience with a superior technology to make the use of that new technology worthwhile.

In addition to requiring openness to divergent views and a critical attitude toward past practices, learning requires the adoption of an experimental, inquiry-oriented approach to decision making of the sort proposed for assessments of strategic design programs (Chapter 7). This approach entails learning through inquiry, in the sense of adapting decisions and strategies to emerging realities in the field (Pascale, 1984). In a learning organization, managers regard their actions as tests of current understandings, models, and hypotheses about the organization and its environment. The effects of managerial action provide data about the accuracy of the original conceptions and suggest ways to modify them (Schon, 1983).

In summary, here are the main features of organizational cultures that support second-level learning:

- Acceptance of error
- Interpersonal relations that are high on trust and low on defensiveness
- Tolerance of ambiguity and uncertainty
- Critical attitude, which questions current achievements and does not take future success for granted
- Encouragement of risk taking and experimentation
- Inquiry-driven decision making and action
- Valuing of multiple viewpoints and perspectives on problems, including inputs from customers and other groups outside the organization
- Preservation of paradox and complexity in the framing of issues for action
- Granting authority based on experience and expertise, rather than on a basis of seniority or formal position

In contrast, most bureaucratic organizations contain cultural norms and assumptions that block learning. These cultures are averse to risk and error, resist new and different ideas, emphasize control over subordinates and action, call for expressions of loyalty to current goals and practices, reduce complexity by sorting people and events into a limited number of agreed-upon categories, and grant substantial authority to a limited number of high-level managers.

Practitioners of diagnosis can apply this emerging model of the conditions for learning in much the same way that they apply the model of conditions for innovativeness. However, the cultural conditions for learning run deep and are harder to change than are those supporting innovation.

Consultants and managers may therefore seek to *enhance* an organization's learning capacity rather than just assessing its current capacity. To do so, they can use diagnostic interventions in which consultants help members of the client organization learn to diagnose organizational challenges and decide on appropriate actions (e.g., Chapter 4; see also Case 13.2). To promote enduring learning, consultants must help participants in diagnostic workshops to move beyond their immediate decision tasks. The participants also need to become aware of the prospects and difficulties of enhancing type two learning and to consider ways to build greater learning capacity into their organization.

Diagnostic approaches and techniques can contribute to organizational learning more readily if consultants and clients define diagnosis as a *learning process*. To view diagnosis in this way, both the practitioners of diagnosis and the recipients of diagnostic feedback need to free themselves from the assumption that decision making and managerial action should necessarily proceed sequentially through the stages of diagnosis, planning, implementation, and evaluation. Instead, diagnostic thinking and problem solving can be redefined as *iterative forms of inquiry and hypothesis testing* (Chapter 7). By conducting quick mini-diagnoses *throughout* the processes of decision making, planning, and action, managers can review and reassess their understandings of questions like these:

What is the nature of our main problems and challenges?
How did these challenges develop?
What are we trying to accomplish?
What actions have we taken so far?
Why do we expect our current or future actions to produce the results we want to achieve? What causal models underlie these expectations?

What are the results so far of our past actions?

What do these results suggest about our original analysis of the problem, about the appropriateness of the actions taken so far, and about our causal models?

When decision makers employ diagnostic thinking and problem solving in this way, they can develop a self-correcting, results-oriented style of learning about the circumstances facing them and can more readily discover effective ways of confronting current challenges. In this way, decision makers start analyzing unclear and changing conditions as soon as they encounter them and keep track of the accumulating evidence about these conditions and about possible ways of dealing with them. As suggested in Chapter 7, managers need not wait until the final evaluation report is in to begin shifting their tactics and actions or to start revising their models. If an early assessment of a program's implementation reveals hidden hazards—such as pockets of resistance or changing competition—management can and should shift course in mid-stream.

Awareness of the models and theoretical frames underlying diagnosis and conscious use of them can also contribute directly to organizational learning. In particular, system thinking, which lies at the heart of many diagnostic models, can help decision makers develop the kind of complex thinking that facilitates learning (Senge, 1990). Users of the systems frame learn to look for configurations of variables and complex, systemic interactions, as opposed to simple causal chains made up of a few variables. Once they adopt a systems approach, decision makers become aware that actions in one part of a system can have delayed consequences in other, distant parts of that system. By helping to break down conceptual boundaries between organizations and units, systems analysis encourages people to consider possible forms of cross-boundary cooperation and linkage that were ruled out by more traditional forms of managerial thinking. Other diagnostic models, such as those based on the political and cultural frames, also contain many insights that are counterintuitive for managers who draw their implicit frames and models of organizational life from a single discipline or functional specialization, such as accounting, finance, law, or industrial engineering. Diagnostic thinking and inquiry can also foster organizational learning by introducing decision makers to the benefits of approaching organizational challenges from the vantage point of divergent theoretical perspectives and models. By using multiple models and perspectives, as we did in our treatment of organization design, decision makers may become aware of ways of thinking and acting that were previously neglected in their organization. For example, the resistance of veteran employees to the upgrading of an office computer system may be hard to explain from an instrumental, cost-benefit perspective. But viewing the employees' reactions in terms of the political and symbolic implications of the upgrade may quickly shed light on the sources of resistance and on possible ways to deal with it. In a similar fashion, combining familiar frames, such as the structural frame, with the political frame—and, in particular, with the stakeholder approach to effectiveness—can sensitize clients to the need to strive simultaneously to satisfy conflicting constituencies, incommensurate objectives, and divergent criteria of organizational effectiveness.

Conclusion

This chapter showed how behavioral science consultants can make valuable contributions to strategy formation—a field that traditionally has been viewed as the province of business consultants and industry experts. First, we presented a contingency model that can help consultants and clients decide when it is feasible and appropriate for managers to formulate strategy deliberately. This model shows the conditions in which it is reasonable to apply the guidelines for systematic strategic planning contained in many texts and training programs. Then, we pointed to ways that consultants can provide support for deliberate strategy formation and the emergence of strategy through bottom-up and horizontal interaction among many separate actors. That discussion also introduced ways that top managers can craft emergent strategies, and it provided guidelines for supporting these crafting activities. The last part of the chapter presented models of the conditions facilitating organizational innovation and learning and identified steps that consultants can take to enhance organizational capacities in these vital areas. In particular, we stressed the potential contributions of diagnostic inquiry to organizational learning.

Chapter 14 explores the applications of diagnosis to a realm that has received very little attention in the past: diagnosing an entire institutional sector. That chapter applies diagnostic models to the analysis of interorganizational relations, an area of growing importance to policymakers and business managers.

Notes

1. The first two terms are from Mintzberg (1987), and the third comes from Miles and Snow (1978). The discussion that follows draws on those sources and on Harrison and Phillips (1991), where a more complex, fourfold typology is examined. For a thorough review of recent approaches to strategy, see Mintzberg, Quinn, and Voyer (1995).

2. See Chapter 11 on the difficulties of carrying out long marches toward strategic change. On the complexities of implementation in the public sector, see Kenis and Schneider (1991) and Pettigrew et al. (1992).

3. There is strong empirical and theoretical support for some of the contingent relations shown in the table, but not for all of them. For example, there are conflicting findings on the relations between decision rationality, environmental instability, and decision effectiveness (Dean & Sharfman, 1996).

4. The terminology of the first three phases and their subroutines draws, with modifications, on research on strategic decision processes by Mintzberg et al. (1976). On the planning of operational programs, controls, and measures, see, for example, Kaplan and Norton (1992, 1993).

5. For clarity and consistency, we have summarized the 7-S framework using terms defined in Chapter 2. Waterman, Peters, and Phillips label the components of the internal system in terms of seven Ss—strategy, superordinate goals, structure, (administrative and operating) systems, (management) style, staff (values and orientations), and (organizational) skills.

6. See, for example, Chapter 8, Assessing HRM's Strategic Contribution.

7. The following discussion of ways to recast traditional SWOT analysis draws on Hamel and Prahalad (1994); Mintzberg et al. (1994); and on Smircich and Stubbart (1985).

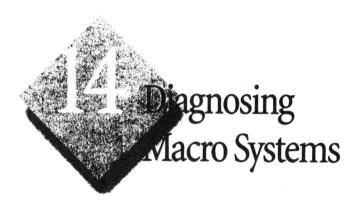

14 Diagnosing Macro Systems

A ll of the preceding chapters in this book examined ways of diagnosing single organizations, subsystems, or functions within them, such as the labor relations system and the human resources function. Yet diagnosis can also contribute to planning changes in networks of organizations and in whole institutional sectors.

The diagnosis of such macro systems is in keeping with a growing number of applications of organization development concepts to organizational networks and other systems that encompass many separate organizations (e.g., Gray, 1989; Johnson & Cooperrider, 1991; Motamedi & Cummings, 1984; Tichy, 1978). Unfortunately, public policy makers rarely take advantage of the potential contributions of diagnosis of macro systems to policy making, program planning, and implementation.

This chapter illustrates the possible contributions of macro-system diagnosis by constructing a diagnostic model of a national health care system. The proposed macrolevel diagnostic model rests on the procedures and techniques of sharp-image diagnosis that were presented in the first part of this book. The procedures used here to develop the diagnostic model can readily be applied to the diagnosis of other macro systems, such as a country's educational and social welfare systems.

Why have we chosen a national health system to illustrate the diagnosis of macro systems? In most industrialized countries in the West, the health care system has several distinct traits. It is projected to grow continuously in the next decade to become one of the largest national industries. It affects every citizen, and it has been the subject of much political contention. Furthermore, in most countries, the health system has been a target of reform efforts (Abel-Smith, Figueras, Holland, McKee, & Mossialos, 1995; OECD, 1992; Seedhouse, 1995).

Reforms in health care systems are usually introduced by politicians, whose policy-making processes may be influenced by a variety of stakeholders and ideological agendas. These reforms have been driven by concerns over the rising costs of health care; aging of the population; new definitions of health; and shifting and rising expectations about health care quality, availability, and patient rights. It is very likely that these forces will continue to generate pressure for increasing the effectiveness of publicly funded health care systems. Although politicians are driving health system reforms, professionals, such as staff experts in the government ministries, as well as consultants, often become involved in the planning and implementation of reforms.

Rather than considering actual reform efforts, this chapter concentrates on one of the prerequisites for the success of health system reform: a valid diagnosis of the system under consideration. The macrolevel diagnostic model presented here is proposed as a conceptual tool to be used by professionals and consultants concerned with reforming a macrolevel system, such as a health care system. Two premises underlie the development of this model. First, without an adequate diagnosis, it is difficult to design an appropriate systemwide reform. Second, a simple and easily understood diagnostic model provides both a useful heuristic device for professionals working on health care reform and an effective point of entry into the policy-making process.

Diagnostic models and organization development interventions have been used in the past to increase the effectiveness of both single and multiple health care organizations (Boss, 1989; Margulies & Adams, 1982; Tichy, 1978; Wieland, 1981). However, we are not aware of any explicit attempt to construct a diagnostic model for a country's entire health care system or a section thereof, such as its geriatric or psychiatric health services.

The construction of the diagnostic model is presented in several successive steps, each step accompanied by a specific guideline and by illustrations and examples based on a diagnosis of the Israeli health care system. The first part of this chapter proposes that effectiveness in health care systems be defined in terms of system outcomes. The main section of the chapter is devoted to guidelines for constructing a model for diagnosing a health system. In this section, the construct of system ineffectiveness is used to identify each "*outcome in need of overhaul*." In the rest of this chapter, each such ineffective outcome is represented by the onomatopoeic acronym of OINO (pronounced "Oy, no!"), or, in the plural form, OINOs. The open-systems approach is then used to delineate a health care system's components, specify its boundaries, identify major relations among components, and describe system-environment interactions. Procedures are also developed for identifying system features that give rise to important OINOs. The discussion section identifies some constraints on the use of diagnostic models, such as the one illustrated here, and examines advantages and limitations of the model.

Focusing on System Outcomes

Sharp-image diagnosis of macro systems, such as health care systems, advocates focusing on system outcomes—and, in particular, on ineffective outcomes and their antecedent conditions (Chapters 1, 3, and 12). Focusing on outcomes in health systems is appropriate on both theoretical and practical grounds. Following the multiple stakeholder approach to effectiveness (Chapter 3), it could be argued that a health care system's main strategic task is to add value to its environment in order to ensure its legitimacy and obtain the continued support of stakeholders. The system's added value consists mainly of its outcomes. The practical benefit of focusing on outcomes in diagnosis is that outcomes are very salient to diagnostic clients, policy makers, and other system stakeholders. Furthermore, by focusing on outcomes, investigators can avoid being overwhelmed by the complexity revealed by the whole open-systems framework (Chapter 2).

How does the focus on outcomes tie in with a health care system's effectiveness? Reforms introduced in a health care system may take many forms, such as changes in system organization or financing. By and large, these reforms are designed to enhance the system's effectiveness (Frenk, 1994). Therefore, at the outset, diagnosis of a health care system requires a working definition of effectiveness. Like most definitions of organizational effectiveness (see Chapter 3), the effectiveness of a health care system is a multidimensional construct. In the past, effectiveness has been defined in terms of any combination of the following criteria: (a) adequacy of inputs into the system, that is, of resources such as hospital beds or physicians per capita; (b) optimal operation of organizational processes, such as absence of waiting lines for surgery or smooth and full communication between physicians and patients; (c) effective structural arrangements that ensure desired results, such as coordination and transfer of information among primary, secondary, and tertiary medical services; (d) ongoing adaptation to the environment and to new medical technologies; and (e) optimal achievement of outcomes, such as the net impact of the system on the incidence of specific illnesses and rates of mortality in the population (Ham, Robinson, & Benzeval, 1990; Rosenthal & Frenkel, 1992). As a result of initiatives by the World Health Organization (WHO, 1985), the last mentioned effectiveness dimension—the optimal achievement of a set of outcomes—has now been incorporated into national health care plans. Therefore, the focus on outcomes proposed above appears well grounded in current health planning theory and practice. It should be noted that measures of outcome effectiveness are often supplemented by measures of efficiency involving outcomes/inputs ratios and by measures of the accessibility of health care (OECD, 1987). The diagnostic model developed below is thus based on an extended definition of outcomes effectiveness—one that includes criteria reflecting outcomes, efficiency, and accessibility.

This discussion leads to the first diagnostic guideline:

1. *Focus on the set of outcomes of the health care system. Use either the outcomes selected in your nation's health planning effort or WHO health targets. Include among the outcomes the overall cost of obtaining them (i.e., the system's economic efficiency) and their accessibility to the residents of the country.*

A set of possible outcomes of a health care system is illustrated in the right-hand panel of Figure 14.1, below. These include outcomes defined in terms of attitudes and behaviors of consumers and providers of health care (OECD, 1992). The treatment of accessibility as an outcome involves some imprecision because accessibility is clearly a process-related characteristic of the system. It was included in the outcome group because in most nations, universal access to health care is defined as a highly important target to be achieved by the system.

What yardstick should one use to gauge the effectiveness of achieving specific outcomes? Most outcomes have been defined operationally by health planners (e.g., WHO, 1985) in terms of readily available yardsticks. Examples include reducing the rate of infant mortality and increasing the coverage of the population by health insurance schemes. The price tag on these outcomes, that is, the system's economic efficiency, is customarily measured by the proportion of the gross national product that is directed to health care services (OECD, 1992). There are outcomes, such as increasing the longevity of the population, that need to be desegregated into a set of composite indicators (e.g., reducing chronic diseases, increasing health-enhancing behaviors). Yet another problem concerns the choice of an appropriate standard of comparison. As discussed in Chapter 3, several standards of comparison are available, including other comparable systems, past performance, future targets, or normative judgments.

It is intuitively appealing to use other, comparable systems as the standard of comparison for a health care system. However, there are several reasons for exercising caution when making such comparisons. First, it is well known that every country's health care system reflects cultural priorities, characteristics of the political system, stage of economic growth, and the level of professionalization of health care personnel. As an illustration, the outcome of infant mortality, as measured by the yardstick of the annual mortality rate per 100,000 newborn infants, is generally interpreted as a reflection of standard of living, lifestyle, and genetics, as well as reflecting the performance of the health care system (Rosenthal & Frenkel, 1992, p. 331). Second, we are not aware of a health care system that can be used as an ideal standard of comparison for all other systems.

For these reasons, a more adequate standard of comparison between countries would be the level of effectiveness achieved by a group of comparable systems. One such standard is the average level of performance on a given outcome for the 24 OECD countries. If there is concern that ineffective outliers within the OECD group may draw averages down, then comparisons can be made to the average level of outcomes among the upper third of the 24 OECD countries (Schieber, Poullier, & Greenwald, 1994). For most OECD countries, such a standard would set a realistic level of aspiration that encourages excellence. For other types of outcomes, such as accessibility of services, the system's past record or desired level of accessibility are often used as standards of comparison. For outcomes having to do with consumer or producer satisfaction, cross-service comparisons or averages may provide suitable benchmarks.

Constructing a Diagnostic Model

Identifying Ineffective Outcomes

Construction of a diagnostic model for a health system starts with the identification of a subset of ineffective outcomes. This subset should be placed in the panel of outcomes in the diagnostic model (thus replacing the examples of outcomes provided in Figure 14.1). For several reasons, this focus on ineffective outcomes, which corresponds to the focus for sharp-image diagnosis presented in Chapter 1, is very relevant to health care systems. First, ineffective outcomes are very relevant to high-ranking decision makers in public agencies (Golembiewski & Eddy, 1978). Second, ineffectiveness is more critical than effectiveness to the long-term survival of publicly funded health care systems. Third, ineffective outcomes are easier to identify and describe than are effective ones. Therefore, people involved in planning health care reforms can reach agreement on them more readily.

The identification of ineffective outcomes and the subsequent steps for constructing a diagnostic model will be illustrated with reference to Israel's health system. The first group of system outputs, labeled in Figure 14.1 as Outputs of Health Care, consists of outcomes commonly used in cross-country comparisons of health care systems (e.g., Raffel, 1984). It is thus reasonable to compare their effectiveness in Israel with the average for OECD countries (OECD, 1987, 1993). The same standard will be used to gauge the extent to which these outcomes were achieved at a reasonable cost to the economy.

Before discussing the Israeli case, some background information should be provided (see also Shuval, 1991). Since the passage of the National Health Insurance Law in January 1995, the Israeli health care system has been financed by a compulsory tax paid by most adult residents of the country, by allocations from the national budget, and by consumers' out-of-pocket payments. The new law provides all residents with access to a comprehensive basket of services without regard to a patient's financial status. These services generally meet high standards. Because citizens purchase much care that is not provided under the National Health Insurance Law, income differences do affect the total amount of care received by individuals and the quality of that care. Since the 1980s, the government's contributions to health care have declined, and out-of-pocket contributions by individuals have grown, producing greater inequalities and more market-like features within the health

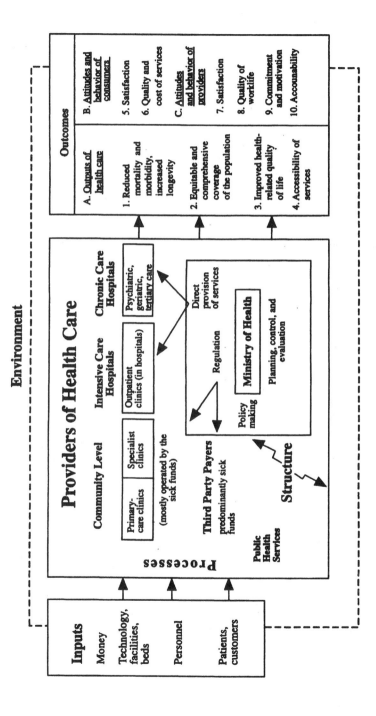

Figure 14.1 Components of a Health Care System: The Israeli Case.
SOURCE: Modified from Shirom (1996). Copyright 1996 by JAI. Reprinted by permission.

system. Total expenditure on health care, around 8% of gross domestic product (GDP), is on a par with OECD countries (OECD, 1993). However, this figure is somewhat misleading because of Israel's relatively low GDP. For a society that places high priority on health care, the low absolute per capita expenditures, which are far below the OECD average, constitute a serious social problem.

The major providers of individual and community-level health services are the Ministry of Health and four sickness funds, the largest of which is Kupat Holim Clalit (KHC). Aside from bearing the usual ministerial responsibilities, the Ministry of Health owns and operates about one half of the country's acute care and psychiatric beds and about 20% of the long-term care (geriatric institutions') beds. As of June 1997, KHC insured about 62% of Israel's population. KHC also owns and operates about one third of the country's acute care hospital beds. KHC provides its members with comprehensive care (excluding only a few services, such as dental care) through a network of the community clinics staffed by salaried physicians and nurses. Another 38% of the population is insured by the three smaller sickness funds, which operate clinics and maintain panels of physicians on contract.

When the outcomes of health care in Israel are compared to those of the OECD countries, a relatively satisfactory picture emerges. Life expectancy is comparable to the OECD average (OECD, 1987), and in most areas of the country, there is easy accessibility to the health care delivery system. Comparisons for each of the major system outcomes allows identification of ineffective outcomes. In Israel's case, they include poor dental health among the elderly, infant mortality in the Arab sector, insufficient coverage of long-term geriatric care and poor accessibility to it, and growing inequality in the distribution of health resources among different socioeconomic strata.

It is more difficult to select an appropriate yardstick to identify OINOs among the other subset of system outputs shown in Figure 14.1, namely, the subset of outcomes referred to as Attitudes and Behaviors of Consumers and as Attitudes and Behaviors of Providers. Qualitative goals set for the system often serve as possible yardsticks. One such goal states that "more than 70% of those insured by state-supported sickness funds should express satisfaction with the health services provided to them by their sickness fund" (WHO, 1985, p. 37). In general, in setting qualitative standards and in establishing priorities among OINOs, the normative judgments of a group of experts can supplement assessments based on objective data. This group of experts could represent important stakeholders in the diagnostic process, thus increasing the accountability and acceptability of the diagnostic process.[1] The major task of this group would be to rate the relative importance of the list of ineffective outcomes thus identified, providing inputs to the next step of the diagnosis. To enhance the objectivity of this process, the group of experts may be given specific instructions. For example, they could be told that the importance of outcomes is to be assessed by the size of the gap between the current level of performance on each outcome and the benchmark set for it.

The second diagnostic guideline may now be formulated:

2. *Identify the subset of ineffective outcomes using a predetermined standard of comparison.*

For many outcomes, averages for a group of comparable nations can be used as standards. For some outcomes, the collective judgments of experts can be used.

An overall comparison of the identified OINOs with effective system outcomes can be instructive. In the analysis of the Israeli health care system, this comparison showed that many OINOs belong to the category of attitudes and behaviors among consumers and providers of health care. To illustrate, labor unrest, including strikes by physicians, nurses, and other health care employees for better salaries and employment conditions, has been common in the system. Strikes in the health care system were responsible for a substantial portion of Israel's total of work days lost because of strikes in recent years. Patients expressed dissatisfaction with long lines for elective surgery, and health care professionals were dissatisfied with underutilization of facilities. Long waiting lists and lines gave rise to under-the-table, "black" medicine and to "gray" practices—such as advancing patients in waiting lists in exchange for donations to the department involved. These developments, in turn, led to an inequitable distribution of hospital resources, with better treatment for the haves and growing dissatisfaction among the have-nots.

Notwithstanding these dysfunctional aspects of the Israeli health care system, comparison of Israel's OINOs with effective outcomes led to an important conclusion: It is not necessary to transform or massively restructure this system in order to improve it. This conclusion contradicts that reached by some observers of the Israeli scene, who focused exclusively on its ineffective outcomes (OINOs) and ignored its many effective outcomes. The diagnostic approach followed here can be summed up in the following guideline:

3. *Compare OINOs with effective outcomes in order to obtain an indication as to the general type of reforms needed to improve the OINOs—for example, system transformation versus incremental readjustments.*

Once a general strategy for reform has been determined in keeping with this third guideline, all subsequent steps for constructing the diagnostic model are focused on the OINOs and their roots in the health care system. It is often advisable to focus on the most important or critical OINOs, as identified by a group of experts, so as to concentrate diagnosis and planned change on the most critical problems and challenges. Focusing on the most critical OINOs reflects a reality wherein decision makers in social systems tend to sort issues between those requiring action and those on which action can be deferred (Nutt, 1979). Action on less important OINOs can probably be safely deferred. Here again, a sharp-image diagnosis can lead to the construction of a more coherent and fruitful diagnostic model than could other, more conventional diagnostic approaches.

Focusing on a small set of issues is particularly useful in the diagnosis of health care systems because of the tremendous complexity of these systems. This complexity shows up in a multiplicity of occupational specializations, in multiple and dynamic health care technologies, in organizational structures, and in standard operating procedures. By conducting a highly focused diagnosis, investigators can avoid being overwhelmed by the complexity of this macro system. This approach is summarized in the next diagnostic guideline:

4. *Direct further diagnostic efforts to the more important and pressing OINOs.*

Explaining Ineffective Outcomes

The next step in constructing the diagnostic model involves tracing the antecedents of OINOs. This step forms the core of the model because it is essential for planning effective interventions into the system. To plan appropriate interventions to improve OINOs, it is necessary to understand the conditions that gave rise to these ineffective outcomes. For each OINO, a diagnostic search must be undertaken for its causal antecedents. These are the factors that will have to be modified to improve this ineffective system outcome. For this purpose, the diagnostician should develop an overall framework relating each of the OINOs to other system components. A method for handling this diagnostic task is described below. It is based upon the notions of the open-systems approach as presented in Chapter 2. Therefore, only those modifications made necessary by applying the open-systems framework to macro systems will be discussed here.

The application of open-systems approaches to health care has a long history that is readily available elsewhere (Frenk, 1994). The systems approach has been used in many attempts to compare different countries' health care services (e.g., Rosenthal & Frenkel, 1992, pp. 323-339). It has been used extensively in the analyses of health care delivery processes (e.g., Moos & Schaefer, 1987; Siler-Wells, 1987). Applied to health care, it leads to the following propositions. A health care system may be described in terms of a set of components, elements or features within components, and relations among components and elements.[2] Components refer to the building blocks of a health care system, whereas relations among them include their exchanges with one another and the environment. Any health care system may be viewed as importing patients, physicians, other health professionals, money, and other inputs from the environment, and transforming these inputs through internal processes into outputs that are subsequently exported into the environment for new inputs.

Figure 14.1 presents the application of the systems approach to the Israeli health care system. This figure depicts features of the Israeli health system but does not provide a diagnostic model of the system. Instead, the figure serves as a stepping-stone to the identification of system components and features that produce OINOs. These system components are represented by the panels in Figure 14.1.[3] The figure also helps diagnosticians conceptualize the relations between system features and OINOs. These relations are represented (in Figure 14.1) by the closeness or remoteness of the panels from one another and by arrows showing influence paths, such as those radiating from the Ministry of Health toward several other system elements.

The next step in constructing a diagnostic model involves linking OINOs to antecedent conditions. To do this, each OINO should be connected by arrows to the specific aspects of the components of process, structure, inputs, and system environment that were shown to be related to it on the basis of systematic data gathering and analysis. Each OINO should thus be understood as a function of a set of interrelated, antecedent system components and elements.[4] This step is essentially an application of the open-systems approach to the health care system under discussion. The guideline that expresses this principle is the following:

5. *For each of the OINOs in the outcomes panel, provide a graphic representation*
of related features within other system components and elements (including other
OINOs).

Although Figure 14.1 is not a complete diagnostic model, it can illustrate
the above step. In preparing Figure 14.1, we tried to position the elements
making up the system's processes so as to reflect their causal relations.
Suppose infant mortality in the Arab sector of the country is considered an
OINO. The Ministry of Health and a few municipalities are responsible for
operating a network of "mother-and-child" clinics that provide preventive
health services to newborn children and prenatal care to their mothers.
Currently, this network is not linked effectively to community clinics operated
by the sickness funds. This condition is probably related to the high rate of
infant mortality in the country's Arab sector. Figure 14.1 depicts this lack of
continuity in service delivery by omitting arrows linking the Ministry of
Health to providers at the community level.

The fifth diagnostic guideline does not tell us how to organize those
components and their elements that are related to an OINO. In the next
diagnostic step, the logic of the systems approach is applied to arrange system
components and their elements in relation to each of the OINOs. OINOs are
shaped primarily by the health care system's processes and structure. These
system components serve as mediating factors between inputs and outputs.
The relations among components and their elements operate in a dynamic,
interactive pattern with feedback loops that, for simplicity, were omitted from
Figure 14.1. This logic may explain why proposed and implemented reforms
in health care delivery systems, in Israel and elsewhere, have often focused
on changing processes in order to mitigate OINOs. One example is the
incorporation of five government hospitals in Israel, begun in 1991, along
lines resembling Britain's hospital trusts.

The diagnostic strategy proposed is to construct, for each of the OINOs, a
flowchart relating it to features of the system's processes, structure, and
inputs, in that order. This strategy is summarized in the following guideline:

6. *Arrange system components, elements, and problem areas related to each OINO*
in a flowchart representing possible causal chains and allowing for dynamic and
multidirectional patterns of influence. Put system processes that lead to an OINO
closest to the OINO and then proceed to influential structural elements, inputs,
and, finally, environmental features.

Any particular OINO can be explained by competing theories. These theories depend on the complex context and environment of the health care sector of the country under consideration. Choice among competing explanations should be based on data gathering and analysis. At this juncture, diagnosticians can bring their knowledge of social science methods and inference processes to bear on diagnostic analysis.

In essence, the sixth guideline means that to explain any specific OINO, the set of explanatory elements should be arranged in a flowchart, preferably organized as separate subsystems. The procedure recommended here adapts the sharp-image approach to diagnosing macro systems and is parallel to Cameron's suggestion to proceed through a fault-tree analysis, which leads from description of the symptoms of ineffectiveness toward an analysis of their causes (Cameron, 1984).

The example of dental health further illustrates this crucial diagnostic step. In several surveys of the dental health of adolescents, it was found that their average number of cavities was the highest among OECD countries. Staff experts sought to develop a number of competing theories to explain this OINO. A series of in-depth interviews conducted with key informants in the dental health area pointed to three processual features that were related to dental health: deficient water fluoridation procedures, insufficient resources directed to dental health education, and lack of or poor quality of school-affiliated dental care clinics. These characteristics were linked in turn to the Ministry of Health, which exercised inadequate control over the dental services purchased for the schools by the municipalities. Other structural and input-related elements were also implicated. An important environmental condition was the failure of the Ministry of Education to develop a national health education curriculum. As this example may illustrate, the development of competing explanations for an OINO can become quite complex and specific. Once these explanations have been developed, conventional forms of data analysis and inference allow diagnosticians to choose among them.

Once the conditions producing OINOs are understood, analysts can create flowcharts for each OINO. These separate flowcharts need to be integrated, that is, compiled into a single, comprehensive flowchart. The integrative flowchart, or the diagnostic model, is a synthesized representation of the series of separate flowcharts. One way of integrating the separate flowcharts is by putting them side by side, without changing any of them substantively. When the flowcharts, one for each OINO, are juxtaposed, this often reveals major causal factors responsible for several OINOs. This leads to the final guideline offered to diagnosticians:

7. *Integrate and emphasize in the model common antecedents of several OINOs.*

This guideline, which shows how to complete the construction of the diagnostic model, may be illustrated by the diagnosis of the role of the Ministry of Health in the Israeli health care system. Metaphorically, the Ministry might be considered the system's brain because it is supposed to regulate, control, and give direction to the other components. In reality, the Ministry of Health is preoccupied with running hospitals that are owned and controlled by the government and does not effectively carry out most of its ministerial functions. Health planning, control, and evaluation by the Ministry of Health are very weak because the Ministry lacks essential managerial data (such as information on the demand for health services, supply of health professionals, and diffusion of medical technology). This situation is shown in Figure 14.1 by an absence of arrows originating from the Ministry's functions of policy making, planning, control, and evaluation.

To be more specific, Israel's inequitable distribution of acute-care hospital beds and the relative scarcity of long-term geriatric hospital beds are both related to the weakness of the Ministry's planning, budgeting, and control functions. This is why several governmental committees that examined the country's health care system cited transformation of the Ministry of Health as a necessary condition for reform of the system as a whole (Shuval, 1991).

Table 14.1 summarizes the steps in the proposed diagnosis of macro systems. Each step corresponds to one of the guidelines set out above.

Conclusion

The diagnostic procedures described in Table 14.1 provide conceptual tools to be used by professionals and consultants concerned with reforming a macrolevel system, such as a country's educational or welfare system. These diagnostic procedures were illustrated by the diagnosis of a specific health care system. Each step in the construction of a diagnostic model of a health care system was accompanied by a conceptual guideline and by examples of its use in diagnosing the Israeli health care system.

Health care systems are particularly appropriate for diagnostic study be-cause they have been and will probably continue to be targets for organiza-

Table 14.1 Steps in the Diagnosis of a Health Care System

Step	Guideline
1. Focus on preferred system outcomes.	Using the WHO-proposed health targets and/or your nation's health plan, identify the outcomes to be achieved by your health care system.
2. Identify OINOs.	Identify ineffective outcomes in need of overhaul (OINOs) by applying a predetermined standard of comparison.
3. Compare OINOs with effective outcomes.	Compare OINOs with effective outcomes to provide an indication of the general type of reform needed.
4. Focus on important OINOs.	Direct further diagnostic efforts at the more important and pressing OINOs.
5. Examine and depict relations between OINOs and system features.	Use the systems approach to delineate the major components, and elements thereof, that are related to OINOs.
6. Explain each OINO.	Explain each OINO and create a flow chart showing (from right to left) the effects of processual elements (problem areas), then of structural elements, and finally of system inputs.
7. Model common causes of OINOs.	Create a model that integrates and emphasizes the common antecedents of important OINOs.

tional and systemwide reforms. The diagnostic model of a health system was presented in several steps. First, the concepts of macro-system effectiveness and of ineffective system outcomes (OINOs) were defined. Subsequently, we described the steps that form the core of the model, including the identification of the system components and elements that lead to each of the OINOs.

In developing the diagnostic model and guidelines, we have taken into consideration constraints that are likely to impinge on any macro-system diagnosis. These constraints include limited resources allocated to the diagnostic project. There may also be limitations on the information that can be searched, distilled, and appraised by the diagnostician. For instance, no survey has ever been conducted in Israel on several important determinants of the demand for health services, including health-related behavior such as smoking, and the population's functional or perceived health status.

The following discussion considers some of the advantages and limitations of the procedures recommended here for diagnosing macro systems. The diagnostic model developed here can be generalized, with appropriate modifications, to other macro systems in the public sector, such as the social welfare system. Due to space limitations, this avenue for developing the core ideas of the model was not followed, and the discussion focused on health care systems.

To begin with the advantages, models like the one constructed here can be used profitably by staff experts, consultants, and other professionals involved in the reform of health care systems. These professionals may serve on public committees, commissions of inquiry, or any other politically neutral body assigned the task of developing a blueprint for reforming a health care system. The model should yield useful recommendations because it cuts through to the causes of critical system problems rather than producing very complex but hard-to-apply findings. The focus on OINOs incorporates a valid and tried lesson of past health reforms: Do not change aspects of the health care system that function more or less adequately (Ham et al., 1990). Focusing on OINOs may have other side benefits, including motivating proactive thinking (Cowan, 1986) and facilitating communication and consensus building among those involved in health reforms.

Another advantage of the proposed model is that it takes account of the needs of policy makers, including senior administrators in public agencies, to obtain clear explanations for critical problems. These officials are engaged in a never-ending struggle to contain costs, regulate biotechnological innovations, meet consumers' rising expectations, and cater to the needs of an aging population. In Israel, they are also occupied with daily emergencies involving the operation of government-run hospitals. For all of these reasons, health care officials and politicians are prone to put the cart of intervention before the horse of diagnosis, thus easily losing view of the target to be reformed. Recent research in problem identification by policymakers provides evidence of this tendency. It shows that type three errors—in which policy makers solve the wrong problem—are perhaps the most important and most overlooked errors in decision making (Shrivastava & Mitroff, 1984). A salient feature of the model developed in this chapter is that it builds in protection against type three error. By identifying important, policy-relevant OINOs and linking these to clear causes, the model discourages policymakers from trying to solve the wrong problems. Furthermore, by emphasizing that solutions must attack the causes of problems, this type of diagnosis discourages policymakers from framing problems in unconstructive ways and from applying inappropriate solutions to problems.

The diagnostic model was constructed in a way that takes into account roles that staff experts, particularly organizational scientists, play in planning systemwide reforms. These professionals integrate their specialized knowledge of the organizational sciences into the diagnosis and intervention processes (Tichy, 1983). They apply the methods and inferential techniques of the social sciences to enhance the rationality of decision-making processes and then make relevant data available to policymakers. They advise elected officials who control planned reforms. They can help policymakers in the politically charged field of policy formation by providing a basis for common understandings among diverse groups of stakeholders (Wildavsky, 1979a).

Despite these strengths, the diagnostic model developed here contains several limitations and deficiencies. One is that it needs to be further refined and expanded. Interrelationships among the OINOs need to be considered and depicted in flowcharts. More detail is needed on system features that contribute to OINOs. For example, in the Israeli case, problems within the structure and functioning of the four sickness funds should be added to the model because these features contribute to the OINO of consumer dissatisfaction.

The diagnostic model presented here did not explicitly incorporate political elements, such as those described in Chapter 5. Admittedly, this is a major limitation. In Western democracies, reforms involving systemwide changes in the public sector are invariably decided upon, announced, and carried out by elected public officials. Therefore, the design of reforms becomes part of the public policy-making process. The goals and means of reform are influenced by many interests, ideologies, and political alignments. Future developments and applications of the model will need to make explicit the values and interests reflected in problem definitions and other phases of diagnosis. For example, defining consumer satisfaction as an important health outcome involves an implicit value stance with which some participants in the health system might take issue. If the terms of public debate permit, diagnosticians might try to make their own value positions clear to allow for honest debate among users of the diagnostic model. In addition, where appropriate, the diagnostic model can be extended to examine the values and political forces that come into play once proposals for reform are made explicit or are implemented (see Chapter 5).

The model presented in this chapter lacks any accompanying blueprint for implementation. In practice, the whole diagnostic process would gain in effectiveness if it followed the tradition of action research (Boss, 1989;

Chisholm & Elden, 1993). In this case, each of the diagnostic steps would involve interaction and collaboration between diagnostic investigators and health policy makers. This type of collaboration would add credibility and relevance to the diagnostic findings and would help diagnostic practitioners avoid assuming the mindset of dissociated experts (Cowan, 1990).[5]

Admittedly, every health care reform is politically shaped. Ultimately, the interplay of political stakeholders determines which reforms are implemented. This chapter proposed that a systematic diagnosis become one of the factors in decision making about reform. Constructing a diagnostic model like the one provided here can provide staff experts and consultants with an appropriate entry point into the policy-making process. Furthermore, the sharp-image approach developed here would seem to possess substantial analytical and practical advantages over popular models for policy analysis that concentrate on the consumption and allocation of health resources.

This chapter brings to a close the third part of this book, which explored the diagnosis of macro-organizational functions and conditions and the diagnosis of macro systems. These topics have not generally enjoyed the attention they deserve in other treatments of diagnosis, assessment, and planned change. Chapter 15 synthesizes some of the main themes that emerged in all three parts of the book and proposes ways to combine multiple theoretical frames within diagnosis.

Notes

1. For further details, see the discussion of stakeholder analysis and search conferences in Chapter 5.

2. Note that in this chapter, in contrast to others, the term *system element* is reserved for features contained within a system component, such as the various providers of health care who are jointly responsible for creating system throughputs.

3. To avoid additional complexity, the health system's technological component is treated here as an input. System behavior and culture are subsumed within the Processes component.

4. To keep the model simple, we excluded possible causal paths and feedback loops among OINOs.

5. See Chapter 4 for a discussion of contingencies affecting the use of collaborative approaches and practical difficulties of applying collaborative techniques such as action research.

PART IV BRIDGING THEORY AND PRACTICE

15 Applying Multiple Theoretical Frames

One of the reasons that so many problems are intractable is that they are formulated in such a way as to defeat any solution.

(Beer, 1985, p. xiii)

This book has examined ways to frame and model organizational problems and challenges so as to help decision makers discover workable solutions, rather than defeating solutions in advance. The diagnostic models and procedures developed in this book can uncover the roots of ineffectiveness and the nature of critical organizational challenges. Moreover, these diagnostic approaches can help consultants and their clients decide on feasible steps toward solving problems and enhancing organizational performance.

Systematic diagnosis thus offers an alternative to overreliance on uncreative and self-defeating ways of defining problems—such as blaming them on personality conflicts, intransigent unions, or unclear rules and regulations. Diagnosis can also help managers and other decision makers, including governmental policymakers, avoid the hazards of "acting first and evaluating

405

later"—implementing fashionable management techniques or even launching full-scale reorganizations without first diagnosing their organization's challenges, needs, and capacities for change. Furthermore, by fostering a reflective and inquiry-oriented approach to managing change, the diagnostic approach developed in this book can help both consultants and decision makers cope with the surprises and paradoxes of planned change and even learn from the implementation process.[1]

This concluding chapter extends the treatment of diagnostic frames and models into new territory. Here, we explicitly treat possibilities for applying multiple theories, models, and analytical techniques during diagnosis and assessment. Use of multiple theoretical frames can enrich the ways in which consultants and clients understand organizations and planned change. Multiple framing can thereby enhance the ability of diagnostic practitioners and decision makers to discover workable solutions to problems. Moreover, this approach can help decision makers learn to cope with future challenges.

By incorporating multiple frames into their work, consultants and applied researchers can take advantage of important new developments within organizational and management studies. These adaptations to recent theoretical trends can make diagnosis more responsive to rapidly changing organizational conditions and contribute to both client and consultant learning.

Although it can enrich diagnosis, the use of divergent theoretical frames also exposes consultants and applied researchers to new conceptual and methodological difficulties. In particular, theoretical perspectives such as postmodernism and social constructionism challenge widely held assumptions about social research and consultation. Social constructionism looks at organizational "realities," like all other social activities, through an interpretive frame and defines these realities as products of socially created meanings (Berger & Luckmann, 1967). Sometimes, these meanings become so taken for granted that they seem objectively real, but all knowledge, including that of social researchers and consultants, is socially constructed. Postmodernism goes even further in its critique of conventional views of science and knowledge (Alvesson & Deetz, 1996). This set of diverse views shows how linguistic and conceptual distinctions contribute to social construction. Postmodernists attack experts, such as researchers and consultants, for aiding powerful actors in imposing their own self-serving constructions of reality on others. Postmodernists celebrate the myriad possible ways of thinking and feeling that become possible once traditional sources of knowledge and expertise have been stripped of their authority.

This chapter explores the use of multiple frames under four headings. First, we examine potential benefits of using multiple frames in diagnosis. Second, we consider the implications for diagnosis of the emergence of competing and possibly incommensurable theoretical perspectives within the fields of management and organization studies. This section considers challenges that the newer theoretical approaches pose to conventional philosophical and methodological premises about research and consultation. Third, we explore criteria for choosing appropriate theoretical approaches for use in diagnosis. Several approaches stand out for their broad applicability, analytical power, and ability to contribute to constructive change. These are open-systems diagnoses of fits, gaps, and interdependencies; political assessments of stakeholder interests, power, and reactions to proposed changes; and interpretive analyses of cultural differentiation. Fourth, we examine procedures for combining multiple frames during the main phases of diagnosis.

Before turning to these tasks, we will briefly survey how we applied divergent frames and models in preceding chapters. Throughout this book, we recommended drawing on more than one theoretical perspective to construct diagnostic models. The preceding chapters took a mid-range approach to the possibilities and challenges of applying diverse theoretical perspectives in diagnosis. These chapters examined a set of separate theoretical starting points for diagnosis and provided guidelines as to when each theoretical approach might prove useful.

Many of the chapters explained how to conduct sharp-image diagnoses, in which consultants develop diagnostic models directly in response to the focal organization's critical problems, challenges, and capacities—rather than simply choosing a diagnostic model from the available literature. Chapters 2 and 4 presented the open-systems frame as the most useful frame for developing a broad overview of organizational needs, problems, and capacities. These and subsequent chapters further developed diagnostic principles and procedures and presented specific models that sharpen the focus of the open-systems frame and can add diagnostic power to it (e.g., Chapters 6, 12, and 13). Chapter 14 showed how the open-systems frame and the sharp-image approach to diagnosis can be applied to macro systems comprised of entire societal sectors or networks of organizations. Chapter 11 added a developmental perspective to the open-systems frame in order to deal with diagnosis across the organizational life cycle. Chapter 13 explored links between the open-systems frame and theories of competitive strategy. Special attention was given to techniques such as SWOT analysis, which assesses internal and organization-environment fits in terms of the concept of competitive advantage. Chapters 9 and 10 showed how the interpretive and negotiation frames add depth to diagnosing emergent behavior and organizational culture.

Several chapters suggested ways to combine models and frames in the analysis of a single problem or focal issue. Chapters 3 and 8 pointed to the benefits of combining three distinctive theoretical views on effectiveness: a structural view that focuses on goal attainment; a systems view that examines internal processes, environmental adaptation, and resource acquisition; and a political view that emphasizes the need to satisfy multiple stakeholders. Chapter 7 showed how interpretive and political analyses can help account for design patterns that seem paradoxical when viewed from a purely structural and instrumental frame.

Additional uses of multiple framing occurred in the treatment of programs of strategic change. In Chapters 7 and 13, we suggested surfacing options for change with the help of techniques grounded in the open-systems and structural frames. Then, stakeholder analysis or force field analysis (Chapter 5), both of which draw on a political view of organizations, can be used to guide the assessment of the feasibility of change options and the planning of change. Chapter 12, which developed a model for diagnosing management-union relations, provided yet another illustration of combining the open-systems and political frames. In Chapter 13 we saw that structural and open-systems ideas can guide initial formulations of deliberate strategy, but that emergent processes, which are best viewed through a negotiations frame, are critical to strategy implementation and the formation of crafted strategies. The interpretive frame also helped us analyze the crafting of strategy. By articulating a strategic vision, change strategists shape the ways that actors in and outside the organization define its organizational challenges, opportunities, and capacities.

Chapter 9 provided an even more explicit example of the benefits and complexities of multiple framing. There, we showed that organizational culture can be usefully diagnosed using four divergent theoretical approaches. The cultural ambiguity and cultural differentiation perspectives elaborate variations on the interpretive frame, whereas the institutional and cultural integration perspectives draw on both the interpretive and system frames.

Advantages of Multiframe Diagnosis

There are several major benefits to using multiple frames in diagnosis. First, each theoretical frame and each variant on a frame provides consultants and members of the client organization with a distinctive theoretical guide to viewing organizational problems and searching for possible solutions. Frames work like cognitive maps or scripts (Huff & Schwenk, 1990): They sensitize users to certain phenomena and relations while playing down the importance of other phenomena.

One of the mechanisms that lies behind this sensitizing process is the use of metaphors and other figures of speech (Palmer & Dunford, 1996; Schon & Rein, 1994). These suggest that the organization is like the object or process to which it is compared. For example, metaphors that describe organizational change in terms of engineering imply that change agents can anticipate and control the change process, whereas metaphors drawn from the realm of gardening (e.g., planting, nurturing, pruning, gathering) encourage thinking about change as a less predictable, more participative, and more exploratory process (Sackmann, 1989).

Adding frames thus reveals features of the organization that would otherwise be hidden. Consider, for example, the assessment of the power of actors and stakeholders in and around a focal organization. Chapters 3 and 5 viewed power through a political frame, that is, embedded within a broad structural-functional paradigm (Burrell & Morgan, 1979; see Chapter 1). From this standpoint, power derives from formal authority, network location, and control over critical resources and organizational contingencies. By adding an interpretive frame, consultants can discover aspects of power that would not be evident if power were examined only structurally. For instance, the interpretive frame helps consultants see how clients construct reality in ways that enhance their power (Bradshaw-Camball, 1989). The negotiations frame adds yet a third view of power. According to this view, a manager's power depends on the willingness of subordinates to act in ways that confirm and reinforce the manager's power. If subordinates fail to play by the manager's rules of the game—for example, by withholding vital information from their boss or by not bothering to make their boss look good—they may gradually undermine the manager's ability to exercise power over them and others. Developments such as these sometimes lie behind the ability of subordinates to resist the implementation of unpopular changes.

Second, using multiple frames can help consultants and clients become aware of their own taken-for-granted perspectives (Armenakis & Bedeian, 1992) and move beyond them. Many managers and some enterprising consultants seem to rely on an implicit theory containing two rather strong and hard-to-substantiate assumptions (Abrahamson & Fairchild, 1997). The first is that introducing a popular management technique—usually known by a catchy acronym such as TQM, QCs, or BPR—will solve nearly all current problems and radically boost performance.[2] The second assumption is that techniques that (presumably) succeeded in some other well-known organization will produce similar results in the manager's own organization. Diagnosis using approaches such as fit assessment, stakeholder analysis, and examination of organizational culture can quickly reveal the risks in making decisions based on so naive a theory of organizational effectiveness and change.

Even when consultants and organizational members apply more sophisticated frames to problems and new situations, these frames reflect their training and their past experience, as well as being influenced by empirical conditions and constraints. Consultants, like organizational members, often become committed to specific frames and to diagnostic and intervention techniques that reflect a single theory-in-use (Argyris & Schon, 1996). As a result, consultants sometimes view both organizations and the consulting process very narrowly and inflexibly.

Overreliance on a single frame can sometimes lead to stereotypical thinking, poor decisions, and actions that bring unintended consequences (Bolman & Deal, 1991; Schon, 1993). This risk is particularly great when decision makers use self-reinforcing frames that help them save face and justify their own actions, thereby blocking honest inquiry by themselves or others and making it hard to learn from experience (Argyris & Schon, 1996). These self-reinforcing frames can give rise to self-defeating formulations of problems, such as those described in the chapter's opening quotation.

One frame that is commonly overused in this way treats organizations as political jungles and blames problems on people's thirst for power and their unwillingness to compromise. This interpretation militates against honest confrontations and explorations of interpersonal differences that reflect people's distinctive experiences, functional specializations, and values. The jungle view leads managers to despair of finding ways that members of an organization can work together despite their differences. Instead, users of this frame try to solve problems through coercion or managerial fiat. As a result, they face intractable cycles of conflict or chronic states of alienation and dissent.

Bureaucratic models and metaphors are also frequently used unselectively and uncritically to frame important problems and issues. Managers and policymakers who rely exclusively on this structural model define the process of organizing in terms of the development of clear rules and procedures for coordinating work, defining responsibilities in an organizational hierarchy, and ensuring accountability. Other means of mobilizing people for effective joint action are ignored.

Framing problems in a particular way often implies solutions that seem natural or self-evident (Bolman & Deal, 1991; Schon, 1993). When viewed through a bureaucratic frame, problems are readily defined as resulting from too much fragmentation or too much red tape and rigidity. In either case, the solution lies in improving and rationalizing rules and policies. Another popular theory regards organizational performance as directly dependent on individual traits and behavior, such as leadership and motivation. This frame leads users to blame organizational problems on people's incompetence or on their bad attitudes and personalities. Better training and personnel selection then are seen as virtually self-evident and universal solutions to organizational problems.

Consultants and clients alike become aware of the frames they use and of the frames' limitations when they participate actively in a diagnosis that uses several frames, or when they receive feedback based on multiple frames. By analyzing the same set of events from several viewpoints, the participants discover which views come naturally to them and which seem surprising and alien. For instance, many consultants and managers unconsciously adopt structural frames that treat organizations and even systems of organizations as goal-directed tools. As they talk about designing procedures and structures to promote attainment of "the organization's goal," these analysts assume that members of an organization can be led to direct their behavior toward a limited number of agreed-upon and clearly defined goals. The limitations of these integrative and instrumental assumptions become evident when this view is contrasted with "bottom-up" views provided by multiple-stakeholder analysis, examinations of emergent behavior, or analyses of sources of cultural differentiation.

A third potential benefit of multiple framing is that reframing can help expand problem definitions and can point to a broader range of factors affecting ineffective outcomes and capacity to meet challenges. By expanding definitions and explanations of problems, analysts can sometimes overcome the limitations of familiar frames and discover new action possibilities (Barrett & Cooperrider, 1990; Schon, 1993). Consider, for instance, a diagnosis of problems of turnover and low productivity among mostly female clerical workers in a public agency. Analyses of group processes and individual behavior within the open-systems frame often assume that turnover reflects low morale (Chapter 6). Morale, in turn, is explained with reference to rewards, supervisory behavior, and group climate. A consultant schooled in this approach recommends steps to improve these sources of morale. Follow-up shows that employee attitudes have improved, but turnover remains unchanged. Adding a feminist perspective to the diagnosis might provide an alternative explanation and point to more workable routes to improvement. The feminist view directs attention to gendering practices that construct a "glass ceiling" that blocks the movement of women into management (Chapter 9). From this viewpoint, high turnover among clerical workers may reflect their limited opportunities for mobility within the firm. This analysis could lead the consultant to recommend dealing with turnover and morale problems by opening up opportunities for female clerical workers to gain access to entry-level managerial positions.

Fourth, using multiple paradigms and perspectives can foster more "complicated understanding" among clients (Bartunek, Gordon, & Weathersby, 1983) and more context-sensitive forms of problem solving. If clients and other organizational members learn to apply these forms of thinking to future problems and programs for change, organizational learning will be enhanced. When more than one frame is applied simultaneously to a situation, people become aware that each frame—including ones that they had relied upon previously—provides only partial accounts of organizational life, rather than revealing "the whole truth" about the organization. Reframing events and contrasting the views obtained by alternative frames thereby encourage critical inquiry into the concepts, assumptions, and implications for action that are embedded within each frame (Bolman & Deal, 1991; Chia, 1996; Martin & Frost, 1996; Morgan, 1986, 1996; Schon, 1993).

Theoretical Diversity and Diagnosis

Depending on one's point of view, organizational and management studies during the past two decades have been distinguished by their extraordinary diversity and creativity (Burrell, 1996)—or by their lamentable fragmentation and lack of consensus (Pfeffer, 1993; for literature reviews, see Clegg, Hardy, & Nord, 1996; Reed, 1992). The political and interpretive frames posed the initial challenge to the dominance of structural-functionalism in American organizational research. Further challenges came from feminist approaches and from (initially) European streams of thought, such as radical humanism and radical structuralism (Burrell & Morgan, 1979; Calas & Smircich, 1996). In recent years, some of the most powerful challenges to prevailing organizational paradigms derive from postmodernism and deconstruction (Alvesson & Deetz, 1996; Cooper, 1989). There have also been calls to bring race, class, and ethnicity into sharper focus, much as feminist work has illuminated the gendering of organizations (Ferguson, 1994).

Responding to Diversity

The new paradigms and perspectives that emerged during the 1980s called into question many of the basic methods and approaches of structural-functionalism. These developments shook the faith of many scholars in the ability of structural-functionalism and positivism to provide the foundation for an empirical science of management and administration.

Organizational and management scholars have debated vigorously the implications of the emergence of so many competing paradigms and perspectives. These debates concern the desirability of theoretical divergence, the commensurability of competing paradigms (e.g., Schultz & Hatch, 1996; Weaver & Gioia, 1994; Willmott, 1993a, 1993b), and the feasibility of simultaneously applying multiple paradigms and theories (e.g., Gioia & Pitre, 1990; Hassard, 1991; Martin & Frost, 1996; Parker & McHugh, 1991).

Unfortunately, many organizational consultants and applied researchers remained on the sidelines of these debates and continued uncritically to use the dominant functionalist paradigm and to adopt its strong positivist assumptions.[3] We believe that practitioners of diagnosis, organizational assessment, and applied research cannot reasonably remain aloof from the debates occurring within organization studies. New theoretical perspectives are particularly relevant to diagnosis because the framing of organizational conditions is central to diagnosis and because diagnostic practitioners derive their frames and methods directly from social and behavioral science knowledge about organizations, management, and change.

Four responses have been proposed to the growing theoretical diversity within organizational studies. Only one, which favors *combining* frames, provides much promise for diagnosis. Before considering this option, let us consider the other, less promising alternatives in turn.[4] *Conservatism* aims at retaining and even enhancing positivist methods (Donaldson, 1985), and at developing a flexible yet coherent and consensual version of the structural-functional approach (Pfeffer, 1993; for critiques, see Canella & Paetzold, 1994; Perrow, 1994). The conservative response essentially calls on researchers and consultants to forget much of what they learned about organizations once the fortress of Parsonian structural-functionalism began to crumble beneath the onslaught of competing perspectives. Practitioners of diagnosis who adopt this stance would be able to apply only a very narrow range of frames to the problems they encounter.

In contrast, *radicalism* accepts and even endorses the multiplication and fragmentation of theoretical approaches and the incommensurability of competing paradigms. This response, which draws inspiration from the postmodernist critique of positivism, celebrates the loss of the certainties that characterized organization studies in the 1960s and 1970s and announces with approval that "science seems to have run out of steam" (Burrell, 1996, p. 657). From this vantage point, the myriad analytical frames and theories that now compete within organizational theory provide investigators with multiple lenses for viewing organizational life, each of which brings different features into focus. To put it another way, the multiplication of theoretical frames and concepts grants managers and consultants with opportunities to play many language games through which they interpret and justify their activities (Astley & Zammuto, 1992). By shifting rapidly between frames, investigators can learn to avoid assigning objective status to their own social constructions (Chia, 1996, p. 142).

The radical response to diversity provides an appealing counterpoint to the dogmatic forms of positivism that formerly captured large portions of social science. However, taken to the extreme, the radical approach to diversity can lead to theoretical and methodological anarchy and can totally undermine the legitimacy of consultation and applied research. The acknowledgment that all accounts, images, frames, and conceptual distinctions are social constructions is sometimes taken to mean that none offers "privileged" definitions of reality and that all theories and conceptualizations provide equally good—or bad— starting points for inquiry (Chia, 1995). Newton (1996) clearly demonstrates some of the consequences of this view in his postmodernist critique of feminist theory:

> There is no easy reconciliation between postmodernism and action, whether the action is aimed at changing society or merely one organization. . . . Action inevitably implies choice, and . . . some basis must be found for that choice. The problem is in determining that basis, since this implies the end of endless self-reflexivity and a move towards the postmodernly [*sic*] abhorrent notion of closure. All this reinforces the question of whether there can ever be a postmodern feminist or any kind of postmodern reconstructionist. (p. 15)

Taking postmodernism to its logical extreme can leave consultants and clients without guidelines for choosing theories, combining or contrasting the accounts flowing from different frames, and knowing when their analysis has produced valid results. Furthermore, if all theories and concepts provide potentially valid ways of looking at and talking about organizations (as Astley & Zammuto, 1992, seem to suggest), then the applied practitioner and change agent run the risk of becoming nothing more than storytellers or witch doctors. At its most extreme, the radical approach to diversity thus undermines the capacity for reasoned social action (Parker, 1995).

Another response to theoretical diversity involves a quest for *integration* of existing frames and paradigms into one synthetic and comprehensive approach (e.g., Lee, 1991; Torbert, 1995). After examining the basic assumptions, methods, and concepts within currently competing theories, advocates of this approach seek to create a common framework on which to construct an overarching theory that incorporates elements of currently competing ones. Giddens (1984) is perhaps the strongest exponent of integrating interpretive and structural-functional paradigms. Many others have proposed midrange integrations of theories reflecting more than one theoretical perspective (e.g., Barley, 1986; Gamson, 1968; Harrison & Phillips, 1991; Pettigrew, 1985; Slappendel, 1996).

To date, neither the conservative nor the integrationist responses to theoretical diversity have made much progress toward generating highly coherent and cumulative bodies of theory and research. What is more, little progress toward these ends seems likely. Students of organizations are deeply divided in their political goals and values, philosophical views, methodological assumptions and techniques, intellectual traditions, cultural orientations (Hofstede, 1996), network ties (Reed, 1992), and personal agendas. Hence, it seems unlikely that anyone can define a new or renewed integrative paradigm capable of bringing consensus, clarity, and substantial conformity to the entire field of organizational studies.

In light of the limitations of the conservative, radical, and integrationist agendas, we advocate a fourth response to theoretical diversity: *combining frames*. This approach provides a way for diagnosis to benefit from frame divergence without succumbing to the pitfalls of radical responses to diversity and without attempting to force very disparate frames into a single integrative system. Perhaps the most influential advocate of this approach is Morgan (1986), whose book *Images of Organizations* elegantly presents possibilities for interpreting organizational life through the lenses of multiple theoretical metaphors. We and other advocates of frame combination concur with Morgan that it is possible "to develop and model a postmodern approach to organization and management that thrives on continuous construction, deconstruction, and reconstruction without adopting the intellectual trappings of the professional postmodernist" (Morgan, 1996, p. 236).

To combine frames, investigators both note conflicts between frames and explore possibilities for using frames in complementary ways. This approach is similar, but not identical, to the interplay strategy proposed by Schultz and Hatch (1996), who examine theoretical contrasts and connections between frames. In our view, contrasts between frames can often yield complementary understandings during diagnosis and during other forms of research. Conflicts between frames, on the other hand, often reflect wide gaps in fundamental premises, assumptions, norms, and values. The last two sections of this chapter examine in detail complementary and conflicting relations between frames and procedures for combining them.

Challenges in Using Multiple Frames

Serious theoretical and practical challenges confront consultants who would depart from exclusive reliance on structural functionalism with its strong, postivist assumptions. Despite their potential contributions to diagnosis, some of the newer theoretical approaches threaten to undermine fundamental assumptions shared by many consultants. Interpretive, deconstructionist, and postmodernist approaches all call into question the ability of both researchers and consultants to ascertain objective truths about organizations through the use of positivistic methods. In its most radical form, the postmodern position views science as mere rhetoric (Alvesson, 1995) and questions whether social science research provides a better way of understanding and changing organizations than each individual's subjective perceptions and conceptions.[5]

In contrast, to claim honestly that they can help clients solve problems and enhance organizational effectiveness, consultants and applied researchers must adopt at least a "soft" realist position, even as they incorporate social constructionist views and reject many of the bolder claims of traditional positivist social science. This compromise position works on the following premises: All conceptions of reality—including those produced by social and behavioral scientists—are socially constructed. However, people can use constructed concepts to learn about external reality and to reach provisional agreements about reality, even if they can never ascertain the total or absolute truth about the things they are studying. These agreements provide the basis for reasoned action. The social and behavioral sciences cannot establish the goals or values that guide choice and action. Nor can organizational scholarship provide much inspiration for those creative and innovative decisions that can affect organizational strategy decisively. However, the social and organizational sciences can help consultants and managers develop more systematic understandings of organizational behavior and dynamics than they would have gained without the aid of these fields. Furthermore, these understandings will usually provide a more consistent basis for reasoned action and planned change than will other valuable sources of understanding, such as personal experience, common sense, the fine arts, or journalism. Unless applied researchers and consultants are prepared to adopt this methodological and philosophical stance and to work hard to demonstrate its benefits, their clients may legitimately question the wisdom of purchasing their services. Moreover, consultants and applied researchers who do not see any particular advantage in their approach to problem solving should be legitimately concerned that their applied activities may do more harm than good.

The interpretive, radical humanist, and radical political paradigms marshall yet another challenge for consultation and applied research. These frames cast doubt on the ability of consultants to adopt a politically neutral stance during diagnosis and planned change. These frames show that consultants often contribute to client power by helping clients impose their own definitions of reality on other members of the organization. From this viewpoint, when consultants define problems in ways that fit client needs and support clients' assumptions, the consultants implicitly take sides in subtle negotiations about the meanings of events and about current organizational conditions. Moreover, consultants contribute to their clients' power by providing relevant and valid feedback on organizational operations and environmental conditions.

In responding to criticisms like these, behavioral science consultants have explored the political implications of consultation (e.g., Cobb & Margulies, 1981; Greiner & Schein, 1988). Moreover, theoreticians and practitioners of organization development (e.g., Huse & Cummings, 1985, p. 461) have acknowledged that diagnosis and change often benefit clients and other powerful members of an organization more than weaker stakeholders (see Chapter 5). In consequence, most diagnostic consultations sustain ongoing power relations rather than pose major challenges to them.

Despite the well-taken criticisms of social constructionism and postmodernism, consultants need not conclude that diagnosis merely performs political and symbolic functions. Instead, practitioners of diagnosis can continue to aspire to uncover useful findings about client organizations without claiming to reveal politically neutral or ontologically absolute truths about them.[6] Clearly, consultants and applied researchers who take social constructionist and postmodern ideas seriously will have to adopt a reflexive and nondogmatic view of their own theoretical assumptions and will need to remain alert to the implications of their choices and applications of diagnostic frames (Palmer & Dunford, 1996).

Choosing Frames

Consultants who want to apply multiple perspectives face difficult choices among the wide range of available options. In principle, many frames can provide useful guides to diagnosis. But in practice, combining too many analytical frames at once can create an overly fragmented approach, which places a heavy cognitive and practical burden on most analysts. Consultants and advanced students with whom we have worked have difficulty applying more than four or five frames to the same problem. Clients accustomed to looking at their organization from just one or two viewpoints are not likely to feel comfortable using more than two or three frames at once. An additional difficulty is that many theoretical perspectives are very abstract and hard to apply.

Hence, we suggest choosing just a few frames. On what grounds, other than past experience and familiarity with a particular approach, can diagnostic investigators choose their frames? One possibility is to judge each analytically appropriate frame in terms of its ability to contribute to an effective diagnosis. As suggested in Chapter 1, the effectiveness of a diagnosis can be evaluated in terms of the goals set for it or in terms of its contributions. Potential contributions include empowering clients to reduce ineffectiveness and face challenges, fostering organizational adaptation, and enhancing client and organizational learning (Chapters 7 and 13). For the most part, diagnosis can aim most appropriately at middle-range goals, such as eliminating critical ineffective outcomes or helping an organization or focal unit meet specific challenges. These challenges might include threats or opportunities caused by sudden changes in governmental policies, technological change, changing customer expectations, or the appearance of new competitors. Less frequently, diagnosis and assessment can support managerial attempts to produce major strategic change or organizatlonal transformations (Chapters 7, 11, and 13). In keeping with the emphasis throughout the book, the discussion that follows concentrates on midrange goals for diagnosis. At its conclusion, we consider the contribution of diagnostic framing to organizational learning.

Effective diagnosis requires simultaneous attention to three distinctive facets of diagnosis: analysis, methods, and interactions between clients and consultants and among members of the focal organization (Harrison, 1994; see also Chapter 1). To help diagnostic practitioners consider the potential contribution of theoretical frames, we will note the requirements for handling each of these three facets of diagnosis separately. Then, we will examine the ability of alternative frames to meet these requirements. No diagnostic frame will meet all of the requirements, just as no diagnosis will optimize all aspects of diagnostic effectiveness. It is also likely that a particular frame may prove more useful in one phase of diagnosis, such as problem formulation, than during some other phase, such as feedback.

First, consider criteria for effectively handling the analytical tasks of diagnosis: No matter what the goals of a diagnosis, it will prove effective only if it provides clients with useful and valid feedback on organizational problems and challenges. This feedback will call attention to features of the organization that produce ineffective outcomes or that can enhance effectiveness. Moreover, feedback will help decision makers identify workable routes to improvement, or it will contain explicit recommendations about feasible action options. Diagnosis is also more likely to help clients when feedback motivates recipients to take appropriate actions.

Many, but not all, frames successfully direct attention to crucial organizational features that produce ineffectiveness or shape effectiveness. Consider, for example, the ability of frames to illuminate the sources of intergroup tension within interdisciplinary management teams in a high-tech firm in the United States. The cultural differentiation approach can help analysts understand the sources and nature of subgroup differences within a highly educated workforce (e.g., Kunda, 1992). In contrast, a radical structural frame (Burrell & Morgan, 1979) might lead investigators to seek links between intergroup tension and manifestations of class conflict within the focal organizations. Yet in the United States, the dynamics of class are not felt strongly inside firms that mainly employ college graduates. Hence, in this instance the application of a radical structuralist frame could be ruled out on empirical grounds.

Ability to separate symptoms from underlying causes or configurations is a cardinal feature of good diagnosis, which sets it apart from commonsense approaches to organizational problems. The open-systems frame is justly popular for its ability to help users untangle linkages that lie beneath pressing problems (e.g., Senge, 1990). Among the features of the frame that are particularly helpful for separating symptoms from underlying patterns are the focus on organization-environment exchanges and the diagnosis of system fits, gaps, and interdependencies. One limitation in the system frame is its failure to direct attention to emergent and subterranean organizational patterns. A related problem is that the open-systems frame leads analysts to look at organizational features and patterns that are found in most organizations, as opposed to patterns that are distinctive to the focal organization. Hence, open-systems analyses often need to be supplemented by additional frames that focus on more unique and emergent features of the client organization. Among the many frames that can contribute to this type of fine-grained analysis are those focusing on negotiations and emergent behavior, cultural differentiation, cultural ambiguity, organizational politics, gendering (Chapter 9), and workgroup processes.

No feature is more critical to diagnostic effectiveness than the capacity to help decision makers find workable routes to organizational improvement. The ability of a diagnostic frame to meet this requirement often turns on the degree to which the frame fits the problem, the client's position and power, and the focal organization. Suppose, for example, that managers in a financial services firm seek to reduce complaints about the handling of customer inquiries and ask an in-house consultant to examine the issue. The consultant approaches the question by assessing whether organizational behavior and human resource practices are well aligned with the tasks of handling customer inquiries (see Chapter 8). This framing of the diagnostic question directs attention to staff behavior and ways to improve it. If diagnosis showed that staff behavior did indeed lie behind many of the customer complaints, the consultant might suggest using human resource techniques such as selection, training, and rewards to improve behavior. In contrast, the diagnostic practitioner could approach the same problem by using a structural frame that focuses on organization design. This frame might help the investigator uncover problems in the routing of customer inquiries to appropriate personnel, in routines for locating the information needed to handle inquiries, and in procedures for responding to inquiries. If diagnosis confirmed these findings, action op- tions would include redesigning rules, job descriptions, and information- processing techniques, as well as ensuring that human resource practices supported these design changes. The workability of these two very different approaches depends on several contingencies besides the nature of the problem. These include the clients' power, their propensity for particular types of action, anticipated costs of alternatives, and the likely reactions of other powerful actors.

The feasibility of options for action also depends greatly on the goals and values of power stakeholders in the client organization. For example, frames oriented toward radical change in power relations and toward fundamental organizational change may point to feasible options for organizations dedicated to egalitarian values and social change (e.g., Chisholm & Elden, 1993). However, these same frames would be unlikely to reveal feasible options for reorganizing conventional businesses or public sector bureaucracies.

Now consider the contribution of frames to motivating clients and other organizational members to take appropriate steps toward improvement. Both the open-systems frame and the structural frame are well suited to motivate steps toward change. These frames direct attention to ineffectiveness, poor fits, and performance gaps—findings that well reflect client concerns. On the other hand, the interpretive frame could divert attention toward deep cultural patterns that are very resistant to change. Focusing diagnosis on hard-to-change conditions can increase frustration and even lead members to conclude that change is impossible.

Having considered some of the analytical and motivational implications of choosing one frame or another, let us now consider more briefly the contributions of diagnostic frames to the second facet of diagnosis—its methodology. The prime methodological requirement for effective diagnosis is that it generate valid data. Although many frames can meet this requirement, not all can do so at present. Deconstruction (Kilduff, 1993), for example, might indeed increase the investigator's understanding of the assumptions that members of a management team build in to their statements to one another. However, there is little agreement in the literature so far about the methods of deconstruction and about ways to evaluate the validity of its inferences. There are other frames that raise methodological problems of a more pragmatic sort: They direct attention to phenomena that are hard to study, very costly, or very sensitive. For these reasons, consultants usually rule out gathering a lot of data that would prove relevant to frames focusing on cultural differentiation, cultural ambiguity, negotiation, political processes, and power distribution.

The third set of requirements for effective diagnosis relates to the development of constructive interactions among consultants and clients and among members of the client organization. Diagnosis can succeed only if top managers support it and become committed to its findings. To generate support for their work, practitioners of diagnosis may use at least one organizing frame that is compatible with the ways that top managers view their organization or subunit. The open-systems frame can often meet this requirement, as can the structural frame, with its emphasis on organization design. If managers are particularly concerned with strategy formation, consultants may supplement the broad open-systems frame with a more focused one that directly considers issues relevant to the formation and implementation of strategy.

Sometimes, an analytically valuable frame must not be made explicit because it contains assumptions that powerful clients will reject outright. Attempts to introduce clients to the frame will undermine their support for the study and heighten resistance to feedback. Some of the assumptions and values embedded in feminist theories, for example, can produce fierce resistance among (mainly male) managers. Another analytically powerful frame that seems poorly suited to consultation is the dramaturgic approach to organizations (Goffman, 1959), which has provided generations of researchers with insights into subtle principles of emergent interpersonal and intergroup behavior. Unfortunately, many people react defensively to descriptions of their behavior that use metaphors from the theater, such as performances, props, and fronts. These metaphors are taken to mean that people typically behave inauthentically and even dishonestly. Managers in a client organization are likely to resent this implication, or if they accept it, to become even more suspicious of the consultant and of their fellow members than they were prior to exposure to this frame!

Now let us consider the ability of frames to contribute to client and organizational learning, as opposed to promoting midrange diagnostic goals. The requirements for attaining midrange goals, which were just reviewed, form necessary, but not sufficient, conditions for learning. If, for example, a diagnostic study does not ensure the support and trust of clients, it cannot contribute to their capacity to learn how to analyze and solve problems on their own. Similarly, if diagnostic frames evoke defensive reactions in clients, the frames will not help clients see themselves and their organization in new ways. Nor will the frame help members reduce reliance on familiar, self-defeating frames.

Frames and diagnostic techniques must be clear and easy to learn if clients are to learn to use them independently. Moreover, to be well suited for use in management development and training, frames should rest on a substantial body of research and practice and should employ widely understood and agreed-upon concepts and methods. Organizational consultants have had much experience in applying the open-systems frame to organizational problems and in teaching clients to use the frame. Techniques and models derived from this frame that are well developed and hold promise for use in training and client learning include analysis of competitive advantage (Chapter 13); assessment of fits among system features (Chapter 2); assessment of fits between system features and deliberate strategies (Chapters 8 and 13); gap analysis (Chapter 2); Hackman's model of group task performance (Chapter 6); open-systems planning (Chapter 4); and Weisbord's six-box model (Chapter 4). Other frames holding special promise for client learning include the political frame and, in particular, the techniques of stakeholder analysis and force field analysis, as well as examinations of cultural integration and differentiation. Some frames, such as the negotiations and cultural ambiguity frames, require further specification before they can contribute directly to client learning. Others, such as the life cycle and labor relations models discussed in Chapters 11 and 12, are suited to very specific types of organizations or types of conditions. Unfortunately, many of the newer theoretical frames, such as postmodernism and deconstruction, are very abstract and lack clear implications for diagnosis and action. In time, researchers and consultants may develop the implications of these newer frames and translate them into terms that nonspecialists can readily grasp and use.

If diagnostic frames are to contribute to type two learning (Chapter 13), they need to help clients break out of modes of thought that define problems as intractable or that produce interim solutions that just generate additional problems. Sometimes, the very process of examining the same issue from multiple perspectives helps people develop a less defensive and more self-reflective posture toward sensitive issues. Juxtaposing several perspectives on the same condition or issue can encourage a more playful approach to problem solving and can help participants realize that there need not be a single, comprehensive truth about organizational conditions or a single path to solving problems.

Open-systems analyses can sometimes help members of an organization break out of self-defeating cycles of blame by recasting issues at the group or organizational levels of analysis (e.g., Case 1.2). Moreover, feedback stressing system interdependencies can help organizational members stop trying to pin the blame for organizational problems on a particular group or function.

A related route toward type two learning is to foster openness among clients and other organizational members toward alternative points of view that are present within the organization and in its environment. Honest dialogue between individuals or between divergent subgroups becomes possible when members of a group acknowledge the legitimacy of the distinctive needs, objectives, and viewpoints held by people in some other group (Barrett & Cooperrider, 1990). But many theories-in-use delegitimate alternative viewpoints and interests.

The open-systems frame can sometimes provide an alternative to theories-in-use that block honest communication. With open-systems theories, the stress on adaptation to external change can make people more aware of the need to take alternative views seriously. In addition, the frame focuses on the contribution to overall system functioning of divergent subcomponents and subgroups. On the other hand, the system frame's unitary and abstract view of system conditions and of "system needs" can divert users from the diversity of behavior and interpretations that prevail within an organization and in its environments. This tendency toward abstraction and reification can tempt users of the system frame to assume that top management correctly interprets and presents the path to system effectiveness. This assumption can result in failure to attribute much importance to competing definitions of effectiveness, alternative ways of enhancing effectiveness and reducing ineffectiveness, and divergent stakeholder interests and goals.

Specifications of the interpretive and political frames may prove more effective than the systems frame at promoting understanding of subgroup diversity and at creating respect for the views and goals of others. In particular, consultants can draw on the cultural differentiation approach and on multiple-stakeholder models of effectiveness to heighten awareness of subgroup divergences and to strengthen respect for them. Both approaches draw attention to the ubiquity of subgroup differences. Moreover, these two approaches suggest that organizational effectiveness can be enhanced through cooperation among divergent subgroups in and around the focal organization. Such cooperation requires members to understand and respect group and individual differences.

Barrett and Cooperrider (1990) provide an illustration of this type of reframing process within a hotel's management team. With the help of the consultants, team members gradually abandoned a frame that delegitimated differences among them and blamed team ineffectiveness on unsolvable interpersonal conflicts. Stimulated by a task force report on a very successful hotel, the managers gradually adopted a new frame that concentrated on achieving excellence in their own hotel. This new frame emphasized shared objectives, accepted diversity as legitimate, and recognized that diverse views could contribute to joint problem solving.

As practitioners of diagnosis evaluate the capacity of frames to contribute to diagnostic analysis, methods, and interactions, they need to consider the potential *mix* of frames to be used, as well as the contribution of individual frames. In choosing frames, it is important to weigh the possible analytical benefits of shifting between radically disjunctive frames against the risks of using very incompatible frames. Clients concerned with "bottom-line" issues can find it confusing and frustrating to be confronted by very divergent frames—such as the structural frame, with its highly instrumental view, and the interpretive frame, with its symbolic approach.[7] A diagnosis using such a juxtaposition of frames may contribute less to client understanding, problem solving, and learning than would a diagnosis based on more familiar frames containing more complementary perspectives.

A further consideration in selecting an appropriate mix of frames concerns the degree to which each frame adds value to the other selected frames. Each frame or diagnostic technique should contribute distinctive insights or lead to an important line of inquiry that could not be sustained by the frames that are already in use. For example, stakeholder analysis adds a perspective that is sorely lacking in the organization-design and open-systems frames. On the other hand, both the stakeholder and the cultural differentiation approaches point to subgroup differences. If a diagnosis has already analyzed stakeholder orientations, it would not be worthwhile to examine cultural differentiation just to reinforce awareness of subgroup goals. On the other hand, the cultural differentiation frame will add value to the stakeholder frame if investigators need to examine subgroup norms, values, and interpretations—features that are not usually considered during stakeholder analyses.

Combining Frames

Complementary Versus Conflicting Components

To combine frames successfully, diagnostic investigators need to pay close attention to the degree to which frames complement or oppose one another, to the specific elements within frames that create conflicting and complementary perspectives, and to possible ways of handling divergence between frames. Apparent conflicts between frames can produce complementary perspectives if the conflicts stem from concentration on different levels of analysis. In this case, combining the frames can illuminate crucial interactions

between levels. A particularly useful combination of this type joins a frame
that readily focuses on the total organization, such as open-systems, to a frame
that focuses most easily and powerfully on interpersonal interactions or
interpretations—as the negotiation frame does, and as do the cultural differentiation and ambiguity versions of the interpretive frame (Barley, 1986;
Giddens, 1984).[8] When the open-systems frame is applied to an entire organization or division, it directs attention to macro conditions, including the
organization's environment, resource flows, structure, and technology. The
frame thus provides a vantage point enjoyed mainly by top management and
highly placed outsiders. In contrast, frames stressing negotiation, politics,
cultural differentiation, and cultural ambiguity all provide a bottom-up, actor-
focused view that draws attention to microlevel interactions between individuals and small groups. This microlevel view helps reveal fine-grained differences between subgroups or hierarchical levels in interpretations of events and
in prevailing rules of the game. In addition, interpretive approaches direct
attention to the ways that members of the organization interpret their environments and enact (i.e., define and shape) them through their own interpretations
and behavior (Smircich & Stubbart, 1985).

Simultaneously framing organizations at both the macro and micro levels
can produce insight into organizational features and cross-level interactions
that would be missed if only one frame were used. Moreover, combining the
two types of frames contains a very practical implication for managers and
governmental policymakers, who often rely heavily on macro-oriented
frames, such as the structural frame: People in the middle and lower levels of
an organization are likely to reinterpret and renegotiate programs, plans, and
mandates imposed from above. These modifications can be so substantial that
little of the original program is actually implemented, and many unintended
and unanticipated consequences emerge (Chapter 7).

Conflicts between frames can stem from many specific components that
are embedded within the frames—philosophical and methodological foundations, empirical expectations (testable hypotheses), (untestable) premises
concerning causality and prevailing empirical conditions, implied and declared norms and values, and assumptions about appropriate problem-solving
techniques. When users of multiple diagnostic frames encounter tension or
opposition between frames, they need to identify the components of the
frames that produce this opposition.

Once they uncover the underlying components and sources of frame
conflicts, investigators can decide on tactics for handling them. Some conflicts

can be resolved logically by spelling out the chain of argument embedded in a frame and by clearly defining key terms. Conflicts between empirical expectations that are embedded in frames can sometimes be translated into opposing, testable hypotheses. Framing organizations in terms of cultural integration, for instance, leads investigators to anticipate finding cultural norms and values that are shared throughout an organization, whereas framing in terms of cultural differentiation leads to the expectation that the organization will be divided into subcultures. These opposing expectations can be investigated empirically during diagnoses and applied research studies, as well as in academic research. Unfortunately, until now, few researchers or consultants have pitted empirical predictions about cultural unity and differentiation against one another in a single investigation. For example, most quantitative studies of culture assume the existence of cultural integration without actually testing this assumption (Rousseau, 1990a).[9]

The well-known contrast between frames stressing strategic choice and those focusing on environmental selection and determinism (Astley & Van de Ven, 1983) can also be restated to give rise to useful issues that can be investigated empirically during diagnosis and applied research. Some ecological theories argue that managers typically lack the information needed to guide adjustment to environmental shifts, and that managers lack the power to change their organizations. In contrast, strategic-choice theories assume that top managers can, in principle, obtain necessary information and use it effectively.[10] This debate points to issues that could be investigated empirically in diagnosis. For example, during investigations of organizational decline and other fundamental upheavals (Chapter 11), diagnostic practitioners can examine how much organizational members know and learn about their environments, whether they develop clear understandings of how to cope with upheavals, and whether top managers can overcome political barriers and lead turnarounds or other major strategic changes.

Unfortunately, many clashes between frames cannot be resolved by empirical study or logical analysis. Instead, many organizational and policy controversies resist resolution because participants use frames that reflect divergent norms, values, and theories-in-use. The users of these conflicting frames interpret problems and experiences selectively, apply divergent criteria for setting priorities and weighing evidence, and advocate incompatible actions (Schon, 1993; Schon & Rein, 1994). Consider, for example, the clash between feminist perspectives on work and the family and mainstream American views of human resource management and organizational control. American managers typically view part-time employees as less central to their organization. Moreover, managers regard employees who work long hours and are rarely absent as more committed and more desirable employees. These employees are more likely to be retained when firms cut staff and are more likely to be promoted than are equally qualified peers who devote less time to their work. Researchers and consultants reinforce prevailing managerial views when they treat absenteeism or preference for part-time work as indicative of low organizational commitment.

Feminist critics, such as Bailyn (1993), argue that prevailing managerial views and practices rest on several taken-for-granted assumptions: Time spent at work can be equated with commitment; greater time investment by employees invariably enhances individual and organizational productivity; and direct supervision is required to ensure that employees work productively.

Bailyn challenges these prevailing assumptions, pointing out that they are based on mechanistic views of organizational control processes and of the causes of competitiveness and productivity. According to this critique, these assumptions might have been appropriate for assembly-line production, but they do not reflect the requirements for competitive performance in knowledge-based organizations. Instead, demands for working long hours at the office or for extensive travel are often simply convenient for the firm, rather than absolutely necessary. Particularly in knowledge work, productivity derives from "working smart" rather than from putting in long hours at the office. From the feminist perspective, the traditional managerial approach perpetuates the value that an employee's time belongs primarily to the employer. By doing so, traditional norms and assumptions disadvantage women, who continue to retain primary responsibility for child care. Moreover, resistance to working at home and to other flexible work arrangements reflects the assumption that direct, personal supervision is necessary to ensure productivity.

Instead, say the feminists, technical, managerial, and professional employees should be given substantial operational autonomy, including opportunities to work at home. Their productivity should be evaluated directly, rather than through surrogate measures that perpetuate male advantages in the workplace.

Some of the issues underlying this clash between traditional and feminist views of management could be examined empirically in ways that are illustrated below. However, in many businesses and knowledge-based organizations, it is taken for granted that organizational success depends on the willingness of professionals, technical specialists, and managers to put work ahead of personal priorities (e.g., Kunda, 1992). People who take this assumption as axiomatic are likely to discount potentially discrediting evidence. Furthermore, empirical findings can never resolve the underlying value issue of how much employees can be expected to sacrifice their personal goals for the sake of corporate ones.

An even more basic tension occurs between frames that accept the status quo and those that seek radical change in organizations and in society as a whole (Burrell & Morgan, 1979). Frames such as radical feminism and those derived from neo-Marxism posit that the purpose of understanding organizations is to change their power structure and their relation to society. These radical frames also assume that one way to understand organizations is to try to change them. In contrast, stability-oriented frames usually take power distributions in and around organizations as given and seek understanding or organizational improvement within these constraints.

What is to be done when conflicts between frames reflect such divergent or even opposing premises, assumptions, and fundamental values? One option is for investigators to create dialogue or interplay between opposing positions so as to articulate the major dimensions or components on which the frames diverge (Aldrich, 1992; Reed, 1996). Once these dimensions have been identified, it becomes possible to examine gray areas—instances in which one frame contains emphases or assumptions that were thought to be the exclusive province of the other frame (Gioia & Pitre, 1990; Schulz & Hatch, 1996). For example, the integrative approach to culture assumes the presence of clearly defined cultural meanings, whereas the cultural ambiguity approach anticipates lack of clarity about the meaning of events and symbols. Nevertheless, we can easily find gray areas that do not readily fit this dichotomy: Top managers sometimes foster cultural integration by using ambiguous slogans and mission statements. Ostensible agreement over ambiguous symbols masks gaps between individuals or groups holding divergent goals and operating assumptions (Astley & Zammuto, 1992; Meyerson & Lewis, 1992).

Consultants and organizational members can also handle frame conflict by building bridges between frames at the level of organizational practice. This approach rests on the search for pragmatic moves that combine elements from opposing frames or provide ways of overcoming or bypassing frame conflicts (Schon, 1993; Schon & Rein, 1994). Abstract analytical frames rarely produce unique and unambiguous implications for practice. Instead, two different frames can support the same action implication. The introduction of self-managed teams, for example, can be based on theories of motivation and peer interaction that fit well with open-systems thinking; on structural analyses of designs for coordinating work (Chapter 7); and on cognitive-interpretive views of organizational learning, such as those developed in this chapter and in Chapter 13. This type of meeting of two or more frames at the level of practice opens up possibilities for participants to discover constructive overlaps between frames.

In a similar fashion, a single theoretical frame can give rise to several different action options. For example, Galbraith's information-processing model leads to several alternative design prescriptions (Chapter 7). As managers and consultants explore such options, they can discover continuities and complementarities between the guiding frame and other frames that might not have been evident in the abstract.

Users of divergent frames can discover pragmatic ways to resolve interframe controversy only if they trust one another and communicate openly. Moreover, to bridge between frames through practice, participants in organizational decision making need to avoid defensive postures and to be open to learning from feedback concerning the results of their actions. In this way, participants will be able to reframe some of their actions and may even begin to put themselves in the shoes of other actors who draw on divergent frames. This learning process can help actors to appreciate and value frame diversity and can lead them to discover mutually beneficial, win-win solutions to problems.

How might frame bridging work in practice? Suppose that a diagnosis of productivity problems shows that a consumer products firm is not tapping the full potential of women working in managerial and technical positions.[11] Faced with stiff workloads and long hours, some of the best qualified women are leaving or cutting back their workloads in order to give more time to their families. This pattern reduces productivity and raises costs for staff recruitment, placement, and training. Discussion of diagnostic feedback and possible solutions to this problem might quickly turn into a conflict between two camps, each of which draws on conflicting theories-in-use. One camp employs an essentially feminist frame. Its members claim that working mothers need more control over their time in order to raise their families properly, and that the company must radically change its expectations about work hours and conditions so as to accommodate to these needs. Otherwise, the firm will go on losing good people. The other camp consists of defenders of current practices, who retain essentially structural and bureaucratic ideas about coordination and control. These people argue that without strict supervision and standard working hours, individual productivity will fall, and it will become impossible to coordinate work activities. Moreover, they argue that overtime work is necessary to meet deadlines that are imposed on the firm by its competitive environment. Any attempt to resolve this conflict in the abstract is likely to go around in circles, because the members of each camp base their views on very divergent assumptions and values. In addition, the diagnostic findings could be seen as supporting both ways of framing the problem.

To avoid a deadlock, the firm's managers set up a task force to look for a practical means to meet two sets of objectives: First, introduce greater flexibility in locating and scheduling work; and second, maintain or even enhance current levels of work productivity and quality. Members of the task force meet to examine different types of tasks and to interview people about work supervision and coordination. The task force reports that some tasks require higher levels of supervision and coaching than do others. In like manner, the requirements for face-to-face coordination vary between tasks. Electronic mail and computer networking techniques can substitute for much, if not all, of the required interactions in many task areas. In light of these findings, the task force recommends setting up a computer network and introducing flexible work hours among office workers.

Management responds by setting up an experimental network for staff members whose main task involves preparing technical manuals. This task requires coordination among people who are dispersed both geographically and functionally. The participants in the experiment will be allowed to work on the manuals wherever and whenever they want as long as the job gets done quickly and standards remain high. To assist them in cooperating with other staff members, they are given new networking software for their personal computers. Some people take their computers home, whereas others work from their desks. Some of the latter group maintain regular nine-to-five hours, wherease others take advantage of flexible hours. The experiment will be monitored by the task force, with the assistance of the consultant who conducted the original diagnosis. Management will consider extending networking to other tasks if the experimental network succeeds in producing manuals in the same or less time than was previously required and if it maintains quality standards. Networking may also be expanded if the experiment turns up additional promising possibilities for using this technology.

By carefully analyzing the results of this experiment and the processes by which participants in the experiment managed their work, the advocates and opponents of home work and flexible hours will see whether granting employees greater autonomy can be justified in terms of productivity. In addition, they will better understand how to accomplish this design change. In the end, both parties to the original argument may also learn more about how to control the outcomes of work rather than its inputs or processes.

Procedures for Combining
Frames During Diagnosis

So far, we have concentrated more on the logical relations among frames and their components than on procedures for combining them during diagnosis. To facilitate this discussion, we will refer to six analytical phases of diagnosis: scouting, contracting, study design, data gathering, analysis, and feedback (Harrison, 1994). In practice, these phases can overlap, repeat, and vary in sequence. Nevertheless, distinguishing among them brings to light features relating to four alternative procedures for combining and sequencing multiple frames during diagnosis.

The first procedure combines two or three frames and then uses these frames during all phases of diagnosis. For example, as explained in Part 1 of this book, many diagnostic studies combine open-systems and political frames. Models and procedures based on the open-systems frame guide design, data gathering, analysis, and feedback. Political analyses contribute to definitions of effectiveness criteria and to assessments of the feasibility of action alternatives.

Another way to combine frames throughout diagnosis is to introduce clients to frame combination during diagnostic workshops. The consultant introduces the concept of frame combination and helps participants choose appropriate frames. Then, participants are helped to use the frames to analyze current problems and challenges, design ways to gather additional needed information, analyze their findings and understandings of the situation, and formulate plans for action. If the political and interpersonal climate favors cooperation and reflective inquiry, workshops like this can help members of an organization learn to use new frames and to combine frames.[12] However, workshops typically provide fewer opportunities for systematic data gathering and analysis. Moreover, workshop participants often encounter difficulties in transferring skills learned in workshops to their regular work settings.

A second combinatorial procedure introduces frames in a sequence and limits the use of frames to specific phases of diagnosis. For instance, during data gathering, consultants can draw on the open-systems frame to guide a broad survey of potential sources of effectiveness and ineffectiveness. Then, on the basis of these findings, they can add another frame, model, or diagnostic technique to sharpen the analysis of existing data and guide further data gathering and analysis. For example, when diagnostic feedback leads clients to consider programs of planned change, stakeholder analysis can be added during feedback and action planning. This technique can help decision makers identify actors who may support and resist change and plan ways of dealing with them. The second and third parts of the book contain many other examples of models and diagnostic approaches that can be applied to specific issues that emerge from an initial diagnosis.

A third procedure, which is well suited to sharp-image diagnosis, employs multiple frames in only one diagnostic phase or in just a few phases. By concentrating frame combination on one or more critical diagnostic phases, this procedure avoids the complexities of employing multiple frames throughout diagnosis. Consultants who adopt this approach can cooperate with clients to choose frames during the scouting, contracting, and design phases of the diagnosis. Then, the consultant can gather appropriate data and synthesize the findings into a single diagnostic model that provides the basis for feedback to clients. Suppose, for example, that a consultant diagnoses fits among system elements and also examines the political feasibility of reducing serious misfits. Rather than explicitly presenting the political frame during feedback, the consultant could simply create a systems model that reflected the insights gained from the political analysis. This model would emphasize those sources of poor fit that clients could deal with without encountering opposition.

Rather than starting with multiple frames and concluding with a synthetic model, consultants can also reduce ambiguity for clients by introducing them to frame combination only at the conclusion of the diagnosis, during the feedback stage. By encouraging clients to use multiple frames in reacting to feedback and planning appropriate action, the consultant may stimulate creative thinking about available options for action. This procedure rests on the assumption that diagnostic feedback stimulates action planning but does not provide a comprehensive guide to decision making. Instead, participants ordinarily supplement feedback during action planning by gathering and analyzing additional information and by drawing on their own experience and knowledge.

A fourth procedure for frame combination uses different sets of frames during the early and later phases of diagnosis. This approach allows consultants and clients to employ frames that are particularly appropriate to different stages in diagnosis and meet different criteria for effective diagnosis. To launch a diagnostic study successfully, consultants must first win the support of the top managers in the unit to be studied. If consultants initially propose using frames that clash with client perspectives, the clients may not approve the study. However, once consultants have gained the support and trust of clients, the consultants may introduce these discordant frames in order to stimulate creative thinking and problem solving.

Alternatively, once support has been obtained, consultants can choose frames for data gathering and analysis that are most likely to yield a rich and powerful understanding of organizational problems and conditions. In contrast, during feedback and analysis, the consultant can choose frames that are likely to motivate desire for improvement while helping members to identify feasible options for action and mobilizing support for these actions. When enhancing organizational learning is an important objective, frames and frame combinations may be chosen because of their ability to enhance complicated thinking and provide clients with diagnostic and analytical tools that they can use in the future.

To illustrate this procedure for sequencing of frames, consider the potential contribution of the negotiations frame to a diagnosis of an organization facing serious difficulties in coordinating customer services across separate departments. The negotiations frame might indeed help consultants understand how each department had evolved its own ways of dealing with customers and why emergent practices in one department do not fit those in another. However, when clients discuss diagnostic feedback and look for ways to deal with these problems, they are likely to find that other frames—such as the structural frame, with its focus on design tools, and the political frame, with its focus on multiple stakeholders—provide more practical guidelines than does the negotiations frame.

In sequencing frames in this fashion, consultants need to pay close attention to variations among approaches and techniques that are embedded within the same broad frame and to the subtle messages that frames, models, and analytical techniques convey to clients. Some messages contribute to the consulting process, whereas others can be destructive (Armenakis & Bedeian, 1992; Larwood, 1992). For instance, when consultants use feedback to unfreeze people's prior conceptions and theories-in-use, the consultants need to frame the feedback in ways that will not invoke defensiveness. Consider, for example, the messages that are embedded within two closely related variants of the political frame. Consultants viewing an organization from a pluralistic political standpoint might describe the organization as a "battlefield" of conflicting interest groups. This military metaphor could lead recipients of feedback to feel that only a fight to the finish can produce change. On the other hand, consultants could cast the same findings within a stakeholder frame that defined organizations as "polities." This approach suggests that managers earn the loyalty of stakeholders by being fair and responsive to them. This framing of the situation can help feedback recipients define the interests of other actors as legitimate. Furthermore, the stakeholder frame can enhance members' willingness to confront differences openly and to negotiate mutually satisfactory resolutions of conflict.

Practitioners need to consider one additional issue in formulating procedures for frame combination. This issue concerns the desirability and feasibility of standardizing procedures for selecting frames and frame combinations, as opposed to grounding decisions about appropriate frames in the investigator's emerging understanding of organizational conditions, problems, and prospects for change. Consultants can reduce the level of ambiguity faced by themselves and their clients by developing a repertoire of frames and combinations in advance of any particular consulting assignment and then choosing from this repertoire during the design of each successive diagnostic study. As suggested earlier, it is often possible to combine a system-based model or frame with one that illuminates subgroup differences, such as frames that highlight cultural differentiation or stakeholder expectations. Where greater depth is sought, both the stakeholder and the cultural differentiation approaches can be used. Standardizing or programming multiframe diagnosis can produce both benefits and disadvantages for clients and consultants. By using the same set of frames repeatedly, consultants can streamline and enhance their diagnostic skills and techniques, more readily train new consultants and organizational members in the use of multiple frames, and reduce the costs of diagnosis.

Unfortunately, consultants may obtain these benefits at the expense of creatively matching frames to the unique circumstances prevailing within each client organization. To maximize creativity and sensitivity to local conditions, investigators will choose and evoke frames as they carry out the diagnosis. For example, a diagnosis of a philanthropic organization might begin with a single, comprehensive frame, such as the open-systems frame. If initial inquiries suggested that the organization was losing support among its donors and among influential people in the government, then the investigators could draw on institutional theory (Chapter 10) or stakeholder analysis to illuminate the nature of these threats to the organization. Subsequent analyses might use an information-processing frame (Morgan, 1986) to examine how the organization gathers and processes information about the expectations of key stakeholders.

The obvious advantage of this type of grounded and emergent framing lies in its capacity to facilitate sharp-image diagnosis. Grounded framing helps the investigator remain constantly alert to emerging possibilities for analyzing organizational problems and challenges and to possibilities for helping clients deal constructively with diagnostic findings. This grounded approach can help consultants and clients respond creatively and quickly to unique and unforeseen organizational conditions and features. On the other hand, consultants need conceptual and methodological agility to accomplish this type of study, and they must be adept at explaining and justifying their approach to clients. Clearly, a very grounded approach to frame combination is not appropriate for beginning practitioners or for veterans who want to standardize their diagnostic procedures, rather than developing them anew during each consulting assignment.

Conclusion

This chapter, like those that preceded it, invited consultants and managers who engage in diagnosis to combine theoretical frames and use grounded research methods as they diagnose and assess organizations. This flexible and pluralistic approach deviates from much previous work on planned change that elaborated systems models in advance of diagnosis (e.g., Chapter 4) and gathered data with standardized survey instruments (e.g., Seashore et al., 1983; Van de Ven & Ferry, 1980). By combining multiple theoretical frames, consultants and their clients can break out of conventional ways of analyzing problems and challenges and discover new possibilities for action. In addition, users of multiple frames gradually become accustomed to thinking more reflexively and more critically about their own perspectives and diagnoses. This type of critical thinking contributes to richer and more flexible consultation and managerial decision making and to greater responsiveness to contingencies and dynamic developments affecting planned change. In our view, practitioners of diagnosis and their clients can reap the benefits of frame combination without adopting philosophical and methodological stances that preclude systematic inquiry and reasoned action.

Framing organizational problems forms an integral part of solving them. Even where diagnostic practitioners provide feedback without making any action recommendations, the very process of gathering, analyzing, and presenting findings in terms of particular frames and models suggests that some solutions to problems and some action options are appropriate, while ruling out others. Hence, consultants and their clients need to attend closely to their choices and applications of frames and models during diagnosis and decision making.

Current trends in consultation and organizational decision making indicate that consultants, managers, and governmental policymakers too often neglect diagnosis when they face complicated organizational challenges and problems. In their enthusiasm for management fashions, they respond to poorly understood symptoms and complex environmental changes by applying overly simple, ready-made solutions, such as quality assurance, benchmarking, outsourcing, reengineering, and privatization. Such uncritical implementation of off-the-shelf management techniques can lead to negative and unanticipated consequences. At least some of these outcomes can be avoided through diagnosis. Systematic diagnosis can help decision makers understand underlying sources of problems and the nature of external threats and challenges. Diagnosis can also contribute to better assessments of workable options for planned change.

In concentrating on the potential contributions of diagnosis to organizational problem solving, consultants and decision makers cannot reasonably overlook cognitive constraints on systematic decision making and ignore limitations of the knowledge base on which diagnosis rests. Nor would it be prudent to ignore the many political, behavioral, and operational forces that constrain and divert systematic decision making in management and government. Diagnostic studies and diagnostic thinking cannot eliminate these conditions, but diagnosis can help managers and other decision makers anticipate and deal with these constraints.

In this way, diagnosis can help managers gain greater freedom of movement and enhance their capacity to manage change. By examining problems, challenges, and the sources of ineffectiveness carefully, managers can more successfully envision desirable paths toward organizational improvement. This view of a desired direction for action will help them keep track of their destination even as they encounter barriers and make detours. By engaging in diagnostic inquiry during planned change, and by conducting periodic assessments of change programs, managers can respond more quickly and appropriately to emerging developments. In addition, this inquiry approach will help them learn more about their own managerial views and practices, their organization, and planned change.

Even more importantly, as managers and other organizational members develop their own capacity for diagnostic analysis, they equip themselves to confront as yet unforeseen problems and challenges. One thing is certain in today's uncertain world: New challenges will confront decision makers long before they have finished dealing with current ones.

Notes

1. In particular, see Chapters 7 and 13 for discussions of how diagnosis and assessment can contribute to learning during programs of strategic change.

2. The acronyms refer to Total Quality Management, Quality Circles, and Business Process Reengineering, respectively. See Chapters 1 and 7 for further discussions of management fads.

3. Torbert (1995) and Ramirez and Bartunek (1989) are important exceptions to this trend.

4. Reed (1996) discusses the conservative and radical responses to diversity, along with ways of preserving and highlighting differences among perspectives.

5. An increasing number of scholars who view social theories and concepts in constructionist terms explicitly reject the tendency of some postmodernist thinking to treat all language as purely rhetorical and to adopt radically subjectivist ontologies (e.g., Alvesson, 1995; Beyer, 1992; Martin, 1992).

6. From this standpoint, utility, rather than validity (Argyris, 1970; Bowen, 1977), becomes the ultimate test of the value of diagnostic feedback. However, invalid diagnostic findings seem very unlikely to lead to actions that prove useful in the long run.

7. Such analytical juxtapositions (e.g., Aldrich, 1992) can, of course, be very illuminating for organizational theorists and researchers.

8. The interpretive frame can be applied at any level of analysis, as can the open-systems frame and other abstract frames. But these frames diverge in terms of the levels to which they can easily and powerfully be applied.

9. One possible outcome of the simultaneous investigation of predictions derived from the cultural integration and cultural differentiation frames might be that integration is more prevalent in less complex organizations. In complex organizations, integration across subgroups may occur at the level of deep, unarticulated assumptions, whereas subgroup differentiation prevails in articulated norms and meanings.

10. Much of the divergence between these two frames stems from the use of different levels of analysis, rather than from divergent empirical predictions at the organization level (see Astley & Van de Ven, 1983). To the extent that the frames focus on different levels, they are more complementary than conflicting.

11. This case is based loosely on one reported by Bailyn (1993, p. 95). However, the decision process leading to the experiment is not reported by her. Moreover, in the original experiment, reduction of work-family conflict was an unintended consequence for a single employee, rather than a planned outcome for all participants.

12. See Chapter 4 on the conditions supporting collaborative diagnoses.

References

Abel-Smith, B., Figueras, J., Holland, W., McKee, M., & Mossialos, E. (1995). *Choices in health policy: An agenda for the European Union.* Luxembourg: Office for Official Publications of the European Communities, and Aldershot, England: Dartmouth Publishing.

Abrahamson, E. (1991). Managerial fads and fashions: The diffusion and rejection of innovations. *Academy of Management Review, 16,* 586-612.

Abrahamson, E. (1996). Management fashion. *Academy of Management Review, 21,* 254-285.

Abrahamson, E., & Fairchild, G. (1997). *Management fashion: Lifecycles, triggers, and collective learning processes.* Unpublished manuscript, Columbia University, Graduate School of Business. (Summary in *Academy of Management Proceedings,* 254-257).

Abrahamsson, B. (1977). *Bureaucracy or participation: The logic of organization.* Beverly Hills, CA: Sage.

Adams, S. (1996). *The Dilbert principle.* New York: Harper Business.

Adizes, I. (1988). *Corporate lifecyles: How and why corporations grow and die and what to do about it.* Englewood Cliffs, NJ: Prentice Hall.

Adler, N., & Bartholomew, S. (1992). Managing globally competent people. *Academy of Management Executive, 6*(3), 52-65.

Adler, N., & Jelinek, M. (1986). Is "organization culture" culture bound? *Human Resource Management, 25,* 73-90.

Aldrich, H. (1979). *Organizations and environments.* Englewood Cliffs, NJ: Prentice Hall.

Aldrich, H. (1992). Incommensurable paradigms? Vital signs from three perspectives on organizations. In M. Reed & M. Hughes (Eds.), *Rethinking organizations: New directions in organizational theory and analysis* (pp. 16-45). London: Sage.

Alinsky, S. (1971). *Rules for radicals.* New York: Random House/Vintage.

All in the same bunch. (1997, May 31). *Economist,* p. 66.

Alvesson, M. (1995). The meaning and meaninglessness of postmodernism: Some ironic remarks. *Organization Studies, 16,* 1047-1075.

Alvesson, M., & Deetz, S. (1996). Critical theory and postmodern approaches in organization studies. In S. Clegg, C. Hardy, & W. Nord (Eds.), *Handbook of organization studies* (pp. 191-217). London: Sage.

439

Amburgery, T., Kelly, D., & Barnett, W. (1993). Resetting the clock: The dynamics of organizational change and failure. *Administrative Science Quarterly, 38*, 51-73.

Ancona, D. G. (1990). Outward bound: Strategies for team survival in organizations. *Academy of Management Journal, 33*, 334-365.

Ancona, D., & Caldwell, D. (1992). Demography and design: Predictors of new product team performance. *Organization Science, 3*, 321-341.

Ancona, D., & Chong, C. (1992). *Entrainment: Cycles and synergy in organizational behavior* (Working paper 3443-92 BPS). Cambridge: MIT Sloan School.

Anderson, P., & Tushman, M. (1990). Technological discontinuities and dominant designs: A cyclical model of technological change. *Administrative Science Quarterly, 35*, 604-633.

Andrews, K. (1980). *The concept of corporate strategy* (Rev. ed.). Homewood, IL: Dow-Jones, Irwin.

Argyris, C. (1970). *Intervention theory and method.* Reading, MA: Addison-Wesley.

Argyris, C., & Schon, D. (1974). *Theory in practice: Increasing professional effectiveness.* San Francisco: Jossey-Bass.

Argyris, C., & Schon, D. (1996). *Organizational learning II: Theory, method, and practice.* Reading, MA: Addison-Wesley.

Armenakis, A. A., & Bedeian, A. G. (1992). The role of metaphors in organizational change. *Group & Organization Management, 17*, 242-248.

Ascari, A., Rock, M., & Dutta, S. (1995). Reengineering and organizational change: Lessons from a comparative analysis of company experiences. *European Management Journal, 13*, 1-30.

Ashby, W. R. (1956). *An introduction to cybernetics.* London: Methuen.

Ashforth, B., & Lee, R. (1990). Defensive behavior in organizations. *Human Relations, 43*, 621-648.

Ashkenas, R., Ulrich, D., Jick, T., & Kerr, S. (1995). *The boundaryless organization: Breaking the chains of organizational structure.* San Francisco: Jossey-Bass.

Ashmos, D. P., & Huber, G. P. (1987). The system paradigm in organization theory: Correcting the record and suggesting the future. *Academy of Management Review, 12*, 607-621.

Astley, W., & Van de Ven, A. (1983). Central perspectives and debates in organization theory. *Administrative Science Quarterly, 28*, 245-273.

Astley, W., & Zammuto, R. (1992). Organization science, managers, and language games. *Organization Science, 3*, 443-460.

Austin, M. (1982). *Evaluating your agency's programs.* Beverly Hills, CA: Sage.

Bacharach, S. (1989). Organizational theories: Some criteria for evaluation. *Academy of Management Review, 14*, 496-515.

Bacharach, S. B., & Lawler, J. E. (1980). *Power and politics in organizations.* San Francisco: Jossey-Bass.

Bailyn, L. (1993). *Breaking the mould: Women, men and time in the new corporate world.* New York: Free Press.

Baird, L., & Meshulam, I. (1988). Managing two fits of strategic human resource management. *Academy of Management Review, 13*, 116-128.

Bamberger, P., & Phillips, B. (1991). Organizational environment and business strategy: Parallel versus conflicting influences on human resource strategy in the pharmaceutical industry. *Human Resource Management, 30*, 153-182.

Banta, D. (1995). Health care technology as a policy issue. In H. Banta, R. Battista, H. Gelband, & E. Jonsson (Eds.), *Health care technology and its assessment in eight countries.* Washington, DC: Office of Technology Assessment.

Barley, S. (1986). Technology as an occasion for structuring: Evidence from observations of CT scanners and the social order of radiology departments. *Administrative Science Quarterly, 31*, 78-108.

Barney, J. (1991). Firm resources and sustained competitive advantage. *Journal of Management, 17,* 99-120.

Baron, J., & Cook, K. (1992). Process and outcome perspectives on the distribution of rewards in organizations. *Administrative Science Quarterly, 37,* 191-197.

Baron, R. (1994). The physical environment: Effects on task performance, interpersonal relations, and job satisfaction. *Research in Organizational Behavior, 16,* 1-46.

Barrett, F., & Cooperrider, D. (1990). Generative metaphor intervention: A new approach for working with systems divided by conflict and caught in defensive perception. *Journal of Applied Behavioral Science, 26,* 219-239.

Bartlett, C., & Ghoshal, S. (1990). Matrix management: Not a structure, a frame of mind. *Harvard Business Review, 68*(4), 138-145.

Bartunek, J. M. (1984). Changing interpretive schemes and organizational restructuring: The example of a religious order. *Administrative Science Quarterly, 29,* 355-372.

Bartunek, J. (1993). The multiple cognitions and conflicts associated with second order organizational change. In J. K. Marnighan (Ed.), *Social psychology in organizations: Advances in theory and research* (pp. 322-349). Englewood Cliffs, NJ: Prentice Hall.

Bartunek, J., Gordon, J., & Weathersby, R. (1983). Developing "complicated understandings" in administrators. *Academy of Management Review, 8,* 273-284.

Bartunek, J., Lacey, C., & Wood, D. (1992). Social cognition in organizational change: An insider-outsider approach. *Journal of Applied Behavioral Science, 28,* 204-223.

Bartunek, J., & Louis, M. R. (1988). The interplay of organization development and transformation. *Research in Organizational Change and Development, 2,* 97-134.

Bartunek, J., & Louis, M. (1996). *Insider/outsider team research.* Thousand Oaks, CA: Sage.

Bartunek, J. (1990). *Creating alternative realities at work: The quality of work life experiment at FoodCom.* New York: Harper.

Bass, B., & Avolio, B. (1990). The implications of transactional and transformational leadership for individual, team, and organizational development. *Research in Organizational Change and Development, 4,* 231-272.

Baum, J. (1996). Organizational ecology. In S. Clegg, C. Hardy, & W. Nord (Eds.), *Handbook of organization studies* (pp. 77-114). London: Sage.

Becker, B., & Gerhart, B. (1996). The impact of human resource management on organizational performance: Progress and prospects. *Academy of Management Journal, 39,* 779-801.

Beckhard, R. (1969). *Organization development: Strategies and models.* Reading, MA: Addison-Wesley.

Beckhard, R., & Harris, R. (1977). *Organizational transitions: Managing complex change.* Reading, MA: Addison-Wesley.

Bedeian, A. (1987). Organization theory: Current controversies, issues, and directions. In C. Cooper & I. Robertson (Eds.), *International review of industrial and organizational psychology* (pp. 1-33). New York: Wiley.

Beer, M. (1980). *Organizational change and development—A systems view.* Santa Monica, CA: Goodyear.

Beer, M., & Eisenstat, R. (1996). Developing an organization capable of implementing strategy and learning. *Human Relations, 49,* 597-619.

Beer, M., & Eisenstat, R. (1997, August). *Organizational fitness profiling: A new diagnostic process that meets the criteria for an effective method of organizational diagnosis.* Paper prepared for the annual meeting of the Academy of Management, Boston.

Beer, S. (1985). *Diagnosing the system for organizations.* Chichester, UK: Wiley.

Benfari, R., & Knox, J. (1991). *Understanding your management style: Beyond the Meyers-Briggs Type Indicators.* Lexington, MA: Lexington Books.

Ben Zeev, N. (1993, September 29). One last chord and the race is on to the parking lot. *Haaretz,* p. B-9. (in Hebrew)

Berger, P., & Luckman, T. (1967). *The social construction of reality.* Garden City, NY: Doubleday.

Bernstein, W., & Burke, W. (1989). Modeling organization meaning systems. *Research in Organizational Change and Development, 3,* 117-159.

Bertalanffy, L. von (1968). *General system theory: Foundations, development, and applications.* New York: George Braziller.

Bettman, J., & Weitz, B. (1983). Attributions in the board room: Causal reasoning in corporate annual reports. *Administrative Science Quarterly, 28,* 165-183.

Beyer, J. (1992). Metaphors, misunderstandings, and mischief: A commentary. *Organization Science, 3,* 467-474.

Biasatti, L. L., & Martin, J. E. (1979). A measure of the quality of union-management relationships. *Journal of Applied Psychology, 64,* 387-390.

Black, A. (1983). Some factors influencing attitudes toward militancy, membership solidarity, and sanctions in a teachers' union. *Human Relations, 36,* 973-986.

Blackburn, R., & Rosen, B. (1993). Total quality and human resource management: Lessons learned from Baldrige award-wining companies. *Academy of Management Executive, 7*(3), 49-66.

Blake, R., & Mouton, J. (1964). *The managerial grid.* Houston, TX: Gulf.

Block, P. (1981). *Flawless consulting.* San Diego, CA: University Associates.

Block, R., Kleiner, M., Roomkin, M., & Salsburg, S. (1987). Industrial relations and the performance of the firm: An overview. In M. Kleiner, R. Block, M. Roomkin, & S. Salsburg (Eds.), *Human resources and the performance of the firm* (pp. 319-343). Madison, WI: Industrial Relations Research Association.

Bluedorn, A., Johnson, R., Cartwright, D., & Barringer, B. (1994). The interface and convergence of the strategic management and organizational environment domains. *Journal of Management, 20,* 201-262.

Bluedorn, A., & Keon, T. (1985). Precursors of employee turnover—A multiple-sample causal analysis. *Journal of Occupational Behavior, 6,* 259-271.

Bluedorn, A., & Lundgren, E. (1993). A culture-match perspective for strategic change. *Research in Organizational Change and Development, 7,* 137-179.

Bodenheimer, T. (1996). The HMO backlash—Righteous or reactionary? *New England Journal of Medicine, 335,* 1601-1604.

Bolman, L. G., & Deal, T. (1991). *Reframing organizations: Artistry, choice, and leadership.* San Francisco: Jossey-Bass.

Boss, R. W. (1989). *Organization development in health care.* Reading, MA: Addison-Wesley.

Boudreau, J. (1988). Utility analysis. In L. Dyer (Ed.), *Human resource management* (pp. 621-745). Washington, DC: Bureau of National Affairs.

Boudreau, J. (1991). Utility analysis for decisions in human resource management. In M. Dunnette & L. Hough (Eds.), *Handbook of industrial and organizational psychology* (2nd ed., Vol. 2, pp. 621-745). Palo Alto, CA: Consulting Psychologists Press.

Boulding, K. E. (1956). General system theory: The skeleton of science. *General Systems, 1,* 11-17.

Bourdieu, P. (1989). Social space and symbolic power. *Sociological Theory, 7,* 14-25.

Bourgeois, L. J., & Jemison, D. (1982). Analyzing corporate culture in its strategic context. *Exchange: The Organizational Behavior Teaching Journal, 7*(3), 37-41.

Bowen, D. (1977). Value dilemmas in organization development. *Journal of Applied Behavioral Science, 13,* 543-556.

Bowen, D., & Lawler, E. (1992). The empowerment of service workers: What, why, how, and when. *Sloan Management Review, 33*(3), 31-39.

Boyacigiller, N. A., & Adler, N. (1991). The parochial dinosaur: Organization science in a global context. *Academy of Management Review, 16,* 262-290.

Bradshaw-Camball, P. (1989). The implications of multiple perspectives on power for organization development. *Journal of Applied Behavioral Science, 25,* 1-34.

Brass, D., & Burkhardt, M. (1993). Potential power and power use: An investigation of structure and behavior. *Academy of Management Journal, 36,* 441-470.

Bromiley, P., & Cummings, L. (1995). Organizations with trust: Theory and measurement. In R. Bies, B. Sheppard, & R. Lewicki (Eds.), *Research in negotiations* (Vol. 5). Greenwich, CT: JAI.

Bryson, J. (1988). *Strategic planning for public and nonprofit organizations.* San Francisco: Jossey-Bass.

Buckley, W. (1967). *Sociology and modern systems theory.* Englewood Cliffs, NJ: Prentice Hall.

Buenger, V., Daft, R. L., Conlon, E. J., & Austin, J. (1996). Competing values in organizations: Contextual influences and structural consequences. *Organization Science, 7,* 557-576.

Buono, A. (1991, Summer). Managing strategic alliances: Organizational and human resource considerations. *Business in the Contemporary World,* pp. 92-101.

Buono, A., & Bowditch, J. (1990, Autumn). Ethical considerations in merger and acquisition management: A human resource perspective. *SAM Advanced Management Journal,* pp. 18-23.

Buono, T., & Bowditch, J. (1989). *The human side of mergers and acquisitions: Managing collisions between people, cultures, and organizations.* San Francisco: Jossey-Bass.

Burke, W. W. (1982). *Organization development.* Boston: Little, Brown.

Burke, W. W. (1994). Diagnostic models for organizational development. In A. Howard & Associates (Eds.), *Diagnosis for organizational change: Methods and models* (pp. 53-85). New York: Guilford.

Burke, W. W., Clark, L. P., & Koopman, C. (1984). Improve your OD project's chances of success. *Training and Development Journal, 38*(4), 62-68.

Burkhart, P., & Reuss, S. (1993). *Successful strategic planning: A guide for nonprofit agencies.* Newbury Park, CA: Sage.

Burns, T. (1961). Micropolitics: Mechanisms of institutional change. *Administrative Science Quarterly, 6,* 256-281.

Burns, T., & Stalker, G. M. (1961). *The management of innovation.* London: Tavistock.

Burrell, G. (1996). Normal science, paradigms, metaphors, discourses and genealogies of analysis. In S. Clegg, C. Hardy, & W. Nord (Eds.), *Handbook of organization studies* (pp. 642-659). London: Sage.

Burrell, G., & Morgan, G. (1979). *Sociological paradigms and organizational analysis.* London: Heinemann.

Butler, R., Astley, W., Hickson, D., Mallory, G., & Wilson, D. (1977-1978). Organizational power, politicking, and paralysis. *Organization and Administration Sciences, 8,* 45-60.

Calas, M., & Smircich, L. (1996). From "The Woman's" point of view: Feminist approaches to organization studies. In S. Clegg, C. Hardy, & W. Nord (Eds.), *Handbook of organization studies* (pp. 218-257). London: Sage.

Cameron, K. (1980). Critical questions in assessing organizational effectiveness. *Organizational Dynamics, 9,* 66-80.

Cameron, K. (1984). The effectiveness of ineffectiveness. *Research in Organizational Behavior, 6,* 235-285.

Cameron, K. (1994). Strategies for successful organizational downsizing. *Human Resource Management, 33,* 189-211.

Cameron, K., & Freeman, S. (1991). Cultural congruence: Strength and types: Relations to effectiveness. *Research in Organizational Change and Development, 5,* 23-58.

Cameron, K., Freeman, S., & Mishra, A. (1991). Best practices in white-collar downsizing: Managing contradictions. *Academy of Management Executive, 5*(3), 57-73.

Cameron, K., Kim, M. U., & Whetten, D. (1987). Organizational effects of decline and turbulence. *Administrative Science Quarterly, 32,* 222-240.

Cameron, K., & Quinn, R. E. (1988). Organizational paradox and transformation. In R. E. Quinn & K. Cameron (Eds.), *Paradox and transformation: Toward a theory of change in organization and management* (pp. 1-18). Cambridge, MA: Ballinger.

Cameron, K., Sutton, R., & Whetten, D. (1988). Issues in organizational decline. In K. Cameron, R. Sutton, & D. Whetten (Eds.), *Readings in organizational decline: Frameworks, research, and prescriptions* (pp. 3-19). Cambridge, MA: Ballinger.

Cameron, K., & Whetten, D. (1983). Models of the organizational life cycle: Applications to higher education. *Review of Higher Education, 6,* 269-299.

Campbell, D. (1977). On the nature of organizational effectiveness. In P. Goodman & J. Pennings (Eds.), *New perspectives on organizational effectiveness* (pp. 13-55). San Francisco: Jossey-Bass.

Canella, A., & Paetzold, R. (1994). [Dialogue:] Pfeffer's barriers to the advance of organizational science: A rejoinder. *Academy of Management Review, 19,* 331-341.

Capon, N., Farley, J., & Hulbert, J. (1994). Strategic planning and financial performance: More evidence. *Journal of Management Studies, 31,* 105-110.

Carlisle, H. (1974, July). A contingency approach to decentralization. *SAM Advanced Management Journal.*

Cartwright, S., & Cooper, C. (1993). The role of cultural compatibility in successful organizational marriage. *Academy of Management Executive, 7*(2), 57-70.

Cascio, W. (1993). Downsizing: What do we know? What have we learned? *Academy of Management Executive, 7*(1), 95-104.

Chaison, G. N., & Rose, J. B. (1991). The macroeconomics of union growth and decline. In G. Strauss, D. G. Gallagher, & J. Fiorito (Eds.), *The state of the unions* (pp. 3-47). Madison, WI: Industrial Relations Research Association.

Charon, J. (1995). *Symbolic interactionism: An introduction, an interpretation, an integration.* Englewood Cliffs, NJ: Prentice Hall.

Checkland, P. B. (1981). *Systems thinking, systems practice.* Chichester, UK: Wiley.

Checkland, P. B., & Scholes, J. (1990). *Soft systems methodology in action.* Chichester, UK: Wiley.

Cheng, C. (1996). Selected annotated bibliography of books on diversity within and among organizations. *Academy of Management Review, 21,* 580-582.

Chesler, M., Crawfoot, J., & Bryant, B. (1978). Power training: An alternative path to conflict management. *California Management Review, 21,* 84-91.

Chia, R. (1995). From modern to postmodern organizational analysis. *Organization Studies, 16,* 579-603.

Chia, R. (1996). Metaphors and metaphorization in organizational analysis: Thinking beyond the unthinkable. In D. Grant & C. Oswick (Eds.), *Metaphor and organizations* (pp. 127-146). London: Sage.

Child, J. (1977). *Organization: A guide to problems and practice.* New York: Harper & Row.

Chimezie, A. B., & Osigweh, Y. (Eds.). (1989). *Organizational science abroad: Constraints and perspectives.* New York: Plenum.

Chin, R., & Benne, K. (1985). General strategies for effecting changes in human systems. In W. Bennis, K. Benne, & R. Chin (Eds.), *The planning of change* (4th ed., pp. 22-45). New York: Holt, Rinehart & Winston.

Chisholm, R., & Elden, M. (1993). Features of emerging action research. *Human Relations, 46,* 275-298.

Church, A. H., & Burke, W. W. (1995). Practitioner attitudes about the field of organization development. *Research in Organization Change and Development, 8,* 1-46.

Churchill, N., & Lewis, V. (1983). The five stages of small business growth. *Harvard Business Review, 60*(3), 30-50.

Clark, J. McLouglin, I., Rose, H., & King, R. (1988). *The process of technological change: New technologies and social choice in the workplace.* Cambridge, UK: Cambridge University Press.

Clegg, S., Hardy, C., & Nord, W. (Eds.). (1996). *Handbook of organization studies.* London: Sage.

Clemons, E., Thatcher, M., & Row, M. (1995). Identifying sources of reengineering failures: A study of behavioral factors contributing to reengineering risk. *Journal of Management Information Systems, 12,* 9-26.

Cobb, A. (1984). An episodic model of power: Toward an integration of theory and research. *Academy of Management Review, 9,* 482-493.

Cobb, A. (1986). Political diagnosis: Applications of organizational development. *Academy of Management Review, 11,* 482-497.

Cobb, A., & Margulies, N. (1981). Organization development: A political perspective. *Academy of Management Review, 6,* 49-59.

Colwill, N. (1982). *The new partnership: Women and men in organizations.* Palo Alto, CA: Mayfield.

Connolly, E., Conlon, E., & Deutsch, S. (1980). Organizational effectiveness: A multi-constituency approach. *Academy of Management Review, 5,* 211-218.

Cooke, R., & Rousseau, D. (1988). Behavioral norms and expectations: A quantitative approach to the assessment of organizational culture. *Group & Organization Studies, 13,* 245-273.

Coombs, G. (1992). Organizational demography: Implications for the organization development practitioner. *Research in the Sociology of Organizations, 10,* 199-220.

Coombs, R., Knights, D., & Willmott, H. (1992). Culture, control, and competition: Towards a conceptual framework for the study of information technology in organizations. *Organization Studies, 13,* 51-72.

Cooper, R. (1989). Modernism, postmodernism and organizational analysis: The contribution of Jacques Derrida. *Organization Studies, 10,* 479-502.

Cowan, D. A. (1986). Developing a process model of problem recognition. *Academy of Management Review, 11,* 763-776.

Cowan, D. A. (1990). Developing a classification structure of organizational problems: An empirical investigation. *Academy of Management Journal, 33,* 366-390.

Cox, T. (1991). The multicultural organization. *Academy of Management Executive, 5*(3), 34-47.

Cranny, C. J., Smith, P., & Stone, E. (Eds.). (1992). *Job satisfaction: How people feel about their jobs and how it affects their performance.* New York: Lexington Books.

Cummings, T. G. (1993). Sociotechnical systems consultation. In R. T. Golembiewski (Ed.), *Handbook of organizational consultation* (pp. 129-136). New York: Dekker.

Cummings, T., & Worley, C. (1993). *Organization development and change* (5th ed.). St. Paul, MN: West.

Cusamano, M. (1994). The limits of "lean." *Sloan Management Review, 34*(Summer), 27-32.

Cyert, R. M., & March, J. G. (1963). *A behavioral theory of the firm.* Englewood Cliffs, NJ: Prentice Hall.

Daft, R. (1995). *Organization theory and design* (5th ed.). Minneapolis, MN: West.

Daft, R., & Weick, K. (1984). Toward a model of organizations as interpretive systems. *Academy of Management Review, 9,* 284-295.

Dalton, M. (1959). *Men who manage.* New York: Wiley.

D'Aveni, R. (1994). *Hypercompetition: Managing the dynamics of strategic maneuvering.* New York: Free Press.

D'Aveni, R., & MacMillian, I. (1990). Crisis and the content of managerial communications: A study of the focus of attention of top managers in surviving and failing firms. *Administrative Science Quarterly, 35,* 634-657.

Davenport, T. (1993). *Process innovation: Reengineering work through information technology.* Boston: Harvard Business School Press.

Davis, L., & Cherns, A. (1975). *The quality of working life* (Vols. 1 & 2). New York: Free Press.

Davis, S. (1984). *Managing corporate culture.* Cambridge, MA: Ballinger.

Davis, S., & Lawrence, P., with Kolodny, H., & Beer, M. (1977). *Matrix.* Reading, MA: Addison-Wesley.

Dean, J., & Sharfman, M. (1996). Does decision process matter? A study of strategic decision-making effectiveness. *Academy of Management Journal, 39,* 368-396.

Deephouse, D. (1996). Does isomorphism legitimate? *Academy of Management Journal, 39,* 1024-1039.

Delbecq, A., & Mills, P. (1985). Managerial practices that enhance innovation. *Organizational Dynamics, 14*(1), 24-34.

Deming, W. (1986). *Out of crisis.* Cambridge: MIT-CIAS.

Denison, D. (1996). What IS the difference between organizational culture and organizational climate? A native's point of view on a decade of paradigm wars. *Academy of Management Review, 21,* 619-654.

Denison, D., Hart, S., & Kahn, J. (1996). From chimneys to cross-functional teams: Developing and validating a diagnostic model. *Academy of Management Journal, 39,* 1005-1023.

Denison, D., & Mishra, A. (1995). Toward a theory of organizational culture and effectiveness. *Organization Science, 6,* 204-223.

Denison, D., & Spreitzer, G. (1991). Organization culture and organizational development: A competing values approach. *Research in Organizational Change and Development, 5,* 1-21.

DiMaggio, P., & Powell, W. (1983). The iron cage revisited: Institutional isomorphism and collective rationality in organizational fields. *American Sociological Review, 48,* 147-160.

Dodgson, M. (1993). Learning, trust, and technological collaboration. *Human Relations, 46,* 77-95.

Donaldson, L. (1985). *In defense of organizational theory: A reply to the critics.* Cambridge, UK: Cambridge University Press.

Donaldson, T., & Preston, L. (1995). The stakeholder theory of the corporation: Concepts, evidence, and implications. *Academy of Management Review, 20,* 85-92.

Dougherty, D. (1992). Interpretive barriers to successful product innovation in large firms. *Organization Science, 3,* 179-202.

The downsizing of America: The company as family, no more. (1996, March 4). *New York Times* [On-line]. Available: www.nytimes.com/downsize/glance.html.

Dunlop, J. T. (1958). *Industrial relations system.* New York: Holt, Rinehart & Winston.

Dunphy, D., & Stace, D. (1988). Transformational and coercive strategies for planned organizational change: Beyond the OD model. *Organization Studies, 9,* 317-334.

Dunphy, D., & Stace, D. (1993). The strategic management of corporate change. *Human Relations, 46,* 905-920.

Dutton, J., & Dukerich, J. (1991). Keeping an eye on the mirror: Image and identity in organizational adaptation. *Academy of Management Journal, 34,* 517-554.

Dutton, J., Dukerich, J., & Harquail, C. (1994). Organizational images and identification. *Administrative Science Quarterly, 39,* 239-263.

Eden, D. (1986). Team development: Quasi-experimental confirmation among combat companies. *Group & Organization Studies, 11,* 33-46.

Eden, D. (1990). *Pygmalion in management.* Lexington, MA: Lexington Books.

Eisenhardt, K., & Tabrizi, B. (1995). Accelerating adaptive processes: Product innovation in the global computer industry. *Administrative Science Quarterly, 40,* 84-110.

Eisenhardt, K., & Westcott, B. (1988). Paradoxical demands and the creation of excellence: The case of Just-in-Time manufacturing. In R. E. Quinn & K. Cameron (Eds.), *Paradox and transformation: Toward a theory of change in organization and management* (pp. 169-193). Cambridge, MA: Ballinger.

Eisenhardt, K., & Zbaracki, M. (1992). Strategic decision making. *Strategic Management Journal, 13,* 17-37.

Emery, F., & Trist, E. (1973). *Toward a social ecology.* New York: Plenum.

Enz, C. (1989). The measurement of perceived intraorganizational power: A multi-respondent perspective. *Organization Studies, 10,* 241-251.

Epstein, C. (1988). *Deceptive distinctions: Sex, gender, and the social order.* New Haven, CT: Yale University Press.

Farberman, H., & Perinbanayagam, R. (Eds.). (1985). *Studies in symbolic interaction (Foundations of interpretive sociology: Original essays in symbolic interaction)* (Suppl. 1). Greenwich, CT: JAI.

Ferguson, K. (1994). On bringing more theory, voices, and more politics into the study of organizations. *Organizations, 1,* 81-99.

Fiedler, F. E. (1967). *A theory of leadership effectiveness.* New York: McGraw-Hill.

Fiegenbaum, A. (1990). Prospect theory and the risk-return association: An empirical examination of 85 industries. *Journal of Economic Behavior and Organization, 14,* 187-203.

Fiegenbaum, A., Hart, S., & Schendel, D. (1996). Strategic reference point theory. *Strategic Management Journal, 17,* 216-236.

Finkelstein, S. (1992). Power in top management teams: Dimensions, measurement and validation. *Academy of Management Journal, 35,* 505-538.

Fishbein, M., & Ajzen, I. (1975). *Beliefs, attitudes, intention, and behavior.* Reading, MA: Addison-Wesley.

Fisher, C., & Locke, E. (1992). The new look in job-satisfaction research and theory. In C. J. Cranny, P. Smith, & E. Stone (Eds.), *Job satisfaction: How people feel about their jobs and how it affects their performance* (pp. 165-194). New York: Lexington Books.

Fitz-Enz, J. (1980). Quantifying the human resources function. *Personnel*(AMACOM), pp. 41-52.

Fitz-Enz, J. (1984). *How to measure human resources management.* New York: McGraw-Hill.

Flamholtz, E. (1986). *How to make the transition from an entrepreneurship to a professionally managed firm.* San Francisco: Jossey-Bass.

Flanagan, J. (1954). The critical incident technique. *Psychological Bulletin, 51,* 327-358.

Florida, R., & Kenney, M. (1991). Transplanted organizations: The transplantation of Japanese industrial organization to the U.S. *American Sociological Review, 56,* 381-398.

Floyd, S., & Woolridge, B. (1992). Managing strategic consensus: The foundation of effective implementation. *Academy of Management Executive, 6*(4), 27-39.

Fombrun, C., Tichy, N., & DeVanna, M. (Eds.). (1984). *Strategic human resource management.* New York: Wiley.

Forrester, J. W. (1961). *Industrial dynamics.* Cambridge: MIT Press.

Forrester, J. W. (1975). *Collected papers of Jay W. Forrester.* Portland, OR: Productivity Press.

Fottler, M. (1981). Is management really generic? *Academy of Management Review, 6,* 1-12.

Fottler, M. (1987). Health care organizational performance: Present and future research. *Journal of Management, 13,* 367-391.

Fox, A. (1974). *Beyond contract: Work, power and trust relations.* London: Faber and Faber.

French, J., & Raven, B. (1959). The bases of social power. In D. Cartwright (Ed.), *Studies in social power*. Ann Arbor: University of Michigan Press.

French, W., & Bell, C. (1995). *Organization development* (5th ed.). Englewood Cliffs, NJ: Prentice Hall.

Frenk, J. (1994). Dimensions of health systems reform. *Health Policy, 27,* 19-34.

Friedlander, F., & Pickle, H. (1967). Components of effectiveness of small organizations. *Administrative Science Quarterly, 13,* 289-304.

Frost, P., & Egri, C. (1991). The political process of innovation. *Research in Organizational Behavior, 13,* 229-295.

Frost, P., Moore, L., Louis, M. R., Lundberg, C., & Martin, J. (Eds.). (1991). *Reframing organizational culture.* Newbury Park, CA: Sage.

Fry, L. W., & Smith, D. A. (1987). Congruence, contingency, and theory building. *Academy of Management Review, 12,* 117-132.

Fry, R. (1982). Improving trustee, administrator, and physician collaboration through open systems planning. In M. Plovnick, R. Fry, & W. Burke (Eds.), *Organization development: Exercises, cases and readings* (pp. 282-292). Boston: Little, Brown.

Fulk, J., Schmitz, J., & Steinfeld, C. (1990). A social influence model of technology use. In J. Fulk & C. Steinfeld (Eds.), *Organizations and communication technology* (pp. 117-142). Newbury Park, CA: Sage.

Gaertner, G. H., & Ramnarayan, S. (1983). Organizational effectiveness: An alternative perspective. *Academy of Management Review, 8,* 97-107.

Galbraith, J. (1977). *Organization design.* Reading, MA: Addison-Wesley.

Galbraith, J., Lawler, E., & Associates. (1993). *Organizing for the future: The new logic for managing complex systems.* San Francisco: Jossey-Bass.

Gamson, W. (1968). *Power and discontent.* Homewood, IL: Dorsey.

Gamson, W., Fireman, B., & Rytina, S. (1982). *Encounters with unjust authority.* Homewood, IL: Dorsey.

Gersick, C. (1991). Revolutionary change theories: A multilevel exploration of the punctuated equilibrium paradigm. *Academy of Management Review, 16,* 10-36.

Ghani, U. (1996). Holistic reengineering. *Management Review, 85*(1), 62-63.

Ghoshal, S., & Bartlett, C. (1990). The multinational corporation as an interorganizational network. *Academy of Management Review, 15,* 603-625.

Giddens, A. (1984). *The constitutions of society: Outline of the theory of structuration.* Berkeley: University of California Press.

Gilfillan, D. P. (1980). Characteristics of middle range organizational theories and their implications for operationalization and testing. In C. C. Pinder & L. F. Moore (Eds.), *Middle range theory in the study of organizations* (pp. 45-60). Boston: Martinus Nijhoff.

Gioia, D., & Pitre, E. (1990). Multiparadigm perspectives on theory building. *Academy of Management Review, 15,* 584-602.

Glanz, E. F., & Dailey, L. K. (1992). Benchmarking. *Human Resource Management, 31,* 9-20.

Glaser, B., & Strauss, A. (1967). *The discovery of grounded theory: Strategies for qualitative research.* Chicago: Aldine.

Goffman, E. (1959). *The presentation of self in everyday life.* Garden City, NY: Doubleday.

Goldratt, E. M. (1990). *The haystack syndrome.* New York: North River Press.

Golembiewski, R. T., & Eddy, W. (1978). *Organization development in public administration.* New York: Dekker.

Goodman, P. S. (1977). Social comparison processes. In B. Staw & G. Salancik (Eds.), *New directions in organizational behavior* (pp. 1-13). Chicago: St. Clair.

Goodman, P. S., & Pennings, J. (1980). Critical issues in assessing organizational effectiveness. In E. Lawler, D. Nadler, & C. Cammann (Eds.), *Organizational assessment* (pp. 185-215). New York: Wiley.

Goodstadt, B., & Kipnis, D. (1970). Situational influences on the use of power. *Journal of Applied Psychology, 54,* 201-207.

Gordon, J. (1996). *Organizational behavior: A diagnostic approach* (5th ed.). Upper Saddle River, NJ: Prentice Hall.

Grant, R. M., Shani, R., & Krishnan, R. (1994). TQM challenge to management theory and practice. *Sloan Management Review, 34*(Winter), 25-37.

Gray, B. (1989). *Collaborating: Finding common grounds for multiparty problems.* San Francisco: Jossey-Bass.

Gray, B., & Ariss, S. (1985). Politics and strategic change across organizational life cycles. *Academy of Management Review, 10,* 707-723.

Greening, D. W., & Gray, B. (1994). Testing a model of organizational response to social and political issues. *Academy of Management Journal, 37,* 467-498.

Greenlagh, L. (1982). Organizational decline. *Research in the Sociology of Organizations, 1,* 231-276.

Greenlagh, L. (1986). Managing conflict. *Sloan Management Review, 26*(Summer), 45-51.

Gregory, K. (1983). Native-view paradigms: Multiple cultures and culture conflicts in organizations. *Administrative Science Quarterly, 28,* 359-376.

Greiner, L. (1972). Evolution and revolution as organizations grow. *Harvard Business Review, 50*(4), 37-46.

Greiner, L., & Schein, V. (1988). *Power and organization development: Mobilizing power to implement change.* Reading, MA: Addison-Wesley.

Gresov, C. (1989). Exploring fit and misfit with multiple contingencies. *Administrative Science Quarterly, 34,* 431-453.

Grey, C., & Mitev, N. (1995). Re-engineering organizations: A critical appraisal. *Personnel Review, 24,* 6-18.

Griffen, R. (1991). Effects of work redesign on employee perceptions, attitudes, and behaviors: A long-term investigation. *Academy of Management Journal, 34,* 425-435.

Griner, P., Mayers, D., & McKiernan, P. (1988). *Sharpbenders: The dynamics of releasing corporate potential.* London: Basil Blackwell.

Grover, V., Jeong, S., Kettinger, W., & Teng, J. (1995). The implementation of business process reengineering. *Journal of Management Information Systems, 12,* 109-144.

Guzzo, R. A., & Dickson, M. (1996). Teams in organizations: Recent research on performance and effectiveness. *Annual Review of Psychology, 46,* 307-338.

Guzzo, R., & Salas, E. (Eds.). (1995). *Team effectiveness and decison making in organizations.* San Francisco: Jossey-Bass.

Guzzo, R., & Shea, G. (1993). Group performance and intergroup relations in organizations. In M. Dunnett & L. Hough (Eds.), *Handbook of industrial and organizational psychology* (Vol. 3, pp. 269-314). Palo Alto, CA: Consulting Psychologists Press.

Hackman, J. R. (1987). The design of work teams. In J. Lorsch (Ed.), *Handbook of organizational behavior* (pp. 315-342). Englewood Cliffs, NJ: Prentice Hall.

Hackman, J. R. (Ed.). (1991). *Groups that work (and those that don't).* San Francisco: Jossey-Bass.

Hackman, J. R., & Wageman, R. (1995). Total quality management: Empirical, conceptual, and practical issues. *Administrative Science Quarterly, 40,* 309-342.

Hackman, R., & Oldham, G. (1980). *Work redesign.* Reading, MA: Addison-Wesley.

Halachmi, A. (1995). Reengineering and public management: Some issues and considerations. *International Review of Administrative Sciences, 61,* 329-341.

Hall, G., Rosenthal, J., & Wade, J. (1993). How to make reengineering really work. *Harvard Business Review, 71*(6), 119-131.

Hall, R. (1987). *Organizations: Structure, process, and outcomes* (4th ed.). Englewood Cliffs, NJ: Prentice Hall.

Ham, C., Robinson, R., & Benzeval, M. (1990). *Health check: Health care reform in an international context.* London: King's Fund Institute.

Hamel, G., & Prahalad, C. K. (1994). *Competing for the future.* Boston: Harvard Business School Press.

Hammer, M. (1990). Reengineering work: Don't automate, obliterate. *Harvard Business Review, 68*(4), 104-112.

Hammer, M., & Champy, J. (1993). *Reengineering the corporation: A manifesto for business revolution.* New York: Harper.

Handy, C. (1995). *The age of paradox.* Boston: Harvard Business School Press.

Hannan, M., & Freeman, J. (1984). Structural inertia and organizational change. *American Sociological Review, 49*, 149-164.

Harari, O. (1993). Ten reasons why TQM doesn't work. *Management Review, 82*(1), 33-38.

Harrison, M. (1991). The politics of consulting for organizational change. *Knowledge and Policy, 4*, 92-107.

Harrison, M. (1994). *Diagnosing organizations: Methods, models, and processes* (2nd ed.). Thousand Oaks, CA: Sage.

Harrison, M. (1995). *Implementation of reform in the hospital sector: Physicians and health system reforms in four countries.* Tel Hashomer, Israel: Israel National Institute for Health Policy and Health Services Research.

Harrison, M., & Phillips, B. (1991). Strategic decision making: An integrative explanation. *Research in the Sociology of Organizations, 9*, 319-358.

Hassard, J. (1991). Multiple paradigms and organizational analysis. *Organization Studies, 12*, 275-299.

Hausser, C., Pecorella, P., & Wissler, A. (1975). *Survey guided development: A manual for consultants.* Ann Arbor: University of Michigan, Institute for Social Research.

Haverman, H. (1992). Between a rock and a hard place: Organizational change and performance under conditions of fundamental environmental transformation. *Administrative Science Quarterly, 37*, 48-75.

Hayes, R., & Abernathy, W. (1980). Managing our way to economic decline. *Harvard Business Review, 58*, 67-77.

Hearn, J., & Parkin, P. (1983). Gender and organizations: A selective review and a critique of a neglected area. *Organization Studies, 4*, 219-242.

Hedberg, B. (1980). How organizations learn and unlearn. In P. Nystrom & W. Starbuck (Eds.), *Handbook of organizational design* (Vol. 1, pp. 3-27). New York: Oxford University Press.

Hedley, B. (1977). Strategy and the "business portfolio." *Long Range Planning, 10.*

Heilpern, J., & Nadler, D. (1992). Implementing total quality management: A process of cultural change. In D. Nadler, J. Heilpern, R. Shaw & Associates (Eds.), *Organizational architecture: Designs for changing organizations* (pp. 137-153). San Francisco: Jossey-Bass.

Heneman, H. G., III, Schwab, D., Fossum, J., & Dyer, L. (1989). *Personnel/Human Resource Management* (4th ed.). Homewood, IL: Irwin.

Herman, J., Morris, L., & Fitz-Gibbon, C. (1987). *Evaluator's handbook—Program evaluation kit* (Vol. 1). Beverly Hills, CA: Sage.

Hickson, D., Butler, R., Cray, G., Mallory, G., & Wilson, D. (1986). *Top decisions: Strategic decision making in organizations.* San Francisco: Jossey-Bass.

Hickson, D., Hinings, C., Schneck, R., & Pennings, J. (1971). A strategic contingencies theory of intraorganizational power. *Administrative Science Quarterly, 16,* 216-229.

Hill, M., Mann, L., & Wearing, A. J. (1996). The effects of attitude, subjective norm and self-efficacy on intention to benchmark: A comparison between managers with experience and no experience in benchmarking. *Journal of Organizational Behavior, 17,* 313-327.

Hill, R. (1993). When the going gets rough: A Baldrige award winner on the line. *Academy of Management Executive, 7*(3), 75-79.

Hirschorn, L., & Gilmore, T. (1992). The new boundaries of the "boundaryless" company. *Harvard Business Review, 70*(3), 104-115.

Hoffman, J. (1974). Nothing can be done: Social dimensions of the treatment of stroke patients in a general hospital. *Urban Life and Culture, 3,* 50-70.

Hofstede, G. (1980). *Culture's consequences.* Beverly Hills, CA: Sage.

Hofstede, G. (1993). Cultural constraints in management theories. *Academy of Management Executive, 7*(1), 81-94.

Hofstede, G. (1996). An American in Paris: The influence of nationality on organization theories. *Organization Studies, 17,* 525-537.

Hofstede, G., Neuijen, B., Ohayv, D., & Sanders, G. (1990). Measuring organizational cultures: A qualitative and quantitative study across twenty cases. *Administrative Science Quarterly, 35,* 286-316.

House, R., Rousseau, D., & Thomas-Hunt, M. (1995). The meso paradigm: A framework for the integration of micro and macro organizational behavior. *Research in Organizational Behavior, 17,* 71-114.

How to identify and enhance core competencies. (1994). *Planning Review, 22*(6), 24-26.

Howard, A. (1994). Diagnostic perspectives in an era of organizational change. In A. Howard & Associates (Eds.), *Diagnosing for organizational change: Methods and models.* (pp. 3-27). New York: Guilford.

Howard, A., & Associates (Eds.). (1994). *Diagnosing for organizational change: Methods and models.* New York: Guilford.

Howe, M. A. (1989). Using imagery to facilitate organizational development and change. *Group & Organization Studies, 14,* 70-82.

Hrebiniak, L. G., & Joyce, W. F. (1985). Organizational adaptation: Strategic choice and environmental determinism. *Administrative Science Quarterly, 30,* 336-349.

Huber, G., Miller, C., & Glick, W. (1991). Developing more encompassing theories about organizations: The centralization-effectiveness relationship as an example. *Organization Science, 1,* 11-40.

Huff, A. S., & Schwenk, C. (1990). Bias and sense-making in good times and bad. In A. S. Huff (Ed.), *Managing strategic thought* (pp. 89-109). New York: Wiley.

Hunter, J., Schmidt, F., & Jackson, G. (1982). *Meta-analysis—Cumulating research findings across studies.* Newbury Park, CA: Sage.

Huse, E., & Cummings, T. (1985). *Organization development and change* (3rd ed.). St. Paul, MN: West.

Huselid, M. (1995). The impact of human resource management practices on turnover, productivity, and corporate financial performance. *Academy of Management Journal, 38,* 635-672.

Huselid, M., & Becker, B. (1997). The impact of high performance work systems, implementation effectiveness, and alignment with strategy on shareholder wealth. *Academy of Management Proceedings,* pp. 144-148.

Huselid, M., Jackson, S., & Schuler, R. (1997). Technical and strategic human resource management effectiveness as determinants of firm performance. *Academy of Management Journal, 40,* 171-188.

Ibarra, H. (1993). Network centrality, power, and innovation involvement: Determinants of technical and administrative roles. *Academy of Management Journal, 36,* 471-501.

Ironson, G. (1992). Job stress and health. In C. J. Cranny, P. Smith, & E. Stone (Eds.), *Job satisfaction: How people feel about their jobs and how it affects their performance* (pp. 219-239). New York: Lexington Books.

Izraeli, D. N. (1975). The middle manager and tactics of power expansion—A case study. *Sloan Management Review, 16,* 56-70.

Jackson, M. C. (1992). *System methodology for the management sciences.* New York: Plenum.

Jackson, M. C. (1995). Beyond the fads: System thinking for managers. *Systems Research, 12,* 25-42.

Jackson, S. E., & Schuler, R. (1995). Understanding human resource management in the context of organizations and their environments. *Annual Review of Psychology, 46,* 237-264.

Jaeger, A. (1986). Organization development and national culture: Where's the fit? *Academy of Management Review, 11,* 178-190.

Jamieson, D., & O'Mara, J. (1991). *Managing workforce 2000: Gaining the diversity advantage.* San Francisco: Jossey-Bass.

Janssens, M., Brett, J., & Smith, F. (1995). Confirmatory cross-cultural research: Testing the viability of a corporation-wide safety policy. *Academy of Management Journal, 38,* 364-382.

Jayaram, G. (1976). Open systems planning. In W. Bennis, K. Benne, R. Chin, & K. Corey (Eds.), *The planning of change* (3rd ed., pp. 275-283). New York: Holt, Rinehart & Winston.

Jenkins, C. (1983). Resource mobilization theory and the study of social movements. *Annual Review of Sociology, 9,* 527-553.

Jimenez, J., Escalante, J., & Aguirre-Vazquez, J. (1997). Application of the search conference methodology to planning in higher education. *System Practices, 10,* 255-271.

Johnson, P. C., & Cooperrider, D. L. (1991). Finding a path with heart: Global social change organizations and their challenge for the field of organization development. *Research in Organizational Change and Development, 5,* 223-284.

Judd, C., Smith, E., & Kidder, L. (1991). *Research methods in social relations* (6th ed.). New York: Holt, Rinehart & Winston.

Kakabadse, A., & Parker, C. (Eds.). (1984). *Power politics and organizations: A behavioral science view.* Chichester, UK: Wiley.

Kaminka, S. (1983). *On some characteristics of plants with successful labor relations* (Report No. 83-10). Tel Aviv, Israel: Tel-Aviv University, Institute for Social and Labour Research.

Kanfer, R. (1990). Motivation theory and industrial/organizational psychology. In M. D. Dunnette & L. M. Hough (Eds.), *Handbook of industrial dnd organizational psychology* (2nd ed., Vol. 1, pp. 75-170). Palo Alto, CA: Consulting Psychologists Press.

Kanfer, R. (1992). Work motivation: New directions in theory and research. In C. L. Cooper & I. T. Robertson (Eds.), *International review of industrial and organizational psychology* (Vol. 7, pp. 1-53). New York: Wiley.

Kanter, R. (1977). *Men and women of the corporation.* New York: Basic Books.

Kanter, R. (1979). Power failure in management circuits. *Harvard Business Review, 57*(4), 65-75.

Kanter, R. (1983). *The change masters: Innovation for productivity in the American corporation.* New York: Simon & Schuster.

Kanter, R., & Brinkerhoff, D. (1981). Organizational performance. *Annual Review of Sociology, 7,* 321-349.

Kanter, R., Stein, B., & Jick, T. (1992). *The challenge of organizational change: How companies experience it and leaders guide it.* New York: Macmillan.

Kanter, R. M., & Summers, D. (1987). Doing well while doing good: Dilemmas of performance measurement in nonprofit organizations and the need for a multiple-constituency approach.

In W. Powell (Ed.), *The nonprofit sector: A research handbook* (pp. 154-166). New Haven, CT: Yale University Press.

Kaplan, R., & Norton, D. (1992). The balanced scorecard: Measures that drive success. *Harvard Business Review, 70*(5), 71-79.

Kaplan, R., & Norton, D. (1993). Putting the balanced scorecard to work. *Harvard Business Review, 71*(5), 134-147.

Katz, D., & Kahn, R. (1978). *The social psychology of organizations* (2nd ed.). New York: Wiley.

Katz, H. C., Kochan, T., & Weber, M. (1985). Assessing the effects of industrial relations systems and efforts to improve the quality of working life on organizational effectiveness. *Academy of Management Journal, 28,* 509-526.

Keen, P. (1990). Telecommunications and organizational choice. In J. Fulk & C. Steinfeld (Eds.), *Organizations and communication technology* (pp. 295-312). Newbury Park, CA: Sage.

Kelly, J. (1992). Does job re-design theory explain job re-design outcomes? *Human Relations, 45,* 753-774.

Kenis, P., & Schneider, V. (1991). Policy networks and policy analysis: Scrutinizing a new analytical toolbox. In B. Marin & R. Mayntz (Eds.), *Policy networks: Empirical evidence and theoretical considerations* (pp. 25-59). Boulder, CO: Westview.

Kerr, J., & Slocum, J. (1987). Managing corporate culture through reward systems. *Academy of Management Executive, 1*(5), 98-108.

Kerr, S. (1995). On the folly of rewarding A, while hoping for B. *Academy of Management Executive, 9*(1), 7-14.

Ketchen, D., Combs, J., Russell, C., Shook, C., Dean, M., Runge, J., Lohrke, F., Naumann, S., Haptsonstahl, D., Baker, R., Beckstein, B., Handler, C., Honig, H., & Lamoureux, S. (1997). Organizational configurations and performance: A meta-analysis. *Academy of Management Journal, 40,* 223-240.

Ketchen, D., Thomas, J., & Snow, C. (1993). Organizational configurations and performance: A comparison of theoretical approaches. *Academy of Management Journal, 36,* 1278-1313.

Khandwalla, P. (1977). *The design of organizations.* New York: Harcourt Brace Jovanovich.

Khaneman, D., Slovic, P., & Tversky, A. (Eds.). (1982). *Judgement under uncertainty: Heuristics and biases.* London: Cambridge University Press.

Kidder, T. (1981). *The soul of a new machine.* Boston: Little, Brown.

Kilduff, M. (1993). Deconstructing organizations. *Academy of Management Review, 18,* 13-31.

Kilmann, R. (1977). *Social systems design: Normative theory and the MAPS Design Technology.* New York: Elsevier North-Holland.

Kilmann, R. (1985). Five steps for closing culture gaps. In R. Kilmann, M. Saxton, R. Serpa, & Associates (Eds.), *Gaining control of the corporate culture* (pp. 351-369). San Francisco: Jossey-Bass.

Kilmann, R., Covin, T., & Associates. (1988). *Corporate transformations: Revitalizing organizations for a competitive world.* San Francisco: Jossey-Bass.

Kilmann, R., & Saxton, M. (1981). *Kilmann-Saxton Culture-Gap Survey.* Tuxedo, NY: Organization Design Consultants (Xicom Inc., Distrib.).

Kilmann, R., Saxton, M., Serpa, R., & Associates (1985). *Gaining control of the corporate culture.* San Francisco: Jossey-Bass.

Kitay, J., & Marchington, M. (1996). A review and critique of workplace industrial relations typologies. *Human Relations, 49,* 1263-1290.

Klein, K., & Sorra, J. S. (1996). The challenge of innovation implementation. *Academy of Management Review, 21,* 1055-1080.

Kline, S. J. (1995). *Conceptual foundations for multidisciplinary thinking.* Stanford, CA: Stanford University Press.

Kluger, A., & DeNisi, A. (1996). The effects of feedback intervention on performance: A historical review, meta-analysis, and preliminary feedback intervention theory. *Psychological Bulletin, 119*, 254-284.

Kochan, T. (1980). *Collective bargaining and industrial relations.* Homewood, IL: Irwin.

Kochan, T., & McKersie, R. (1992). Human resources, organizational governance, and public policy: Lessons from a decade of experimentation. In T. Kochan & M. Useem (Eds.), *Transforming organizations* (pp. 169-187). New York: Oxford University Press.

Kolb, D., & Frohman, A. (1970). An organization development approach to consulting. *Sloan Management Review, 12*, 51-65.

Kolodny, H., & Sternberg, T. (1986). The change process of innovative work designs: New design and redesign in Sweden, Canada, and the United States. *Journal of Applied Behavioral Science, 22*, 287-301.

Kotter, J. P. (1978). *Organizational dynamics: Diagnosing and intervention.* Reading, MA: Addison-Wesley.

Kotter, J. P. (1995). Leading change: Why transformation efforts fail. *Harvard Business Review, 73*(2), 59-67.

Kotter, J., & Heskett, J. (1992). *Corporate culture and performance.* New York: Free Press.

Kotter, J., & Schlesinger, L. (1979). Choosing strategies for change. *Harvard Business Review, 57*(2), 106-114.

Kowalski, R. M. (1996). Complaints and complaining: Functions, antecedents, and consequences. *Psychological Bulletin, 119*, 179-196.

Kramer, R., & Tyler, T. (Eds.). (1995). *Trust in organizations.* Thousand Oaks, CA: Sage.

Krantz, J. (1985). Group processes under conditions of organizational decline. *Journal of Applied Behavioral Science, 21*, 1-18.

Krauss, H. (1995). Attitude and the prediction of behavior: A meta-analysis. *Personality and Social Psychology Bulletin, 21*, 58-75.

Kunda, G. (1992). *Engineering culture: Control and commitment in a high-tech corporation.* Philadelphia: Temple University Press.

Lammers, C. (1990). Sociology of organizations around the globe: Similarities and differences between American, British, French, German, and Dutch brands. *Organization Studies, 11*, 179-205.

Larwood, L. (1992). Don't struggle to scope those metaphors yet. *Group & Organization Management, 17*, 249-254.

Lasswell, H. (1936). *Politics: Who gets what, when, how.* New York: McGraw-Hill.

Lawler, E. (1977). Reward systems. In J. Hackman & J. Suttle (Eds.), *Improving life at work: Behavioral science approaches to organizational change* (pp. 166-226). Santa Monica, CA: Goodyear.

Lawler, E. (1986). *High involvement management: Participative strategies for improving organizational performance.* San Francisco: Jossey-Bass.

Lawler, E. (1990). *Strategic pay: Aligning organizational strategy and pay systems.* San Francisco: Jossey-Bass.

Lawler, E., & Bacharach, S. (1983). Political action and alignments in organizations. *Research in the Sociology of Organizations, 2*, 83-108.

Lawler, E., & Drexler, J. (1980). Participative research: The subject as co-researcher. In E. Lawler, D. Nadler, & C. Cammann (Eds.), *Organizational assessment* (pp. 535-547). New York: Wiley.

Lawler, E., & Galbraith, J. (1994). Avoiding the corporate dinosaur syndrome. *Organizational Dynamics, 23*(Autumn), 5-17.

Lawler, E., Mohrman, S., & Ledford, G. (1992). *Employee involvement and total quality management: Practices and results in Fortune 1000 companies.* San Francisco: Jossey-Bass.

Lawler, E., Nadler, D., & Cammann, C. (Eds.). (1980). *Organizational assessment.* New York: Wiley.

Lawler, E., Nadler, D., & Mirvis, P. (1983). Organizational change and the conduct of organizational research. In S. Seashore, E. Lawler, P. Mirvis, & C. Cammann (Eds.), *Assessing organizational change* (pp. 19-48). New York: Wiley.

Lawler, E., & Rhode, J. (1976). *Information and control in organizations.* Santa Monica, CA: Goodyear.

Lawrence, P., & Lorsch, J. (1969). *Organization and environment.* Homewood, IL: Irwin.

Leach, J. (1979). The organizational history: A consulting analysis and intervention tool. In G. Gore & R. Wright (Eds.), *The academic consultant connection* (pp. 62-69). Dubuque, IA: Kendall/Hunt.

Leana, C., & Feldman, D. (1992). *Coping with job loss.* New York: Lexington Books.

Lee, A. (1991). Integrating positivist and interpretive approaches to organizational research. *Organization Science, 2,* 342-365.

Lefkowitz, J. (1994). Sex-related differences in job attitudes and dispositional variables: Now you see them . . . *Academy of Management Journal, 37,* 323-349.

Lengnick-Hall, C., & Lengnick-Hall, M. (1988). Strategic human resources management: A review of the literature and a proposed typology. *Academy of Management Review, 13,* 454-470.

Levitt, B., & March, J. (1988). Organizational learning. *Annual Review of Sociology, 14,* 319-340.

Lewin, A., & Minton, J. W. (1986). Determining organizational effectiveness: Another look, and an agenda for research. *Management Science, 32*(5), 514-538.

Lewin, K. (1951). *Field theory in social sciences.* New York: Harper.

Lewin, K. (1958). Group decision making and social change. In E. E. Maccoby, T. M. Newcomb, & E. L. Hartley (Eds.), *Readings in social psychology* (3rd ed., pp. 197-211). New York: Holt, Rinehart & Winston.

Likert, R. (1967). *The human organization.* New York: McGraw-Hill.

Lindbloom, C. (1959). The science of muddling through. *Public Administration Review, 19,* 79-88.

London, M., & Beatty, R. (1993). 360-degree feedback as a competitive advantage. *Human Resource Management, 32*(2-3), 353-372.

Louis, M., & Sutton, R. (1991). Switching cognitive gears: From habits of mind to active thinking. *Human Relations, 44,* 55-76.

Low, M. (1991). Performance and between-group goal consensus. In J. Wall & L. Janch (Eds.), *Academy of Management best papers 1991* (pp. 178-182). Ada, OH: Academy of Management.

Lowstedt, J. (1993). Organizing frameworks in emerging organizations: A cognitive approach to the analysis of change. *Human Relations, 46,* 501-526.

Lubatkin, M., & Chatterjee, S. (1994). Extending modern portfolio theory into the domain of corporate diversification: Does it apply? *Academy of Management Journal, 37,* 109-136.

Lubatkin, M., & Lane, P. (1996). Psst . . . the merger mavens still have it wrong. *Academy of Management Executive, 10*(2), 21-37.

Lundberg, C. C. (1989). On organizational learning: Implications and opportunities for expanding organizational development. *Research in Organizational Change and Development, 3,* 61-82.

Lundberg, C. (1990). Innovative organization development procedures. Part 2: Surfacing organizational culture. *Journal of Managerial Psychology, 5*(4), 19-26.

Macy, B. A., & Izumi, H. (1993). Organizational change, design, and work innovations: A meta-analysis of 131 North American field studies, 1961-1991. *Research in Organizational Change and Development, 7,* 235-313.

Mainero, L. (1986). Coping with powerlessness: The relationship of gender and job dependency to empowerment-strategy usage. *Administrative Science Quarterly, 31,* 633-653.

Maines, D., & Charlton, J. (1985). The negotiated order approach to the analysis of social organization. In H. Farberman & R. Perinbanayagam (Eds.), *Studies in symbolic interaction (Foundations of interpretive sociology: Original essays in symbolic interaction)* (Suppl. 1, pp. 263-270). Greenwich, CT: JAI.

Manganelli, R., & Klein, M. (1994). *The reengineering handbook: A step-by-step guide to business transformation.* New York: AMACOM.

Manzini, A. (1988). *Organizational diagnosis: A practical approach to company problem solving and growth.* New York: AMACOM.

March, J., & Sproull, L. (1990). Technology, management, and competitive advantage. In P. Goodman, L. Sproull, & Associates (Eds.), *Technology and organizations* (pp. 144-173). San Francisco: Jossey-Bass.

March, J., & Weissinger-Baylon, J. (1986). *Ambiguity and command: Organizational perspectives on military decision making.* Marshfield, MA: Pitman.

Margulies, N., & Adams, J. D. (Eds.). (1982). *Organization development in health care organizations.* Reading, MA: Addison-Wesley.

Marshak, R. (1993). Managing the metaphors of change. *Organizational Dynamics, 22*(Summer), 44-56.

Martin, J. (1992). *Cultures in organizations: Three perspectives.* New York: Oxford University Press.

Martin, J., & Frost, P. (1996). The organizational culture war games: A struggle for intellectual dominance. In S. Clegg, C. Hardy, & W. Nord (Eds.), *Handbook of organization studies* (pp. 599-621). London: Sage.

Mason, D. (1994). Scenario-based planning: Decision model for the learning organization. *Planning Review, 22*(6), 7-12.

Mayes, B., & Allen, R. (1977). Toward a definition of organizational politics. *Academy of Management Review, 2,* 672-678.

McAllister, D. (1995). Affect- and cognition-based trust as foundations for interpersonal cooperation in organizations. *Academy of Management Journal, 38,* 24-59.

McDaniel, R., Thomas, J., Ashmos, D., & Smith, J. (1987). The use of decision analysis for organizational design: Reorganizing a community hospital. *Journal of Applied Behavioral Science, 22,* 337-350.

McGregor, D. (1960). *The human side of enterprise.* New York: McGraw-Hill.

McKersie, R., & Walton, R. (1991). Organizational change. In M. S. Morton (Ed.), *The corporation of the 1990s: Information technology and organizational transformation* (pp. 244-277). New York: Oxford University Press.

McKinley, W. (1993). Organizational decline and adaptation: Theoretical controversies. *Organization Science, 4,* 1-9.

McMahan, G. C., & Woodman, R. W. (1992). The current practice of organization development within the firm: A survey of large industrial corporations. *Group & Organization Management, 17,* 117-134.

Mealiea, L., & Lee, D. (1979). An alternative to macro-micro contingency theories: An integrative model. *Academy of Management Review, 4,* 333-346.

Meyer, A., Tsui, A., & Hinnings, C. (1993). Configurational approaches to organizational analysis. *Academy of Management Journal, 36,* 1175-1195.

Meyer, J., & Rowan, B. (1977). Institutionalized organizations: Formal structure as myth and ceremony. *American Journal of Sociology, 83,* 340-363.

Meyer, M., & Zucker, L. (1989). *Permanently failing organizations.* Newbury Park, CA: Sage.

Meyerson, D., & Lewis, S. (1992, August). *Cultural tolerance of ambiguity and its organizational consequences.* Paper presented at the annual meeting of the Academy of Management, Las Vegas, Nevada.

Miles, M., & Huberman, A. M. (1994). *Qualitative data analysis: An expanded sourcebook of new methods* (2nd ed.). Thousand Oaks, CA: Sage.

Miles, R. E., & Snow, C. (1978). *Organizational strategy, structure, and process.* New York: McGraw-Hill.

Miles, R. E., & Snow, C. (1986). Organizations: New concepts for new forms. *California Management Review, 28,* 62-73.

Miller, D. (1992). Environmental fit versus internal fit. *Management Science, 38,* 159-178.

Miller, D., & Friesen, P. (1984a). A longitudinal study of the corporate life cycle. *Management Science, 30,* 1161-1183.

Miller, D., & Friesen, P. (1984b). *Organizations: A quantum view.* New York: Prentice Hall.

Miller, D., & Mintzberg, H. (1983). The case for configuration. In G. Morgan (Ed.), *Beyond method: Strategies for social research* (pp. 57-73). Beverly Hills, CA: Sage.

Miller, J. G. (1978). *Living systems.* New York: McGraw-Hill.

Miller, J. G., & Miller, J. C. (1991). A living systems analysis of organizational pathology. *Behavioral Science, 36,* 239-252.

Milliken, F., & Martins, L. (1996). Searching for common threads: Understanding the multiple effects of diversity in organizational groups. *Academy of Management Review, 21,* 402-433.

Millman, J., Von Glinow, M., & Nathan, M. (1991). Organizational life cycles and strategic international human resource management in multinational companies: Implications for congruence theories. *Academy of Management Review, 16,* 318-339.

Mills, A. (1988). Organization, gender, and culture. *Organization Studies, 9,* 351-369.

Mills, A., & Tancred, P. (Eds.). (1992). *Gendering organizational analysis.* Newbury Park, CA: Sage.

Mills, D. Q. (1991). *Rebirth of the corporation.* New York: Wiley.

Mintzberg, H. (1979). *The structuring of organizations.* Englewood Cliffs, NJ: Prentice Hall.

Mintzberg, H. (1983). *Power in and around organizations.* Englewood Cliffs, NJ: Prentice Hall.

Mintzberg, H. (1984). Power and organizational life cycles. *Academy of Management Review, 9,* 207-224.

Mintzberg, H. (1987). Crafting strategy. *Harvard Business Review, 67*(4), 66-75.

Mintzberg, H. (1994). *The rise and fall of strategic planning.* New York: Free Press.

Mintzberg, H., & McHugh, A. (1985). Strategy formation in adhocracy. *Administrative Science Quarterly, 30,* 160-197.

Mintzberg, H., Quinn, J. B., & Voyer, J. (1995). *The strategy process.* San Francisco: Jossey-Bass.

Mintzberg, H., Raisinghani, D., & Theoret, T. (1976). The structure of "unstructured" decision processes. *Administration Science Quarterly, 21,* 246-275.

Mintzberg, H., & Westley, F. (1992, Winter). Cycles of organizational change. *Strategic Management Journal, 13*(Special issue), 17-38.

Mirvis, P., & Berg, D. (1977). *Failures in organization development and change: Cases and essays for learning.* New York: Wiley.

Mitroff, I. I., Mason, R. O., & Pearson, C. M. (1994). *Framebreak: The radical redesign of American business.* San Francisco: Jossey-Bass.

Moch, M., Cammann, C., & Cooke, R. (1983). Organizational structure: Measuring the degree of influence. In S. Seashore, E. Lawler, P. Mirvis, & C. Cammann (Eds.), *Assessing organizational change* (pp. 177-202). New York: Wiley.

Moch, M., & Bartunek, J. (1987). First-order, second-order, and third-order change and organization development interventions: A cognitive approach. *Journal of Applied Behavioral Science, 23,* 483-500.

Moch, M., Feather, J., & Fitzgibbons, D. (1983). Conceptualizing and measuring the relational structure of organizations. In S. Seashore, E. Lawler, P. Mirvis, & C. Cammann (Eds.), *Assessing organizational change* (pp. 203-228). New York: Wiley.

Moos, R., & Schaefer, J. (1987). Evaluating health care work settings: A holistic conceptual framework. *Psychology and Health, 1,* 97-122.

Morgan, G. (1986). *Images of organizations.* Newbury Park, CA: Sage.

Morgan, G. (1996). An afterword: Is there anything more to be said about metaphor. In D. Grant & C. Oswick (Eds.), *Metaphor and organizations* (pp. 227-240). London: Sage.

Morgan, G. (1997, August). *Metaphor: The DNA of organization and management.* Paper presented at the annual meeting of the Academy of Management, Boston.

Morrione, T. (1985). Situated interaction. In H. Farberman & R. Perinbanayagam (Eds.), *Studies in symbolic interaction (Foundations of interpretive sociology: Original essays in symbolic interaction)* (Suppl. 1, pp. 161-192). Greenwich, CT: JAI.

Morris, W. L., & Sashkin, M. (1976). *Organizational behavior in action.* St. Paul, MN: West.

Morton, M. (Ed.). (1991). *The corporation of the 1990's: Information technology and organizational transformation.* New York: Oxford.

Motamedi, K., & Cummings, T. G. (1984). Transorganizational development: Developing relations among organizations. In D. D. Warrick (Ed.), *Contemporary organizational development.* Glenview, IL: Scott, Foresman.

Nadler, D. (1977). *Feedback and organization development: Using data-based methods.* Reading, MA: Addison-Wesley.

Nadler, D. A. (1980). The role of models in organizational assessment. In E. E. Lawler, D. A. Nadler, & C. Cammann (Eds.), *Organizational assessment: Perspectives on measurement of organizational behavior and quality of work life* (pp. 119-131). New York: Wiley.

Nadler, D. (1988). Organizational frame bending: Types of change in the complex organization. In R. Kilmann, T. Covin, & Associates, *Corporate transformations: Revitalizing organizations for a competitive world* (pp. 66-83). San Francisco: Jossey-Bass.

Nadler, D., Gerstein, M., & Shaw, R., & Associates. (1992). *Organizational architecture: Designs for changing organizations.* San Francisco: Jossey-Bass.

Nadler, D., & Lawler, E. (1983). Quality of work life: Perspectives and directions. *Organizational Dynamics, 11*(Winter), 20-30.

Nadler, D., Mirvis, P., & Cammann, C. (1976). The ongoing feedback system: Experimenting with a new management tool. *Organizational Dynamics, 4,* 63-80.

Nadler, D., Shaw, R., Walton, A. E., & Associates. (1995). *Discontinuous change: Leading organizational transformation.* San Francisco: Jossey-Bass.

Nadler, D., & Tushman, M. (1980a). A congruence model for diagnosing organizational behavior. In E. Lawler, D. Nadler, & C. Cammann (Eds.), *Organizational assessment* (pp. 261-278). New York: Wiley.

Nadler, D., & Tushman, M. (1980b, Autumn). A model for diagnosing organizational behavior. *Organizational Dynamics, 9,* 35-51.

Nadler, D., & Tushman, M. (1989). Leadership for organizational change. In A. M. Mohrman, S. A. Mohrman, G. E. Ledford, Jr., T. Cummings, & E. Lawler (Eds.), *Large scale organizational change* (pp. 100-119). San Francisco: Jossey-Bass.

Naisbit, J., & Aburdene, P. (1990). *Megatrends 2000.* New York: Avon.

Nay, J. N., et al. (1976). If you don't care where you get to, then it doesn't matter which way you go. In C. C. Abt (Ed.), *The evaluation of social programs* (pp. 97-98). Beverly Hills, CA: Sage.

Nayyar, P. (1992). Performance effects of three foci in service firms. *Academy of Management Journal, 35,* 985-1009.

Nees, D., & Greiner, L. (1985, Winter). Seeing behind the look-alike management consultants. *Organizational Dynamics, 13,* 68-79.

Neilsen, E. H. (1984). *Becoming an OD practitioner.* Englewood Cliffs, NJ: Prentice Hall.

Nelson, R. E. (1988). Social network analysis as an intervention tool. *Group & Organization Studies, 13,* 39-58.

Nelson, R., & Mathews, K. M. (1991). Cause maps and social network analysis in organizational diagnosis. *Journal of Applied Behavioral Science, 27,* 379-397.

Nemetz, P., & Christensen, S. (1996). Toward a theory of communicative interactions in culturally diverse workgroups. *Academy of Management Review, 21,* 434-462.

The new industrial relations. (1981, May 11). *Business Week,* pp. 85-93.

Newman, G. A., Edwards, J. E., & Raju, N. S. (1989). Organizational development interventions: A meta-analysis of their effects on satisfaction and other attitudes. *Personnel Psychology, 42,* 461-489.

Newton, T. (1996). Postmodernism and action. *Organization, 3,* 7-29.

Nicholson, N. (1977). Absence behavior and attendance motivation: A conceptual synthesis. *Journal of Management Studies, 14,* 231-253.

Nightingale, O., & Toulouse, J. (1977). Toward a multi-level congruence theory of organization. *Administrative Science Quarterly, 22,* 264-280.

Nkomo, S. (1992). The emperor has no clothes: Rewriting "race in organizations." *Academy of Management Review, 17,* 487-513.

Nord, W., & Tucker, S. (1987). *Implementing routine and radical innovations.* Lexington, MA: Lexington Books.

Nutt, P. (1979). Calling out and calling off the dogs: Managerial diagnosis in public service organizations. *Academy of Management Review, 4,* 203-214.

Nystrom, P., & Starbuck, W. (1984). To avoid organizational crisis: Unlearn. *Organizational Dynamics, 12*(Spring), 53-65.

Ohlott, P., Ruderman, M., & McCauley, C. (1994). Gender differences in managers' developmental job experiences. *Academy of Management Journal, 37,* 46-67.

O'Leary-Kelly, A., Martocchio, J., & Frink, D. (1994). A review of the influence of group goals on group performance. *Academy of Management Journal, 37,* 1285-1301.

O'Reilly, B. (1992, January 28). Preparing for leaner times. *Fortune,* pp. 40-47.

O'Reilly, C., Chatman, J., & Caldwell, D. (1991). People and organizational culture: A profile comparison approach to assessing person-organization fit. *Academy of Management Journal, 34,* 487-516.

Organization for Economic Cooperation and Development (OECD). (1987). *Financing and delivering health care.* Paris: Author.

Organization for Economic Cooperation and Development (OECD). (1992). *The reform of health care: A comparative analysis of seven OECD countries* (Health Policy Studies No. 2). Paris: Author.

Organization for Economic Cooperation and Development (OECD). (1993). *OECD health systems. Facts and trends, 1960-1991* (Health Policy Studies No. 3, Vol. 1). Paris: Author.

Orton, J., & Weick, K. (1990). Loosely coupled systems: A reconceptualization. *Academy of Management Review, 15,* 203-223.

Osborn, R., & Baughn, C. (1993). Societal considerations in the global technological development of economic institutions: The role of strategic alliances. *Research in the Sociology of Organizations, 11,* 113-150.

Osterman, P. (1994). How common is workplace transformation and who adopts it? *Industrial and Labor Relations Review, 47,* 173-188.

Ostroff, C. (1993). Relationship between person-environment congruence and organizational effectiveness. *Group and Organization Management, 18,* 103-122.

Ovretveit, J. (1992). *Health service quality: An introduction to quality methods for health services.* Oxford, UK: Basil Blackwell.

Palmer, D., Jennings, P. D., & Zhou, X. (1993). Late adoption of the multidivisional form by large U.S. corporations: Institutional, political, and economic accounts. *Administrative Science Quarterly, 38,* 100-131.

Palmer, I., & Dunford, R. M. (1996). Conflicting uses of metaphors: Reconceptualizing their use in the field of organizational change. *Academy of Management Review, 21,* 691-718.

Parker, M. (1995). Critique in the name of what? Postmodern and critical approaches to organization. *Organization Studies, 16,* 553-564.

Parker, M., & McHugh, G. (1991). Five texts in search of an author: A response to John Hassard's "Multiple paradigms and organizational analysis." *Organization Studies, 12,* 451-456.

Pascale, T. (1984). Perspectives on strategy: The real story behind Honda's success. *California Management Review, 26,* 47-72.

Passmore, W. A. (1988). *Designing effective organizations.* New York: Wiley.

Passmore, W. J., Petee, J., & Bastian, R. (1986). Sociotechnical systems in health care: A field experiment. *Journal of Applied Behavioral Science, 22,* 329-339.

Patton, M. Q. (1986). *Utilization-focused evaluation* (2nd ed.). Beverly Hills, CA: Sage.

Pearson, C., & Mitroff, I. (1993). From crisis prone to crisis prepared: A framework for crisis management. *Academy of Management Executive, 7*(1), 48-60.

Pennings, J. (1992). Structural contingency theory: A reappraisal. *Research in Organizational Behavior, 14,* 267-309.

Pennings, J., & Harianto, F. (1992). Technological networking and innovation implementation. *Organization Science, 3,* 356-382.

Perrow, C. (1994). [Dialogue:] Pfeffer slips! *Academy of Management Review, 19,* 191-194.

Peters, T., & Waterman, R. (1982). *In pursuit of excellence.* New York: Harper & Row.

Peterson, R., & Tracy, L. (1976). A behavioural model of problem-solving in labour negotiations. *British Journal of Industrial Relations, 14,* 159-173.

Peterson, R., & Tracy, L. (1977). Testing a behavioral theory model of labor negotiations. *Industrial Relations, 16,* 35-50.

Pettigrew, A. (1975). Towards a political theory of organizational intervention. *Human Relations, 28,* 191-208.

Pettigrew, A. (1985). Examining change in the long-term context of culture and politics. In J. Pennings & Associates (Eds.), *Organizational strategy and change* (pp. 290-310). San Francisco: Jossey-Bass.

Pettigrew, A., Ferlie, E., & McKee, L. (1992). *Shaping strategic change in large organizations—The case of the National Health Service.* London: Sage.

Pfeffer, J. (1981a). Management as symbolic action: The creation and management of organizational paradigms. *Research in Organizational Behavior, 3,* 1-52.

Pfeffer, J. (1981b). *Power in organizations.* Marshfield, MA: Pitman.

Pfeffer, J. (1992). *Managing with power: Politics and influence in organizations.* Boston: Harvard Business School Press.

Pfeffer, J. (1993). Barriers to the advancement of organizational science: Paradigm development as a dependent variable. *Academy of Management Review, 18,* 559-620.

Pfeffer, J., & Salancik, G. (1978). *The external control of organizations.* New York: Harper & Row.

Phillips, B. (1991). Significant events: An applied sociologist learns to play the corporate game. *Sociological Practice Review, 1,* 59-67.

Plovnick, M., Fry, R., & Burke, W. (1982). *Organization development: Exercises, cases, and readings.* Boston: Little, Brown.

Pondy, L. (1967). Organizational conflict: Concepts and models. *Administrative Science Quarterly, 12,* 296-320.

Poole, M. (1986). *Industrial relations: Origins and patterns of national diversity.* London: Routledge.

Porras, J. I. (1987). *Stream analysis.* Reading, MA: Addison-Wesley.

Porras, J. I., & Robertson, P. (1992). Organization development: Theory, practice, and research. In M. D. Dunnette & L. M. Hough (Eds.), *Handbook of industrial and organizational psychology* (2nd ed., Vol. 3, pp. 719-822). Palo Alto, CA: Consulting Psychologists Press.

Porras, J., & Silver, R. (1991). Organization development and transformation. *Annual Review of Psychology, 42,* 51-78.

Porter, L., Allen, R., & Angle, H. (1981). The politics of upward influence in organizations. *Research in Organizational Behavior, 3,* 109-150.

Porter, M. (1980). *Competitive strategy: Techniques for analyzing industries and competitors.* New York: Free Press.

Porter, M. (1985). *Competitive advantage.* New York: Free Press.

Porter, M. (1996). What is strategy? *Harvard Business Review, 74*(6), 61-78.

Powell, W. (1990). Neither market nor hierarchy: Network forms of organization. *Research in Organizational Behavior, 12,* 295-336.

Prahalad, C. K., & Hamel, G. (1990). The core competencies of the corporation. *Harvard Business Review, 68*(3), 79-91.

Pressman, J., & Wildavsky, A. (1973). *Implementation.* Berkeley: University of California Press.

Price, J., & Mueller, C. (1986). *Handbook of organizational measurement.* Marshfield, MA: Pitman.

Pruitt, D. (1981). *Negotiation behavior.* New York: Academic Press.

Purser, R., & Passmore, W. (1992). Organizing for learning. *Research in Organizational Change and Development, 6,* 37-114.

Quinn, J. B. (1977). Strategic goals: Process and politics. *Sloan Management Review, 19,* 21-37.

Quinn, J. B. (1980). *Strategies for change: Logical incrementalism.* Homewood, IL: Irwin.

Quinn, J. B. (1985). Managing innovation: Controlled chaos. *Harvard Business Review, 63*(3), 73-84.

Quinn, R. E. (1988). *Beyond rational management.* San Francisco: Jossey-Bass.

Quinn, R. E., & Cameron, K. (1983). Organizational life cycles and shifting criteria of effectiveness: Some preliminary evidence. *Management Science, 29,* 33-51.

Quinn, R. E., & Cameron, K. (Eds.). (1988). *Paradox and transformation: Toward a theory of change in organization and management.* Cambridge, MA: Ballinger.

Quinn, R. E., & McGrath, H. R. (1982). Moving beyond the single solution perspective: The competing values approach as a diagnostic tool. *Journal of Applied Behavioral Science, 18,* 463-472.

Quinn, R. E., & Rohrbaugh, J. (1983). A spatial model of effectiveness criteria: Toward a competing values approach to organizational analysis. *Management Science, 29,* 363-377.

Quinn, R. E., & Spreitzer, G. (1991). The psychometrics of the competing values culture instrument and an analysis of the impact of organizational culture on quality of life. *Research in Organizational Change and Development, 5,* 115-142.

Raffel, M. W. (Ed.). (1984). *Comparative health system: Descriptive analysis of fourteen national health systems.* University Park: Pennsylvania State University Press.

Ramirez, I. L., & Bartunek, J. (1989). The multiple realities and experiences of organization development consultation in health care. *Journal of Organizational Change Management,* 2(1), 40-57.

Rashford, N., & Coghlan, D. (1994). *The dynamics of organizational levels: A change framework for managers and consultants.* Reading, MA: Addison-Wesley.

Reed, M. (1992). *The sociology of organizations.* Hemmel Hempstead, UK: Harvester Wheatsheaf.

Reed, M. (1996). Organizational theorizing: A historically contested terrain. In S. Clegg, C. Hardy, & W. Nord (Eds.), *Handbook of organization studies* (pp. 31-57). London: Sage.

Rice, A. K. (1963). *The enterprise and its environment: A system theory of management and organization.* London: Tavistock.

Ridgeway, C. (1997). Interaction and the conservation of gender inequality. *American Sociological Review, 62,* 218-235.

Robbins, S. P. (1978). Conflict management and conflict resolution are not synonymous terms. *California Management Review, 21,* 67-75.

Roberts, N. (1986). Organizational power styles: Collective and competitive power under varying organizational conditions. *Journal of Applied Behavioral Science, 22,* 443-458.

Robertson, P. J., Roberts, D. R., & Porras, J. I. (1993). An evaluation of a model of planned organizational change: Evidence from a meta-analysis. *Research in Organizational Change and Development, 7,* 1-39.

Rogers, E. (1995). *Diffusion of innovations* (3rd ed.). New York: Free Press.

Romanelli, E., & Tushman, M. (1994). Organizational transformation as punctuated equilibrium: An empirical test. *Academy of Management Journal, 37,* 1141-1166.

Rosenthal, M., & Frenkel, M. (Eds.). (1992). *Health care systems and their patients.* Boulder, CO: Westview.

Rossi, P., & Freeman, H. (1993). *Evaluation: A systematic approach* (5th ed.). Newbury Park, CA: Sage.

Rousseau, D. (1985). Issues of level in organizational research: Multi-level and cross-level perspectives. *Research in Organizational Behavior, 7,* 1-37.

Rousseau, D. (1990a). Assessing organizational culture: The case for multiple methods. In B. Schneider (Ed.), *Climate and culture* (pp. 153-192). San Francisco: Jossey-Bass.

Rousseau, D. (1990b). Normative beliefs in fund-raising organizations: Linking culture to organizational performance and individual responses. *Group & Organization Studies, 15,* 448-460.

Rousseau, D. (1997). Organizational behavior in the new organizational era. *Annual Review of Psychology, 48,* 515-546.

Rubenstein, D., & Woodman, R. (1984). Spiderman and the Burma Raiders: Collateral organization theory in action. *Journal of Applied Behavioral Science, 20,* 1-21.

Sackmann, S. (1989). The role of metaphors in organization transformation. *Human Relations, 42,* 463-485.

Sackmann, S. (1992). Cultures and subcultures: An analysis of organizational knowledge. *Administrative Science Quarterly, 37,* 140-161.

Sankar, Y. (1991, November). Implementing information technology: A managerial audit for planning change. *Journal of Systems Management, 15,* 32-37.

Sashkin, M., & Burke, W. (1990). Understanding and assessing organizational leadership. In K. Clark & M. Clark (Eds.), *Measures of leadership* (pp. 297-325). West Orange, NJ: Leadership Library of America.

Sathe, V. (1985). *Culture and related corporate realities.* Homewood, IL: Irwin.

Savage, G., Nix, T., Whitehead, C., & Blair, J. (1991). Strategies for assessing and managing organizational stakeholders. *Academy of Management Executive, 5*(2), 61-75.

Sayles, L. (1979). *Leadership.* New York: McGraw-Hill.

Schaffer, R. (1988). *The breakthrough strategy: Using short-term successes to build the high performance organization.* New York: HarperBusiness.

Schein, E. (1971). The individual, the organization, and the career: A conceptual scheme. *Journal of Applied Behavioral Science, 7*, 401-426.

Schein, E. (1985). *Organizational culture and leadership.* San Francisco: Jossey-Bass.

Schein, E. (1988). *Process consultation: Its role in organization development* (2nd ed.). Reading, MA: Addison-Wesley.

Schein, E. H. (1993). Models of consultation: What do organizations of the 1990's need? In R. Golembiewski (Ed.), *Handbook of organizational consultation* (pp. 653-661). New York: Marcel Dekker.

Schein, E. (1994). Cultures in organizations: Three perspectives [Book review]. *Administrative Science Quarterly, 39*, 339-342.

Schieber, G., Poullier, J., & Greenwald, L. (1994). Health systems performance in OECD countries, 1980-1992. *Health Affairs, 13*, 100-113.

Schilit, W., & Locke, E. (1982). A study of upward influence in organizations. *Administrative Science Quarterly, 27*, 304-316.

Schlesinger, L., & Heskett, J. (1991). The service-driven service company. *Harvard Business Review, 69*(5), 71-81.

Schneider, B. (1985). Organizational behavior. *Annual Review of Psychology, 36*, 573-611.

Schneier, C., Shaw, D., & Beatty, R. (1991). Performance measurement and management: A tool for strategy execution. *Human Resource Management, 30*, 279-301.

Schon, D. (1983). *The reflective practitioner: How professionals think in action.* New York: Basic Books.

Schon, D. (1993). Generative metaphor: A perspective on problem-setting in social policy. In A. Ortony (Ed.), *Metaphor and thought* (pp. 137-163). New York: Cambridge University Press.

Schon, D., & Rein, M. (1994). *Frame reflection: Toward the resolution of intractable controversies.* New York: Basic Books.

Schuler, R., & MacMillan, I. (1984). Gaining competitive advantage through human resource management practices. *Human Resource Management, 23*, 241-255.

Schultz, M., & Hatch, M. (1996). Living with multiple paradigms: The case of paradigm interplay in organizational culture studies. *Academy of Management Review, 21*, 529-557.

Schwartz, H., & Davis, S. M. (1981). Matching corporate culture and business strategy. *Organizational Dynamics, 10*(Summer), 30-48.

Schwenk, C. (1995). Strategic decision making. *Journal of Management, 21*, 471-493.

Scott, B. (1971). *Stages of corporate development—Part 1* (HBS Case No. 9-371-294). Boston: Harvard Business School Case Services.

Scott, J. (1991). *Social network analysis: A handbook.* Newbury Park, CA: Sage.

Scott, K. D., Bishop, J., & Casino, L. (1997, August). *A partial test of Hackman's (1987) normative model of group effectiveness.* Paper presented at the annual meeting of the Academy of Management, Boston.

Scott, S., & Bruce, R. (1994). Determinants of innovative behavior: A path model of individual innovation in the workplace. *Academy of Management Journal, 37*, 580-607.

Scott, W. R. (1987). The adolescence of institutional theory. *Administrative Science Quarterly, 32*, 493-511.

Scott, W. R. (1992). *Organizations: Rational, natural, and open systems* (3rd ed.). Englewood Cliffs, NJ: Prentice Hall.

Seashore, S., Lawler, E., Mirvis, P., & Cammann, C. (Eds.). (1983). *Assessing organizational change.* New York: Wiley.

Seedhouse, D. (Ed.). (1995). *Reforming health care: The philosophy and practice of international health reform.* Chichester, UK: Wiley.

Senge, P. (1990). *The fifth discipline: The art and practice of the learning organization.* New York: Doubleday.

Shea, G. (1986). Quality circles: The danger of bottled change. *Sloan Management Review, 26*(Spring), 33-46.

Shenhav, Y. (1995). From chaos to systems: The engineering foundations of organization theory, 1879-1932. *Administrative Science Quarterly, 40,* 557-585.

Sheridan, J. (1992). Organizational culture and employee retention. *Academy of Management Review, 5,* 1036-1056.

Shirom, A. (1980). On the dimensionality of the attitudinal militancy of local union officers. *Journal of Occupational Behavior, 1,* 285-296.

Shirom, A. (1983). Toward a theory of organizational development interventions in unionized work settings. *Human Relations, 36,* 743-764.

Shirom, A. (1993). A diagnostic approach to labor relations in organizations. *Research in the Sociology of Organizations, 12,* 211-243.

Shirom, A. (1994). The system perspective in labor relations: Toward a new model. *Advances in Industrial and Labor Relations, 6,* 37-62.

Short, J., & Venkatraman, N. (1992). Beyond business process redesign: Redefining Baxter's business network. *Sloan Management Review, 34*(Fall), 7-21.

Shrivastava, P., & Mitroff, I. I. (1984). Enhancing organizational research utilization: The role of decision makers' assumptions. *Academy of Management Review, 9,* 18-26.

Shuval, J. T. (1991). Political processes in health care: A case study of Israel. *Research in the Sociology of Health Care, 9,* 275-304.

Siler-Wells, G. (1987). An implementation model for health system reform. *Social Science and Medicine, 24,* 821-832.

Silverman, D. (1970). *The theory of organizations: A sociological perspective.* London: Heinemann.

Singh, J., Tucker, D., & House, R. (1986). Organizational legitimacy and the liability of newness. *Administrative Science Quarterly, 31,* 171-193.

Sitkin, S., & Roth, N. (1993). Explaining the limited effectiveness of legalistic "remedies" for trust/distrust. *Organization Science, 4,* 367-392.

Slappendel, C. (1996). Perspectives on innovation in organizations. *Organization Studies, 17,* 107-129.

Smircich, L. (1983). Concepts of culture and organizational analysis. *Administrative Science Quarterly, 28,* 339-358.

Smircich, L., & Stubbart, C. (1985). Strategic management in an enacted world. *Academy of Management Review, 10,* 724-736.

Smith, G. F. (1995). Classifying managerial problems: An empirical study of definitional content. *Journal of Management Studies, 32,* 679-706.

Smith, K. G., Smith, K. A., Olian, J., Sims, H., O'Bannon, D., & Scully, J. (1994). Top management team demography and process: The role of social integration and communication. *Administrative Science Quarterly, 39,* 412-438.

Smith, P. (1992). In pursuit of happiness: Why study general job satisfaction. In C. J. Cranny, P. Smith, & E. Stone (Eds.), *Job satisfaction: How people feel about their jobs and how it affects their performance* (pp. 5-20). New York: Lexington Books.

Spanier-Golan, F. (1993). *Investigation of activities of quality circles in an industrial plant.* Unpublished master's thesis, Department of Sociology and Anthropology, Bar-Ilan University, Ramat-Gan, Israel. (In Hebrew with English abstract)

Sparrow, P., Schuler, R., & Jackson, S. (1994). Convergence or divergence: Human resource practices and policies for competitive advantage worldwide. *International Journal of Human Resource Management, 5,* 267-299.

Spreitzer, G. (1996). Social structural characteristics of psychological empowerment. *Academy of Management Journal, 39,* 483-504.

Sproull, L., & Goodman, P. (1990). Technology and organizations: Integration and opportunities. In P. Goodman, L. Sproull, & Associates. *Technology and organizations* (pp. 254-266). San Francisco: Jossey-Bass.

Starbuck, W., Greve, A., & Hedberg, B. (1978). Responding to crisis. *Journal of Business Administration, 9,* 111-137.

Starbuck, W., & Nystrom, P. (1986). Why the world needs organisational design. *Journal of General Management, 6,* 3-17.

Staw, B. M. (1975). Attribution of the "causes" of performance: A general alternative interpretation of cross-sectional research on organizations. *Organizational Behavior and Human Performance, 13,* 414-432.

Staw, B., Sandelands, L., & Dutton, J. (1981). Threat-rigidity effects in organizational behavior: A multi-level analysis. *Administrative Science Quarterly, 26,* 501-524.

Stebbins, M. W., & Shani, A. B. (1989). Organization design: Beyond the Mafia model. *Organizational Dynamics, 17,* 18-30.

Steel, R., & Jennings, K. (1992). Quality improvement technologies for the 90s: New directions for research and theory. *Research in Organizational Change and Development, 6,* 1-36.

Stein, B., & Kanter, E. R. (1980). Building the parallel organization: Creating mechanisms for permanent quality of work life. *Journal of Applied Behavioral Science, 16,* 371-388.

Stewart, J. (1984). *Managing a successful business turnaround.* New York: American Management Association.

Stone, D., & Colella, A. (1996). A model of factors affecting the treatment of disabled individuals in organizations. *Academy of Management Review, 21,* 352-401.

Strauss, A., Schatzman, L., Ehrlich, D., Boeker, R., & Sabshin, M. (1963). The hospital and its negotiated order. In E. Friedson (Ed.), *The hospital in modern society* (pp. 147-169). Glencoe, IL: Free Press.

Strauss, G. (1977). Managerial practices. In J. Hackman & T. Suttle (Eds.), *Improving life at work* (pp. 297-363). Santa Monica, CA: Goodyear.

Strauss, G. (1982). Workers' participation in management: An international perspective. *Research in Organizational Behavior, 4,* 173-265.

Strebel, P. (1996). Why do employees resist change? *Harvard Business Review, 74*(3), 86-94.

Survey: Management consultancy. (1997, March 22). *Economist,* pp. 1-22.

Susman, G. I. (1981). Planned change: Prospects for the 1980s. *Management Science, 27,* 139-154.

Sutton, R. (1990). Organizational decline processes: A social psychological perspective. *Research in Organizational Behavior, 12,* 205-253.

Taylor, J., & Bowers, D. (1972). *Survey of organizations: A machine scored standardized questionnaire instrument.* Ann Arbor: University of Michigan, Institute for Social Research.

Taylor, S. E. (1991). Asymmetrical effects of positive and negative events: The mobilization-minimization hypothesis. *Psychological Bulletin, 110,* 67-85.

Tett, R. P., Meyer, J. P., & Roese, N. J. (1994). Applications of meta-analysis: 1987-1992. *International Review of Industrial and Organizational Psychology, 9,* 71-112.

Thach, L., & Woodman, R. (1994). Organizational change and information technology: Managing on the edge of cyberspace. *Organizational Dynamics, 23,* 30-46.

Thomas, C. (1994a). Learning from imaging the years ahead. *Planning Review, 22*(6), 6-10, 44.

Thomas, C. (1994b). Scenario planning at a finance and insurance company. *Planning Review, 22*(6), 11.

Thomas, K., & Velthouse, B. (1990). Cognitive elements of empowerment: An "interpretive" model of intrinsic task motivation. *Academy of Management Review, 15,* 666-681.

Thomas, R. (1992a). Organizational change and decision making about new technology. In T. Kochan & M. Useem (Eds.), *Transforming organizations* (pp. 281-298). New York: Oxford University Press.

Thomas, R. (1992b). Organizational politics and technological change. *Journal of Contemporary Ethnography, 20,* 442-477.

Thompson, J. D. (1967). *Organizations in action.* New York: McGraw-Hill.

Tichy, N. M. (1978). Diagnosis for complex health care delivery systems: A model and a case study. *Journal of Applied Behavioral Science, 14,* 305-321.

Tichy, N. (1983). *Managing strategic change: Technical, political, and cultural dynamics.* New York: Wiley.

Tichy, N., & DeVanna, M. (1986). *The transformational leader.* New York: Wiley.

Tichy, N. M., & Hornstein, H. A. (1980). Collaborative model building. In E. Lawler, D. Nadler, & C. Cammann (Eds.), *Organizational assessment: Perspectives on measurement of organizational behavior and quality of work life* (pp. 300-316). New York: Wiley.

Tichy, N., Hornstein, H., & Nisberg, J. (1976). Participative organization diagnosis and intervention strategies: Developing emergent pragmatic theories of change. *Academy of Management Review, 1,* 109-120.

Tichy, N., Tushman, M., & Fombrun, C. (1980). Network analysis in organizations. In E. Lawler, D. Nadler, & C. Cammann (Eds.), *Organizational assessment* (pp. 372-398). New York: Wiley.

Torbert, W. (1981). The role of self-study in improving managerial and institutional effectiveness. *Human Systems Management, 2,* 72-82.

Torbert, W. (1995, August). *A scientific paradigm that integrates quantitative, qualitative, and action research.* Paper presented at the annual meeting of the Academy of Management, Vancouver, BC, Canada.

Tornow, W. (1993). Editor's note: Introduction to special issue on 360-degree feedback. *Human Resource Management, 32,* 211-219.

Triandis, H. (1994). Cross-cultural industrial and organizational psychology. In H. Triandis, M. Dunnette, & L. Hough (Eds.), *Handbook of industrial and organizational psychology* (Vol. 4, pp. 103-172). Palo Alto, CA: Consulting Psychologists Press.

Trice, H., & Beyer, J. (1984). Studying organizational cultures through rites and ceremonial. *Academy of Management Review, 9,* 653-669.

Trice, H., & Beyer, J. (1993). *The cultures of work organizations.* Englewood Cliffs, NJ: Prentice Hall.

Tsui, A. (1990). A multiple-constituency model of effectiveness: An empirical examination at the human resource subunit level. *Administrative Science Quarterly, 35,* 458-484.

Tsui, A. (1994). Reputational effectiveness: Toward a mutual responsiveness framework. *Research in Organizational Behavior, 16,* 257-307.

Tsui, A., Egan, T., & O'Reilly, C. (1992). Being different: Relational demography and organizational attachment. *Administrative Science Quarterly, 37,* 549-579.

Tucker, F., Zivan, S., & Camp, R. (1987). How to measure yourself against the best. *Harvard Business Review, 65*(1), 8-10.

Turner, A. (1982). Consulting is more than giving advice. *Harvard Business Review, 60*(5), 120-129.

Tushman, M. (1977). A political approach to organizations: A review and rationale. *Academy of Management Review, 2,* 206-216.

Tushman, M., & Nadler, D. (1978). Information processing as an integrative concept in organizational design. *Academy of Management Review, 3,* 613-624.

Tushman, M., & O'Reilly, C. (1996). The ambidextrous organization: Managing evolutionary and revolutionary change. *California Management Review, 38,* 1-23.

Tushman, M., & Romanelli, E. (1985). Organizational evolution: A metamorphosis model of convergence and reorientation. *Research in Organizational Behavior, 7,* 171-222.

Two cheers for loyalty. (1996, January 6). *Economist,* p. 55.

Ulrich, D. (1997). *Human resource champions.* Boston: Harvard Business School Press.

Ulrich, D., Brockbank, W., & Yeung, A. (1989). Beyond belief: A benchmark for human resources. *Human Resource Management, 28,* 311-339.

Ulrich, D., Brockbank, W., Yeung, A., & Lake, D. (1995). Human resource competencies: An empirical assessment. *Human Resource Management, 34,* 473-495.

Ulrich, D., Yeung, A., Brockbank, W., & Lake, D. (1993). *Human resources as a competitive advantage: An empirical assessment of HR practices and competencies in global firms.* Unpublished manuscript, University of Michigan.

Useem, M., & Kochan, T. (1992). Creating the learning organization. In T. Kochan & M. Useem (Eds.), *Transforming organizations* (pp. 391-406). New York: Oxford University Press.

Uttal, B. (1983, October 17). Corporate culture vultures. *Fortune,* pp. 66-72.

Vaill, P. (1989). *Managing as a performing art: New ideas for a world of chaotic change.* San Francisco: Jossey-Bass.

Van de Ven, A., & Drazin, R. (1985). The concept of fit in contingency theory. *Research in Organizational Behavior, 7,* 333-365.

Van de Ven, A., & Ferry, D. (1980). *Measuring and assessing organizations.* New York: Wiley.

Van Maanen, J. (Ed.). (1979). Qualitative methodology [Special issue]. *Administrative Science Quarterly, 24*(4).

Venkatraman, N. (1989). The concept of fit in strategy research: Toward verbal and statistical correspondence. *Academy of Management Review, 14,* 423-444.

Venkatraman, N. (1991). IT-induced business reconfiguration. In M. Morton (Ed.), *The corporation of the 1990s: Information technology and organizational transformation* (pp. 122-158). New York: Oxford University Press.

Von Glinow, M. (1993). Diagnosing "best practice" in human resource management practices. *Research in Personnel and Human Resources Management* (Suppl. 3), 95-112.

Von Glinow, M. (1996). Presidential address: On minority rights and majority accommodations. *Academy of Management Review, 21,* 346-350.

Walker, J., & Bechet, T. (1994). Addressing future staffing needs. In A. Howard & Associates, (Eds.), *Diagnosis for organizational change: Methods and models* (pp. 113-138). New York: Guilford.

Walton, A. E. (1995). Generative strategy: Crafting competitive advantage. In D. Nadler, R. Shaw, A. Walton, and Associates *Discontinuous change: Leading organizational transformation* (pp. 121-137). San Francisco: Jossey-Bass.

Walton, E., & Nadler, D. A. (1994). Diagnosis for organizational design. In A. Howard & Associates (Eds.), *Diagnosis for organizational change: Methods and models* (pp. 85-113). New York: Guilford.

Walton, R. (1975). Quality of working life: What is it? *Sloan Management Review, 15,* 11-21.

Walton, R., & Dutton, J. (1969). The management of interdepartmental conflict: A model and review. *Administrative Science Quarterly, 14,* 73-84.

Walton, R., & McKersie, R. (1965). *A behavioral theory of labor negotiations.* New York: McGraw-Hill.

Waterman, R., Peters, T., & Phillips, J. (1980, June). Structure is not organization. *Business Horizons,* pp. 14-26.

Watson, W., Kumar, K., & Michaelsen, L. (1993). Cultural diversity's impact on interaction process and performance: Comparing homogeneous and diverse task groups. *Academy of Management Journal, 36,* 590-602.

Weaver, G., & Gioia, D. (1994). Paradigms lost: Incommensurability vs. structurationist inquiry. *Organization Studies, 15,* 565-590.

Webb, E., Campbell, D., Schwartz, R., & Sechrest, L. (1966). *Unobtrusive measures: Nonreactive research in the social sciences.* Chicago: Rand McNally.

Weick, K. (1979). *The social psychology of organizing* (2nd ed.). Reading, MA: Addison-Wesley.

Weick, K. (1985). Sources of order in underorganized systems: Themes in recent organizational history. In Y. Lincoln (Ed.), *Organizational theory and inquiry* (pp. 106-137). Beverly Hills, CA: Sage.

Weick, K., & Roberts, K. (1993). Collective mind in organizations: Heedful interacting in flight decks. *Administrative Science Quarterly, 38,* 357-381.

Weisbord, M. R. (1976). Diagnosing your organization: Six places to look for trouble with or without theory. *Group & Organization Studies, 1,* 430-447.

Weisbord, M. R. (1988). Toward a new practice theory of OD: Notes on snapshooting and moviemaking. *Research in Organization Change and Development, 2,* 59-96.

Weitzel, W., & Jonsson, E. (1989). Decline in organizations: A literature integration and extension. *Administrative Science Quarterly, 34,* 91-109.

Weitzel, W., & Jonsson, E. (1991). Reversing the downward spiral: Lessons from W. T. Grant and Sears Roebuck. *Academy of Management Executive, 5*(3), 7-22.

Welsh, D., Luthans, F., & Sommer, S. (1993). Managing Russian factory workers: The impact of U.S.-based behavioral and participative techniques. *Academy of Management Journal, 36,* 58-79.

Whetten, D. (1987). Organizational growth and decline processes. *Annual Review of Sociology, 13,* 335-358.

Whitney, J. (1987). Turnaround management every day. *Harvard Business Review, 65*(5), 49-55.

Wick, C., & Leon, L. (1995). From ideas to action: Creating a learning organization. *Human Resource Management, 34,* 299-311.

Wieland, G. (Ed.). (1981). *Improving health care management.* Ann Arbor, MI: Health Administration Press.

Wildavsky, A. (1972). The self-evaluating organization. *Public Administration Review, 32,* 509-520.

Wildavsky, A. (1979a). *The politics of the budgetary process* (3rd ed.). Boston: Little, Brown.

Wildavsky, A. (1979b). *Speaking truth to power: The art and craft of policy analysis.* Boston: Little, Brown.

Wilkins, A. (1983). The culture audit: A tool for understanding organizations. *Organizational Dynamics, 12*(Autumn), 24-38.

Willmott, H. (1993a). Breaking the paradigm mentality. *Organization Studies, 14,* 681-721.

Willmott, H. (1993b). Paradigm gridlock. *Organizational Studies, 14,* 727-731.

Wofford, J. C. (1994). An examination of the cognitive processes used to handle employee job problems. *Academy of Management Journal, 37,* 180-192.

Wood, D., & Gray, B. (1992). Toward a comprehensive theory of collaboration. *Journal of Applied Behavioral Science, 27,* 139-162.

Woodman, R. (1989). Organizational change and development: New arenas for inquiry and action. *Journal of Management, 15,* 205-228.

World Health Organization (WHO). (1985). *Targets for health for all* (European Health for All Series No. 1). Copenhagen: WHO Regional Office for Europe.

Yeung, A., Brockbank, J., & Ulrich, D. (1991). Organizational culture and human resource practices. *Research in Organizational Change and Development, 5,* 59-81.

Yin, R. (1981). Life histories of innovations: How new practices become routinized. *Public Administration Review, 41,* 21-28.

Yulevitz, G. (1997). *Organizational image and identification.* Unpublished master's thesis, Department of Sociology and Anthropology, Bar-Ilan University, Ramat-Gan, Israel. (In Hebrew with English abstract)

Zald, M., & Berger, M. (1978). Social movements in organizations: Coup d'etat, insurgency, and mass movements. *American Journal of Sociology, 83,* 823-861.

Zammuto, R. (1984). A comparison of multiple constituency models of organizational effectiveness. *Academy of Management Review, 9,* 606-616.

Zammuto, R., & Cameron, K. (1985). Environmental decline and organizational response. *Research in Organizational Behavior, 7,* 223-262.

Zammuto, R., & Krakower, J. (1991). Quantitative and qualitative studies of organizational culture. *Research in Organizational Change and Development, 5,* 83-114.

Zammuto, R., & O'Connor, E. (1992). Gaining advanced manufacturing technologies' benefits: The roles of organization design and culture. *Academy of Management Review, 17,* 701-728.

Zander, A. (1994). *Making groups effective* (2nd ed.). San Francisco: Jossey-Bass.

Zeira, Y., & Avedisian, J. (1989, Spring). Organizational planned change: Assessing chances for success. *Organizational Dynamics, 17,* 31-45.

Zmud, R. (1990). Opportunities for strategic information manipulation through new information technology. In J. Fulk & C. Steinfeld (Eds.), *Organizations and communication technology* (pp. 95-116). Newbury Park, CA: Sage.

Zuboff, S. (1988). *In the age of the smart machine: The future of work and power.* New York: Basic Books.

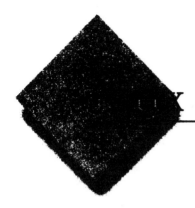

About the Authors

Michael I. Harrison, Associate Professor of Sociology at Bar-Ilan University in Ramat-Gan, Israel, is head of the Graduate Program in Organizations and former department chair. After receiving his B.A. from Columbia and his doctorate from the University of Michigan, he taught at SUNY, Stony Brook. He has also twice served as Visiting Associate Professor in the School of Management at Boston College and has been a Visiting Scholar at Harvard Business School, the Institute for Health Policy of Brandeis University, and the Nordic School for Public Health in Gothenburg, Sweden. Professor Harrison has worked as a consultant and has conducted research in a wide variety of organizations in the public and private sectors. His research on health professions and organizations, planned change, organizational analysis, and social institutions has been published in many prominent academic journals. His first book, *Diagnosing Organizations: Methods, Models, and Processes* (1994) made a major contribution to defining and advancing diagnostic practice. He is currently completing a book on *Implementing Heath System Reforms in Europe,* to be published by Sage, London.

Arie Shirom is Professor of Organizational Behavior and Health Care Management in the Faculty of Management of Tel Aviv University, Israel. He received his doctorate from the University of Wisconsin at Madison. He has twice been a Visiting Professor at the University of Michigan and at Cornell University. He has published extensively on organizational stress, organizational diagnosis, labor relations, and health care administration. He is cur-

485

rently a member of the editorial boards of the *Journal of Organizational Behavior* and several other periodicals. He also has distinguished himself in organizational consultation, applied research, and policy development. From 1988 through 1990 he served as a member of Israel's State Commission of Inquiry into the Functioning and Effectiveness of the Health Care System. His current research in organizational behavior focuses on work-related stress and its effects on performance and health; theory construction in organizational diagnosis and development; and using diagnosis to enhance effectiveness in health care organizations.